Arthur Dyott Thomson

The Gospel History and Doctrinal Teaching Critically Examined

Arthur Dyott Thomson

The Gospel History and Doctrinal Teaching Critically Examined

ISBN/EAN: 9783743399198

Manufactured in Europe, USA, Canada, Australia, Japa

Cover: Foto ©Lupo / pixelio.de

Manufactured and distributed by brebook publishing software (www.brebook.com)

Arthur Dyott Thomson

The Gospel History and Doctrinal Teaching Critically Examined

THE

GOSPEL HISTORY

AND

DOCTRINAL TEACHING

CRITICALLY EXAMINED

BY THE

AUTHOR OF 'MANKIND, THEIR ORIGIN AND DESTINY'

LONDON
LONGMANS, GREEN, AND CO.
1873

CONTENTS.

INTRODUCTION.

The Codex Sinaiticus—Selection of the canonical gospels—Selection of the Jewish canonical books—The Jewish traditional law—Origin of the Septuagint Version—Its reception in Judæa—The Sibylline Oracles—Admissions of Eusebius—Justin's Apology—Dishonesty of Church writers—Origen on the Gospel History—Ancient Theophanies—Alterations in the text of the gospels—The Apocryphal gospels—The Judæo-Christian gospels—Bishop Marsh's hypothesis—Examination of the fourth gospel—The dogma of Original Sin—The Talmud opposed to this dogma—The story of the Fall examined—Philo and Origen explain it allegorically . . . . PAGE 1

CHAPTER I.

Birth of John the Baptist—The names of the angels Persian—The genealogies of Christ examined—The descent of Christ from David impossible—Contradictions in the narratives of the birth of Christ—Isaiah's prophecy examined—Jewish Messianic expectations—The early Christians were all Jews—The Messianic Star—The Massacre of the Innocents unhistorical—Christ in the Temple 53

CHAPTER II.

Date of the birth of Christ—The taxing of Joseph and Mary unhistorical—The Messianic idea among the Essenes—The baptism of Christ—Contradictions in the narrative—Examination of the chronology of the third gospel—The Temptation—The call of the apostles—Nature of the office—The power of binding and loosing explained 77

CHAPTER III.

The Sermon on the Mount examined—Origin of the Beatitudes—Observance of the Mosaic Law enjoined—The doctrine of purgatory taught—Asceticism enjoined—Misquotation of the Old Testament—Origin of the Lord's Prayer—The teaching of Hillel 100

CHAPTER IV.

The Essenes—Philo's account of them—Origin of the Pharisees—The Assideans—Origin of the Essenes—Their religious practices—Their exorcisms and miraculous cures—The Ebionites—Jewish expectations of the Messiah—Early Christian miracles—The Talmud on miracles 116

CONTENTS.

CHAPTER V.

The Transfiguration—The Triumphal entry of Christ into Jerusalem—The Betrayal of Christ—Pontius Pilate—Caiaphas—The trial of Jesus—Contradictions in the narrative—The forged order for his crucifixion—The mocking and crucifixion of Jesus—Jewish and Roman practices at executions—The inscriptions on the cross—The prophecy of Jonah—The crucifragium unhistorical . . . . PAGE 133

CHAPTER VI.

The darkness at the Crucifixion—The Apostles' Creed—The Jewish School—Jewish ideas of the resurrection—Man a Microcosm—The burial of Jesus—Contradictions in the narrative—Pilate's letter to Tiberius—The ascension not mentioned in the original gospels—The passage in Tacitus respecting Christ—Irenæus ignores the Crucifixion—The Sibylline predictions—Cassini's astrological system—Misquotations in the gospels 157

CHAPTER VII.

Eusebius's period—Meaning of the word Evangel—The Evangelium Eternum—The doctrine of vicarious punishment—The Day of Atonement—The letter of Publius Lentulus—Forged letters from heaven—The Ebionites reformed Jews—Meaning of the words Son of God—Dialogue between Peter and Paul—The Acts and Epistles contradict each other—Nature of Inspiration . . 184

CHAPTER VIII.

Augustine on Original Sin—Philo's doctrine of the Logos—The Calvinistic doctrine—Initiation adopted by the Church—Persecution of the Pagans by the Christians—Doctrinal teaching of the Egyptians and of Orpheus—Speculations of the philosophers on the origin of evil—Philo on the origin of evil—The war of the rebel angels—Ascent and descent of souls according to the ancients—Plato's division of souls 207

CHAPTER IX.

The Metempsychosis a Jewish belief—Destiny of the soul according to the Fathers—Cardinal Bellarmine on Purgatory—Universal Redemption taught by many of the Fathers—Origin of the demons and of Satan—Augustine and Origen on the literal interpretation of Scripture—Examination of the Apocalypse—Allegorical meaning of the word Babylon—Two Messiahs expected by the Jews—Prophecies invented by the Fathers—Incorporeal nature of Christ asserted by Augustine—Origin of Mithraism—Antiquity of Christianity 229

THE GOSPEL HISTORY.

INTRODUCTION.

THE LIFE of JESUS CHRIST is contained in four evangels (εὐαγγέλια), or "good tidings," the earliest known manuscript of which is the Codex Sinaiticus, which belongs to the earlier part of the fourth century. This manuscript is of great importance, both on account of its antiquity and because it is in all probability one of the fifty copies of the Scriptures which Constantine ordered to be made in Byzantium in A.D. 331, under the superintendence of Eusebius. These evangels, or gospels, were originally anonymous, and even so late as the time when the Codex Sinaiticus was written their titles are simply, "After Matthew," &c. These evangels make no allusion to any supernatural help, or Divine inspiration, but show from the manner in which they unhesitatingly contradict each other that the idea of infallibility, or canonicity, such as was given in their time to the books of the Old Testament in the synagogue, was entirely foreign to the authors with respect to their own writings. The following pages, some portions of which have already appeared in print, contain the results of modern critical enquiry, combined with original investigation, into the origin and historical value of these biographical narratives.

The canonicity of our present gospels was not established till the Council of Nice in A.D. 325. Pappus, in his Synodicon to the Council, tells us how it set about choosing the gospels which it intended to adopt out of the immense number of gospels then in existence. He says:—" Having promiscuously put all the books that were referred to the Council for determination under the communion table in a church, they besought the Lord that the inspired writings might get upon the table while the spurious ones remained underneath, and that it happened accordingly." The gospels which Gelasius ought to burn remained, we are told, under the table, and the four inspired ones got upon it, and were declared to be canonical! Subsequently to this Council, however, a general revision and correction of the gospels was made at Constantinople in A.D. 506, by order of the Emperor Anastasius. This extraordinary order runs as follows:—

"Messalâ V. C. consule, Constantinopoli jubente Anastasio imperatore, sancta evangelia, tanquam ab idiotis evangelistis composita, reprehentur et emendantur."

"The illustrious Messala being consul, by order of the Emperor Anastasius, the holy gospels as having been written by idiotic evangelists, are censured and corrected." Signed Victor, Bishop of Tunis, in Africa. (See Cave, Hist. Lit., vol. I. p. 415.)

The Council of Nice was composed of the mystical number of 318 bishops, and presided over by the "pious" Constantine. Sabinus, the bishop of Heraclea, affirms, however, that "excepting Constantine himself, and Eusebius Pamphilus, they were a set of illiterate simple creatures, that understood nothing." Constantine, however, said that what was approved by these bishops could be nothing else than the will of God himself, since the Holy Spirit, residing in such great and worthy souls, unfolded to them the Divine will (Socr. Schol. Eccl. Hist. l. I. c. 9). The mystic number 318 is explained as follows in the Epistle of Barnabas (VIII. 10-14), which was very generally held, especially by Origen and Jerome, to be canonical and genuine:—

"Understand, therefore, children, these things more fully, that Abraham, who was the first that brought in circumcision, looked forward to Jesus, circumcised, having the mystery of three letters. For the Scripture says that Abraham circumcised three hundred and eighteen men of his own house. But what, therefore, was the mystery made known to him? Mark first the eighteen, and then the three hundred. For the numeral letters of ten and eight are I H. And these denote Jesus. And because the cross was that by which we were to find grace, therefore he adds three hundred, the root of which is T (the figure of his cross). Wherefore by two letters he signified Jesus, and by the third his cross. He who has put the engrafted gift of his doctrine within us, knows that I never taught anyone a more certain truth: but I guess that ye are worthy of it."

Cotelerius has shown that many of the Fathers agreed with the author of this sublime specimen of reasoning on this subject, and it was of course recognised by those who convened the Council of Nice.

The Jewish canonical books were selected from the rest by much the same process as the gospels. The learned Jew Spinoza says in his Tractatus Theologico-Politicus,—" I presume to conclude, from all that precedes, that before the time of the Maccabees there was no canon of Holy Writ extant, but that the books we have were selected from amongst many others by and on the authority of the Pharisees of the second temple, who also instituted the formula for the prayers used in the synagogue." The Talmud (Treatise Sabath. l. II.) says: "The wise men wished to suppress the book of Ecclesiastes, because its words contradict each other. But, having well considered the matter, they did not do so, *because the beginning and end of it are words from the Thorah* (the Pentateuch). They also wished to suppress for ever Solomon's Proverbs." It is not stated why this was not done, but perhaps Meghunja, the son of Hiskias, who prevented the destruction of Ezekiel's writings, preserved this work also.

The grand synagogue which decided upon the canon of Scripture did not assemble until after the subjection of Asia to the Macedonian power. Like the Christian council, its decrees became binding on the faithful, and came to be regarded as a Sinaitic revelation, or, as it is expressed theologically, they became Halacha le Mosché mi-Sinaï. Eusebius says that it was not allowed among the Jews that everyone should determine who was guided by the Divine Spirit to write the sacred books, but that only a few persons were charged with this duty, *who were also divinely inspired,* and that THEY ALONE determined what books were sacred and prophetic, and rejected those which were not. The only means, therefore, of ascertaining whether a book of the Old Testament is inspired is, that an unknown Jew, who says that he is divinely inspired, shall be able to say that it is so!

The same process, as Josephus and Eusebius inform us, was adopted with regard to the historical parts of the Old Testament, which Josephus says were not allowed to be written by anyone. "This," he says, "was reserved for the prophets, who knew by divine inspiration what was future and distant from them, and who also wrote what happened in their own time." No doubt it required a great deal of inspiration to assert, for instance, that Solomon employed 153,600 workmen for seven years to build the temple, which Villapandus has proved cost, according to the text, six thousand nine hundred millions of pounds sterling (6,900,000,000*l.*)! Yet Herodotus, who travelled through Syria, knew nothing of Solomon's empire, though we are told (2 Chron. ix. 23, 24) that "*all the kings of the earth. . . . brought every man his present, vessels of silver and vessels of gold, and raiment, harness and spices, horses and mules, a rate year by year.*" Josephus found the neglect of the temple by Alexander so unsatisfactory that he found it expedient to forge a story of his having visited Jerusalem, where he never was.

The doctors who composed the synagogue say: "Moses received the law on Sinai: it was transmitted from Moses to Joshua, from Joshua to the elders, from the elders to the prophets, and from the prophets to the members of the great synagogue." This is intended to include, not only the sacred writings, but also the oral or traditional law said to have been given to Moses on Sinai, and committed to memory by Aaron and the rulers of the congregation. The Talmud is emphatic on this subject. It says (Treatise Berachoth, 1. 1.), "Whoever shall transgress a command of the wise men is deserving of death." And that there may be no mistake as to who the wise men are, it repeats in Treatise Erobin, 1. I., "Whoever transgresses a command of the scribes (Sopherim) is deserving of death." When the great synagogue assembled these sopherim had obtained almost absolute authority in spiritual matters. The Talmud (Treatise Berachoth, 1. I.) also says that the traditional law is of equal authority with the books of Moses: "It is written, 'Jehovah said unto Moses, Come up to me into the mount, and be there, and I will give thee tables of stone, and the Thorah, and the Mitzvah (commandments) which I have written that thou mayest teach them.' The 'tables' mean the Decalogue;

the 'Thorah' means the Pentateuch; the 'Mitzvah' means the Mischnah; 'which I have written' means the prophets and hagiographers; 'that thou mayest teach them,' means the Gemarah (the Talmud). Hence we conclude that all this was given to Moses on Mount Sinai." This and other passages show that the traditional law, taught by the general assemblies which were first instituted by Ezra and Nehemiah, were invested with the same authority as the written law.

Rabbi Michel Weill says, "What is certain, what results from several traditional passages (Talmud, Meguilla, fol. 3 and 7) which have never been the subject of any serious doubt, is that the holy books were first arranged in the time of Ezra." Irenæus (l. III. c. 15), Eusebius (l. I. c. 8), Clemens Alexandrinus (Strom. l. I. c. 2), Tertullian (De habitu mulierum, l. I. c. 3), Basil (Letter to Chilo), and others of the Fathers go much beyond this, for they hold that the books of the law had been burnt by Nebuchadnezzar, and that Ezra was really the author of these books. It is certain that the law of Moses is not once alluded to in the Old Testament till the time of Malachi, who wrote in the time of Nehemiah, and is not mentioned again until Dan. ix., a chapter which speaks of the repair of the fortifications of the temple and of Jerusalem 69 weeks, or 490 lunar years after the sentence had been issued that the Jews might return from captivity. The books which Moses wrote, according to the references to them in the Pentateuch, differ from any of the five books now ascribed to him. They are "The War against the Amalekites," which we are told (Exod. xvii. 14) that Moses wrote by God's command; "The Book of the Agreement" (Exod. xxiv. 4, 7); and "The Book of the Law of God," subsequently augmented by Joshua by an account of another covenant (Josh. xxiv. 25, 26). The Book of the Agreement, which has perished, was to be esteemed imperative upon all, and even upon posterity (Deut. xxix. 14, 15), and Moses, it is said, ordered the book of this second covenant to be religiously preserved for future ages.

The preface to the Mischnah tells us how the traditional law was committed to memory. It says that the Jewish mysteries were revealed orally to Moses on Mount Sinai; that Moses communicated them in the same way to his brother Aaron; that afterwards, placing himself on Aaron's right hand, he called Eleazar and Shumar, Aaron's sons, and went over them again with them in his presence; that afterwards he sent for the seventy elders and repeated to them what he had said to the others; and that at length he caused the whole people (about three millions in number) to be assembled, and once more proclaimed what had been revealed to him.

The Hebrew Scriptures were unknown to the Gentile world until the Greek translation of them, known as the Septuagint, was published. As this version is used alternately with the Hebrew version by the evangelists, it is necessary to introduce here a short account of its origin and peculiarities.

About two centuries before the Christian era, foreign conquest and domestic dissensions had led to a very general dispersion of the Jews. Jewish colonisation in Egypt was favoured by the Ptolemies, and Alexandria, where this Jewish population principally resided, became the centre of an active propaganda in favour of Judaism. The genius of the religion thus became mingled with that of Greece, and this was the origin of the influence which the Greeks afterwards exercised upon Christianity. By degrees Alexandria became a sort of metropolis for the Jews of the Dispersion, and it became more so than ever when distinguished refugees fled thither in order to escape from the hated rule of the Syrians.

Onias IV., who was the son of the last high priest of the sacerdotal branch of Joshua ben Jozadok, and whose family had supported the interests of the Ptolemies against those Jews who were in favour of the Syrians, was among those who sought refuge in Egypt (Jos. Ant. XXII. III. 1). Onias was welcomed by Philometor, who considered him to be the representative of a political party which might be of use to him. Eventually Onias and Dositheus, who also belonged to the priestly caste (Esther XI. 1), and had accompanied Onias to Egypt, became the generals of Philometor (Jos. Ant. Apion, II. 5), and having placed themselves at the head of the Egyptian Jews, they repulsed the king's brother, who had taken up arms against him, and restored the throne of Egypt to Philometor, who had fled to Cyprus. The grateful king gave Onias a sort of supremacy over the Jews in Egypt, with the title of Ethnarch. This supremacy resembled that of the Prince of the Captivity (Resch Galouta) at Babylon, who was ruler over the Jews of the Euphrates.

Onias, seeing the precarious condition of the Jews in Palestine, and relying on Isaiah xix. 19, "In that day shall there be an altar to the Lord in the midst of the land of Egypt," obtained from Philometor some land in the neighbourhood of Heliopolis; and the temple of Onias (Beth Chonjo) was erected in the small town of Leontopolis, on the ruins of an ancient temple. The new temple did not resemble the temple of Jerusalem externally, for it was a species of tower built of brick, but the interior resembled it in every respect, except that a gold chandelier, suspended from the roof by a chain of the same metal, replaced the seven-branched candlestick of the older temple. The priests and Levites who had fled from Judæa conducted the sacrifices and ministrations of the new temple, which Philometor endowed with the revenues of the town of Heliopolis and its neighbourhood. Ewald fixes the date of the inauguration of the temple of Onias at 160 B.C. The whole of the surrounding district formed from this time a small sacerdotal government called Onion (Jos. Ant. XIII. 1, Bell. Jud. VII. VIII, 5).

Philometor, struck by seeing so many distinguished refugees from Palestine voluntarily exiling themselves from their country, began to interest himself in them. Aristobulus, a Jewish philosopher, who had studied Greek philosophy, and who belonged to the Peripatetic school, held many conversations with the king respecting Judaism, and at length Philometor ordered him to translate the Pentateuch. An old Jewish tradition says that the Pentateuch was translated into Greek by five wise men. There is no doubt that the translation was made by more than one person. Aristobulus was one of the translators, and Lysimachus, the son of Ptolemy, of Jerusalem, who translated the Book of Esther for Philometor, was another. Whatever the number of the translators may have been, it is certain that they went to the island of Pharos, near Alexandria, in order to complete their work in retirement.

Aristobulus wrote a species of preface, or dedication to the king, which was intended to prevent misconceptions relative to certain biblical expressions respecting God. Certain passages which might have given offence to the king if translated literally, have been altered. Thus, out of regard to the king's ancestor Lagos, who gave his name to the dynasty of Lagides, the literal translation of the Hebrew word Arnebet, the Greek equivalent of which is the word λαγὼς (a hare), was abandoned in order to avoid classing that quadruped among the unclean animals! The name of Jehovah was altered into "The Lord" in order to avoid writing the word Jehovah in Greek letters. This practice has been followed by the writers of the New Testament, so that Christ is made to speak of God in the words of the Septuagint version. The quotations from the Old Testament in the gospels are almost always in the words of this version, which the orthodox Jews had the greatest horror of, and from which it is impossible that Christ can have quoted. Another alteration was an addition to the ages of the patriarchs, which made the creation of the world to have taken place in 5890 B.C. instead of 4121 B.C. as our version has it. Both these dates, however, differ from that which is assigned to this event by Josephus, who fixes it at 5688 B.C., which he must have taken from the Temple copy of the Scriptures which Titus made him a present of soon after the fall of Jerusalem, and which he had had in his possession twenty-eight years when he published his "Antiquities of the Jews." Another remarkable alteration is, that the east wind mentioned in Exod. xiv. 21 as dividing the waters of the Red Sea, has been altered into the south wind, ἐν ἀνέμῳ νότῳ.

The Egyptian Jews were so much pleased with the interest the king took in their religion, and with the opportunity which the Septuagint translation afforded of making it known among the Greeks, that the day on which the Greek version of the Pentateuch was presented to the king was kept as a festival, and the anniversary was commemorated by a pilgrimage to the island of Pharos. This anniversary soon became a popular festival, which commenced with prayers and hymns, and terminated with eating and drinking in booths or in the open air, and eventually the whole population of Alexandria used to take part in this national festival of the Egyptian Jews. Those Jews who remained in Palestine, however, looked upon the translation of the sacred idiom into another language, in which it was impossible to express its meaning, as a profanation, and they kept this same anniversary as a day of national mourning. The 8th of December, therefore, became a day of national rejoicing in Egypt, and a day of fasting and of mourning in Judæa.

The name Septuagint has been given to this version of the Scriptures owing to a legend, which says that the curiosity of Ptolemy Philadelphus had been excited by his librarian, Demetrius of Phalera, who presented the books of Moses to him as being worthy of a place in his royal library, and of the honour of being translated. The king is said to have sent two ambassadors, Aristeas and Andreas, at his instigation to Eleazar, who was then high priest at Jerusalem, with rich presents, and with instructions to obtain from him some learned men who understood both Latin and Greek. The king, it is said, was so anxious to gain his point, that he bought at his own expense, and set at liberty, all the Jewish slaves whom his father Ptolemy I. had captured. Eleazar, overwhelmed with these proofs of goodwill, chose seventy-two men of the greatest learning among the Jews, six out of each tribe, and sent them to Alexandria. These seventy-two men completed the translation of the Pentateuch in seventy-two days, and read it in the presence of the king and their fellow-countrymen. It was also said that each of them was shut up in a cell that they might not communicate with each other, and yet that in spite of this their version was perfectly identical, and that all present were compelled to recognise this translation as the result of Divine inspiration!

Constantine, who presided over the Council of Nice, and who is called the first Christian emperor, never became a Christian until the remembrance of his crimes drove him to embrace a faith which promised to save him from the consequences of them on his death-bed. The rest of his life was a strange mixture of Paganism and Christianity, in which the former predominated. When he completed the building of Constantinople (A.D. 344), which he says (Cod. Th. l. XIII. tit. 5) that a divine revelation impelled him to build, he had its horoscope drawn by the astrologer Valens on the eighth day of the festival of its dedication, which took place on the 11th of May (Adren.). He worshipped Apollo, or the Sun-god, whose altars were covered with his votive offerings. The people were brought to believe that the emperor beheld the visible image of Apollo with his own eyes. He published two edicts in the same year, the first of which enjoined the observance of the Dies Solis, or Day of the Sun [Sun-day] (Ad. Theodos. l. II. tit. viii. leg. 1 ; Cod. Justinian, l. III. tit. xii. leg. 3), to which his Pagan subjects can have had no objection, while the second directed the regular consultation of aruspices (Cod. Theodos. l. XVI. tit. 10). Tertullian (Apol. c. 21) says that the Christians in his time used to assemble in the morning on the day of the sun for religious purposes out of hatred to the Jews, who used to meet on the Sabbath; and that the Christians were forbidden to abstain from work on that day that they might not imitate the Jews. One of Constantine's medals, which was struck in A.D. 315, bears the inscription, Solis Invicto Comiti, "To the Invincible Companion of the Sun." Another medal has his bust on one side and the god Anubis on the other. He always retained the title and prerogative of Pontiff, which gave him absolute jurisdiction in matters relating to the Pagan religion. Many of the medals give him the title of God, with which the monogram of Christ (which is also that of Jupiter Ammon) was associated. The title, ensigns, and prerogatives of Sovereign Pontiff were accepted without hesitation by seven Christian emperors, and Paganism was tolerated from Constantine down to Gratian, who was the first of the emperors who refused the title and dress of Pontifex Maximus as inconsistent with being a Christian.

Constantine murdered his eldest son, Crispus, in the same year that he presided over the Council of Nice. He had previously murdered his wife's father, Maximian, his sister Anastia's husband, Bassanius, and Licinianus, his nephew by his sister Constantia. He had also drowned his unoffending wife, Fausta, in a bath of boiling water, besides murdering his friend Sopater, and Licinius, his sister Constantia's husband. Eusebius (Life of Constantine, l. III. c. 73) says that a coin was struck to perpetuate the memory of this holy personage, "whereon was engraven the effigy of this blessed man, with a scarf bound round his head, on one side, and on the other he was represented sitting and driving in a chariot, and a hand reached down from heaven to take him up"! The real reason why he inclined to and ultimately adopted Christianity is to be found in Zosimus and Sozomen, who say that he applied to his faithful friend Sopater, a Pagan priest, whom he afterwards murdered, to free him from the consequences of his crimes. Sopater, however, refused to administer spiritual consolation, saying that the purity of the gods admitted of no compromise with crimes like his, and Constantine then turned to the Christian bishops, "who promised him that by repentance and baptism they would cleanse him from all sin," and he was at length baptized during his last illness.

Niebuhr (Hist. Rome, vol. V. p. 359) says of Constantine: "The religion which he had in his head must have been a strange compound indeed. The man who had on his coins the inscription Sol invictus, who worshipped pagan divinities, consulted the haruspices, indulged in a number of pagan superstitions, and, on the other hand, built churches, shut up pagan temples, and interfered with the Council of Nicæa, must have been a repulsive phenomenon, and was certainly not a Christian. He did not allow himself to be baptized till the last moments of his life, and those who praise him for this do not know what they are doing. He was a superstitious man, and mixed up his Christian religion with all sorts of absurd superstitions and opinions. When, therefore, certain Oriental writers wish to call him ἰσαπό-στολος, they do not know what they are saying, and to speak of him as a saint is a profanation of the word."

In Constantine's Oration to the Clergy (c. 18) we find the following extraordinary statement of what was to him the truest evidence of the Christian religion:—

"Here we must needs mention a certain testimony of Christ's divinity, fetched from those who were aliens and strangers to the faith. For those who contumeliously detract from him, if they will give evidence to their own testimonies, may sufficiently understand thereby that he is both God and the Son of God. For the Erythræan Sibyl, who lived in the sixth age after the Flood, being a priestess of Apollo, did yet, *by the power of Divine inspiration*, prophesy of future matters that were to come to pass concerning God, and by the first letters, which are an acrostic, declared the history of Jesus."

In the next chapter he says:—"The truth of the matter doth manifestly appear, for our writers have with great study and accuracy compared the times, that none can suspect that this power was made and came forth after Christ's coming, and therefore they are convicted of falsehood who blaze abroad that these verses were not made by the Sibyl." In

c. 20, which is entitled " Other verses of Virgil concerning Christ, in which under certain veils (as poets use) this knotty mystery is set forth," he speaks of the fourth Bucolic of Virgil as the ultimate proof and main evidence of the Christian religion! This, however, sinks into insignificance beside the recognition of the inspiration of these books by the Apostle Paul himself. Clemens Alexandrinus (Strom. l. III.) says:—

"As God, out of his desire to save the Jews, gave them prophets, so raising up prophets also to the Greeks from their own nation and language, as far as they were capable of receiving that good gift of God, He separated them from the vulgar, *as not only the preaching of Peter, but the Apostle Paul also* declares, speaking thus:—' Take the Greek books into your hands, and look into the Sibyl, how clearly she speaks of one God and of things to come; then take Hystaspes [an ancient king of the Medes] also, and read, and you will find the Son of God much more clearly and evidently described, and that many kings shall employ all their force against Christ, out of hatred to him and to all that call upon His name.' "

Augustine makes the Erythræan Sibyl to be a citizen of God's holy city! He also says that Homer spoke truly of God, and that he borrowed many of his verses from one Daphne, a Sibyl, who lived at the taking of Thebes. Josephus also quotes the oracles respecting the building of the Tower of Babel and the confusion of tongues. He also quotes Histiæus as mentioning the plain of Shinar in Babylonia, "for he says, 'such of the priests as were saved took the sacred vessels of Jupiter Enyalius and came to Shinar of Babylonia.'" Eusebius, Justin, Jerome, Lactantius, and many others, both Pagans and Christians, recognise these oracles as inspired. Last, but not least, the Roman Catholic Church has sanctioned these Pagan impostures by placing the Erythræan Sibyl in the Sistine Chapel at Rome, as well as over the door of the Casa Santa at Loretto; by having their figures beautifully inlaid in the marble floor of the cathedral at Sienna; by having their statues placed in a church at Venice which formerly belonged to the bare-footed Carmelites, and by placing their oracular utterances on a level with those of David in the hymn beginning " Dies iræ, dies illa."

Eusebius, who presided over and directed the Council of Nice in conjunction with Constantine, is considered by Petavius to have been an Arian. He held that Jesus Christ created the substance of the Holy Ghost. Cave says that "there are many unwary and dangerous expressions in his writings," and adds, that "He subscribed the Nicene Creed as he would have subscribed any other, though contrary to his convictions and to the sense of his writings both before and after that council." The reason of this pliability was no doubt his anxiety to please Constantine, who, he says, "alone of all the Roman emperors was beloved of God, and hath left us the idea of his most pious and religious life as an inimitable example for other men to follow at a humble distance"! Constantine, who had espoused the views of the orthodox party, had issued the following proclamation to "the bishops, pastors, and people wheresoever:"—

"Moreover we thought good, that if there can be found extant any work or book compiled by Arius, the same should be burned to ashes, so that not only his damnable doctrine may thereby be wholly rooted out, but also that no relic thereof may remain to posterity. This also we straitly command and charge, that if any man be found to hide or conceal any book made by Arius, and not immediately bring forth the said book, and deliver it up to be burned, that the said offender shall die the death. For as soon as he is taken, our pleasure is that his head be stricken off his shoulders. God keep you in his tuition."—(Socr. Schol. l. I. c. 6.)

Such were the means by which the orthodox faith was established by "Constantine, the puissant, the mighty and noble emperor," as he styles himself in the title of this edict. Lardner compassionates the time-serving Eusebius, whose regard for his head seems to have outweighed his conscientious scruples, and thinks that "better had it been that the bishops of that council (of Nice) had never met together, than that they should have tempted and prevailed upon a Christian bishop, or anyone else, to prevaricate and act against conscience."

The admissions of Eusebius are of the most startling description. "It is wonderful," says Lardner, "that Eusebius should think that Philo's Therapeutæ were Christians, and that their ancient writings should be our gospels and epistles." The wonder, however, is less that he should have held that opinion than that he should have given utterance to it, though Jerome (De viris illustribus, c. 8) has said the same thing. Eusebius probably forged the celebrated testimony to Jesus Christ in Josephus, for while it is quoted in two of Eusebius's works, it is not to be found in any of the ancient apologists for Christianity. The letters that passed between Jesus Christ and Abgarus, king of Edessa, which are translated into Greek in his Ecclesiastical History (l. I. c. 13), and which he says he himself found at Edessa, written in Syrian, were also probably forged by him. In his Ecclesiastical History (l. VII. 19) he says that the Christians at Jerusalem preserved and worshipped the episcopal throne of James, their first bishop! He also pretends (ib. VII. 18) that he had himself seen in one of the streets of Jerusalem the monument which the woman who had an issue of blood had erected to Jesus Christ, as also an unknown plant, which grew beside it, and which cured all diseases. He unfortunately forgot that we are expressly told that the woman had spent all that she had on physicians (Mark v. 25 et sqq.); Luke viii. 45). The monument he speaks of was no doubt one which had been erected in honour of the Emperor Adrian (see Heinichen, Exa. ad Euseb.; H. E. vol. III. pp. 412 and 396).

It seems strange to us that an emperor who was still a Pagan Pontiff, and who in that capacity officiated during his whole life as a priest of the gods, as Constantine did, should preside over an assembly of Christian bishops. But independently of the personal reasons which led Constantine to favour Christianity, the broad line of demarcation which now separates Paganism from Christianity did not then exist. Justin Martyr addressed an Apology in A.D. 141, "Unto the autocrat Titus Ælius Adrianus; unto Antoninus Pius, most noble Cæsar and true philosopher; unto Lucius, son of the philosopher Cæsar, and adopted of Pius, favourers of learning; and unto the Sacred Senate, with all the people of Rome, on behalf of the Christians," in which he says:—

"If we hold some opinions near of kin to the poets and philosophers in greatest repute among you, why are we unjustly hated? For in saying that all things were made in this beautiful order by God, what do we seem to say more than Plato? When we teach a general conflagration, what do we teach more than the Stoics? By opposing the worship of the work of men's hands, we concur with Menander the comedian, and by declaring Logos to be the first-begotten of God, our Master Jesus Christ to be born of a Virgin without any human mixture, and to be crucified and dead, and to have risen again and ascended into heaven, we say no more in this than what you say of those whom you style the Sons of Jove.

"For you need not be told what a number of sons the writers most in vogue among you assign to Jove. Mercury, the interpreter of Jove, in imitation of the Logos, is worshipped among you. [It is necessary to observe that Mercury had been styled the Logos, or "the word that in the beginning was God, and that also was a God," Centuries before this Justin wrote his Apology.] You have Æsculapius, the physician, smitten by a thunderbolt, and afterwards ascended into heaven. You have Bacchus torn to pieces, and Hercules burnt to get rid of his pains. You have Pollux and Castor, the sons of Jove by Leda, and Perseus by Danae. Not to mention others, I would fain know why you always deify the departed emperors, and have a fellow at hand to make affidavit that he saw Cæsar mount to heaven from the funeral pile. As to the Son of God, called Jesus, should we allow him to be nothing more than man, yet the title of the Son of God is very justifiable on account of his wisdom, considering you have your Mercury in worship under the title of the Logos and the Messenger of God.

"As to the objections of our Jesus being crucified, I say that suffering was common to all the fore-mentioned sons of Jove, only they suffered another kind of death. As to his being born of a virgin, you have your Perseus to balance that. As to his curing the lame, and the paralytic, and such as were cripples from their birth, this is little more than what you say of your Æsculapius."

In this as in other Christian writings of this and later periods, no attempt is made to deny the existence of the heathen deities, or the truth of the popular beliefs respecting them. Justin, the author of this Apology, owes his title of Martyr to an absurd story told by Eusebius (H. E. l. IV. c. 15) of his being knocked on the head by Crescens, a cynical philosopher, because Justin had accused him of an infamous offence.

Clemens Alexandrinus says in his Stromata, "Those who

lived according to the Logos were really Christians, though
they have been thought to be atheists, as Socrates and
Heraclitus were among the Greeks, and such as resembled
them." In another passage of the same work he says that
there is no difference between a true Gnostic and a perfect
Christian. Origen (Adv. Cels. l. VI.) says, " For God showed
these things unto them, and whatsoever things have been
well spoken," and in the same work (l. I. c. 6) he reproaches
Jesus Christ with having borrowed several things from Plato!
In a letter to St. Gregory Thaumaturgus, he says that by
ordering the Israelites to steal from the Egyptians that they
might have wherewithal to contribute to the worship of
Jehovah, God seems to have wished the Christians to steal
Pagan philosophy, *in order to make it appear like Christianity*.
St. Augustine (Confessions, l. VII. c. 9, 13, 20) admits that
the commencement of the fourth gospel is the teaching of
Plato. In another place (ib. c. 19) he also admits that it was
the dogmas of Plato that made him adopt those of the Christians; that he learned from the Platonists, " that the Word
existed before all things, that he was from all eternity with
God, that he created all things, that he is the only son of the
Father, and lastly, that he is equal to the Father, being of
the same substance as the Father."

Arnobius goes so far as to say that " If Cicero's works had
been read as they ought to have been by the heathen, there
would be no need of Christian writers." Ludovicus Vivus, a
learned Catholic writer, confesses that "there can be found
no other difference between Pagan and Popish worship before
images, but only this, that names and titles are changed."
The Manichæans, of whom St. Augustine was one until he
left them through disgust at not being admitted to the higher
grades, and who were the most distinguished for learning
and intelligence of all the Christian sects, possessed a work
called the " Theosophy, or Wisdom of God," the purport of
which was to show that Judaism, Paganism, and Manichæism,
or Christianity, were one and the same religion (Fabricius,
vol. I. p. 354). The celebrated eclectic philosopher Ammonius
Saccas, whose teaching was approved of by Athenagoras,
Pantænus, Clemens Alexandrinus, and all who had the care
of the public school belonging to the Christians of Alexandria,
and which was afterwards adopted by Longinus, Plotinus,
Heremius, Origen, Porphyry, Jamblichus, Sopater, Julian

the Apostate, and Chrysanthius his master, Hierocles, Proclus, and many others, both Pagans and Christians, held that there was no difference between the Pagan and Christian systems. He held that the religions of Melchizedek, of Pythagoras, and of Jesus were the same, and that Justin Martyr spoke nothing but the truth when he declared that Socrates was a Christian.

Mosheim says that in the fourth century, "it was an almost universally received maxim that it was an act of virtue to deceive and to lie when by such means the interest of the Church might be promoted." As to the fifth century, he says, "The simplicity and ignorance of the generality in those times furnished the most favourable occasion for the exercise of fraud, and the impudence of impostors in contriving false miracles was artfully proportioned to the credulity of the vulgar, while the sagacious and wise, who perceived these cheats, were overawed into silence by the dangers that threatened their lives and fortunes if they should expose the artifice." In another part of his history he traces the origin of this flagrant dishonesty to the Platonists and Pythagoreans, who, he says, held it as a maxim that it was not only lawful, but praiseworthy to deceive, and even to use the expedient of a lie, in order to advance the cause of *truth* and *piety*! The Egyptian Jews received this maxim from them before the Christian era, and the Christians became infected with this pernicious error from both these sources. This is why the Fathers and others assert that what they teach is often only true in a spiritual sense, that is, that it is a pure invention. Thus Origen (Comm. in Joan., vol. X. § 4) says that every passage of Scripture has a spiritual meaning, but that every passage has not a literal meaning; that there is often a spiritual truth under a literal lie—$\Sigma\omega\zeta o\mu\acute{\epsilon}\nu o\upsilon$ πολλάκις τοῦ ἀληθοῦς πνευματικοῦ ἐν τῷ σωματικῷ, ὡς ἂν εἴποί τις, ψεύδει. He also says that the Scriptures have incorporated into their history many things which never took place, and that a person's understanding must be limited who did not see for himself that the Scriptures relate events which could not possibly have occurred in the manner in which they are narrated. This, he says, is especially the case both with those which give a too human character to God, and with those in which persons who are represented as enjoying the particular favour of God are said to have been guilty of wicked acts. "Quae nobis aedificatio erit," he observes, "legentibus Abraham tantum patriarcham non solum mentitum esse Abimelech regi, sed et pudicitiam conjugis prodidisse? Quid nos aedificat tanti patriarchae uxor, si putatur contaminationibus exposita per conniventiam maritalem? Haec" (that is, that Sarah was exposed by her husband to impurity) "Judaei putant, et si qui cum eis, sunt literae amici, non spiritûs." (Hom. 6 in Gen. iii.) He uses the same language with respect to the New Testament. He says (Contra Celsum, I. 42) :—

"In almost every history, however true it may be, it is difficult, and sometimes impossible, to demonstrate the reality of it. Let us suppose, in fact, that some one should take upon himself to deny that there was a Trojan war on account of the improbabilities which are connected with that history, such as the birth of Achilles from a sea-goddess, &c. How could we prove the reality of it, overwhelmed as we should be by the evident inventions which in some unknown manner have been mixed up with the generally admitted idea of a war between the Greeks and Trojans? What alone is practicable is that he who wishes to study history with judgment, and to remove illusions from it, must consider how much of that history he can believe without more complete information; how much, on the contrary, he must only understand symbolically (τίνα δὲ προπολογῆσαι), bearing in mind the intention of the narrator, *and how much he must mistrust altogether, as being merely dictated by the desire of pleasing.* It has been my wish to put forward these remarks as preliminary to the subject of the entire history of Jesus as given in the gospels, not with the view of leading clear-sighted people to a blind and unauthorised belief, but of showing that this history requires to be studied with judgment, and examined with care, and that we must, so to speak, bury ourselves in the meaning of the writer, in order to discover for what purpose each separate thing has been written."

In another passage (De principp. IV. 16) he says that, generally speaking, the New Testament is the work of the same spirit as that which dictated the Old, which spirit has acted in the one in the same way as it has in the other; that is to say, that it has incorporated with things which have actually happened other things which have not happened, in order to bring us back to the spiritual meaning:

Οὐ μόνον δὲ περὶ τῶν πρὸ τῆς παρουσίας ταῦτα τὸ πνεῦμα ᾠκονόμησεν, ἀλλ', ἄτε τὸ αὐτὸ τύγχανον καὶ ἀπὸ ἑνὸς θεοῦ, τὸ ὅμοιον καὶ ἐπὶ τῶν εὐαγγελίων πεποίηκε, καὶ ἐπὶ τῶν ἀποστόλων, οὐδὲ τούτων πάντῃ ἄκρατον τὴν ἱστορίαν τῶν προσυφασμένων κατὰ τὸ σωματικὸν ἐχόντων, μὴ γεγενημένον.

The Fathers seem to have held much the same opinion as Strabo, who says, "It is not possible for a philosopher to lead by reasoning a multitude of women, and of the low vulgar, and thus incite them to piety, holiness, and faith; but the philosopher must also make use of superstition, and not omit the invention of fables, and the performance of miracles. For the lightning, and the ægis, and the trident, and the thyroleuchal arms of the gods, are but fables, *and so is all ancient theology.* But the founders of states adopted them as bugbears to frighten the weak-minded."

All ancient legislators, when they wished to give a divine sanction to their laws, pretended that a theophany had taken place. Bacchus in Euripides (Bacch.) answers Pentheus, who asks him whence he derived his new worship, that he has derived them from Bacchus the son of Jupiter, who has ordered him to propagate them (Pentheus not having recognised him); that Jupiter has manifested himself to him, and has dictated the laws of this religious institution to him himself. Rhadamanthus (Strabo, l. X., Diod., l. V. c. 75) says that he received the laws which he gave to Crete from Jupiter. Minos shut himself up in a cave in order to compose his code of laws, which he also said he had from heaven. Zoroaster (Hyde, de Vet. Pers. rel., p. 317) did the same when he wished to establish the Magian doctrines, and said that the Zend-Avesta came down from heaven. Josephus (Adv. Apion, l. II. § 17) says of Moses, "When he had first persuaded himself that his actions and designs were favourable to God's will, he thought it his duty to impress above all things that notion on the multitude. He was no impostor, no deceiver, as his revilers say, *but such a one as they brag Minos to have been among the Greeks, and other legislators after him,* for some of them suppose that they had their laws from Jupiter, while Minos said that the revelation of his laws was to be referred to Apollo, and to his oracle at Delphi, *whether they really thought that they were so deceived, or supposed, however, that they could persuade the people easily that so it was.*"

Varro says that "there are many truths which it is useless for the vulgar to know, and many falsehoods which it is not fit the people should know to be falsehoods." Christian bishops have spoken with equal plainness. Bishop Synesius (A.D. 400) writes, "The people will be deceived; you cannot manage them otherwise. The old Egyptian priests always acted on those principles, hence they shut themselves up in their temples when they carried on their mysteries. If the people had been initiated in them they would have felt indignant at the deception. I, for my part, shall always be a philosopher in my private capacity, but a priest before the people." Gregory of Nazianzen writes to Jerome, "A flow of words is alone requisite for making an impression on the people. The less they understand the more they admire. Our fathers and teachers have not always said what they thought, but what the occasion required." The Therapeutan monks expounded their scriptures allegorically, and in the Epistle to the Galatians the same method of expounding the most simple and obvious apparent facts of the Old Testament is adopted. Thus, the two sons of Abraham are to be understood as two covenants; his mistress Agar is a mountain in Arabia, and the mountain in Arabia is Jerusalem. This principle was carried to such an extent by the Fathers that they did not hesitate to admit that the gospels could not be defended as true according to the literal text. Origen (Hom. 7 in Is., fol. 106, D) says "There are things contained therein, which, taken in their literal sense, are mere falsities and lies." St. Gregory (Comment. on 2 Kings, c. vii.) asserts of the whole Divine letter that "it is not only dead, but deadly," and Athanasius (Quæst. ad Antiochum, vol. II. p. 357 D) admonishes his readers that "should we understand Sacred Writ according to the letter, we should fall into the most enormous blasphemies."

Even the oldest ecclesiastical writers can give us nothing but vague traditions respecting the origin of the canonical gospels. Mosheim says: "The opinions, or rather the conjectures, of the learned concerning the time when the books of the New Testament were collected into one volume, as also about the *authors* of that collection, are extremely different.... This important question is attended with great labours and almost insuperable difficulties to us in these later times." This question is further complicated by the admission of Bishop Marsh (Michaelis's "Introduction to the New Testament," by Bishop Marsh, vol. II. p. 365), that "it is a certain fact that several readings in our common printed text are nothing but alterations made by Origen, whose authority was so great in the Christian Church that emendations which he proposed, though, as he himself acknowledges, they were supported by the evidence of no manuscripts, were very generally received." Words, phrases, and sometimes whole verses, have also been taken from one gospel and put into another, as has been done with Matt. xxiii. 14; Mark, vi. 14; Luke, i. 28, iv. 4, ix. 56, xi. 2, 14, 15, &c. (Conf. Tischendorf, Nov. Test. Græce, vol. VII. ad hos locos, et prolegom. p. 399 sqq.). Texts which favoured the opinions of heretics have also been changed (Conf. Volkmar, Das Evang. Marcions, Hilgenfeld, Theol. Jahrbuch, vol. XII. (1853) p. 215 sqq.). Others have been inserted in support of some special dogma, of which the well-known text, 1 John, v. 7, 8, which was formerly relied upon to establish the doctrine of the Trinity, is an example. The original text, as it stands in the Codex Sinaiticus, is, "For there are three that bear record, the Spirit, and the water, and the blood, and these three agree in one." This is also the text in the Alexandrian, Vatican, and other codices, and the whole of the passage respecting the Father, the Word, and the Holy Ghost, is a later insertion.

The Epistle to the Galatians is the oldest of the canonical writings, but before it was written there was in existence a body of other writings of which we know nothing but by name. Some of the titles of these works, such as "The Mystery," "The Living Gospel," &c., occur in the Epistles. All the communities addressed in the Epistles are spoken of as being already Christians. In Gal. i. 8, the author of that epistle speaks of a gospel which "we have preached," and desires that if an angel from heaven should preach any other gospel he may be cursed. It is evident, however, from the epistle itself that this gospel was not only not the same in substance, but that it did not in the least resemble any of our gospels. Any resemblance must in fact have been out of the question, for St. Justin tells us that party feeling ran so high that many who followed the Pauline teaching thought it their duty to avoid even associating with the Jewish Christians. Justin says that he himself is not so intolerant, provided that his Judaizing brethren do not endeavour to make proselytes of and excommunicate those of more liberal opinions, and he concludes by saying that in his opinion both parties will be saved (Dial. cum Tryph. n. 45). Notwithstanding this, however, he abstains from quoting from the Pauline writings, and even from mentioning the name of Paul, and he attributes the conversion of the Gentiles not to Paul, but to the Apostles (Apol. prima, c. 39). He also says (Dial. cum Tryph. c. 35), that he will not be in communion with those who eat meals sacrificed to idols (εἰδωλόθυτα), and say that they have received no injury from them (καὶ μηδὲν ἐκ τούτου βλάπτεσθαι λέγειν), thus condemning the teaching of the Epistle to the Corinthians (1 Cor. viii. 8–10, x. 23 and sqq.). Papias does not speak of Paul as having any authority in the Church, or as one whose words were worth remembering, and the Ebionites, or Judæo-Christians, rejected all his writings, and held him to be an apostate from the law, the father of all heresies, and the chief enemy of the faith.

The curse in the Galatians, therefore, lights upon writings that have not come down to us. There is a quotation from one of them in Acts xx. 35, "Remember the words of the Lord Jesus, how he said, It is more difficult to give than to receive." These words are not in any of the gospels, and the quotation is important as showing that the author of the Acts recognised other writings than those which we possess as canonical. The Epistle of Jude also refers to a book which is now lost, the "Assumption of Moses," and quotes the book of Enoch as authentic and inspired. Tertullian (De cultu fœm. I. 8) appeals to some Messianic texts which had been inserted in this book, and reproaches the Jews with rejecting it, for he says that it might have survived the Deluge, or have been re-written by Noah under the inspiration of the Holy Ghost!

St. Clement says that Christ, having been asked when his kingdom would come, answered, "It will only come when two and two make one, when the outside resembles the inside, and when there is neither male nor female." Fabricius shows that Clement does not name the person who interrogated Christ, nor the gospel from which he took these words. Clemens Alexandrinus, however, mentions the gospel according to the Egyptians, and says that Christ's answer began: "When you shall trample under foot the dress of modesty, and when two shall be one," &c. There is another quotation in the Epistle of Ignatius to the Smyrnæans (c. iii.) : "And when the Lord came to those who were round Peter, he said to them, Take hold of me, and touch me, and see that I am not an incorporeal demon. And straightway they touched him, and they believed, being convinced by his flesh, and by the Spirit." Eusebius (H. E. l. III.) admits that he does not know from what gospel this passage is quoted, but Jerome (In Catalog. Script. Eccl.) says it is taken from a gospel which he had recently translated, and reproduces it, with the omission of the words after "and they believed." He quotes these latter words in his Proem in c. xviii. Isaiæ, as taken from the Gospel to the Hebrews.

The gospels which have been called Apocryphal since the Council of Nice, but which are quoted from by the Fathers with as much reverence as they quote from those which are now called canonical, have this remarkable feature about them, that they entirely ignore the latter, while the canonical gospels contain large portions of the apocryphal, though frequently in an altered and distorted form. These gospels are full of fabulous wonders, but they contain a narrative which, however incredible, is at least free from the contradictions which the canonical gospels are full of. The simplicity and artlessness of these compositions is strongly in favour of their antiquity. The Fathers certainly did not consider these gospels and other writings as apocryphal. Justin makes use of one or several uncanonical gospels under the name of "Memorials of the Apostles" (Hitzenfeld, Die Evang. Justins; Volkmar, Ueber Justin der Martyrer, p. 12 sqq.; Zeller, Theol. Jahrbuch, 1857, p. 138 sqq.). He also refers to the Acts of Pontius Pilate as containing an account of the miracles of Jesus. Eusebius (H. E. IV. 22) says that Hegesippus, in the middle of the second century, made use of the Gospel to the Hebrews, and the Epistle of Ignatius to the Smyrnæans is also quoted by Clemens Alexandrinus and Origen. Clemens Alexandrinus considers the preaching of Peter to be the authentic production of that apostle. The Apocalypse of Peter is considered in the Commentaries of Clemens Alexandrinus to be as authentic as the Catholic Epistles. It was read publicly at Rome towards the close of the second century, and in the time of Sozomenes certain churches in Palestine still held it to be canonical. Irenæus, who was the disciple of Papias, considers the Shepherd of Hermas to be a sacred book, and Origen (Comment. in Epist. ad Rom. l. X. n. 31) says that it is a divinely inspired writing. Origen, Jerome, and others consider the Recognitions to be an authentic work by Clemens Romanus, and Epiphanius only quotes from the Apostolic Constitutions by the words "The Apostle said," or "The Divine Word said."

The first in date of these gospels which have come down to us is that of the Birth of Mary, which is contained in the works of St. Jerome. Epiphanius and Augustine also mention this gospel, which several Christian Churches received as genuine and authentic. A gospel very much resembling this was attributed to St. Matthew, and was also received as genuine by several of the Christian Churches. The second is the Protevangelion, which is attributed to James the Lesser, and which contains the greater portion of the preceding gospel. It is frequently alluded to by the Fathers in a way which shows that it was very generally accepted. It is supposed to have been originally composed in Hebrew. Postellus, who brought the text of this gospel from the Levant, says that it was publicly read as canonical in the Eastern Churches. Joseph is represented in it as being a widower with children before his marriage with Mary. This belief was held by all the Latin Fathers till the time of Ambrose, and by the Greek Fathers afterwards.

The First Gospel of the Infancy of Jesus Christ was received by Eusebius, Athanasius, Epiphanius, Chrysostom, &c., who accredit several of its relations. Peter Martyr, who was bishop of Alexandria in the third century, says that the place in Egypt to which Jesus was banished is now called Matarea, about ten miles beyond Cairo. This gospel says that when Joseph and his family drew near a great city in Egypt the idol fell down, and all the inhabitants of Egypt, besides others, ran together. Eusebius (Demon. Evang. l. VI. c. 20) and Athanasius (De Incarnat. Verbi) also tell this story. They say that when Joseph and Mary arrived in Egypt they went to dwell in a city of the Thebais, in which there was a superb temple of Serapis, and that on their going into the temple with Jesus all the statues fell flat on their faces. Mathura, which Ptolemy calls Matura Deorum, is where the Indian Christna was born. His statue, which is in the temple, is black, like the Bambino at Loretto and Rome, and the temple, which is built in the form of a cross, stands due east and west. Matarea in the Eastern languages signifies the sun, and it is mentioned in Isa. xxx. 4, where it is called הנס *hns*, or Hanes, and in the LXX. Heliopolis. Ahmed Ibn Idris, a Mahomedan divine, says that this gospel was used by some Christians in common with the canonical gospels, and Fabricius thinks that it is identical with a Gospel of Thomas, which Orobius de Castro says was read in a very great number of churches in Asia and Africa as the only rule of their faith. The Nestorians in India used it as late as A.D. 1599, when it was condemned by a synod at Angamala, in the mountains of Malabar. The Second Gospel of the Infancy, which is a fragment, was attributed to St. Thomas, and is supposed to have been originally connected with the Gospel of the Birth of Mary.

The Acts of Pontius Pilate, which are now called the Gospel of Nicodemus, are of very great antiquity, and are appealed to by several of the early Christians. They were in use in some churches as late as the latter end of the third century, and were recognised as authentic by Justin, as we have seen, though Eusebius charges the Pagans with having forged a book called the Acts of Pilate, which the Rev. Jeremiah Jones shows there is internal evidence to prove cannot have been the case.

Besides what are usually known as the Apocryphal Gospels, others were in existence long before the canonical Gospels assumed their present form. They are first mentioned in the Talmud by certain doctors who wrote between A.D. 100 and A.D. 130. The Hebrew names given to them are כליובין or אוכלין and כופי הסיכין (Tosifta Sabbat, c. 14, Jerus. Sabbat, c. 16, Babl. Sabbat, 116ª). These Minyan (Judæo-Christian) Gospels seem to have been drawn up in Aramaic, the popular dialect of the Jews in Palestine, which had replaced the ancient Hebrew language at that time, and to have been full of quotations from the Old Testament, for Rabbi Joses of Galilee was of opinion that these writings ought to be burnt after cutting out of them the names of God which they contained, while Rabbi Tarphu thought that they ought to be burnt, names and all.

The first allusion by any ecclesiastical writer to the existence of any gospels is contained in a fragment of a lost writing by Papias, Bishop of Hierapolis, which was written about the middle of the second century. Papias, however, distinctly states that he only derived his information from the verbal statements of men who had been acquainted with certain presbyters and contemporaries of the apostles, who had communicated to him what some of the apostles or other disciples of the Lord had said (εἶπεν). He has gone beyond the testimony of these presbyters to what Aristin and John the Presbyter said (λέγουσιν) in his time. He speaks of them, however, with some contempt, and says that he was not satisfied with their prolix commentaries, and that he found what he had taken from their books less useful than what he had learned by conversation. Eusebius calls him an exceedingly little-minded person (σφόδρα μικρὸς τὸν νοῦν) because he taught that Christ would reign for a thousand years on earth, a doctrine which was preached and universally believed in his time, but had been given up in the time of Eusebius. He was certainly extremely credulous, to say the least of it, for he relates, among other marvels, that a dead man was raised to life where he was, and that a man named Justus, whose surname was Barsabas, drank a rank poison, and by the grace of God suffered no harm. This he says was the same Justus who was set up with Matthias to be elected by lot in the place of Judas Iscariot. In another place he says, "To some of them [the angels] he gave to rule over the administration of the earth, and he enjoined them to rule it well." Afterwards he says, "But it happened that this appointment came to nothing."

Irenæus (Adv. Hier. V. 33, 4) speaks of Papias as of one who had "heard John," but Eusebius doubts, with reason, whether the Apostle John can be meant in this passage, considering that no mention whatever is made of him in the prooemium of Papias, but that he states that he did not derive his narrative directly from the Apostles. Irenæus, however, gives the following specimen of what he alleges Papias to have heard from the Apostle St. John himself:—

"The Lord taught and said that the days shall come in which vines shall spring up, each having ten thousand branches, and in each branch shall be ten thousand arms, and in each arm of a branch ten thousand tendrils, and on each tendril ten thousand bunches, and on each bunch ten thousand grapes, and each grape on being pressed shall yield five and twenty gallons of wine, and when any one of the saints shall take hold of one of these bunches, another shall cry out 'I am a better bunch, take me, and bless the Lord by me.'" This multiplication by ten thousand is extended to grains of wheat, apples, flowers, and animals, and concludes by a saying of Jesus, "And these things are believable by all believers; but Judas the traitor not believing, asked him, 'But how shall things that propagate thus be brought to an end by the Lord?' And the Lord answered him and said, 'Those who shall live in these times shall see.'"

If Papias really wrote this his inventive powers must be on a par with his credulity, and his statements must be received with caution.

The fragment preserved by Eusebius is as follows:—Ματθαῖος μὲν οὖν Ἑβραΐδι διαλέκτῳ τὰ λόγια συνεγράψατο, ἡρμήνευσε δὲ αὐτὰ ὡς ἦν δυνατὸς ἕκαστος. "Matthew put together the logia in the Hebrew dialect, and every one translated them as best he could." These λόγια must, according to the meaning of the word in Acts viii. 31, Rom. iii. 2, Heb. v. 12, and 1 Pet. iv. 11, have been only a collection of sayings which were held to be oracular utterances, or "words of God." The Gospel used by Papias was the Gospel according to the Hebrews, which was also used by Hegesippus, and which is the most ancient gospel we have. Papias gives a story which Eusebius found in c. xix. 3, of that gospel, Γυνή τις ἐπὶ πολλαῖς ἁμαρτίαις διεβλήθη ἀπὸ τοῦ Κυρίου. Eusebius (H. E. III. 25, 27, IV. 22) explicitly separates the καθ' Ἑβραίους εὐαγγέλιον from the λόγια written in Aramaic which Papias speaks of. In the same work Papias speaks of a writing ascribed to Mark, which is distinguished from that of Matthew by its containing not only the sayings, but the acts, of Jesus. Matthew, he says, συνεγράψατο τὰ λόγια, and Mark wrote τὰ ὑπὸ τοῦ Χριστοῦ ἢ λέχθεντα ἢ πράχθεντα. The work attributed to Matthew therefore contained no acts, but only the sayings of Jesus. These λόγια, he says, were written in Hebrew, that is, in the Aramaic dialect. It seems probable that these λόγια were contained in certain divisions, probably five in number. At any rate Papias drew up his Ἐξέγησεις or explanation of these λόγια in five συγγράμματα, perhaps in order to correspond with the Pentateuchal type.

It is evident from what has been said that the canonical gospel of Matthew can only be in part a translation of these Aramaic λόγια. All that can be ascertained is that, according to Papias, there was in existence before the middle of the second century a tradition which came from the παρακολουθήκοτες τοῖς πρεσβυτέροις, the followers of the Presbyters, as the fragment states, and which therefore was at third hand from the apostles or disciples of Jesus, and also that Matthew had compiled a collection of the sayings of Jesus (which will be examined in a subsequent chapter) in Aramaic, but as he says that these λόγια were also written by one of the contemporaries of Jesus, it is impossible to distinguish one from the other.

A five-fold series of discourses is still to be observed in the first gospel, and may be recognised by the formula, "And it came to pass when Jesus had ended these sayings," which occurs five times. We find, however, even in these discourses an admixture of later Christian ideas in c. vii. 22, 23, and c. x. 38, 40, and the quotations from the Old Testament attributed to Jesus in these discourses are almost always in the words of the Septuagint version, which it is not possible that he, as an orthodox Jew, can have made use of, especially as it often differs materially from the Hebrew text. Matthew xiii. 14, is incorrectly quoted from Isa. vi. 9, &c. One of the Fathers attributed the authorship of this gospel to James, while others said that John was the author of it.

The statement of John the Presbyter respecting Mark's Gospel is as follows, according to Papias:—

"Mark, as the intimate friend and interpreter of Peter, described what Christ said and did as far as his memory served him. He did not do this, however, according to the succession of the occurrences, because he had not heard the Lord himself, neither had he heard anything from those who accompanied him, but he was, as I have said, an interpreter (ἑρμηνευτὴς) of Peter, who accommodated his teaching to the exigencies of the moment, and did not, therefore, like Matthew, aim at giving a systematic account of the sayings of the Lord. But Mark omitted nothing, for he wrote down one thing and another (ἔνια) as he remembered them, and he took care respecting them not to forget any of the things that he had heard, and not to narrate anything that was not true" (Euseb. H. E., III. 39).

If this account is held to apply to the canonical gospel of Mark (which ends, as will be shown presently, with c. xvi. 8), we have no authority in the gospel of Mark, the interpreter of Peter, for the miraculous birth, nor for the resurrection and ascension of Christ. It is also remarkable that he should omit Christ's promise of the keys to Peter and the story about paying the tribute out of the fish's mouth, although Peter is put forward on several occasions (c. i. 36, xiii. 3, xxi. 7) when he is not mentioned by the other Evangelists. It is, however, impossible that this statement can apply to the canonical gospel, for not only is the latter, even in its earliest form, and without the additions which have been made to it from time to time, full of mythical narratives, but Papias states further on that Mark wrote οὐ μὲν τῷ τάξει, "not in order," and this expression cannot apply to the most chronologically arranged of the gospels. We must suppose, therefore, that the Presbyter had in view a totally different writing.

The Fathers can tell us nothing respecting the gradual growth of the canonical gospels. Justin, who quotes several passages which occur in Matthew, and one which occurs in Mark, nowhere speaks of either Matthew or Mark as the author of the Memorials (ἀπομνημονεύματα) from which he took several occurrences in the life of Jesus. He only says that they proceeded "from the apostles and their disciples." All that can be said with certainty is that Justin was acquainted with texts which are only found in one of the synoptical gospels, but the words which he says were uttered by the voice from heaven at the baptism of Jesus differ from those in the canonical gospels. It is certain, moreover, that the sources from which he took those texts had no authors' names to them, and that he does not ascribe the writings he made use of to the Evangelists as usually recognised.

Faustus, the learned Manichæan bishop, pressed Augustine with a challenge which he was unable to answer. He says, "It is certain that the New Testament was not written by Christ himself, nor by his apostles, but a long while after them, by some unknown persons, who, lest they should not be credited when they wrote of affairs they were little acquainted with, affixed to their writings the name of apostles, or of such as were supposed to be their companions, asserting that what they had written themselves was written *according to* (secundum) those persons to whom they ascribed it." It is remarkable in connection with this statement that Eusebius says that the Marcus mentioned in 1 Peter v. 13 is Mark the Evangelist. This epistle pretends to be written at Babylon—" The Church at Babylon .... saluteth you " [Cod. Sin.], where there is not the slightest reason to suppose that Peter ever went; besides which, Dr. Coplestone doubts, with reason, whether Peter knew enough Greek to write his epistle. In c. iv. 3 the author says, that in the former part of his life he had been a lascivious, lustful, drunken, riotous, and abominably idolatrous Gentile ! In c. ii. 12 it is said that the Christians were accused of being evil doers, which we know from Pliny's testimony was not the case in the beginning of the second century, and this seems to prove that this epistle must have been composed at a later date than even that period.

In Mark vii. 31 there is an indication of the period when that gospel was compiled. It is there said that Jesus came unto the sea of Galilee " through the midst of the shores of Decapolis." And this name has been inserted into Matthew's gospel (c. iv. 25) merely in order to make it be believed that the fame of Jesus had spread far and wide. Luke, whose description is confirmed both by Josephus and Tacitus, tells us that in the fifteenth year of Tiberius, and during his whole reign, the Jewish territory was divided by the Romans into four tetrarchies ; and Josephus never mentions the name of Decapolis before Vespasian was governor of Syria, and general against the rebellious Jews, in the latter end of Nero's reign. Again, Pliny tells us (Nat. Hist. l. V. c. 10) that the territory which intervenes between these two cities, and which surrounded each of them, was not subject to the same government as the cities themselves, but to the adjoining territories. The Romans had probably been induced to annex the Jewish cities to the Government of Syria in consequence of the insurrection of the Jewish against the Syrian inhabitants of some of those cities. It is evident, therefore, that the Decapolis was not any distinct country or continued district, but merely the general appellation of ten detached, insulated cities, lying all, except Scythopolis, east of the Jordan. Yet Mark and Matthew speak of it as if it were a province, like Galilee or Trachonitis, and as if it were situated north-west of the Sea of Galilee. This gross ignorance of geography shows that the writer cannot have been a native of Palestine, and the insertion of the name renders it probable that both gospels were compiled after the destruction of Jerusalem, as the third certainly was (Luke xix. 41, 43, 44; xxi. 9, 20; xxiii. 29). The verse in the Codex Sinaiticus is, "And again, departing from the coasts of Tyre, he came through Sidon unto the Sea of Galilee."

In order to escape from the difficulties which arise from the errors and contradictions in the gospels, the hypothesis of a common Hebrew document has been resorted to. Bishop Marsh, however, has demonstrated the impossibility of this, and has come to the conclusion that "St. Matthew, St. Mark, and St. Luke, all three used different copies of some common statement, which, before any of our canonical gospels existed, was known as the Gospel to the Hebrews, or the Gospel according to the Twelve Apostles, a gospel of which the ancients speak with great respect; or the Gospel according to the Nazarenes, or the Gospel according to Matthew." Beausobre is of the same opinion. He says, "At the head of the first class [of Scriptures] are to be placed two gospels [that according to the Hebrews and that according to the Egyptians]. In my opinion, the Gospel according to the Hebrews is the most ancient of all. The Nazarenes pretended that this was the original from which the Gospel of St. Matthew was taken. It began with these words, 'It happened in the days of Herod.' . . . That which has been called the Gospel according to the Egyptians is of the same antiquity. Origen has mentioned it; Clemens Alexandrinus had previously quoted it in several places; and if the Second Epistle of Clemens Romanus be authentic, this gospel would have a testimony far more ancient than that of these two doctors. . . . Upon considering the unquestionable fact that it was received by the Christians of Egypt, I have not been able to hinder myself from thinking that it was written by the Essenes, who had believed in Jesus Christ. The religion of these people contained a great deal of the Christian religion. The Gospel according to the Egyptians was full of mysticism, parables, enigmas, and allegories; this has been attributed to the spirit of the nation. For my part I attribute it rather to the Essenean cast of character." This agrees with the statement of Eusebius, that our gospels and epistles were identical with those of the Therapeutæ, or Essenes. The title of one of his chapters (l. I. c. 4) is "The religion published by Jesus Christ is neither new nor strange," and in l. II. c. 17, he states, in the most unqualified terms, that "The ancient Therapeutæ were Christians, and their ancient writings were our gospels and epistles."

None of the Fathers speak of the earlier sources from which the first draft of the canonical gospels originated, and they nowhere show that they had any acquaintance with the Logia which Papias speaks of. There is nothing surprising in this, however, for the knowledge of Aramaic became lost in the Greek Church. Later and more perfect copies of the writings made, we may suppose, the older editions superfluous, and they ultimately were lost or destroyed. The original Gospel of Mark, even after many additions had been made to the short biographical sketch which it contains, must, by reason of its brevity, have been considered inferior to the longer accounts of Matthew and Luke, as is evident from the comparative infrequency with which the text of this gospel is quoted. The ecclesiastical writers of epistles, from Justin downwards, confine themselves to the Gospel according to Matthew, owing to their peculiar theological views; and in some manuscripts the original text of Mark has actually been altered, in order to make it agree with Matthew or Luke.

The original sources of portions of Mark's Gospel are of great antiquity, as is evident from the names of places in it which afterwards fell into disuse, such as Dalmanutha (c. viii. 10), which afterwards became Magadan (Cod. Sin.), or Magdala (Matt. xv. 39), and Bethphage (Mark xi. 1), a reading which has been preserved in Matt. xxi. i., where, however, it is altered into Bethphage and Bethany.

The first edition of this original gospel is of later origin, and indicated a period when mythical narratives were introduced into the text. The account of the resurrection of Jesus points to a period when the older spiritual conception had become developed into a material fact. It belongs to a later date than the Pauline epistles, for a Christian universalism, in the Pauline sense, pervades it, with which the universality of the symbolism (Mark, v. 4 and sqq., vii. 24 and sqq., and elsewhere) is connected, and an unfavourable view of the twelve Apostles is also taken in it. From the junction of this first edition of Mark's Gospel with the Logia, or with portions of them, there arose a writing, the second edition of Matthew, part of which appears in Luke's Gospel, though it does not comprise the narrative of the birth of Jesus, or other legends, which Luke leaves unnoticed. The numerous glosses and alterations which the compiler of the second Matthew allowed himself to make show that dogmatic teaching was already greatly on the increase.

The canonical edition of Matthew's Gospel must have been unknown to the author of St. Luke's Gospel, for the narrative of the birth of Christ, the genealogy, and the account of the death of Judas Iscariot are against the probability of his having read the statements in Matt. i. and ii. and xxviii. 3–10. This last edition of the first gospel appears, in fact, to refer to Luke, and to have been drawn up at a later period. It is pervaded by a strong Judæo-Christian feeling, and this, together with the absence of any explanatory information respecting Palestine, has been thought to show that the author was a Palestinian Christian. It is difficult, however, to reconcile this with the extraordinary mistake in Matt. xiii. 35, in which a quotation from Ps. lxxviii. 2 was attributed to Esaias the prophet, as it still is in the Codex Sinaiticus. Jerome admits that Porphyry had accused the Evangelist of this mis-quotation, and merely says that the name of Isaiah had long been removed from that passage, in which, however, it is still attributed to "the prophet." The canonical Matthew continued to be of authority among the mediæval Jewish Christians, while the Pauline Christians, such as Marcion and others, adhered to Luke's Gospel, so that both these gospels gradually attained to an equal degree of consideration by the fusion of parties which was continually going on in the Church.

The second edition of Mark comes next to the canonical edition of Matthew. In the short preface to the gospel the editor speaks of gospels in which a narrative of the birth of Christ had been inserted. This edition was written for Gentile Christians, as is clearly shown by the nature of its glosses and alterations. It appears to have been written at Rome from certain passages, such as c. x. 12, and xv. 21, in which latter passage Alexander and Rufus are probably Romans, whom the editor was acquainted with (Conf. Romans xvi. 12).

The conclusion of Mark's Gospel (c. xvi. 9–20) is one of the late additions to the Evangelical literature. The genuine conclusion has been lost, for Gregory of Nyssa (A.D. 371) says that in the most exact copies this gospel concludes with c. xvi. 8. Some copies, however, have the following conclusion: "And they told briefly all the things which they were commanded to Peter and those with him, and after that Jesus himself sent forth, through them, from the east to the west, the holy and incorruptible word of eternal salvation." The present conclusion is a compilation from Luke, John, the Acts of the Apostles, and later traditions, and shows itself to be the work of another hand by a style and a meaning attached to words which differs from the other portions of Mark. The copyists of the oldest and best known MSS. did not find this portion of Mark in the MSS. they used. It is wanting, for instance, both in the Codex Sinaiticus and in the Vatican Codex, and it is clear from other versions, and from the testimony of several scholiasts, that it was also deficient in other MSS. This is confirmed by Eusebius (Quæst. 1 and 3 ad Marin. in Script. vet. coll., ed. Aug. Maji, p. 61, 72), by Jerome (Epist. ad Hebid. J. qn. 3), who both distinctly state that almost all the copies that could be depended upon in their time ended with v. 8, and by Gregory of Nyssa (Orat. 2 de resurr. Christi). The present conclusion was in existence before the end of the second century, for Justin (Apol. i. 45) and Irenæus (Cont. Hær. iii. x. 6) were acquainted with it, as was also Hippolytus and the author of the Apostolic Constitutions.

Justin Martyr mentions the visit of the angel Gabriel to the Virgin in the words of Luke i. 35–38, and the agony of Christ in the words of Luke xxii. 42, but does not mention Luke by name. Luke's Gospel is not alluded to in either the Acts or the Epistles, and it is not till A.D. 178 that Luke is mentioned by Irenæus as the author of it. The author has been supposed to be a Palestinian Christian, but in face of the gross blunder in c. iii. 2, where the Jews are made to have two high priests, and in c. xiii. 1, respecting the Galilæans, whose blood Pilate had mingled with their sacrifices, which is a pure invention, it is difficult to believe that the author had ever been in Palestine. If the Acts of the Apostles are by the same author, as Jerome (De viris illustr. c. 7) asserts they were, they contain a speech attributed to Gamaliel (c. v. 35 and sqq.) which he could not possibly have uttered, for no doctor of the law could have said in A.D. 34 or 37 that Theudas rose up before his days; for Josephus (Ant. xx. c. 5) says that Theudas rose up in the procuratorship of Cuspius Tactus, that is, not before A.D. 44. Luke says that, "after this man" Judas of Galilee arose; but the attempt at insurrection by Judas of Galilee took place in A.D. 6 or 7, and the author of the Acts is thus nearly forty years wrong.

Interpolations were made in Luke's Gospel even after the second century, for it appears from Origen that several believers in his time were offended with that part of the gospel which relates to the penitent thief, and declared that that passage was not in the older copies, but was a late addition of some of the interpreters (Ῥᾳδιουργοὶ). Origen does not agree with them, but they are right; for neither Justin, nor Irenæus, nor Tertullian take notice of this remarkable occurrence, though the latter has written a treatise upon the state of souls between death and the resurrection.

It is evident that the fourth Gospel cannot have been written by the Apostle John, the son of Zebedee, and one of "the sons of thunder" (Mark iii. 17), an expression which denotes a fiery nature, which is the very opposite to that attributed to the Apostle in this gospel. It is impossible also to suppose that an "ignorant and unlearned man," as he and Peter are described (Acts iv. 13) to be, who was the son of an obscure Galilæan fisherman, who could only speak his provincial dialect, and did not so much as understand Hebrew, still less any other language, should have written a gospel in indifferent Greek—a remark which applies to other books of the New Testament. In Gal. ii. 6, 9, Paul says distinctly that James, Cephas, and John "added nothing to him;" that is, they could tell him nothing. It is said, moreover, in c. xxi. 24, "This is the disciple which testifieth of these things, and wrote these things, and *we* know that his testimony is true." V. 25, "And then also many other things which Jesus did," &c., is not in the Codex Sinaiticus. The expression, "My Lord and my God" in c. xx. 28, shows that it cannot have been written by the Apostle John, because the latter appellation was not addressed to Christ, either at that time or for many centuries afterwards. Theophilus of Antioch, writing about A.D. 180, says that John was the author of it, but its genuineness was contested even after his time by certain persons whom Epiphanius classes together as "Αλογοι (Hier., 51. Conf. Iren. Adv. hær., iii. xi. 9). It was universally accepted by the Church until long after the Reformation, when the learned and Reverend Dr. Evanson in England, and Eckermann, Vogel, Horst, Cludius, and Ballenstedt in Germany, denied its apostolic origin and its credibility. Dr. Evanson expresses his astonishment that gospels should be received as true which so flatly contradict each other. Bretschneider, in his Probabilia de Evangelii et Epistolarum Johannis indole et origine (1820), gave a severe blow to the orthodox views respecting this gospel.

In c. ix. 7 there is a mistake which no Jewish writer could possibly have made, for Siloam does not signify "sent," but "the place of the sending forth of waters;" that is, "the sluice," or, according to another interpretation, a fountain (שלה). "Sent" is שלחה in Hebrew. The commentators have endeavoured to get the words, "which is by interpretation sent," considered as a marginal note, but they are in all the codices, and are evidently part of the text itself. This miracle is represented as a standing one, frequently repeated in the sheep-market, that is in one of the most public places in Jerusalem, yet no historian, Jewish or Roman, who has given an account of that city, has ever mentioned so extraordinary an occurrence. In c. vii. 53, there is even a greater blunder, for the chief priests and Pharisees are represented as saying, "Search and look, for out of Galilee ariseth no prophet," which they could not possibly have said, for Nahum and Jonah were both Galilæans. Another mistake in this gospel is that Bethsaida is placed in Galilee (c. xii. 21). Josephus and Pliny both say that it was in the district of Ituræa, to which the name of Gaulonitis was given. If John were the author of this gospel he could not possibly have made such a mistake as this, for nearly the whole career of Jesus was passed in Galilee. In order to do away with this mistake the commentators have invented another Bethsaida on the western shore of Lake Gennesaret. But it is evident that the Bethsaida which was afterwards called Julias by Philip the tetrarch, and became his capital (Jos. Ant. xvii. 2, 1), is intended : for in Matt. iv. 25, Decapolis is distinguished from the country "beyond Jordan," and the writer is evidently under the impression that it was on the western side of that river.

In John i. 43 Jesus goes into Galilee on the second day after his baptism, and on the third day he is at Cana (ii. 1); but the synoptical gospels say that he was forty days in the wilderness immediately after his baptism. Again, in c. xi. 49, Caiaphas is represented as being the high priest that year, and as " prophesying " (v. 51) " that Jesus should die for that nation." No Jew could possibly be ignorant that the high priest's office was for life, and that prophesying was no part of his duty. The author of this gospel does not in fact pretend to be a Jew. He speaks of " the Jews " in c. i. 19, ii. 18, v. 15, ix. 18, 22, &c.; of " your law " in c. viii. 17, x. 34; of " their law " in c. xv. 26; of " the Jews' passover " in c. ii. 13; of " a feast of the Jews " in c. v. 1, vi. 4; of " the Jews' feast of tabernacles " in c. vii. 2, and of " the Jews' preparation day " in c. xix. 42, just as a writer would who was a stranger to the nation, to its religious observances, and to its customs.

The chronology of this gospel is hopelessly irreconcilable with that of the others, for it makes the Passover at which Jesus was crucified to be the fourth from the commencement of his ministry. Another circumstance is remarkable. The Churches of Asia Minor all observed the fourteenth Nisan as the day on which the Last Supper took place, and said that they did this on the authority of John, who, they said, had set them an example which they wished to follow (see Euseb. H. E. v. 24), viz., that they should keep that day holy in commemoration of the day on which Jesus ate the Passover in conformity with the Jewish law. This gospel, however, ignores the Passover altogether, and distinctly places (c. xiii. 1) the supper, δεῖπνον, at which he was betrayed, *before* the feast of the Passover. As to the raising of Lazarus, not only is it not mentioned by any of the other Evangelists, although it is said to have taken place in Galilee, where the public life of Jesus was almost exclusively passed, according to them, but we are told that in consequence of it " many of the Jews believed on him," thus contradicting the Acts, which say that all the disciples at his death were Galilæans, and that the whole number was only about one hundred and twenty, which, curiously enough, is the number which constituted the grand synagogue in the time of Esdras.

In c. xxi. 11 Peter brings a net to land which contains 153 great fishes. Jerome (Ad Ezek. c. 47) says that this is an allegory, for this is exactly the number of species of fish which exist, and therefore Peter is represented as catching all the faithful in the world! In c. xii. 17, 18, there is an evident addition to the accounts in Mark and Matthew of the entry into Jerusalem, for it is said that the people met him because they had heard that he had raised Lazarus, while the other gospels are silent on this subject.

The following are some other contradictions between this and the other gospels. According to the synoptical gospels Jesus does not commence his ministry until after John is put into prison (Mark i. 14, Matt. iv. 12, Luke iii. 20). He scarcely leaves Galilee at all, does not cross its southern border, and only goes to Jerusalem at the end of his career. In the fourth gospel, on the contrary, his ministry and his preaching begin long before John's imprisonment, and the scene of them is laid principally in Judæa. He first goes to the Passover a few days after the marriage at Cana (c. ii. 13); then he goes up to "the feast of the Jews" [Cod. Sin.] in c. v. 1; to "the feast of Tabernacles" (c. vii. 2, 10); and to "the feast of Dedication," which took place in winter (c. x. 22). He then goes into Peræa, when John baptized (c. x. 40), and after visiting Bethany he retires to Ephraim, near the wilderness of Judæa (c. xi. 54), until he goes up to Jerusalem before the feast of the Passover (c. xii. 1, 12). According to this gospel, therefore, he had been present at two, if not at four, Passovers, as well as other festivals, previous to his triumphal entry into Jerusalem.

The synoptical gospels represent Jesus as selecting his disciples from among the fishermen on the sea of Galilee (Mark i. 16-20, and parallel passages). In the fourth gospel, on the contrary, Simon and Andrew, two of these very same disciples, are made to be disciples of John, follow Jesus of their own account (i. 35-37), and never quit him again (ii. 2, 11, 12, 17; iii. 22; iv. 2, 8, 27, &c.). According to the synoptical gospels, again (Mark xi. 15, and parallel passages), Jesus cast out the buyers and sellers in the temple, after his triumphal entry into Jerusalem. In the fourth gospel this takes place a few days after the commencement of his ministry (ii. 13). On this occasion Jesus is asked by the Jews what sign he would show, seeing that he did these things, and he answers, "Destroy this temple, and in three days I will build it up" (ii. 18, 19). In the synoptical gospels (Mark xii. 57, 58; Matt. xxvi. 60, 61), this same speech is put into the mouth of false witnesses! In one gospel, therefore, we are told that Jesus uttered this speech, in the other we are told that he did not. In the fourth gospel (iv. 4–42) Jesus is represented as going through Samaria, stopping for two days at Sychar (a city unknown to geography), and making numerous proselytes there. According to the synoptical gospels he has nothing to do with the Samaritans until he goes up to Jerusalem, and in Matt. x. 5 he forbids the apostles to enter into any Samaritan city.

Some ten years before the time that Theophilus of Antioch attributes the authorship of this gospel to John, Apollinaris, Tatian, Athenagoras, the authors of the Epistles of the Churches of Lyons and Vienna, and of the Clementine Epistles, quote from this gospel, but without naming either the book or the author. The earlier writings which pass under the names of Barnabas, Clemens Romanus, and Hermas, do not mention it, and if they admit the doctrine of the Logos at all, it is only in a very elementary form. Marcion, the Gnostic, who would unquestionably have made use of it, if it had been known to him, was obliged to content himself with the third gospel, which he adopted after subjecting it to a complete revision. The texts quoted by Justin Martyr, which many writers have supposed to be taken from the fourth gospel, have, after much discussion, been reduced to seven, or, strictly speaking, to three, which, however, by no means necessarily belong to it; and the only text which really resembles the text of this gospel occurs also in the Homilies and Recognitions of Clement, which were in existence when Justin wrote. In fact the Homilies, the Recognitions, and Justin agree much better with each other than with this gospel; and the text is evidently more accurate, for it speaks of man being born again, while in John iii. 3, Jesus is represented as saying, "Except a man be born from above," ἄνωθεν (Conf. v. 31, where ἄνωθεν is correctly translated "from above"). The question also which is put into the mouth of Nicodemus, "How can a man be born again if he is old?" has nothing to do with the previous assertion of Jesus, that a man must be born from above. The date of this gospel may be nearly ascertained by the Gnostic terms used, such as Λόγος, Μονογενὴς, Ζωὴ, φῶς, Ἀλήθεια, Χάρις, &c., all of which were used by the Gnostic writers to describe a regular series of symbolical personages, and which have been applied by the Evangelist to Christ. Gnosticism became a regular system somewhere about A.D. 120, at which period, according to Hegesippus and Clemens Alexandrinus, the Church first became infected with it. The Valentinian heresy, the terminology of which is so apparent in this gospel, broke out between A.D. 130 and 140.

In the time of Justin the theory of the Logos, which was then in vogue at Alexandria, had begun to infect Christianity, and it was held by him as an essential element of his Christology, but the terms in which he speaks of it are essentially different from those used in the fourth gospel, and he never once quotes from that gospel in support of his favourite doctrine. On the contrary, although he was the first that taught that Christ was the second principle of the Deity, and the Creator of all things, he ascribes his knowledge of that doctrine, not to the Scriptures, but to the special favour of God. He also says that Christ, when he appeared in public, put an end to the preaching and baptizing of John the Baptist, thus formally contradicting John iii. 20-24. In his Apology he speaks of brevity and conciseness as characteristic of the sayings of Jesus, which certainly cannot apply to the long discourses which are attributed to him in the fourth gospel, neither does he mention any of the miracles which are found exclusively in that gospel, not even the raising of Lazarus.

While the synoptical gospels represent Christ as a man who, though in a spiritual sense the Son of God, yet did not contravene the Messianic notions prevalent among the Jews, in the fourth gospel he is God Himself, inferior indeed to the Father (c. vii. 35), but of the same substance (viii. 23, 58; x. 30, &c.). The whole of this teaching may be found in Philo. He says that the Word was the same as God; that he made all things; that he was the Light of the World; that he alone could see God; that he was the first-begotten Son of God; that he was the Son of the Father; that he is anointed with oil (John i. 42, ὁ Χριστὸς); that he was made in the likeness of man; that he is the Seal of God (John vi. 27); that he surrounds and supports all things; that he is the Holy Fountain, by drinking which everlasting life is obtained; that man is raised up by the Logos to be near God in heaven (John vi. 34, 37; xii. 26); and that he is free from all transgressions. A prayer attributed to Thoth shows the Egyptian origin of the doctrine of the Logos. "I call upon thee, O Heaven, thou wise work of the Great God, to be propitious; I call upon thee, Word of the Father, whom he gave utterance to in the beginning, when he established the Universe by his Will; Word of the Father, which he first made heard, his only begotten Word."

The special importance which is attached to the life of Christ is the result of the dogma of Original Sin, and of the teaching founded on that dogma, that it is impossible to escape from the consequences of the state of enmity towards God in which man is supposed to be placed by the sin of Adam, except by faith in the propitiatory sacrifice of Christ as an expiation for it. This dogma is founded on Rom. v. 12 and other passages in that epistle, but it cannot be found in the gospels. It was this dogma, in fact, far more than the disputes respecting circumcision, which led to the antagonism which existed between the Jewish Christians and the followers of Paul. In A.D. 135, after the capture of Bethara in the reign of Adrian, when the final expulsion of the Jews from Palestine took place, the Jewish Christians came to terms with those who followed the teaching of Paul, who were principally congregated at Rome. The quarrel between them was of no ordinary description, as may be inferred from the Clementine Homilies (17–19), where Peter is represented as saying to Paul: "How can Jesus have appeared to thee, who believest the very opposite of what he taught?"

The Epistle to the Romans, however, is not written by Paul. It cannot be supposed that an epistle should be addressed to them in a language of which they were ignorant, and the subscription in our copies, which states that it was written from Corinth, does not exist in the Codex Sinaiticus, in which it is simply "To the Romans." In c. i. 13–15, Paul is represented as writing to the brethren at Rome that he had oftentimes purposed to come unto them; and in c. xv. 25, &c., it is said that the time of Paul's writing this epistle was when he was going to Jerusalem with the contributions for the poor Christians of that city—that is, in the reign of Claudius; and says that when he had performed that office he will come by way of Rome into Spain. The Acts, however, show that Paul never had the least idea of travelling to Spain. Aquila and Priscilla, to whom he sends greetings, had, according to the Acts (xviii. 2), left Rome about, or rather before, the pretended date of this epistle, in obedience to the edict of Claudius, commanding all Jews to depart from Rome. C. xi. 12 shows that it must have been written after the destruction of Jerusalem and the dispersion of the Jews, and verses 15, 21, and 22 also show that this epistle must have been written after these events. It is probably the result of the compromise then arrived at between the two parties.

The General Council of Africa, which was held in A.D. 418, excommunicated all who said that Adam was born mortal. This council held that Adam only became mortal after his fall, and that all children who were born into the world participated in the crime committed by their first parent, and that this natural corruption could only be effaced by baptism. The Council of Florence decided that "the souls of those who die either in natural or original sin, fall straightway into hell, there to be punished by unequal punishments" (pœnis disparibus puniendas). The Council of Trent says: "If any one maintains that Adam, sullied by the crime of disobedience, has only transmitted death and bodily sufferings to the whole human race, and not sin, which is the death of the soul, let him be anathema. If any one denies that this sin of Adam is transmitted to all men by propagation, and not by imitation, or shall deny that it is inherent in each individual, and can only be taken away by the merits of Jesus Christ; if any one say that little children do not derive original sin from Adam, and maintains that so far as they are concerned baptism is not a real remission of sins; if any one denies that the guilt of original sin is effaced by the grace of baptism, let them be anathema."

This dogma is founded on the narrative contained in Gen. ii. and iii. But the better informed among the Jews themselves admit that this narrative is merely an allegory. Maimonides, the most learned of the Rabbis, says of the book of Genesis, " We ought not to take literally that which is written in the Book of the Creation, nor entertain the same ideas of it as are common with the vulgar. If it were otherwise our learned ancient sages would not have taken so much pains to conceal the sense, and to keep before the eyes of the uninstructed the veil of allegory which conceals the truths which it contains. Taken literally, that work contains the most extravagant and absurd ideas of the Deity." (Maimon. More Nevoch, part II. c. 29). In Bereschit Rabba, sect. 21, R. Simeon ben Yohai says respecting the third chapter of Genesis, " Woe to him who takes the biblical narratives for ordinary ones, made to amuse and satisfy the curiosity of the vulgar! If it were so, nothing would prevent us from composing stories which would be much more interesting, and, so to speak, superior to the episodes of Scripture. No. The narratives of the Holy Book are mere coverings which conceal luminous truths. He who takes the bark for the fruit, the exterior of the Thorah for the Thorah itself, is mad. If fools, incapable of looking beyond what is before them, are content with admiring the dress without caring for the being who is clad in it, intelligent persons will nevertheless give all their attention to the ideas which have been thus dressed up. It is the latter which will engage their looks and their meditations."

A legend of the Talmud (Nida XXXI. 2) says that at the moment when the human soul is about to become incarnate in our earthly body, the angels make it swear to maintain its purity in this its ephemeral dwelling-place, in order that it may return pure to its Creator. This Midrasch (explanation) is a poetical affirmation of our primitive innocence, and of the traditional Jewish doctrine on this subject, and is as follows:—

" R. Simlai says: The child in the bosom of its mother resembles folded tablets; its hands rest on its temples, its elbows on its knees, &c. There is a light on its head, and it sees from one end of the world to the other, just as he who sleeps in Judæa can see as far as Spain in his dreams. Never will that child pass happier days than those which it passes in its mother's bosom. It is there that the Thorah is taught it. But as soon as it is born an angel touches it on the mouth, and it forgets all that is past.

" Then this angel exacts an oath from the child. What oath? To live justly, and to avoid impiety. ' Abjure all vanity,' says the angel to the child, 'and even if thou shouldest be called The Just, or the Son of God, promise that thou wilt only consider thyself a sinner. Learn next that the Holy One, blessed be he, is pure, that his children are pure, and that the soul which he giveth thee this day is pure also. Swear therefore to keep thy soul in its native purity, and learn that if thou failest to keep thine oath, thy soul will be taken from thee, and thou wilt become merely matter and nothingness." (Talmud, Nida XXX. 6.)

In the Haggadah it is said, "As God fills the whole universe, so does the soul fill the whole body. As God sustains the whole universe, so does the soul sustain the whole body. As God is pure, so is the soul." The original purity of the soul is frequently set forth in the Talmud in opposition to the doctrine of Original Sin, which it invariably rejects. Thus it says, "There is no death without actual sin; no pain without personal offence. The same Spirit which has said in the Pentateuch, 'The fathers shall not be put to death for the children, neither shall the children be put to death for the fathers,' has also said that no one shall be punished for the sin of another."

The second and third chapters of Genesis, which contain the account of the fall of man, differ from the first in many important particulars. In the first chapter the Elohim or Alcim act; in the others, Jehovah. In the first chapter the earth is covered with water; in the second it is dry and barren, though we find, to our surprise, four rivers watering the garden, although no rain had fallen. In the first chapter the animals are created before man; in the second chapter man is created first, then the animals, and, lastly, woman. In the first chapter the Elohim allow all the fruits of the earth to be eaten without any exception; in the second Jehovah forbids man to eat of the fruit of a tree called the tree of the knowledge of good and evil. In the first chapter the creation is spread over six days; in the second no days are mentioned. In the first chapter (which extends to v. 2 of the second chapter) the seventh day is sanctified because God rested on it from his six days' labour; in the second chapter the seventh day is not mentioned at all. Lastly, in the first chapter, there is no mention of the Garden of Eden; in the second chapter all the events take place in the Garden of Eden, in which they originate.

The fifth chapter of Genesis, which contains the genealogy adopted in the third gospel, ignores the whole story, for it says that "Adam lived 130 years, and begat a son in his own likeness, after his image, and called his name Seth." There is no mention of Eve, or of the serpent, or of Cain, her first-born, or of Abel. The author is evidently referring to the statement in c. i. 27, that God created man "male and female," which is hopelessly irreconcilable with the subsequent statement that woman was created after Adam had been placed in the Garden of Eden, and had given names to the cattle, &c.; and although he speaks of other sons and daughters of Adam, he does so without naming them, and Seth is distinctly put forward as Adam's first-born son. The differences between the two genealogies are as follows:—

CHAPTER V.	CHAPTER IV.
The Elohim create Adam	Jehovah creates Adam
Adam begets Seth	Adam begets Cain, Abel, and Seth
Seth begets Enos	Cain begets Enoch
Enos begets Cainan	Enoch begets Irad
Cainan begets Mahalaleel	Irad begets Mehujael
Mahalaleel begets Jared	Mehujael begets Methusael
Jared begets Enoch	Methusael begets Lamech
Enoch begets Methuselah	Lamech marries
Methuselah begets Lamech	Adah Zillah
Lamech begets Noah	
Noah begets Shem, Ham, and Japheth	Jabal Jubal Tubal, Cain, Naamah

These genealogies contradict each other in every imaginable way. In c. iv. Seth is made to be the third son, and Enoch, the just man, is made to be the son of Cain! In c. v., on the contrary, he is the son of Jared. In c. iv. Enoch begets Irad; in c. v. he begets Methuselah. In chapter v. Lamech is the son of Methuselah, and the grandson of Enoch; in c. iv. three new names are interposed between him and Enoch, viz., Irad, Mehujael, and Methusael. Lastly, Noah is not mentioned in c. iv., and the genealogy of Seth terminates with his son Enos.

We shall confine ourselves to the literal sense of this celebrated narrative, as that is the only one taught at the present day. St. Jerome says that no one who does not believe in the transformation of a rib into a woman can believe in God: "Non potest quispiam credere in conditorem Deum, nisi prius crediderit de sanctis ejus vera esse qua scripta sunt, Adam a Deo plasmatum; Evam ex costâ illius et latere fabricatum." It follows from this that the believers in the literal interpretation must either renounce their belief in physiology or in God. This, however, is not the only difficulty attendant upon the literal interpretation.

The narrative speaks of three guilty individuals, the serpent, the woman, and the man. The serpent is first cursed, and then ordered to go upon his belly, as if a serpent had ever progressed in any other manner, and as if many other animals who were never cursed did not also go upon their bellies. He is then ordered to eat dust—a command which he has never obeyed. It is evident from Isaiah lxv. 25, "Dust shall be the serpent's meat;" and Micah vii. 17, "They shall bite the dust like the serpent" (both chapters written after the Captivity); that this was understood literally; besides which we cannot interpret one portion of a narrative literally, and another allegorically. Perplexed by these difficulties, the Rev. Dr. Adam Clarke has endeavoured in his edition of the Bible to make the serpent to have been a monkey, which, however, agrees just as badly with the interpretation. It is then said that the seed of the serpent is to be at enmity with the seed of the woman, but this is common to the serpent with all other beasts of prey, and it is impossible to understand why the serpent, who was the cause of man's disobedience, should be endowed with a power of injuring him which he did not possess before. Josephus (Ant. l. I. 1) says that God inserted poison under the serpent's tongue, forgetting that many species of serpents are perfectly harmless. The serpent is never identified with Satan till the apocryphal book of Wisdom, which is of a very late date, if it is not a Christian work. "St. Jerome (Præf. in lib. Salominis) says that the wisdom of Solomon resembles the Grecian style, and that ancient authors attributed it to Philo. The general belief on this subject is that Satan came from hell, and took the form of a serpent in order to deceive Eve. But Irenæus states (Adv. Hær. l. V.) "Well did Justin say that before the appearance of our Lord, Satan never ventured to blaspheme God, *because he* did not yet know his own condemnation." The woman is then told that she shall have pain in child-bearing—a pain which she shares with the lower animals—and that her husband shall rule over her, which therefore cannot have been the case previously. Adam, who had been guilty of the crime of disobedience equally with Eve, is, however, not cursed at all, but the earth is cursed for his sake, and the alleged punishment is one of the greatest blessings bestowed upon man by his Creator, and as different in its effects as possible to the lazy sensual life which has always led to the degradation of the human race, and which is indicated in the Vulgate as characteristic of the Garden of Eden by the words, "In Paradiso voluptatis," and in the Septuagint by the words Παράδεισον τῆς τρυφῆς.

The doctrine of Original Sin is opposed to the teaching of all the other parts of the Old Testament. In Deut. viii. 5 Israel is told, "Thou shalt also consider in thine heart that as a man chasteneth his son, so the Lord thy God chasteneth thee." In Prov. iii. 12 it is said, "For whom the Lord loveth he chasteneth, even as a father the son in whom he delighteth." Job (v. 17) says, "Behold, happy is the man whom God correcteth, therefore despise not thou the chastening of the Almighty." In Ps. xciv. 12 we read, "Blessed is the man whom thou chastenest, O Lord." In Isa. xlv. 7 God is represented as saying, "I create evil." Jeremiah (Lam. iii. 38) asks, "Out of the mouth of the Most High proceedeth not evil and good?" And Job asks (ii. 10), "What? shall we receive good at the hand of God, and shall we not receive evil?"

The Talmud is full of this teaching on the subject of evil. Thus it is said in Thaanit, fol. 21, "The just man will take for his model Naham the resigned, who at each blow that he received exclaimed, 'It is for my good.'" In Shabat 88G and Yoma 23 it is said, "They whose acts are all inspired by the love of God, and who find in their sufferings a subject of pious joy, resemble the sun when he arises in his majesty at the dawn of day." In Treatise Berachoth again it is said, "To enjoy the two tables (happiness in this world and the next) is not the lot of all men." R. Eliezer (More Kotan ix. 6) says, "This world is but an inn on the road; the other world is our dwelling-place."

The literal meaning of this narrative was, however, accepted by many among the Jews. The Talmud, that strange assemblage of Jewish ideas and traditions on theology, philosophy, science, and hygiene, is not without traces of the absurdities to which such views of the Divine Nature as are inculcated by the literal meaning reduced the human mind in those days. In Treatise Berachoth we read: "It has been taught (Treatise Synhedr. fol. 70ᵃ) that the tree Adam ate of was, according to R. Meir, the vine, for nothing entices man so much as wine, of which it is said (Gen. ix. 21), 'He drank of the wine and was drunken.' According to R. Nehemiah, however, it was a fig, for the very tree which caused their fall served in part to repair their fault; for it is said (Gen. iii. 7), 'they sewed fig leaves together.'" In another part of this treatise it said that the tree of life was so long that it would take five hundred years to get up it. R. Juda in the name of R. Ha'ï says, "This length is not obtained by adding the length of the branch to it. The tree itself was of this length, and all the streams that were created gushed from its base." Ps. i. 3 is said to allude to the tree of life. It is also said that this tree represented the sixtieth part of the garden, and the garden the sixtieth part of Eden, for it is said (Gen. ii. 10), "A river went out of Eden to water the garden;" the latter is therefore only a portion of Eden.

The origin of blessing the light among the Jews is as follows according to the Talmud. R. Levi says that light, which had been created in the beginning, ceased as soon as Saturday was ended, and darkness began to prevail. "Adam was afraid, and said, 'Now perhaps is the moment when the biblical prediction is about to be realised, according to which I shall tread on the head of the serpent, and he shall bite my heel, and he cried out, Also he will bite me in the dark.' At that moment," says R. Levi, "God caused him to touch two bricks, which he rubbed against one another, and light came forth from them, according to the verse, 'Even the night shall be light about thee,' and he blessed God, saying, 'Praises to him who created the light of fire.' This, says Samuel, is why the light is blessed on Saturday evening, in memory of this creation."—(Treatise Berachoth, c. viii. 8.)

We find this teaching among the Greeks. Solon held that the punishment which a guilty man had not undergone, was merely postponed, and that it would fall upon him in the person of his children. Theognis, protesting against this injustice on the part of the gods, addresses a prayer to them, in which he boldly asks them not to persevere in it, and not to punish virtuous children for the crimes of their fathers any longer. Euripides reproaches the gods with imputing to the children the sins of their fathers. Æschylus, Sophocles, Lucretius, and Horace have dwelt on the sacrifice of Iphigenia, and, though they complain of the injustice of the gods, they never attached the absurd belief on which the story is based. Bion, however (circa B.C. 300), said that if God punished children for the sins of their fathers, he would be more absurd than a physician who should administer to children the remedies necessary to cure their fathers' maladies.

Philo's account of the origin of evil is as follows. He says that it was a very appropriate task for God to create those things which are wholly good, but that it is partly consistent and partly inconsistent with his nature to create beings of a mixed nature, and that this is why God is represented as saying, "Let us make man," which expression, he says, "shows an assumption of other beings to himself as assistants." (De Creat. Mundi, c. 55.)

Speaking in this same work (c. 54 and 56) of the account of the Garden of Eden in Genesis he says, "These statements appear to me to be dictated by a philosophy which is symbolical rather than strictly accurate. . . . I conceive that Moses was speaking in an allegorical spirit, intending by his paradise to intimate the dominant character of the soul, which is full of innumerable opinions as this figurative paradise was of trees. And by the tree of life he was shadowing out the greatest of the virtues—namely, piety towards the gods, by means of which the soul is made immortal, and by the tree of the knowledge of good and evil he was intimating that wisdom and moderation, by means of which things contrary in their nature to one another are distinguished." As to the serpent, the temptation, &c., he says, "These things are not mere fabulous inventions, in which the race of poets and sophists delight; but are rather types shadowing forth some allegorical truths according to some mystical explanation."

Philo pursues the same allegorical method in speaking of the Deluge. The "orthodox" party in this country still teach, in bold defiance of the plainest scientific, historical, and monumental evidences to the contrary, that in B.C. 2348 the summit of the loftiest peak of the Himalayas was fifteen cubits under water, and that there were only eight persons in existence in the world at that time. At this period, according to Herodotus (II. 143, 144), settled government had existed in Egypt for 9,700 years, and he was shown the effigies of priests who had followed each other in regular succession from B.C. 12,053 down to the time of his visit in B.C. 450. According to the learned Mariette Bey the 14th dynasty of the Egyptian kings was then on the throne, and an uninterrupted series of these kings can be traced up to the 1st dynasty of the Thinites in B.C. 5004. Bishop Colenso, after proving the impossibilities and absurdities of the Bible narrative, observes in his Critical Examination of the New Bible Commentary, " It really needs an apology to the common sense of my readers for putting before them in plain words such considerations as these. But I am compelled to enter into these absurd details by the contents of this Commentary, put forth under the sanction of the archbishops and bishops of England. A few years ago there were many who ridiculed the notion of such things being seriously believed in these days, and who condemned my own exposure of such absurdities as utterly unnecessary amidst the light and knowledge of the present age. But here we have this Commentary, set on foot by the Speaker of the House of Commons, and expressing, or supposed very naturally to express, the very mind of the English Episcopate, propounding gravely these childish 'explanations' to satisfy the doubts of devout and earnest inquirers, and Bishop Browne, as one of the most learned members of that body, as the very Coryphæus of the scholarship of England, bringing the English Church into contempt throughout the world by these ineptitudes."

Origen (Philocal. p. 12) asks, " What man of good sense will ever persuade himself that there has been a first, a second, and a third day, and that these days have each of them had their morning and their evening, when there was as yet neither sun, nor moon, nor stars ? What man is there so simple as to believe that God, personifying a gardener, planted a garden in the East ? That the tree of life was a real tree, which could be touched, and the fruit of which had the power of preserving life?" &c. He compares the story of the temptation to the mystic fable of the birth of Love, whose father was Porus, the father of abundance ; and in his answer to Celsus he upbraids that sarcastic infidel with his total want of candour in treating this story as if it had been delivered as historical, Celsus not giving them the words which would have convinced them that they were spoken allegorically (Contra Cels., l. IV.). "It is not reasonable," he says, "to deny to Moses the possession of truth under the veil of allegory, which was then the practice of all Eastern nations." In the same work Origen distinctly admits that there are Arcana Imperii in the Christian religion which are not fit to be entrusted to the vulgar, and in another part of it he speaks in strong terms against the vulgar belief that God punishes the wicked solely in order to avenge disobedience of his commands. He says, "In punishing the wicked God can have no other aim than to bring him back to virtue. These chastisements are nothing but means of education. When the wicked man is punished, he is not deprived of either feeling or reason. The punishments inflicted on him by God are the medicines by which he corrects him, in order to bring him back to him. Such is the belief of sensible Christians."

The oldest evangelical tradition began, not with the birth of Jesus, but with the preaching of John, as is evident from Acts i. 22 and x. 37. We are also told (Epiphan. Hær. xxx. § 13, 4) that the Ebionites and primitive Christians made use of a gospel which did not contain the genealogy of Christ. Mr. Sharpe in his treatise on Egyptian Mythology (p. 89) has pointed out that we have historic evidence that the two first chapters of Matthew's and Luke's Gospels, which receive no support from the other two gospels or from the epistles, formed no part of the original gospels, and that they are of Egyptian origin, being all but identical with the Egyptian ideas of the miraculous conception of their kings, and especially with the miraculous birth of Amunothph III., as shown in a series of sculptures on the wall of the temple of Luxor, which contain the annunciation, the conception, the birth, and the adoration of that king. The account of the mother of Christ being found with child of the Holy Ghost (Matt. i. 18) is contradicted by the passage in c. xii. 46 of that gospel, in which his brethren (not his half-brothers) are spoken of, and by that in c. xiii. 55, 56, in which his sisters are also spoken of, and in which he is called "the carpenter's son." It is impossible also to reconcile the account in c. iii. 16 of the Holy Ghost descending upon Jesus for the first time after his baptism by John with his being the son of the Holy Ghost in the first chapter. The life of Christ therefore begins, strictly speaking, with his baptism by John; but there are many questions connected with these chapters which can best be considered by an examination of them, and we shall therefore begin with them as if they were an integral part of the gospels.

CHAPTER I.

The first incident in the canonical gospels is the miraculous birth of John the Baptist. This marvellous event would not have been introduced into the gospel narrative if it had not been in accordance with the ideas held on this subject by the Jews, and which are thus set forth in the Gospel of the Birth of Mary (c. ii. 5–8): "When God shuts the womb of any person, he does it for this reason, that he may in a more wonderful manner again open it, and that which is born appear to be not the product of lust, but the gift of God. For the first mother of your nation, Sarah, was she not barren even till her eightieth year? and yet even in her old age she brought forth Isaac, in whom the promise was made of a blessing to all nations. Rachel also, so much in favour with God, and beloved so much by holy Jacob, continued barren for a long time, yet afterwards was the mother of Joseph, who was not only governor of Egypt, but delivered many nations from perishing with hunger. Who among the judges was more valiant than Samson, and more holy than Samuel? and yet both their mothers were barren." Josephus, however, who speaks of John the Baptist, never appears to have heard of his miraculous birth.

The narrative in Luke states that the parents of John were "a certain priest named Zacharias, of the course of Abia, and his wife was of the daughters of Aaron, and her name was Elisabeth." In c. i. 36 Elisabeth is said to be the cousin of Mary. This would make the latter to belong to the tribe of Levi instead of that of Judah. In v. 11 it is said that an angel appeared to Zacharias. Many passages, both in the Talmud and in Josephus, show that these appearances were usually to high priests. In the Protevangelion (viii. 4) Zacharias is called the high priest, and in c. ix. 5 it is this high priest who becomes dumb, and Samuel is appointed in his place until he spoke again. This provision was absolutely necessary, for, according to Lev. xxi. 16 et seqq., a dumb priest could not perform any of his priestly functions. Not only, however, is this provision omitted in the third gospel, but Zacharias is represented as accomplishing "the days of his ministration," that is, his weekly service, showing the writer's ignorance of the Jewish law.

The dumbness as represented in the Protevangelion is the effect of the recognition of Mary (Heb. Maryam) by Zacharias as being of the tribe of David, and it is probably founded upon Dan. x. 13, where it is said that Daniel "set his face toward the ground and became dumb" after the angel had spoken to him. This dumbness is inflicted upon Zacharias in this gospel merely for asking a question which Abraham (Gen. xv. 8) and Sarah (Gen. xviii. 12) had asked without receiving any punishment, Abraham having actually fallen on his face and laughed at the promise (Gen. xvii. 17). The angel's anger appears still more extraordinary when we find, in this same chapter, that Mary asks the same question (v. 38) and is not blamed for doing so.

In the Protevangelion Zacharias is murdered because he refuses to tell Herod where John was, and Simeon succeeds him. In Luke, however, neither Zacharias nor Simeon are high priests, but the narrative has been constructed out of the LXX., as is evident from the use of the same expressions. Conf. Luke i. 7, $προσβεβηκότες ἐν ταῖς ἡμέραις αὐτῶν$, with Gen. xviii. 11, $προσβεβηκότες ἡμερῶν$; Luke i. 18, $κατὰ τί γνώσομαι τοῦτο$, with Gen. xv. 8, $κατὰ τί γνώσομαι ὅ τι κληρονομήσω$. Elisabeth (the Greek form of Elisheba), who is said to be of the daughters of Aaron, appears to be taken from Elisheba (LXX. $Ἐλισάβετ$), who was Aaron's wife (Exod. vi. 23). In the Protevangelion she is merely called Mary's cousin. Luke i. 24–26 is applied to Mary, not to Elisabeth, in the Protevangelion. It is there said (c. ix. 23, x. 1) that Mary, "perceiving herself to grow big, and being afraid, went home, and hid herself away from the children of Israel, and was fourteen years old when all these things happened. And when her sixth month was come," &c. The predictions of the angel are principally taken from Judges xiii. John was known to have been an ascetic, therefore the angel is represented as saying, $οἶνον καὶ σίκερα οὐ μὴ πίῃ$. Conf. Judges xiii. 14 (LXX.), $καὶ οἶνον καὶ σίκερα οὐ μὴ πιέτω$. Conf. also

v. 15ᵇ with Judges xiii. 5. In Luke i. 30, John grows, and waxes strong in spirit, and is in the desert. Conf. Judges xiii. 24, 25.

The name of John is given beforehand by the angel just as the names of Ishmael and Isaac are. In Gen. xvi. 11 it is said, Καὶ καλέσεις τὸ ὄνομα αὐτοῦ 'Ισμάηλ; and in Gen. xvii. 19 . . . . 'Ισαάκ. In Luke i. 13 we have the same expression: Καὶ καλέσεις τὸ ὄνομα αὐτοῦ 'Ιωάννην.

In Luke i. 19, the angel who appears to Zacharias announces his name—Gabriel. It is certain, by the admission of the Jews themselves, that they did not know any names of angels before the Captivity. R. Simeon ben Lachish (Treatise Rosch Haschanah, f. 56, 4) says that the names of the angels came to the Jews from Babylon, and he gives as an example the fact that in Isa. vi., which was written before the Captivity, it is said, "There flew one of the seraphim to me," and "above it stood the seraphim," whereas in Dan. ix. 21 "the man Gabriel," and in x. 21 "Michael your prince" are spoken of. In Tobit xii. 15, Raphael is represented as being one of the seven holy angels (a number which corresponds to that of the Persian Amschaspands) "which go in and out before the glory of the Holy One." In Isa. xlv. 5–7, a portion of Isaiah which was written after the return from Captivity, a sort of protest is made against the dualism of the Persian religion, and we are told in Acts xxiii. 9, that the Sadducees did not believe in angels at all; but notwithstanding this, Ormuzd and Ahriman, the good and the evil principle, became adopted into the Jewish system. Ahriman, the prince of darkness, became, it is true, transformed into Satan, but, like Ahriman, Satan has his seven servants, or demons, who execute his commands and lead men into sin; and like Ormuzd, Jehovah has also his seven angels of light, or Amschaspands, who faithfully obey his orders.

The Amschaspands are genii or angels of the first order, who form the retinue of Ormuzd, the beneficent deity, the source of all light. Clemens Alexandrinus (Strom. l. VI.) says that there are seven archangels in the Christian hierarchy, just as there are seven planets in the Chaldæan theology which are appointed to govern the world. It is evident that the Jewish ideas respecting them were astronomical from their Cabala, in which each of those seven angels presides over a planet. The following is their system according to Kircher (Æd. Jud. vol. II. pars 1, p. 310):—

	THEIR ANGELS.	INTELLIGENCES.	SPIRITS.
The Sun	Raphaël.	Nagiel.	Smeliel.
Venus	Hamiël.	Hagiel.	Naguel.
Mercury	Michaël.	Tiriel.	Cochabiel.
The Moon	Gabriel.	Eliniel.	Lemanaël.
Saturn	Zapkiel.	Agiel.	Sabathiel.
Jupiter	Zadykiel.	Sophiel.	Zadakiel.
Mars	Chamaël.	Graphiel.	Modiniel.

These angels, or planets, were held to be ever watching over mortal affairs, as shown in the following table:—

Number of the hours during which, according to the Jews, the angels serve and minister unto man by day and by night throughout the week.

On the Sabbath the Angel of the Sun presides over the first hours, &c.		The Angels of Venus, &c.		The Angels of Mercury, &c.		The Angels of the Moon, &c.		The Angels of Saturn, &c.		The Angels of Mars, &c.	
Hours.		Hours.		Hours.		Hours.		Hours.		Hours.	
On the day of the	☉	4	♀	4	☿	4	☽	3	♄	3	♂	3
Moon	☽	4	♄	4	♃	4	♂	3	☉	3	☿	3
Mars	♂	4	☉	4	♀	4	☿	3	☽	3	♃	3
Mercury	☿	4	☽	4	♄	4	♃	3	♂	3	♀	3
Jupiter	♃	4	♂	4	☉	4	♀	3	☿	3	♄	3
Venus	♀	4	☿	4	☽	4	♄	3	♃	3	☉	3
Saturn	♄	4	♃	4	♂	4	☉	3	♀	3	☽	3

The genealogy of Christ in Luke's Gospel extends beyond David and Abraham, and has an universal tendency. The first portion of this genealogy agrees with that in 1 Chron. i., with three exceptions, as far as Nathan, after which we only meet with two names, Salathiel and Zorobabel, which are mentioned in the Old Testament. Even here, however, the genealogy disagrees with the latter, for it makes Salathiel to be the son of a person named Neri, who is not mentioned in the Old Testament, while in 1 Chron. iii. 7, Salathiel is said to be the son of Zechariah. Again, Rhesa is said to be the son of Zerubbabel, but there is no such name in 1 Chron. iii. 19, 20, where the children of Zerubbabel are enumerated. It has been remarked that this list contains the number seven eleven times by the awkward expedient of reckoning Abraham twice over, but the subjoined list also contains that number eleven times up to Christ without any forcing of the text.

Matthew's genealogy avowedly proceeds upon the number seven as a basis. In the last column, however, beginning with Salathiel, where he says there should be fourteen generations there are only thirteen. This damaging fact is admitted by the Fathers, including Jerome and Augustine, and therefore it is unnecessary to dwell upon modern attempts at explanation by counting David twice over, &c. The following are the genealogies in Luke and Matthew, with the spelling of the Codex Sinaiticus. The genealogy in 1 Chronicles i. is prefixed.

CHRONICLES.	LUKE.	MATTHEW.	CHRONICLES.	LUKE.	MATTHEW.
Adam	Adam		Pharez	Phares	Phares
Sheth	Seth		Hezron	Esrom	Esrom
Enosh	Enos			Arni	
Kenan	Cainam			Adnim	
Mahlaleel	Meleleel		Ram	Aram	Aram
Jered	Jaret		Aminadab	Adam	Aminadab
Henoch	Enoch		Nahshon	Nasson	Naasson
Methuselah	Mathusala		Salma	Sala	Salmon
Lamech	Lamech		Boaz	Booz	Boes
Noah	Noe		Obed	Jobel	Jobed
Shem	Sem		Jesse	Jesse	Jesse
Arphaxad	Arphaxad		David	David	David
	Cainam		Solomon	Nathan	Solomon
Shelah	Sala			Mattatha	Roboam
Eber	Heber		Abia	Menna	'bia
Peleg	Phalec		Asa	Melea	'saph
Reu	Ragau		Jehoshaphat	Eliakim	Josaphat
Serug	Saruch		Joram	Jonam	Joram
Nahor	Nachor			Joseph	Ozias
Terah	Thara			Juda	Joatham
Abram	Abraham	Abraham		Simeon	Achaz
Isaac	Isac	Isaac		Levi	Ezekias
Israel	Jacob	Jacob		Matthat	Manasses

GENEALOGY—continued.

CHRONICLES.	LUKE.	MATTHEW.	CHRONICLES.	LUKE.	MATTHEW.
	Jorim	Amos		Mattathias	
	Eliazer	Josias		Maath	
	Jesu	Jechonias		Nagga	
	Er	Salathiel		Esh	
	Elmadam	Zorobabel		Naum	
	Cosa	Abiud		Amos	
	Addi	Eliakim		Mattathias	
	Melchi	Azor		Joseph	
	Neri	Sadoch		Janne	
	Salathiel	Achim		Melchi	
	Zorobabel	Eliud		Levi	
	Rhesa	Eleazar		Matthat	
	Jonan	Matthan		Heli	
	Joda	Jacob		Joseph	
	Josech	Joseph		Jesus	
	Semein	Jesus			

The variations from the text of the Old Testament in Matthew's list are as follows: The first is in v. 4, where it is said that Rahab the harlot was the mother of Booz. This receives no confirmation from 1 Chron. ii. 13, but in Ruth, which the Jews have always held to be one of the later books, and in which David is made to be the son of a Moabite mother, Salmon, who is the husband of Rahab in Matthew, and who is the great-grandfather of David, is the son of a certain Nahshon, who, according to Numbers i. 7, was in the desert with Moses. In B. C. 1451 (according to the received chronology) Rahab hid the Jewish spies, and thus enabled Joshua to conquer the country. Rahab was held in great estimation by the Jews for this act, and this was probably the reason why she was made an ancestor of David and of Christ. This, however, renders the chronology hopeless, for as David was not born till B. C. 1070, there are only four generations in four hundred years. In the Gospel to the Hebrews, which also begins with the genealogy of Christ, and in which the introductory words are the same, Βίβλος γενέσεως 'Ιησοῦ Χριστοῦ υἱοῦ Δαυὶδ, υἱοῦ 'Αβραάμ, κ. τ. λ., the names of Thamar, Rahab, Ruth, and Bathsheba, in verses 3, 5, and 6, are omitted, and it appears that the Jewish Christians were dreadfully scandalised at the names of such women being inscribed in this genealogy. In v. 8, the Gospel to the

Hebrews has not omitted the three kings, Ahaziah, Jehoash, and Amaziah, between Jehoram and Uzziah, and Jehoiakim, the father of Zechoniah, is inserted between Josiah and Jehoiachin or Zechoniah, but Matthew has omitted him altogether. The reason this has been done is that Jer. xxii. 30 renders the descent of Christ from the line of David impossible, for it is there said, " Thus saith the Lord, Write ye this man childless, a man that shall not prosper in his days ; for *no man of his seed* [Jehoiakim's] shall prosper, sitting upon the throne of David, and ruling any more in Judah." In v. 28 Coniah (Jechoniah) is called a "despised broken idol," and he and his seed are cast out, while Jehoiakim is to be "buried with the burial of an ass," and cast out of the gates of Jerusalem (v. 19). The Epistle of Barnabas, which forms part of the Codex Sinaiticus, and was read throughout, in the churches of Alexandria, as the Canonical Scriptures were, and which is quoted by many ancient Fathers, says positively (xi. 13) that to believe that Jesus Christ is the son of David, is an "error of the wicked." Verse 17, containing the numbering of the generations, is not in this Gospel. The most important thing of all, however, is that the 16th verse is in this Gospel, Ἰακὼβ δὲ ἐγγένησεν τὸν Ἰησοῦν ἐκ τῆς Μαρίας, "And Jacob begat Jesus from Mary." The whole story of the miraculous birth of Christ, of the visit of the Magi, and of Herod's massacre of the children at Bethlehem, is absent from the Gospel to the Hebrews. Joseph has evidently been inserted in order to account for the miraculous birth, &c.

Although the genealogy in the Gospel to the Hebrews resembles that in Chronicles rather than that of Matthew, there are two divergences from the former which are common to them both, viz., that in Chronicles (iii. 19), Zerubbabel is the son of Pedaiah, and not of Salathiel, and that no such person as Abiud the son of Zerubbabel is mentioned.

The Gospel of the Birth of Mary, which has come down to us in the works of Jerome, says that Mary was the daughter of Joachim and Anna ; that her father's family was of Nazareth, and her mother's of Bethlehem ; and that she herself was born at Nazareth, educated at Jerusalem, and was of the royal race of David. The ancient copies, however, differed materially from Jerome's, for Faustus, who was a native of Britain, and bishop of Riez, in France, showed from one of them that Christ was not the Son of God till after his baptism, and that Mary was not of the house of David and tribe of Judah, but of the tribe of Levi, her father being a priest of the name of Joachim; and this agrees with the statement in Luke, that she was the cousin of Elisabeth. In Luke i. 27, the words "of the house of David" refer only to the words immediately preceding them, viz., "a man whose name was Joseph," and not to the words "a virgin espoused." In Luke ii. 4, it is said "Joseph went up .. (because *he* was of the house and lineage of David) to be registered with Mary." If Mary had also been of the lineage of David, the author would have put αὐτοὺς instead of αὐτόν. The descent of Christ from the royal line of David consists, therefore, according to the Gospels, in the fact that a person who was not his father was descended from that line. When Faustus the Manichæan pointed out the absurdity of thus tracing the descent of Jesus through a person who was not his father, the only reply Augustine was able to make was that the masculine gender was of superior dignity!

The Jews said that Jesus was the son of Mary, the plaiter of woman's hair, who was also called Satda, or Stada, and of a man named Pandira, and that the son of Satda was first stoned in Lydda, and then hanged, which is the Jewish punishment for blasphemy (Schoettzenius, Horæ Hebraicæ, 1. ix.) The Rev. Mr. Faber says that Jesus was originally called Jeschua Hammassiah. His name was also Jesus ben Panther. Panthers were the nurses and bringers-up of Bacchus, and Panther was said to be the surname of Joseph's family, according to Epiphanius (Hæres. 78, Antidic. s. 7), who says that Joseph was the brother of Cleophas, the son of James, surnamed Panther.

In the first chapter of Luke's Gospel the angel is represented as telling Mary that the child to be born of her should be called the Son of God; but in the remainder of the Gospel he is never mentioned by that appellation except in the acclamations of the devils in c. iv. 41, which contradicts Mark i. 34, where it is expressly said that he "suffered not the devils to speak," and is evidently a later addition. The Apostles are represented as calling him the Son of God after his ascension, not on account of his supernatural birth, which they do not appear to have so much as heard of, but on account of his being raised from the dead. In Luke Mary is represented as receiving the angel without any surprise. In the Gospel of Mary (vii. 4), however, it is said that "the Virgin ... had before been well acquainted with the countenances of angels." The rest of the narrative in Luke is identical with that in this gospel, except the passages in brackets. The angel says, "Fear not, Mary [as though I intended anything inconsistent with your chastity in this salutation], for thou hast found favour with God [because you make your virginity your choice, therefore, while you are yet a virgin] you shall conceive [without sin] and bring forth a son. He shall be great [because he shall reign from sea to sea, and from the rivers even unto the ends of the earth]. And he shall be called the Son of the Highest [for he who is born in a mean state reigns in an exalted state in heaven]. And the Lord God shall give unto him the throne of his father David, and he shall reign over the house of Jacob for ever, and of his kingdom there shall be no end. [For he is the King of Kings and Lord of Lords, and his throne is for ever and ever. To this discourse of the angel the Virgin replied not as though she were unbelieving, but willing to know the manner of it.] She said, How can that be? For seeing [according to my vow] I have never known any man, [how can I have a child?] To this the angel replied and said, [Think not, Mary, that you shall conceive in the ordinary way. For, without lying with a man, while a virgin, you shall conceive; while a virgin, you shall bring forth; and while a virgin you shall give suck. For] the Holy Ghost shall come upon you, and the power of the Highest shall overshadow you [without any of the heats of lust]. So that which shall be born of you shall be [only] holy [because it is conceived without sin, and being born] shall be called the son of God. Then Mary [stretching forth her hands, and lifting her eyes to heaven], said, Behold the handmaid of the Lord, be it unto me according to thy word."

Faustus, the Manichæan bishop, who charged the orthodox party with falsifying the gospels, says, "Do you receive the gospel? (ask ye). Undoubtedly I do. Why then you also admit that Christ was born. Not so, for it by no means follows that in believing the gospel I should also believe that Christ was born. Do you not think then that he was of the Virgin Mary? Manes hath said, Far be it that I should ever believe that Jesus Christ . . . . . ." The original is,

"Accipis evangelium? Et maxime. Proinde ergo et natum accipis Christum. Non ita est. Neque enim sequitur ut si evangelium accipis, idcirco et natum accipiam Christum. Ergo non putas eum ex Maria Virgine esse? Manes dixit, Absit ut˙Dominum nostrum Jesum Christum per naturalia pudenda mulieris descendisse confitear." (Lardner, vol. IV., p. 20.)

The contradictions in the narratives of the birth of Christ are insuperable. In Matthew the angel is called the "angel of the Lord," as in Genesis, &c.; in Luke he is called Gabriel. In Matthew he appears to Joseph in a dream, and does not appear to Mary at all: in Luke he appears to Mary only. In Matthew he appears to Joseph after Mary had conceived; in Luke he appears to Mary herself before she had conceived. In Matthew Joseph is "minded to put her away privily;" in Luke he is not in the least disturbed by what had occurred.

The Protevangelion (ii. 1) says that Joseph's trade was "building houses abroad," and that it was on his return from that employment that he "found the Virgin grown big." Mark vi. 2, in which Jesus himself is called a carpenter, was not thus in Origen's time; for Celsus, having rallied the Christians on the head of their religion being a carpenter by trade, Origen (Cont. Cels. vi. 56) says that "no doubt Celsus had forgotten that in none of the gospels received by the churches was Jesus called 'a carpenter.'" The ninth Avatar of India was also known by the name of Salivahana, "the carpenter." In Mark iii. 31 we read that the mother and the brethren of Jesus came to seek him. Jesus had brothers and sisters (Matt. i. 25; xii. 46 et sqq.; xiii. 55 et sqq.; John ii. 12; vii. 3, 5, 10; Acts i. 14). Hegesippus, quoted by Eusebius (H. E. iii. 20), mentions one of them, Judas by name, and says that his grandchildren were still living in the time of Domitian. He says that they were brought before Domitian; and having stated that their whole property only amounted to 9,000 denarii (about 270*l.*) and that the kingdom of Christ was a celestial, not a terrestrial one, he dismissed them as simpletons, and ordered the persecution he had commenced to cease. He adds that they continued to live down to the time of Trajan. Jesus appears to have been the eldest of the family (Matt. i. 25; Luke ii. 7). This statement of Hegesippus shows that the statement in Matt.

xiii. 55 that James, Joses, Simon, and Judas were the brothers of the Lord was accepted literally in the time of Eusebius, although Papias, who, however, omits Simon altogether, makes them to have been his cousins. The fourth gospel, which ignores the miraculous birth altogether, makes Joseph and Mary to be the father and mother of Jesus (vi. 42), and says that his brethren advised him to go into Judæa that his disciples might see his works (vii. 3), and adds that they did not believe in him.

The angels in the two gospels use almost exactly the same words as are used in similar communications in the Septuagint version of the Old Testament.

ANNUNCIATION OF ISAAC.

Ἰδοὺ Σάρα ἡ γυνὴ σοῦ τέξεται σοι υἱὸν καὶ καλέσεις τὸ ὄνομα αὐτοῦ Ἰσαάκ.—Gen. xvii. 19.

ANNUNCIATION OF CHRIST.

Τέξεται δὲ υἱὸν, καὶ καλέσεις τὸ ὄνομα αὐτοῦ Ἰησοῦν.—Matt. i. 21.

ANNUNCIATION OF SAMSON.

Καὶ αὐτὸς ἄρξεται σώζειν τὸν Ἰσραὴλ ἐκ χειρὸς Φιλιστιμ.—Judges xiii. 3.

Αὐτὸς γὰρ σώσει τὸν λαὸν αὐτοῦ ἀπὸ τῶν ἁμαρτιῶν αὐτῶν.—Ib.

ANNUNCIATION OF ISHMAEL.

Καὶ εἶπεν αὐτῇ ὁ ἄγγελος Κυρίου· Ἰδού, σὺ ἐν γαστρὶ ἔχεις, καὶ τέξῃ υἱὸν, καὶ καλέσεις τὸ ὄνομα αὐτοῦ Ἰσμαήλ. Οὗτος ἔσται . . .—Gen. xvi. 11.

Καὶ εἶπεν ὁ ἄγγελος αὐτῇ· Ἰδού, συλλήψῃ ἐν γαστρί, καὶ τέξῃ υἱὸν, καὶ καλέσεις τὸ ὄνομα αὐτοῦ Ἰησοῦν. Οὗτος ἔσται. . . Luke i. 31, 32.

In Matt. i. 22, it is said that the angel told Joseph that "all this was done that it might be fulfilled which was spoken of the Lord by the prophet," and a quotation from Isa. vii. 14, is added. The writer has, however, followed the LXX. instead of the Hebrew version, in which the word used does not signify *a* virgin, but generally a young woman. The LXX. have also translated the Hebrew " she calls," " shall call," thus giving a prophetical form to the passage which it does not really possess. The Hebrew " she calls " would not be admissible here, because it is not Mary, but the angel, who is represented as giving the name Emmanuel to the child.

The statement in Isaiah is that Rezin, king of Syria, and Peleah, king of Israel, were in league against Ahaz, king of Judah, and invaded his territory. The heart of Ahaz "was moved, and the heart of his people, as the trees of the wood are moved with the wind." (Isa. vii. 2.) Isaiah is sent to reassure him, but in vain. He is then ordered to tell Ahaz to ask for a sign. "Ask thee a sign of the Lord thy God. Ask it either in the depth, or in the height above. But Ahaz said, I will not ask, neither will I tempt the Lord." Upon this Isaiah tells him that the Lord himself would give him a sign. "Behold the young woman (עלמה) [ἡ παρθένος, LXX.] shall conceive and bear a son, and shall call his name Immanuel" (vii. 14). The word עלמה, alma, signifies a marriageable girl, just as the masculine elem signifies a youth who has attained the age of puberty. The word alma is even used to signify a young woman who is not a virgin in such passages as Prov. xxx. 19, "the way of a man with a maid (alma)." In the Song of Solomon also, where Solomon's harem is described, it is said, "There are three-score queens, and threescore concubines, and maidens (alamoth, the plural of alma) without number." In this passage the queens are the daughters of the neighbouring kings, whom Solomon had married. The concubines are the women of lower rank, whom he had espoused in a less solemn manner; and the young women (alamoth) acted as musicians, perfumers, &c., in the Oriental fashion.

The alma in Isaiah was Isaiah's wife, as is expressly stated in c. viii. 3, "And I approached unto the prophetess, and she conceived, and bare a son." This son receives a name which is applicable to the situation of the people, for he is called Maher-shalal-hash-baz, which signifies "haste, booty, speed, pillage," "for before the child shall have knowledge to cry, My father, and my mother, the riches of Damascus and the spoils of Samaria shall be taken away before the king of Assyria" (v. 4). Gesenius, who considers the translation in Matthew to be incorrect, observes that even if alma did signify a virgin, there would be no miracle unless Mary continued virgin after the birth of a child, which it is evident she did not, for she went through the days of her purification like any other woman who had given birth to a child (Luke ii. 22).

The Jews, according to the Talmud and the Michaschim, expected that there would be terrible and devastating wars before the coming of the Messiah, conducted by Gog and Magog, during which all impious persons would perish (Treatise Soucca, fol. 52ª, Yebamöth, 62ª, Abôda Zara, 5ª, and Middâ, 13ᵇ). Orobio, a learned Jew, maintains, however, that belief in the Messiah is not founded upon any Jewish book, but that it was only a name given to the great and powerful of the earth. Thus Isaiah gives this title to Cyrus; Ezekiel gives it to the king of Tyre; Saul is called "the Lord's anointed," and Herod in later times was held to be the Messiah by the sect called Herodians.

In Luke ii. 7 it is said that Mary, being at an inn in Bethlehem, laid the infant Jesus "in a manger, because there was no room for him in the inn." In other words, the inn being full, Mary was obliged to lay the child in a manger in a stable attached to the inn. This does away with the legend of the birth of Christ in a cave, which is of great antiquity. Justin has proved, to his own satisfaction, that Christ must be born at Bethlehem from the Septuagint version of Isa. xxxiii. 16, "And he shall dwell in a cavern placed on high, made of very hard stone," from which he concludes that Christ was born in a grotto near Bethlehem (Dial. cum Tryph., c. 77). This portion of Isaiah is, however, not written by that prophet, but by a writer who lived after the conquest of Babylon by Cyrus. The Protevangelion (xii. 12 et seqq.) says that Mary said to Joseph, "Joseph, take me down, for that which is within me mightily presses me. And Joseph took her down. And he found there a cave, and let her into it." The visit of the Magi, &c., follows, and finally Mary, alarmed at hearing that Herod was about to kill all the children in Bethlehem, "took the child, and wrapped him in swaddling-clothes, and laid him in an ox-manger, because there was no room for them in the inn" (xvi. 2). The cave at Bethlehem which is shown as that in which Christ was born, according to the Protevangelion, is the cave in which Adonis was formerly worshipped! Jerome (Epist. ad Paulin., p. 564) says, "Bethleem nunc nostrum et augustissimum orbis locum de quo Psalmista canit. Veritas de terrâ orta est, lucus inumbrabat Thamus, id est, Adonidis; et in specu ubi quondam Christus parvulus vagiit, Veneris Amasius planebatur." The ceremonies in the church of the Nativity at Bethlehem are celebrated in this cave, and Dr. Clarke says that they are nearly the same as were celebrated in honour of Adonis in the time of Tertullian and Jerome. This cave had existed at Bethlehem from time immemorial, and Eusebius says that the Emperor Adrian caused a temple to be built over it in honour of Adonis.

The circumcision of Christ is only mentioned in the third Gospel. In c. II. 21, it is said that the name of Jesus (which was a very common one among the Jews) was given to the child by the angel, " before he was conceived in the womb." This is in conformity with what is said in Pirke R. Eliezer, 33 ; " Six men's names have been given before they were born, viz., Isaac, Ishmael, Moses, Solomon, Josiah, and the name of Messiah the king." This applies to the Messianic office generally, but it nevertheless shows that the name of the Messiah was supposed to be settled beforehand. The author, no doubt, had these instances in his mind.

It was of great consequence to the Judæo-Christians that the Messiah should have been circumcised, in other words that he should be a Jew. If, however, the ceremony had really taken place Jesus would, according to Jewish custom, have derived his name from the place of his birth, and have been called Jesus of Bethlehem, or of Nazareth. The name Jesus is in reality Joshua, which signifies literally a preserver, a deliverer; and the LXX. always write Ἰησοῦς for Joshua, as is also done in the English version (see Acts vii. 45; Heb. iv. 8). In c. ii. of the First Gospel of the Infancy we are told that Christ was circumcised in the cave ; that after two days he was taken to Jerusalem; that on the fortieth day from his birth he was presented in the Temple; and that the proper offerings were made for him " according to the law of Moses—namely, that every male which opens the womb shall be called holy unto God " (Exod. xiii. 2, &c.: conf. Luke ii. 23). To this is added in Luke a sacrifice which is enjoined in Lev. xii. 6, 8, after the days of purification are accomplished.

Circumcision was long supposed to be an exclusively Jewish rite, and it is represented in Gen. xvii. 10 et sqq. as being first given to Abraham by God himself as a token of the covenant between them. In that passage (v. 24) it is distinctly laid down that an uncircumcised male child should be cut off from the people. This practice was as common among the heathen as among the Jews. Jer. ix. 24, 25, shows that some of the seven Canaanitish nations were circumcised. The Arabians used to circumcise at thirteen years of age (conf. Gen. xvii. 25). Strabo thinks that the practice originated in Ethiopia, and he quotes a passage from Artemidorus which shows that the operation was differently performed in Egypt from what it was among the Arab tribes. The practice of excision is believed to have also existed among the Jews, as it still does among the Copts and Abyssinians, though they are Christians, and among several of the Arab tribes. Herodotus (II. 3) says that the inhabitants of Colchis, the Egyptians, the Ethiopians, and the inhabitants of Palestine submitted to this operation for sanitary reasons, and that it was also practised by the Phœnicians until they discontinued it in consequence of their intercourse with Greece. In l. VI. c. 104, Herodotus says that "the Syrians of Palestine acknowledged that they adopted this rite from the Egyptians."

It is remarkable that Moses is not represented as regarding this rite as a sign of a covenant with God. On the contrary, he hesitates a long time before circumcising his sons, and only decides upon doing so long after the eighth day from the birth (Exod. iv. 25, 26). It is not enjoined either in the Decalogue or in the commands attributed to Moses. The only two passages in which Moses appears to speak of it are interpolations. Lev. xii. 3 is an evident interpolation, for it is the uncleanness of the mother alone that is in question, and it is not conceivable that so important a law should be mentioned in so incidental a manner. In Exod. xii. 48 it is ordered that no uncircumcised person shall eat of the Passover, but as Moses never enjoined the practice, this is unintelligible. It is certain from Josh. v. 2–4, that no Jew was circumcised during the whole forty years that they are said to have remained in the desert.

Circumcision, however, had become the general practice long before the Christian era, and Eusebius and Sulpitius Severus both state positively that up to the time of the destruction of Jewish nationality under Adrian, that is, up to about A.D. 135, the Church at Jerusalem was composed entirely of circumcised bishops and laity. Eusebius reckons fifteen bishops up to that period, who were all Jews both by birth and by circumcision (ἐκ περιτομῆς), and says that the rest of the Church consisted entirely of believing Jews, ἐξ Ἑβραίων πιστῶν (H. E. IV. 5, 6; V. 12). Sulpitius Severus (Hist. Sacr. II. 31) says: "Tum Hierosolymæ nonnisi ex circumcisione habebat Ecclesia sacerdotem. . . . Quia tum pene omnes Christum Deum sub legis observatione credebant." Jerome says that the primitive Church at Alexandria was also Jewish—"Primam Ecclesiam adhuc judaizantem" (De Vir. Illustr. c. 8). Eusebius (l. IV. c. 6) records the appointment of the first uncircumcised bishop of Jerusalem as follows :—

"In the eighteenth year of the reign of Adrian [A.D. 135], when the war had reached its height at the city of Bethara, a very strong fortress, not very far from Jerusalem, the siege was continued for some time, and the revolters were driven to the last extreme by hunger and famine. The author of their madness had also suffered his just punishment, and the whole nation, from that time, were totally prohibited, by the decree and commands of Adrian, from ever entering the country about Jerusalem, so that they could not behold the soil of their fathers, even at a distance. Such is the statement of Aristo of Pella. The city of the Jews being thus reduced to a state of abandonment for them, and totally stripped of its ancient inhabitants, and also inhabited by strangers, was called Ælia, in honour of the Emperor Ælius Adrian; and when the Church of the Gentiles was collected there, the first bishop after those of the circumcision was called Marcus." From this period the Gentile element began to predominate in the Church, and Judæo-Christian works, such as the Apocalypse of Peter, which Sozomenes says was read in the churches of Palestine; which was publicly read at Rome towards the close of the second century; which Clemens Alexandrinus, and Methudius bishop of Tyre (circa A.D. 312) placed among the inspired writings; and which is mentioned in the Sinaitic index of the sacred books, fell into disrepute.

The narrative in Matthew contradicts that in Luke (ii. 17, 20), according to which the shepherds "made known abroad" what the Angels had told them respecting Christ, for it says that nothing was known of the birth of Jesus until a star revealed it to certain Magi. This revelation by means of a star is inserted here on account of a prophecy said to have been uttered by Balaam (Numb. xxiv., 17), "There shall come a star out of Jacob," &c., which several rabbis held to refer to the Messiah. It is said, however, that this star is to "smite the sides of Moab, and destroy all the children of tumult," and do many other things which cannot possibly apply to the Messiah. The word "star" (Heb. Cocab) is believed to be the origin of the name Maccabee, which was borne by

Judas Maccabæus and his family, whose successors placed a star on their coins. In the latter part of the verse "those that remain in the city" signify the Hellenist party, who still held the citadel of Jerusalem at the time it was written. The expectation of a star was, however, not founded on this prophecy only. In the Testamentum XII. Patriarcharum it is said, Καὶ ἀνατελεῖ ἄστρον αὐτοῦ (of the Messianic ἱερεὺς καινὸς) ἐν οὐρανῷ . . . φωτίζον φῶς γνώσεως, κ. τ. λ. In Pesihta Satarta, f. 48, it is said "Et prodibit stella ab oriente, quæ est stella Messiæ, et in oriente versabitur dies quindecim." The birth of Abraham was also believed to have been heralded by a star. Jalkut Rutuni, f. 32, 3, says, "Quâ horâ natus est Abrahamus pater noster, super quem sit pax, stetit quoddam sidus in oriente, et deglutivit quatuor astra quæ sunt in quatuor cœli plagis." An Arabian author named Maallem says that this wonderful star, which swallowed up four others, was seen by Nimrod.

The account in Matthew differs greatly from that in the Protevangelion. In the latter the Magi came to Bethlehem, not to Jerusalem, where they could have had no business; and thus the unnatural movement of the star from north to south (instead of from east to west like all other stars) as represented in Matthew is avoided. When they arrive at Bethlehem, Herod sends messengers to them and to the priests, and inquires of them what sign it was they saw. They answer: "We saw an extraordinarily large star shining among the stars of heaven, and it so outshined all the other stars that they became not visible, and we knew thereby that a great king was born in Israel, and therefore are we come to worship him" (c. xv. 7). Herod tells them to make inquiry, and if they find the child to bring him word, that he might come and worship him also (conf. Matt. ii. 8); though it is not apparent why Herod should wish to worship a Jewish king. The rest of the account is identical with that in Matthew, except the words in brackets:—

"So the wise men went forth and beheld the star which they saw in the east before them, till it came and stood over [the cave] where the young child was with Mary, his mother. Then they brought forth out of their treasures, and offered unto him gold, and frankincense, and myrrh. And being warned in a dream [by an angel] that they should not return to Herod [through Judæa] they departed into their own country by another way" (xv. 9–11). In Matt. ii. 11 "the house" is substituted for "the cave," but there is not a word about the stable or the manger.

It is wholly unintelligible from Matthew's gospel why the Magi, or Magians, who were idolaters, should have been the first to announce to the Jews that their Messiah was born. The first Gospel of the Infancy explains that they came in consequence of a prophecy by Zoradascht (Zoroaster). The priests of Zoroaster, therefore, the worshippers of Mithra, or the Sun, come to offer to the person foretold by that prophet the identical three gifts which they used to offer to the sun, viz., gold, frankincense, and myrrh. Plutarch (De Iside) speaks of the connection between myrrh and the sun and moon; and Adonis, in whose cave Christ is supposed to be born, was said to have sprung from the incestuous intercourse of Myrrha with her father Cynirus, and she was afterwards changed into a tree of that name, which was consecrated to the sun. Justin explains why the stable was substituted for the cave. After observing that Mithra was born in a grotto and Christ in a stable, he says (Dial. cum Tryph.) "He was born on the day that the sun was born, in stabulo Augiæ," that is, in the station of the Celestial Goat, to which the stable of Augias, in the sixth labour of Hercules, corresponded in the sphere of the labours of Hercules. Justin adds that Christ, after being born in a stable, took refuge in a grotto.

In the time of Leo I. (Leo. Serm. xxi. De Nativ. Dom. p. 148) some of the Fathers of the Church said that "what rendered the festival [of Christmas] venerable was less the birth of Jesus Christ than the return and, as they expressed it, the new birth of the sun. The birth of the Invincible Sun (Natalis Solis Invicti) was celebrated at Rome on the same day, as may be seen in the Roman Calendar published in the reign of Constantine and of Julian (Hymn to the Sun, p. 155). This epithet "invictus" is the same as the Persians give to this god, whom they worshipped by the name of Mithra, and whom, as Justin observes, they caused to be born in a grotto, just as he is represented as being born in a stable, under the name of Christ, in the gospels.

The Roman calendar above mentioned is printed in Father Petau's Uranologia (vol. iii. p. 72). On the 8th of the kalends of January the words N. invicti, C. M. xxiiii. occur, that is the birth-day of the Invincible One. Father Petau in his notes on the hymn of the Emperor Julian to the Sun lays great stress on this correspondence between the birth-day of Christ and the ancient festivals of the birth-day of the sun, and refers to his work called 'Auctarium.' He explains the letters C. M. to signify Circenses missi. The Emperor Julian speaks of the solar festivals which were held at this period of the year. He says (Hymn. ad Solem, p. 292), "Some days before the first day of the year we have magnificent games in honour of the sun, to whom we give the title of Invincible. Why cannot I have the happiness of celebrating them often, O Sun, King of the Universe, Thou whom the supreme Deity engendered from all eternity out of his pure substance?"

Father Petau observes that the Romans also called Jupiter Invincible, and on ancient coins a young child may be seen seated on a goat, or in the sign in which the sun began his course in the solstice, with the legend "Jovi crescenti," which can only apply to the sun, or to the Invincible God, who begins to increase in this sign. As Beausobre (l. 2, p. 798) has remarked, the two equinoxes and the two solstices are marked by two conceptions and two births. John the Baptist is conceived on the 24th of September, and is born on the 24th of June. Christ is conceived on the 25th of March, and is born on the 25th of December.

The birth of Christ at Bethlehem is said (Matt. ii. 5) to be prophesied by Micah. In John vii. 40 et sqq. this is contradicted, for it is there stated that Christ came out of Galilee, and the people are represented as not believing on him because he ought to have come from the village (κώμης) of Bethlehem, "where David was" (v. 42). The portion of Micah here referred to is an addition made in the time of Zerubbabel. In Isa. ii. 2–4, a passage which was also written at this period, some of the words in this portion of Micah are repeated. The prophecy is incorrectly quoted from the LXX., for γῇ Ἰούδα " in the land of Juda" is written instead of οἶκος τοῦ Ἐφραθα, " of the house of Ephratah," and he has inserted a word, οὐδαμῶς " by no means," which is not translated in the English version, and which cannot be found either in the LXX. or in the Hebrew text. In the prophet the contrast is made as follows: " From the little house of Ephratah something great, namely, the fifth king of Israel, shall proceed." The Rabbinistic spirit found "little" an unsuitable word for the birth-place of the Messiah, and, therefore, "little" was changed into "by no means the least."

The Gospel of the Infancy says that the Magi were guided home by an angel in the form of the star which had guided them on their journey, and that Herod, perceiving that they did not return, called the priests and wise men together, and finding that Bethlehem was to be the birth-place of Christ, began to contrive his death in his own mind. An angel, however, appeared to Joseph, telling him to fly to Egypt with the child and his mother as soon as the cock crowed (iv. 14). In Matthew Joseph is made to remain in Egypt until the death of Herod, in order that a prophecy in Hosea might be fulfilled. The writer has here deliberately quoted from the Hebrew text, for the LXX. have τὰ τέκνα αὐτοῦ, "his children," instead of τὸν υἱόν μου, "my son." The former would not have suited the purpose of the evangelist.

The massacre of the children is thus described in the Protevangelion (xvi. 7): "Then Herod, perceiving that he was mocked by the wise men, and being very angry, commanded certain men to go and kill all the children that were in Bethlehem, from two years old and under." In Matthew (ii. 16) there is added to this, "and in all the coasts thereof," the writer being evidently under the impression that Bethlehem was on a lake. Justin (Dial. cum Tryph., c. 78) goes much farther than Matthew, for he says that "Herod, not being able to find the child whom the Magi came to worship, caused *all the children in Bethlehem* to be massacred without exception!" (ἁπλῶς). If this massacre had ever really taken place the fathers and mothers of these innocent children would certainly have appealed to Cyrenius against so frightful a crime. Neither Tacitus, nor any contemporary historian, mention it. Josephus and the Rabbis, who were violent against Herod, are silent respecting it. Macrobius, who lived in the fourth century, is the only heathen author who can be quoted to support the story. Voltaire (Dict. Phil., t. 4) however says that the ancient copies of Macrobius did not contain this passage. Independently of this damaging fact, the passage cannot possibly relate to this massacre, for it confounds the execution of Herod's son Antipater, mentioned by Josephus, with the massacre of the children at

Bethlehem. Antipater himself was so little of a child that he complained that he was becoming gray-headed, and Herod's other sons, Alexander and Aristobulus, whom he caused to be put to death, were both grown-up men.

The passage in Macrobius is as follows: "Cum audisset inter pueros quos in Syriâ Herodes rex Judæorum intra bimatum jussit interfui filium quoque ejus occisum, ait, Melius est Herodi porcum esse quam filium." (Macrob. Sat., l. II. c. 4.) Scaliger, however (ad Euseb. p. 163), is justly sceptical as to such an expression having been made use of by Augustus, for the very intelligible reason that Augustus himself approved of and confirmed the capital sentence which had been passed upon Herod's three sons! The original story is in Ælian (V. H., XII, 56): Διογένης ὁ Σινώπεος ἔλεγε πολλὰ τὴν ἀμαθίαν καὶ τὴν ἀπαιδουσίαν τῶν Μεγαρέων διαβάλλων, καὶ ἐβούλετο Μεγαρέως ἀνδρὸς κριὸς εἶναι μᾶλλον ἢ υἱός. It is pretended (Matt. ii. 17, 18) that this massacre is a fulfilment of Jer. xxxi. 15, but this portion of Jeremiah is an addition by an unknown author, refers to the bringing back of the Jews from Babylon, and has no prophetic meaning whatever. The text follows the LXX. so far that in ὀδυρμὸς πολὺς (Heb. הַמְרוּרִם) (which is omitted in the Codex Sinaiticus) the influence of a Targum is evident, the traces of which are still to be found in Jonathan כְּמָרַד וְדִכְבָן.

Matt. ii. 19, 20 is the parallel passage to Exod. iv. 19 (LXX.). In the Gospel of the Infancy it is said that after dwelling three years in Egypt the family returned without any angelic warning, but that when Joseph came near Judæa he was afraid to enter, because he heard that Archelaus reigned in Judæa in his father's stead. An angel, however, appeared to him, and said, "O Joseph, go into the city of Nazareth, and dwell there." There is an addition to this in Matthew, to the effect that this was done "that it might be fulfilled which was spoken by the prophet, He shall be called a Nazarite," not a Nazarene, as it is commonly translated in the English version. This name does not mean the Hebrew בָּרָךְ (Isa. xi. 1), where a Nazar, or branch, is spoken of, but only the sound of Ναζιραῖος, LXX. (כִּירִי) Judges xiii. 5. This is also the spelling of Nazarite in Lam. iv. 7, and it is evident that the writer had the passage in Judges in view, from the parallel formulas ἰδού, ἐν γαστρὶ ἕξει καὶ τέξῃ υἱὸν (conf. Judg. xiii. 5, 7, with Matt. i. 21, 23). Ναζωραῖος signifies a Nazarite. If the writer had intended to speak of Jesus as an inhabitant of Nazareth, he would have used the word Ναζαρηνός. The marginal reference in our New Testaments to Judges xiii. 5, shows that this is an acknowledged mis-translation. Jesus, however, never was a Nazarite in the sense that Samson and others were, for in Matt. xi. 19 we are told that he came eating and drinking, and was accused of being gluttonous and a wine-bibber, nor is there any such passage in any of "the prophets" as "He shall be called a Nazarite."

Luke (i. 26) makes the city of Nazareth to be the place of residence of Joseph and Mary. In c. ii. 4 he says that they went up from Nazareth to Bethlehem to be taxed, and in v. 39 that they returned to Nazareth as to their own city (πόλις αὐτῶν). In Matthew this is all altered. Bethlehem is represented as their place of residence, and the birth-place of Christ (ii. 1), and Joseph fixes his residence in "a city called Nazareth" (v. 23), solely in consequence of being warned of God in a dream. In John i. 46 et sqq., on the contrary, Nazareth is said to be the birth-place of Jesus, as it is also in Mark vi. 1, and Matt. xiii. 54, in both which passages it is called "his own country" (πατρίς). In Luke xviii. 37 however, he is called a Nazarite, Ἰησοῦς ὁ Ναζωραῖος, and in the inscription on the cross (John xix. 19) he is also called Jesus the Nazarite, which must be considered decisive as to the true appellation of Jesus, especially as after his death the apostles preached "Jesus the Nazarite" (Acts ii. 22), and performed miracles in the name of "Jesus the Nazarite" (Acts iii. 6). John (vi. 4) says that the people objected to his coming from Galilee, and said that he ought to have come "out of the town of Bethlehem, where David was." Nathanael (i. 46) had previously made the same objection, but was allowed to remain under the impression that Jesus was born at Nazareth, as Philip (v. 45) had previously told him. There is not, however, the slightest historical evidence to show that Nazareth was despised at that time. The fact remains that, with the single exception of Matt. ii., the canonical gospels unanimously state that Jesus was born at Nazareth, and not at Bethlehem, thus doing away with the visit of the Magi, the massacre of the children at Bethlehem, and the flight into Egypt. But there is no historical evidence that such a place as Nazareth existed until the first half of the fourth century. Josephus enumerates many of the towns and villages which existed in this district, but says nothing about Nazareth; yet Jotapata, the site of which has been identified, and which was the head-quarters of the army which he commanded during the early part of the Jewish war, was situated close to where this "city" is said to have existed. The whole appears to be a mere play upon words. Jesus was a Nazâra (a Nazarite), which was identical in the Palestinian dialect of the time, and in its Greek equivalent, with Nazarene or Nazarite. The followers of Jesus were long called Nazarenes or Nazarites, as they are still called in Syria and other parts of Western Asia, and it was only at a later period that this became the denomination of an heretical sect (Tertull. adv. Marcion, iv. 8; Epiph. Hæres., xxix. 1). It is remarkable that there was another Bethlehem (Josh. xix. 5) within a few miles of the spot where Nazareth is said to have been.

The first event in the life of Jesus, according to Luke (ii. 42), is his visit to Jerusalem with his parents at the feast of the Passover, when he was twelve years of age. On this occasion his parents lost sight of him for three days, after which they found him in the temple, "sitting in the midst of the doctors, both hearing and asking them questions." This bringing up of Jesus to Jerusalem is in accordance with Exod. xxxiv., 23, "Thrice in every year shall all your men children appear before the Lord God." This, therefore, ought to have been neither his first nor his last appearance in Jerusalem, but according to both Luke and the Gospel of the Infancy, we must assume that it was. The latter gospel says nothing about his being missed on the journey.

All Jewish children were taught to read by the hazzan or reader of the synagogues, which existed in all the Jewish towns. It is surprising, therefore, to hear that after Jesus had been baptized and had taught frequently in the synagogues and the temple, he "never learned letters." (John vii. 15.) His mental superiority is the same as that attributed to Moses, and his resorting to the temple to confer with the doctors instead of engaging in the pastimes usual at his age, was also, according to Philo (De Vitâ Mos.), characteristic of Moses, who, after conferring with many doctors, outstripped them all by the mere force of his genius. According to tradition Moses also left his father's house at twelve years of age. Thus R. Chama says "Moses duodenarius avulsus est a domo patris sui." Twelve years of age was also considered to be the period when a boy attained to maturity. Thus in Treatise Chagiza it is said, "A xii. annis filius censitur maturus," and the same is said in Treatise Joma, f. 82, 1, and Berachoth, f. 24, 1. Samuel also prophesied, according to tradition, from his twelfth year (Jos. Ant. v. 16, 4), and Ignatius (Ep. [interpol.] ad Magnes., c. III.) says that the judgments delivered by Solomon (1 Kings iii. 23 sqq.) and Daniel (Susanna, v. 45, sqq.) were uttered when these personages were twelve years old.

CHAPTER II.

JOHN THE BAPTIST is said by Luke to have appeared in the fifteenth year of Tiberius. The reign of Tiberius began A.D. 14, therefore John must have appeared in A.D. 29. Luke iii. 23, "And Jesus himself was, when he began, about thirty years of age" [Cod. Sin.], shows that according to this gospel Jesus must have been born in the year B.C. 2 or 1, supposing that he was baptized by John, in the same year that he himself appeared. This, however, is impossible, for we are told that John had a great number of disciples to whom he had given forms of prayer (John iv. 1; Luke xi. 1). John, we are told, was cast into prison immediately after the temptation of Jesus (Matt. iv. 12; Mark i. 14), and therefore his preaching must have preceded that event, and the baptism of Jesus. In Luke i. 5, it is stated positively that John was born in the days of Herod the Great. Now as Herod died in the spring of B.C. 3, if we are to take the Gospel statements we must, even upon the supposition that the massacre at Bethlehem took place in the last year of Herod's existence, add two years to that time, because it is evident from them that Jesus might have been two years old at that time. This brings us to B.C. 5, and therefore John would be at least thirty-four years of age at this period. Even upon this supposition, however, he would be a very young man, and one whom it would be impossible to mistake for the prophet Elias.

The date of John's birth is of course nearly identical with that of the birth of Christ. Eusebius (H. E. I. 5) says that this event took place in "the forty-second year of the reign of Augustus, and the twenty-eighth from the subjugation of Egypt and the death of Antony and Cleopatra, when, according to prophetic prediction, our Lord and Saviour Jesus Christ was born in Bethlehem of Judæa." This statement is not very creditable to the accuracy of Eusebius, for

Augustus did not begin his reign till B.C. 30, and therefore Christ would not be born, according to him, till A.D. 12. Cleopatra, however, died in B.C. 30, and twenty-eight years from this would bring us to B.C. 2 as the date of Christ's birth according to Eusebius, which is unfortunately just one year after the death of Herod. Eusebius goes on to say that Christ was born in the same year when the first census was taken, and Quirinius (Cyrenius) was governor of Syria. This refers to the statement in Luke ii. 1, that it took place after a decree had been issued by Cæsar Augustus that the whole inhabited world, πᾶσαν τὴν οἰκουμένην, should be registered, ἀπογράφεσθαι, for the purpose of taxation. Matthew implies (ii. 19) that Jesus was born some time before the death of Herod the Great, for he says that Herod died while Joseph and his family were in Egypt. Josephus (Ant. xvii. 8) says that Herod died in the early part of April in the year of Rome 750 (B.C. 3), at Jericho, five days after the execution of his son Antipater, who had conspired against him. The execution of his other two sons, who were the victims of the intrigues of Salome against them, and whose unmerited fate may have given rise to the story of the massacre at Bethlehem, took place at Samaria in the year B.C. 6.

Herod's son and successor, Archelaus, had reigned about ten years, when he was deposed and banished by Augustus (A.D. 6), after which Judæa became a Roman province. As Herod died in B.C. 3, the registering according to the Gospel account must have taken place in B.C. 4 or 5. But the registering or census made by Quirinius did not take place till A.D. 7, when Judæa was included in the imperial domain after the deposition of Archelaus. It is mentioned by Josephus, who says distinctly that Quirinius was sent to govern " in consequence of the country governed by Archelaus having been made subject to the government of Syria," τῆς Ἀρχελάου χώρας εἰς ἐπαρχίαν περιγραφείσης, or ὑποτελοῦς περιγραφείσης τῇ Συρίων, and who also says (Ant. XVIII. 1, 1) that this census was confined to Judæa, therefore it did *not* extend to Galilee, over which Herod Antipas continued to rule as a prince in alliance with Rome. It follows of course that none of his subjects could be summoned to Bethlehem for the census.

In the Protevangelion (XII. 1) it is said, "And it came to

pass that there went forth a decree from the Emperor Augustus that all the Jews should be taxed who were of Bethlehem in Judæa;" and in the Gospel of the Infancy it is said: "In the three hundred and ninth year of the era of Alexander, Augustus published a decree that all persons should go to be taxed in their own country." This, if we take the era of Alexander to signify the date of his accession, is partially correct, for a decree of Augustus did order an enumeration of the people to take place at that time, viz. B.C. 27.

The assertion that Joseph went up like the rest, "every one into his own city," εἰς τὴν ἰδίαν πόλιν, because he was of the house and family of David, whose city Bethlehem was, is erroneous, for this was a Jewish, not a Roman, custom. The Romans always carried on the census in the places where the persons resided, and in the chief towns of the various districts, for they only conformed to the customs of the vanquished nations as far as suited them; and to cause the whole population to move to places where it would be impossible to test the truth of their declarations, would be contrary to their object. In Luke Mary is made to go up to be taxed with her husband. This is another error. According to the Jewish custom the men alone were enumerated, and according to the Roman custom the names only of the women and children were required, and the husbands did not take them with them.

In A.D. 14 Augustus composed and caused to be engraven on bronze tablets an epitome of his public acts, in order that they might be sculptured on his mausoleum at Rome. This circumstance, which occurred only a few weeks before his death, is mentioned by Suetonius. A copy of this inscription is still extant in the ruined temple of Augustus and Rome at Ancyra, with a Greek version on the outside. In this inscription the enumerations of Roman citizens which took place during his reign are mentioned, and therefore, if there had been a decree that the whole inhabited world should be taxed, it would certainly be found there. As this is not the case, it must be considered as proved that no such taxing ever took place, nor is it at all credible that it should. The three enumerations which did take place were not for the purpose of taxation, and only contained, as might be expected, the names of those who enjoyed the privileges of Roman citizenship. The dates of them are B.C. 27, B.C. 7, and A.D. 14.

Mark i. 4 contains the simple statement that John baptized in the wilderness. In Luke iii. 2 it is said that the word of God came to him in the wilderness, thus contradicting c. i. 15, which says that he should be filled with the Holy Ghost even from his mother's womb. It was taught among a portion of the Jews at this time that the Messiah must have a precursor, and Mark ix. 11 shows that this was a foregone conclusion. It was also held to be essential that the Jews should have repented before the Messiah came. Thus, in Sanhedr. f. xcvii. 1, it is said, "R. Eliezer dixit, Si Israelitæ pœnitentiam agunt, tum per Goëlem liberantur; sin vero, non liberantur." This is why the gospels begin with a baptism of the people by John. The followers of Philo gave a superhuman form to the Messiah. They made him to be a species of angel, who was only visible to pious individuals, and who was to bring the descendants of Jacob back from Greece and other Gentile countries. They also thought that, when the Messiah came, they would be prepared to receive him by a patriarchal holiness of life, and by a purified state of mind, which would render their participation in divine grace certain (Philo de Execrat.). Then grace would again flow as from an eternal spring; the towns which had been deserted would again become populous; the deserts would turn into fertile fields, and the prayers of the living would bring the dead to life again.

It was among the Essenes, however, that the Messianic idea was developed in the most spiritual manner. Their ascetic mode of life was intended to advance the "kingdom of heaven" (Malchuth Schammaïm) and the knowledge of the future world (Olam-ha-Ba). Anyone who claimed to be the Messiah must, according to their ideas, be without sin. He must have renounced the world and its vanities; he must have proved that he was filled with the Holy Spirit (Rouah-ha-kadesch); he must possess power over the devils; and must have adopted a mode of life in which community of goods was recognised, and in which poverty and contempt of wealth were considered to be the greatest of virtues. The Samaritans expect a Messiah who is called Hotah, or Hoshah, the restorer, whom they commonly call Taebah; but they only regard him as a man, and as inferior to Moses, whose law it will be his duty to restore. The Taebah is to be a son of Joseph, of the tribe of Ephraim, and they expect him about A.D. 1910. They say that the Jews, since the Captivity, are a mixed people, and that they have falsified their own history. They also say that the real reading of Gen. xlix. 10 is not Shiloh, but Shulah, and that it refers to Solomon, who transferred the Tabernacle from Mount Gerizim to Jerusalem, thus rendering Ephraim and Judah antagonistic to each other, the former adhering to the Mosaic law, and the latter introducing all sorts of innovations.

Josephus (Ant. xviii. 5, 2) says that John the Baptist induced the Jews, "practising virtue, just to one another, and pure towards God," to come and be baptized. These unions for baptism, however, gave rise to an amount of political and religious excitement which, Josephus says, caused Antipas to fear that a revolution might be brought about by John; and this fear led to his imprisonment, and ultimately to his execution. Baptism had become a sort of initiatory ceremony for proselytes who wished to embrace the Jewish faith (Mischna, Pesachim, viii. 5; Talm. of Babylon, Jebamoth, 466, &c.) Mosheim (Comm. Cent. I. sect. 6) has shown that baptism was an old ceremony of the Israelites long before the Christian era. After baptism they received the sign of the cross, were anointed, and fed with milk and honey (ib. Cent. II. c. iv. sect. 13). The Essenes were called Baptists (Toblé schahenith).

The account of the baptism of Jesus by John differs from that in the Gospel to the Hebrews, as quoted by Epiphanius (Hær. l. xv.), and which is as follows:

"And when he went up out of the water the heavens were opened, and he saw the Holy Spirit of God, in the form of a dove, &c., and a voice was heard, &c., and immediately a great light shone about the place, at the sight of which John said unto him, Who art thou, Lord? And again a voice, &c., and immediately John, falling at his feet, said, I pray thee, Lord, baptize me."

The baptism of John consisted, according to the Fathers, in three immersions of the whole body in water, but the gospels merely state that Jesus "went up out of the water." Mark i. 11 is made up from Psalm ii. 7, and Isaiah xlii. 1. Justin, however, gives a different version, taken from the memorials of the Apostles, which represent the voice as saying, Τἱός μου εἶ σύ· ἐγὼ σήμερον γεγόννηκά σε, "Thou art my son: this day have I begotten thee." This is identical with Ps. ii. 7, but would not suit gospels which stated that Jesus had been already endowed with supernatural powers, and had been miraculously begotten. It is remarkable that Clemens Alexandrinus (Proleg. i. 6) and Augustine (De Consensu Evang. ii. 14) appear to have read these words in copies of the canonical gospels, and some existing MSS. of Luke's Gospel have these words. In the fourth gospel all is altered, and God is represented as telling John (i. 32) that he would recognise Jesus by seeing the Spirit descending from heaven like a dove, and remaining upon him, and Jesus is not baptized by John at all.

The Jew Tryphon (Justin, Dial. c. Tryph. 8) pointed out that baptism was not what was required on this occasion, but unction. He says, "If Christ is born, and exists anywhere, he is unknown; he does not even know himself; and he has no power until Elias comes and anoints him, and makes him visible to all." If Ps. ii. 2, and xiv. 7, are to be regarded as prophetic, it is clear that the Messiah was to be anointed with oil; and kings are represented in the Old Testament as being filled with the Spirit as soon as they were anointed (1 Sam. x. 6, 10, xvi. 13). Nothing is said, however, about Jesus being anointed. It is only said that he was baptized in the presence of the people (Luke iii. 21), who, however, do not appear to have been at all influenced by the opening of the sky and the descent of the dove. This miraculous appearance is in accordance with the Jewish belief that the sky was a solid firmament, which must open before God, who lived above it, could come down to earth. R. Juda says (Talmud of Jerusalem) that it takes fifty years to pass through the firmament. "A man of moderate activity," he continues, "can perform a journey of forty miles a day; therefore, while the sun gets to the summit of the firmament, a man can traverse forty miles." In another part of this Talmud it is said, "Rab says, 'The heavens were moist on the first day, and dried up on the second day.' Rab also says that the words 'Let there be a firmament' mean, Let the sky be solid. After this, let it congeal, let it have layers, and spread itself out."

The dove is mentioned in all the gospels, and it was not only the recognised form in which the Holy Spirit appeared, according to the Rabbis (see Targum Koheleth, 2, 12, where the voice of a dove is interpreted to mean the voice of the Holy Spirit); but it was also compared to the Spirit of God which moved upon the face of the waters (Gen. i. 2). Thus in Treatise Chagiza, c. 2, "Spiritus Dei ferebatur super aquas, sicut columba, quæ fertur super pullos suos, nec tangit illos." Some understand this Spirit to be spoken of as applicable to the Messiah (Bereschit rabba, sect. 2, fol. 4). In Sohar Numer, f. 68, col. 271 sqq., this image of the Spirit of God hovering like a dove over the primeval waters is connected with the Messiah as follows: "If David, according to Ps. lii. 8, is the olive-tree, the Messiah, his descendant, is the olive-leaf: if it is said of Noah's dove that it brought an olive-leaf in its beak, the Messiah will be heralded into the world by a dove." There were, therefore, special Jewish traditions which rendered the appearance of a dove necessary. As to the celestial voice, there was nothing surprising in that to so credulous a people as the Jews. According to Baba Mezia, f. 59, 1, R. Eliezer showed that tradition was in his favour by a celestial sign: "Tum personuit echo cælestis: Quid vobis cum R. Eliesere? Nam ubivis secundum illum obtinet traditio." The Talmud also speaks of a Rabbi seeing Jehovah Zebaoth sitting on his throne, as if it were quite an ordinary occurrence.

In Matthew the very improbable statement is made that many of the Pharisees and Sadducees came to John's baptism. This statement is omitted by Luke, and formally contradicted by Matt. xxvi. 26, and Luke vii. 30, where it is expressly stated that the Pharisees were NOT baptized by John. In Luke iii. 7–9, the reproach, "O generation of vipers," &c., is actually transferred from the Pharisees and Sadducees to the multitude.

John the Baptist was born at Juttah, near Hebron, or perhaps at Hebron. The desert of Judæa was close to Hebron, but Matthew has placed it on the banks of the Jordan. Luke (iii. 4) only says that "he came into all the hill-country about Jordan," but in John (i. 28) the occurrences at the descent of the Holy Spirit are said to have taken place "in Bethany, beyond the river of Jordan." This is the reading in all the old MSS. Origen altered Bethany into Bethabara for no other reason than that there is no such place as Bethany on the other side of the Jordan; but the

MSS. are clear upon this point, and Bethabara is *not* "beyond the river of Jordan." It is clear from c. iii. 16, that a town on the other side of Jordan was intended, for it speaks of him that was with John "beyond Jordan." Peræa, the district beyond the Jordan, was the territory of Antipas, who was hostile to John the Baptist, while Pilate does not seem to have interfered with him in Judæa. Again, in the fourth gospel Jesus and John are brought from the other side of the Jordan to Judæa (iii. 22), thus proving beyond the possibility of doubt that Bethabara, which is in Judæa, cannot be the place meant. We are then told that John and his disciples began to baptize, and this time it is at the place called Œnon, or "the fountains," near to Salim, because there was much water there. This was probably the place where John really did baptize, for there is a locality near the river called Ramet-el-Khalil, near Hebron, which is said to correspond exactly with this account. The Essenes had several colonies here.

Ascetics like John were very common, and Josephus himself became, in A.D. 53, the disciple of one of them, named Banon, who strongly resembles John, and who was probably one of his disciples (Vita, 2). This Banon lived in the desert, was clothed with the leaves of trees, fed on wild plants or fruits, and baptized himself frequently. Josephus says (Ant. xviii. 5, 2) that great crowds, especially of persons belonging to the tribe of Judah, used to resort to Œnon to be baptized by John. His sect were called Hemero-Baptists, and were identical with the Mandaites, Nazoreans, &c., which still exist in the eastern countries, chiefly in the neighbourhood of Bassora, and are the same sect with some slight shades of difference. This sect is named by St. Epiphanius, and is said by him to have been in existence before the time of Christ, and not to have known him.

In all the gospels, except Mark, John describes himself as "the voice of one crying in the wilderness, Make straight the way of the Lord, as saith the prophet Esaias." These words, however, are not written by Isaiah; for the whole of this portion of Isaiah, from c. xl. to c. lix., is the production of some writer who lived after the return from captivity, and its date is some 150 years later than the real Isaiah. The verse quoted in the gospels relates to the return of the captives who had been released by Cyrus, the Lord's anointed.

The quotation is made from the LXX., which could alone be of use to the writer, but he has altered "the paths of our God" into "his paths." The late date of these chapters of Isaiah is evident, not only from the historical facts which they contain, but also from there being, in c. iii. 7, a quotation from Nahum (i. 15) which was written on the occasion of the destruction of Nineveh, B.C. 612. There is, therefore, no pretence for saying, either that this verse was written by Isaiah, or that it has any prophetic meaning. In the added preface to Mark a quotation from Malachi is appended to it, which the later editor found in Matt. xi. 10, and which in the Codex Sinaiticus and other MSS. is attributed, as well as the other quotation, to "Esaias the prophet," which has been altered into "the prophets" by some more accurate editor.

The descent of the Holy Spirit and the recognition of Jesus as the Lamb of God do not, to our surprise, interfere with John's teaching, for he continued to baptize after these events. It would, perhaps, have been too gross a violation of history to represent John as a Christian. The effect of this supernatural appearance upon the disciples of John is equally extraordinary; for after this manifestation of Divine power the only question they ask Jesus is, "Rabbi, where dwellest thou?" The most singular part of the narrative, however, is, that when Jesus knew that the Pharisees had heard that he baptized more disciples than John, he left Judæa and went into Galilee, although John had previously declared (iii. 30) "He must increase, but I must decrease." Jesus thus leaves the field to John, and instead of going into the wilderness to be tempted, during or immediately after which period John was cast into prison, he goes into Galilee while John is still at liberty. The remaining circumstances relative to John are equally inexplicable and contradictory. In Matt. xi. 2, John sends two of his disciples to Jesus while he is in prison; in Luke vii. 19, this takes place before his imprisonment. In Matt. iv. 17, Jesus uses the very same words as John does after he is sent to prison, and Matt. xvi. 7, and xxxii. 32, are merely repetitions of the expressions attributed to John in c. iii. 7. In Matt. xv. 12, it is implied that the two sects were in harmony with each other, for John's disciples inform the disciples of Jesus of his death; but it is evident that neither the supernatural appearance at the baptism nor the miracles of Jesus had had any effect in converting them, and in the Acts (xix. 3) we are told of disciples of John who had never even heard of Christ!

In the synoptical gospels it is said that John recognised Jesus as the Messiah. In the fourth gospel (i. 32) it is expressly said that "John knew him not" until he saw the Spirit descending upon him, and not till then did he bear record "that this is the chosen of God." [Cod. Sin.]

In Luke iii. 1, a show of historical accuracy is made by saying that these things took place when Lysanias was tetrarch of Abilene. Josephus speaks of an Abila of Lysanias, and also of a Lysanias who was ruler of Chalcis, at the foot of Mount Libanus. Abila being in the neighbourhood of Chalcis, Lysanias may have been ruler of it also; but Lysanias was put to death, at the instigation of Cleopatra, no less than thirty-four years before the birth of Jesus, and neither Josephus nor any contemporary historian speaks of any other Lysanias. At the period assigned to the preaching of John, Abilene belonged to the Romans. It has been supposed that the error arose from Luke's inadvertently inserting the name of the last king of the preceding dynasty, because the country was still called the Abilene of Lysanias; but this would not explain his calling Lysanias the tetrarch of Abilene. The object of the writer was to give Jesus a predecessor. It would have been impossible, without violating historical truth, to say that John left off baptizing and became a disciple of Jesus; and therefore a narrative has been drawn up which makes Jesus to have been baptized and recognised as the Lamb of God by John, while he himself continues to baptize as if no such event had taken place, and, after he is cast into prison, actually sends to ask him (Matt. xi. 3) "Art thou he that should come, or do we look for another?" The legend, in its first form, appears to be contained in the Evangelium Infantiæ, c. xxii. 1–3 : "Now from this time Jesus began to conceal his miracles, and gave himself to the study of the law, till he arrived at his thirtieth year, at which time the Father publicly owned him at Jordan, sending down this voice from heaven: 'This is my beloved son, in whom I am well pleased,' the Holy Spirit being also present in the form of a dove."

The verse in which we are told that Jesus came to be baptized of John is a terrible stumbling-block to the supernaturalistic interpretation, for he could not have been baptized by John without confessing his sins. In the Gospel to the Hebrews this difficulty was avoided. It says: "Behold, the mother of the Lord and his brethren said unto him, John the Baptist baptizes for the remission of sins; let us go and be baptized of him. But he said unto them, In what have I sinned that I should go and be baptized of him? unless perchance this very thing that I have said is the speech of an ignorant person? Thus Jesus, who was almost reluctant to do so, was compelled by his mother Mary to receive the baptism of John." The baptism described in Matt. iii. 14–117 is also differently described in the Gospel to the Hebrews. It is there said: "When Jesus was baptized, a fire was seen upon the water. But it happened, when the Lord came up out of the water, that the fountain of All Holy Spirit descended upon him, and said, My son, I have been expecting thee all along from among the prophets, that thou wouldest come, and that I might rest in thee. For thou art my rest, thou art my first-born son, who reignest for ever and ever." It is evident that this is the earlier account, because the Holy Spirit is called in the original Hebrew or Aramaic רוח, as in the second verse of Gen. i., while in the canonical Matthew it is called τὸ πνεῦμα, representing the masculine idea, which came from a totally different source.

Josephus (Ant. xviii. 5, 2) says that John, after remaining some time in prison, was put to death by the order of Herod Antipas, the tetrarch of Galilee. Mark says that he was beheaded by Herod on account of his brother Philip's wife, and Matthew falls into the same error; but Josephus only mentions him by the family name of Herod, and he could not, contrary to all custom, have borne the same proper name as Philip the tetrarch, the brother of Herod Antipas. This is, therefore, a palpable error on the part of the evangelists. Josephus mentions Herod, the son of Mariamne, no less than seven times, and does not once call him Philip. On the contrary, he says: "Now Herod the king [Herod the Great] had at this time nine wives, one of them being Antipater's mother, and another the high-priest's daughter, by whom he had a son *of his own name.*" He also mentions Philip distinctly in the following passage (Ant. xvii. 1, 3): "Herod had also to wife Cleopatra, of Jerusalem, and by her he had two sons, Herod and Philip."

The reason why John was arrested and put to death was the fear of troubles arising from the number of his disciples. Josephus says that the people "pricked up their ears at his words," and that Herod, becoming alarmed, thought it better to cause John to be executed. This is falsely represented in the gospels as taking place in consequence of John's remonstrance against Herod's incestuous marriage; but their accounts are irreconcilable. Mark, who gives the longest account, says that Herod "feared John, knowing that he was a just man, and an holy, and observed him; and when he heard him he hesitated much, and heard him gladly" (Mark vi. 20 [Cod. Sin.]). He represents Herodias as the sole cause of his being put to death. In Matthew, on the contrary, though Herod had "put him into prison for Herodias' sake," he is afraid to put him to death through fear of the multitude (xiv. 5). Thus in Mark Herod is anxious to keep him alive, and Herodias only succeeds by a stratagem, while in Matthew Herod and Herodias are both anxious for his death, but the former is afraid of the people. Both narratives state that the head of John was brought while Herod was at supper. We have therefore to suppose that Herod Antipas, in the presence of the "lords, captains, and chief estates of Galilee" (Mark vi. 21), caused his step-daughter, Salome, a young Roman damsel ($κοράσιον$) of good family, who cannot have been more than ten years old at that time, to dance before the assembled company; after which she receives the head of John in a charger, and carries it to her mother!

The true story is as follows: Herod Antipas went, in A.D. 20, on a visit to Rome, where his half-brother Herod, who was the son of Mariamne, the high-priest's daughter, had lived in retirement since the year B.C. 5, when he was disinherited by Herod the Great (Jos. Antiq. xvii. 4, 2). He had married Herodias, the granddaughter of Herod the Great, who was consequently half-niece to him and to Antipas. Antipas fell violently in love with Herodias, and promised to marry her, and to put away his own wife, who was the daughter of Aretas, the king of Petra, and emir of the tribes which bordered on Peræa. As soon as his wife became aware of his intention, she pretended to wish to undertake a journey to Machærus, a fortress which was then in the possession of Aretas (Jos. Ant. xviii. 5, 1), and he, being warned, made every preparation to aid his daughter's flight, and she was ultimately taken to Petra. In the meantime Herodias left her husband and joined Antipas, taking with her her infant daughter Salome (Jos. Ant. xviii. 6, 1 ; Bell. Jud. i. 30, 7).

The account of the temptation in Matt. iv. and Luke iv. contradicts that in Mark i. 13, which represents Christ as being tempted of Satan for forty days, and says not a word of his fasting. In the fourth gospel the temptation is omitted, and the period between the descent of the Holy Ghost and the first miracle is filled up so as to prevent the possibility of intercalating a period of six weeks, it being distinctly stated that Jesus was in Cana of Galilee on the third day after that event (John iii. 1). The author of this gospel had, therefore, either never heard of the temptation, or regarded it as unhistorical. Mark says that Jesus was forty days in the wilderness, tempted of Satan. Matthew says that he fasted forty days and forty nights, and was tempted, not during that time, but after it. Mark gives no particulars of the temptation, while Luke appears to have endeavoured to reconcile the two accounts. The forty days are taken from the forty days and forty nights that Moses is said to have fasted, neither eating bread nor drinking water (Exod. xxxiii. 28; Deut. ix. 9, 18), and from the fasting of Elijah for a similar period (1 Kings, xix. 8).

The original idea of temptation among the Jews was that it came from God, as in Gen. xxii. 1, where God tempts Abraham; and in Exod. xvi. 4, where he tempts the children of Israel; or as in 2 Sam. xxiv. 1, where he invites David to number Israel. In 1 Chron. xxi. 1, however, God is altered into Satan. This passage, therefore, asserts the identity of Satan with Jehovah. In Job ii. 1, we have Satan in heaven, in company with the sons of God. The different ideas on this subject arise from the Jews having no idea of a devil until after the Babylonish captivity, and are expressed—the first, in what is called the Lord's prayer: "Our Father, who art in heaven . . . lead us not into temptation;" and the second in James i. 13, 14: "Let no man say when he is tempted, I am tempted of God, for God cannot be tempted with evil, *neither tempteth he any man*, but every man is tempted when he is drawn away of his own lust and enticed." Satan, or Shathan, the adversary, the enemy of mankind, had become for the Jews the special adversary of their nation, and consequently the king of all the pagan nations with whom they were in hostility. Thus, in Zachariah ii. 1, Satan resists Joshua, the high-priest, who stands before the angel of Jehovah; and in Vajirha Rabba (Bertholot, Christol. Jud. p. 153) Jehovah, according to R. Jochanan, says to the master of death, that is, to Satan (conf. Heb. ii. 14), "Feci quidem te κοσμοκράτορα, at vero cum populo fœderis negotium nullâ in re tibi est." It was natural, therefore, that if the Jewish people were connected with the Messiah, Satan should be represented as his adversary.

The next great event in the life of Jesus is the call of the apostles. This takes place, according to the synoptical gospels, in Galilee, as do all the other events of the ministry of Jesus until he goes to Jerusalem at the end of his career. It follows from this that he must have neglected all the Jewish festivals, for it is clear from Matt. xvi. 21 that he had not up to that time been to Jerusalem. His ministry, therefore, must have been among a population who were despised by the Jews of Jerusalem; who spoke a dialect which the more cultivated Jews laughed at; who were considered in religious matters to be ignorant and unorthodox; and who were proverbially called "Galilæan fools."

The call of the apostles is described by Mark as follows (Mark iii. 13-19 [Cod. Sin.]): "And he goeth up into a mountain, and calleth unto him whom he would, and they came to him. And he called twelve, whom also he named apostles, that they should be with him, and that he might send them forth to preach, and to have power to cast out devils. And he ordained the twelve, and Simon he surnamed Peter, and James the son of Zebedee, and John the brother of James, and he surnamed them Boanerges, which is, The sons of thunder; and Andrew, and Philip, and Bartholomew, and Matthew, and Thomas, and James the son of Alphæus, and Simon the Canaanite, and Judas Iscariot, which also betrayed him."

This appointment of apostles is usually supposed to be something peculiar to Christianity, as are also the offices in the Christian Church spoken of in the Epistles and in ecclesiastical history. But in fact the early Christian congregations were constituted just as the Jewish congregations were who had the Rabbis or elders (presbyters) instead of priests. Their chiefs were called apostles, or Schelichim (שליחים), and under them were the deacons, or Chazzanim (החזנים). Thus in Acts xx. 17, Paul is represented as addressing himself to the elders of the church, and he afterwards (v. 18) calls these same persons overseers or bishops (ἐπίσκοποι). The same is the case in Phil. i. 1, 1 Tim. iii. 1, 2, and Tit. i. 5–7, in all which passages bishops alone are spoken of; but as it is impossible to suppose that these churches were without priests, we must conclude with Jerome (Epist. 101, Evang.) that the apostle clearly teaches that the presbyters and bishops were identical: "Apostolus perspicue docet eosdem esse presbyteros quam episcopos."

This is also the case in the first epistle of Clement to the Corinthians, which Eusebius says was publicly read in the assemblies of the primitive church, and which is included in the Alexandrine MS. of the Old and New Testament presented by Cyril, the patriarch of Alexandria, to Charles the First in 1628. This epistle, which is certainly not written by the Clement mentioned in Phil. iv. 3, and which probably belongs to the first quarter of the second century, holds the same language respecting the appointment by the apostles of bishops and deacons, using the term bishop in its primitive sense of overseer, in which it was used both in Greece and Rome to denote certain municipal officials (Cic. ad Att. viii. 1), and which at a later period became adopted as the synonym of Rabbi or bishop. The epistle of Clement says (c. xix.), "Thus saith the Scripture in a certain place, I will appoint their overseers in righteousness and their ministers in faith." This is so clear that an attempt has been made to explain it by saying that the bishopric at Corinth was vacant at the time, but there is not the slightest warrant for this assertion. It is evident, therefore, that both at Jerusalem and at Rome there were none but elders or priests in existence in the early church, and that they were on a general footing of equality, so that even the *primus inter pares* was by no means firmly established in his authority.

The term apostle is applied to Jesus himself in Heb. ii. 1, because he is supposed to have exercised the functions of a Rabbi, or elder. The term Rabbi, which was held in great veneration by the Jews, signifies the Master, or the Doctor of the Law. It is clear according to the gospels, in which Jesus is sometimes called Rabbi, that he performed the functions of one, for he taught in the synagogues (Mark i. 21, 39; Matt. iv. 23; Luke iv. 15, 44), and he would of course not be allowed to teach anything that was contrary to the law.

It is remarkable that neither in the above-quoted passage of Mark, nor in the parallel passages, is there any authority given to apostles to baptize. The statement in John iv. 2, that they baptized during the lifetime of Jesus, is therefore inconsistent with the synoptical gospels, as is also the statement in John xii. 6, and xiii. 39, that they carried a box (γλωσσόκομον) with the prohibition against carrying any money with them in Matt. vi. 8. The powers given to the apostles are variously stated. In Mark they have only power to preach and to cast out devils. In Luke the power of curing diseases is added to these. In Matthew they have also power to cleanse the lepers and to raise the dead during the lifetime of Jesus. As they never exercised that power, this must be a later insertion, after the Acts of the Apostles and similar works had been written. A later reading in the Codex Sinaiticus omits the words "raise the dead." The same discrepancies exist as to their equipment. In Mark they are told to take nothing for their journey but a staff, to be shod with sandals, and not to put on two coats. In Matthew (x. 10) they are told not to provide shoes "nor yet a staff" [Cod. Sin.], and in Luke ix. 3 they are again told not to take a staff.

The dress of the lower class among the Jews, to which the apostles exclusively belonged, was white. The upper classes alone wore purple, violet, and crimson robes. The men wore a long and ample tunic with sleeves, which was confined at the waist by a leathern belt, and a white cloth, or turban, was twisted round their heads. They also wore sandals, which left the upper part of the feet bare, and which were strapped on by leathern thongs, and a species of cloak, called simla, resembling the Arab haik, completed their costume. Tzizyt, or fringes, made of violet thread, were fastened to the four corners of this cloak (Numb. xv. 37–41; Deut. vi. 8, xxii. 12; Matt. xxiii. 5); and they also wore, in conformity with the law, a tephilim, or phylactery, in the middle of the forehead, and on the upper part of the arm. A long beard, generally jet black, relieved the monotony of this costume, which was entirely white. The dress of the women differed very little from that of the men. An upper tunic, which was much more ample, covered the lower one almost entirely. Their belts were made of wool instead of leather, and went three or four times round the body. Their cloaks, which were much longer than those of the men, had no tzizyt at the corners. The turban which passed over their foreheads, and to which a white veil was attached, kept up the whole of their hair.

The tzizyt are ordered to be worn in Numb. xv. 37: "And the Lord spake unto Moses, saying, Speak unto the children of Israel, and bid them that they make them fringes on the borders of their garments throughout their generations, and that they put upon the fringe of the border a riband of blue (sky-blue, to remind them of the Deity); and it shall be unto you for a fringe, that ye may look upon it, and remember all the commandments of the Lord, and do them." These fringes, which were attached to the blue ribands, were called tzizyt. Since the dispersion of the Jews they have been put on the four corners of the prayer-cloak (the thalet), and are still worn in this manner.

The tephilim, or phylacteries, as they are called in Greek, were pieces of parchment which all the Jews used to wear on their foreheads and their arms, on which were written Deut. vi. 4, 6, 8; Exod. xiii. 1–16, and xv. 26. This was done in compliance with Deut. vi. 8, "Thou shalt bind them for a sign upon thine hand, and they shall be as frontlets between thine eyes." In Treatise Megilla, 24б, there is a passage which shows that all the Christian sects used to wear these tephilim for a very long period, probably until after the appointment of uncircumcised bishops. Lucian, who wrote circa A.D. 170, shows (De morte Peregr.) how the Christian sects retained the Jewish superstitions and practices. He says, "Peregrinus resumed his wandering life, and was accompanied in his ramblings by a number of Christians, who served him as satellites, and ministered abundantly to his wants. He was supported in this manner for a long time, but afterwards, having violated one of their precepts (I think he had been seen to partake of prohibited flesh), he was abandoned by his attendants and reduced to poverty."

The first apostle mentioned by Mark is Simon, who receives on this occasion the surname of Cephas, a rock, or shore; but as James and John also received surnames on this

occasion, little importance need be attached to this circumstance; and in this gospel Peter has no power given to him over the other apostles. In John i. 40–42 [Cod. Sin.], an account is given of Peter's call which differs essentially from that in the synoptical gospels:—
"One of the two which heard John speak, and followed him, was Andrew, Simon Peter's brother. He first findeth his own brother Simon, and saith unto him, We have found the Messias, which is, being interpreted, Christ. He brought him to Jesus. When Jesus beheld him, he said, Thou art Simon the son of John; thou shalt be called Cephas, which is interpreted Peter."

"The son of John" in this passage has been altered into "the son of Jona," in order to make it agree with Matt. xvi. 17. The explanation of this passage is, that the Christians of the Order of St. John believe that John married and had four children, of whom Simon was one, and later tradition, as given in Luke, made John and Jesus to be cousins. Matt. xvi. 17 is itself an interpolated passage, for it speaks of "the Church of Christ," and of an occasion on which Simon received the surname of Peter, which is not mentioned in Matthew's gospel. In the Gospel of the Nazarenes Peter is also called "the son of John." Luke (vi. 14) and Matthew (x. 2) say that Andrew was Simon Peter's brother, but all the rest of the narrative in both gospels shows that Peter had no brother. Mark says nothing of this relationship, but on the other hand says (iii. 18) that James and John were brothers, and sons of Zebedee. Luke does not mention this, but the Epistle to the Galatians (i. 19) says that James the Apostle was the brother of Jesus—a fact, therefore, of which Mark, the supposed friend and disciple of Peter, was perfectly ignorant. It appears, however, from Acts xii. 2, that the two sons of Zebedee were not apostles at all, but were the two brothers mentioned in the Acts, one of whom was put to death by Herod, and the other of whom was probably the "John whose surname was Mark" mentioned in Acts ii. 25.

Boulanger says that the word Peter, Cephas, or a similar sound, signifies gate or opening in the Eastern languages. This was how this name came to indicate the porter of the Christian heaven. He has also been made a fisherman in order to keep up the allegory of the ship, which is to be seen on medals of Janus. This is the origin of the allegorical fishings in the gospels, and also of the representation of the Church as a vessel without masts, given up to the fury of the winds and waves, which was common among the early Christians. In the mystical language of the fourth gospel, where Peter is again spoken of as the son of John (John xxi. 15 [Cod Sin.]), Peter, the son of John, Joannes, or Oannes, the great Fisherman, inherited the power of ruling the Church from the Lamb of God. The Fisherman succeeded to the Shepherd as Pisces did to Aries.

The passage, Matt. xvi. 17–19, upon which the supposed supremacy of Peter over the other apostles is founded, is, as has been already observed, an evident interpolation, and directly contradicts Matt. xviii. 18, in which the power to bind and to loose is given to *all* the apostles without exception. The words "Thou art Peter" refer to Mark iii. 16, where Simon is stated to have received this surname, and the hand of the compiler is further shown in that he takes care, after the praise of Christ which Peter had commenced, to mitigate the words ἐπετίμησεν αὐτοῖς (Mark viii. 30), and put in their place τότε διεστείλατο (xvi. 20). The power of binding and loosing given to the apostles was an expression well understood at the time, and was merely what is called in the Talmud the Semicha. The Talmud calls declaring a thing to be permitted or forbidden by the law "binding and loosing." Rabbis alone had this power, but they were empowered to transmit it to any of their disciples whom they might think fitted to exercise it. In Treatise Sanhedrin, 5, it is said, "A doctor ought not to pronounce any decision until he has been authorised to do so by his master. The formula of authorisation is as follows: 'Let him decide, let him decide—let him judge, let him judge—let him unbind the first-born, let him unbind.'" Jesus, therefore, is merely represented as using the accustomed formula when he says to his disciples, "Whatever ye shall bind on earth shall be bound in heaven," &c. In other words he is giving them the Semicha, or, as we should say in the present day, the investiture. The Semicha, however, did not allow the slightest breach or abrogation of the law. All that it allowed was the application of the law to the particular cases submitted to the Rabbis or their disciples for decision, and was a mere formal declaration that such a law applied to such a case.

In Mark ii. 14, it is said that Jesus saw Levi the son of Alphæus sitting at the receipt of custom, and said to him, "Follow me." In Matt. ix. 9, this Levi is transformed into Matthew, and in Luke v. 27 he becomes Levi again. Levi, however, in Mark does not become an apostle (see c. iii. 18). The editor of Matthew has altered the name Levi into Matthew, and calls him "the publican" (x. 3), evidently because he took the call of Levi sitting at the receipt of custom to be a call to the apostleship. He has also taken τῇ οἰκίᾳ αὐτοῦ (Mark ii. 15), by which the house of Jesus is indicated, for the house of the publican. Luke (v. 29) makes Levi give a great feast to Jesus in his own house, to which he invites a great number of publicans and others, but does not identify him with Matthew (vi. 15) any more than the author of the Acts does (i. 13). Again, the Gospel of Matthew is attributed to that apostle, but it is utterly inconceivable that he should call himself Matthew if his real name was Levi, or that he should speak of himself as "a man named Matthew."

The third gospel and the Acts contradict the other gospels upon a matter of fact. In Mark and Matthew we have an apostle who is called Thaddæus (Lebbæus, in Matt. x. 3, is an addition, which is not in the Sinaitic or the Vatican Codex). In Luke and the Acts he becomes Judas, the brother of James. The discrepancy is explained by the commentators to arise from Thaddæus being a Syrian word of much the same meaning as Judas, which is used by Luke; but it is certain that the gospels were not originally written in Syriac, and if the author of the first gospel had adopted a Syrian instead of a Hebrew name for this apostle, he would in common consistency have called the last Thaddæus Iscariot also.

It is impossible to suppose that Jesus gave distinguishing epithets to the apostles at a time when he had no experience of them. Matthew, in order probably to give prominence to Peter, has omitted the epithet Boanerges given to the sons of Zebedee, and has altered the representation in Mark x. 35 et sqq., that they occupied so high a rank among the apostles that they asked Jesus to give them the highest place in his father's kingdom, into their mother asking that favour for them. Simon the Canaanite, which is the old reading, and which is derived from the Hebrew קנאי "the zealot" (conf.

Luke vi. 15, ὁ ζηλωτής), has also been altered into Simon the Canaanite, thus making his surname indicate the place of his birth instead of his moral qualities, and leaving Peter alone, in Matthew's Gospel, with an epithet. Judas Iscariot has also undergone a transformation. The word Iscariot is made up of the words איש and קרירה "the man of Karioth," a town in the tribe of Judah, mentioned in Josh. xv. 25. Matthew, though not understanding it, has written Ἰούδας Ἰσκαριώτης in c. x. 4, and elsewhere, as if Iskarioth were the birth-place of Judas. The place where he was really supposed to be born is put beyond question by the correct reading of John vi. 71 [Cod. Sin.], "He spake of Judas the son of Simon, who was of Cariotus."

In Mark iii. 19 [Cod. Sin.] it is said that after the call of the apostles Jesus went into an house. In Luke vi. 17, on the contrary, he comes down from the mountain and stands in the plain, surrounded by his disciples, and by a great multitude of people from Judæa, Jerusalem, Peræa [Cod. Sin.] (conf. Matt. iv. 25, "from beyond Jordan"), from Tyre, and from Sidon. These people, we are told, came to hear him and to be healed of their diseases, and those that had unclean spirits were also healed. Jesus then (v. 20) addresses to his disciples what has obtained the name of the Sermon on the Mount. This sermon, or discourse, is placed much later in this gospel than it is in Matthew, for several journeys and miracles are recorded in it as occurring before the sermon which Matthew places after it, and Matthew makes it precede instead of follow the call of the Apostles. It is impossible to reconcile the two statements, for in Luke, as in Matthew, Jesus goes to Capernaum as soon as the sermon is finished, and heals the centurion's servant.

There are great differences between the two sermons. In Luke the blessings are all of a temporal description, and no spiritual meaning is attached to them. They are conceived in the spirit of the Ebionites, who taught that future happiness was to be the result of bodily suffering in this world. The maledictions which follow in Luke are not in Matthew. The Rabbis attached great importance to the Mosaic blessings and cursings, and these are in conformity with the practice of Moses as represented in the Pentateuch. Matt. v. 14-16 is not in the Sermon on the Mount in Luke, but is inserted, firstly after the parable of the sower and his seed, and secondly in an address to the people in c. xi. 33. Mark (iv. 21) also puts it after the parable of the sower, but puts it not as a parable, but as a question. The parable which Jesus is said to have spoken on this occasion (Luke vi. 39) is represented in Matthew (xv. 14) as being spoken on quite a different occasion, and as not being a parable, and v. 40 is in the charge of Jesus to his disciples long after the Sermon on the Mount (Matt. x. 24). Luke vi. 48 is in an address to the Pharisees in Matt. xii. 34, 35.

The introduction to the Sermon in Matthew states that Jesus "went about . . . healing all manner of sickness and all manner of disease among the people." These words occur again almost identically in c. ix. 35. Even "seeing the multitudes" occurs again in c. ix. 36. The narrative in Matt. ix. 35, 36, precedes a succession of instructions which Jesus gave to the apostles, and these words occur again in the same manner in c. iv. 23 as an introduction to the discourse in the next chapter. The editor, probably the latest one, took c. ix. 35 from Mark vi. 6 and i. 39, and these words have been ingeniously used as an introduction to the Sermon. It is also most improbable that at the very commencement of his ministry the fame of Jesus should have extended over all Syria, and that great multitudes should have followed him, not only from Galilee, but from Decapolis (the error respecting which has already been pointed out), from Jerusalem, and from beyond Jordan. The words "and he goeth up into the mountain" (τὸ ὄρος) (Mark iii. 13) and "he went up into the mountain" (Matt. v. 1) are interchanged. The compiler, who had to find a place for the collection of sayings which he had derived from elsewhere, and which are contained in Matt. v.-vii., took the account of the ascent of the mountain from Mark iii. 13 and the introduction to it (iv. 24, 25) from Mark iii. 7-10.

The choice of the Apostles, which in Mark and Luke follows the ascent of the mountain by Jesus, is placed later by Matthew, according to whom only four disciples had been chosen up to that time (iv. 18-22) and who had not yet been appointed apostles. These four disciples, who according to c. v. 1 were his only hearers, are at the end of the discourse (vii. 28) changed into the multitude which he had endeavoured to avoid by ascending the mountain. In Matt. v. 1, Jesus is represented as seated: in Luke (vi. 17) he is represented as standing.

The Sermon on the Mount is intended as an exposition of doctrine. It is, however, impossible that Jesus can have uttered two dissimilar discourses on the same occasion, and Matt. v. 21 is inconsistent with his telling Peter in c. xvi. 17 that he only knew him to be the Messiah by direct revelation from heaven. When we come to examine this celebrated discourse, we find none of the distinctive doctrines which have been so much insisted upon, but a summary of Jewish doctrines, with some slight alterations, the original sources of which will be given in the next chapter. It is necessary to observe that the first verse is mis-translated, and should be "Blessed in spirit are the poor." The Essenes and Ebionites, whose ideas are represented in this discourse, were essentially poor and humble. The Hebrew word anan, to which the word πτωχὸς corresponds, signifies meek as well as poor (conf. Numb. xii. 3, Ps. xxvii. 11, Prov. xvi. 19, and Isa. xxix. 19), and a spiritual meaning may thus be attached to the word.

CHAPTER III.

MATTHEW, CHAPTER V.	ORIGINAL SOURCES.
VERSE 3. Blessed in spirit are the poor (or meek), for theirs is the kingdom of heaven.	The Lord preserveth the simple.—Ps. cxvi. 6. The Lord is honoured of the lowly. Eccl. iii. 20. Honour shall uphold the humble in spirit.—Prov. xxix. 23. I dwell ... with him that is of a contrite and humble spirit.—Isa. lvii. 15. Wherever the greatness of God is mentioned in the Scriptures, the love of God for the humble is spoken of.—Talmud, Treatise Meguila.
4. Blessed are they that mourn, for they shall be comforted.	The sacrifices of God are a broken spirit: a broken and a contrite heart, O God, thou wilt not despise.—Ps. li. 17. He healeth the broken in heart, and bindeth up their griefs.—Ps. cxlvii. 3.
5. Blessed are the meek, for they shall inherit the earth.	The meek shall inherit the earth.—Ps. xxxvii. 11. He giveth grace to the lowly.—Prov. iii. 34.
6. Blessed are they which do hunger and thirst after righteousness, for they shall be filled.	Lord, who shall abide in thy tabernacle? who shall dwell in thy holy hill? He that walketh uprightly, and worketh righteousness.—Ps. xv. 1. He that walketh righteously ... shall dwell on high.—Is. xxxiii. 15, 16. This gate of the Lord, into which the righteous shall enter.—Ps. cxviii. 8.
7. Blessed are the merciful, for they shall obtain mercy.	He that followeth after righteousness and mercy, findeth life, righteousness, and honour.—Prov. xxi. 21. Whosoever hath mercy on men, on him also hath God mercy. But he who showeth no mercy to men, neither to him will God show mercy.—Treatise Schabbath, fol. 151, 2.

8. Blessed are the pure in heart, for they shall see God.

Who shall ascend into the hill of the Lord? or who shall stand in his holy place? He that hath clean hands and a pure heart. Ps. xxiv. 3, 4.

9. Blessed are the peace-makers, for they shall see God.

Seek peace and pursue it. Ps. xxxiv. 14.

Love peace, and seek it at any price. Hillel-Pirké-Abot, i. 12.

10. Blessed are they which are persecuted for righteousness' sake, for theirs is the kingdom of heaven.

Remember that it is better to be persecuted than to persecute.—Talmud, Treatise Yoma.

If the persecutor were a just man, and the persecuted person an impious one, God always would espouse the cause of the persecuted.—Midrasch, Vayikra Rabba, 27.

It is pleasing to the righteous to suffer afflictions on account of God, for thus are they freed from this state of exile.—Synopsis Sohar, p. 92.

11. Blessed are ye when men shall revile you and persecute you, and shall say all manner of evil against you falsely, for my sake.

12. Rejoice, and be exceeding glad, for great is your reward in heaven, for so persecuted they the prophets that came before you.

Behold, happy is the man whom God chasteneth, therefore despise not thou the chastening of the Almighty.—Job v. 17.

Blessed is the man whom thou chastenest, O Lord.—Ps. xciv. 12.

My son, despise not thou the chastening of the Lord . . . for whom the Lord loveth he chasteneth.—Prov. iii. 11, 12.

Verse 11 here speaks of the blessings which are to fall on the disciples when they are persecuted for Christ's sake. In Luke this is "for the Son of Man's sake;" but Christ had certainly not assumed that title at this period, according to the gospels. On the contrary, it appears from Matt. iv. 17 that he was merely continuing the preaching of John.

13. Ye are the salt of the earth, but if the salt has lost its savour, wherewithal shall it be salted? it is thenceforth good for nothing but to be cast out, and to be trodden under foot of men.

Every oblation of thy meat-offering shalt thou season with salt, neither shalt thou suffer the salt of the covenant of thy God to be absent from thy meat-offering: with all thy offerings thou shalt offer salt.—Lev. ii. 13.

Salt represents incorruptibility, and therefore, in a spiritual sense, eternity. Thus in Numb. xviii. 19, it is said, "It is a covenant of salt for ever before the Lord." In the Talmud (Treatise Kethoubot, f. 66) it is also said, "All food requires to be salted in order to be preserved. Money also requires to be salted in order to be preserved. With what does money require to be salted? With charity." Raschi says, "He who wishes to salt his money, that is to keep it, ought to diminish it incessantly by charity:—to lose in this way is to gain." There was a proverb at Jerusalem, "The salt of money is the diminution ('Heser) by charity ('Hered)." The Talmud attributes this play upon words to a young girl, and it was addressed to R. Johanan ben Zacai, who was born 47 years before Christ. In Luke Christ pronounces this sentence on quite a different occasion, and in Mark (ix. 50) it is connected with a discourse on hell-fire, and the application of the saying is different from what it is in the other two gospels.

14. Ye are the light of the world. A city that is set on an hill cannot be hid.	I will yet make doctrine to shine in the morning, and will send forth her light afar off.—Eccl. xxiv. 32.
15. Neither do men light a candle and put it under a bushel, but on a candlestick, and it giveth light to all that are in the house.	The seal of God is truth.—Talmud, Treatise Yoma, f. 69.
16. Let your light so shine before men that they may see your good works, and glorify your Father which is in heaven.	The path of the just is as the shining light, that shineth more and more unto the perfect day.—Prov. iv. 18.
17. Think not that I am come to destroy the law and the prophets. I am not come to destroy, but to fulfil.	
18. For verily I say unto you, Till heaven and earth pass away, one jot or one tittle shall in no wise pass from the law till all be fulfilled.	

These two verses are very important as showing the early history of Christianity. When Jesus is said (Matt. iv. 23) to have taught in the synagogues, we know that he cannot have taught anything but the law and its accomplishment; and we also know that a very good understanding existed for years between the Jewish Christians and the Jews. In the Recognitions, which are attributed to St. Clement, who is said to have been brought up in the school of Peter, " Beati Petri Apostoli disciplinis imbutus," are the following passages:—

"Between us who believe in Jesus, and the Jews who do not believe on him, there is no difference except as to whether this Jesus is the prophet whom Moses foretold." (c. i. v. 43.)

"The Jews are in error respecting the first advent of the

Lord, and that is the only subject of discussion between us." (Ib. v. 50.)

In Luke xvii. 16 Jesus is made to contradict this assertion, for he says, "The law and the prophets were until John; since that time the kingdom of God is preached."

19. Whosoever therefore shall break one of these least commandments, and shall teach men so, he shall be called the least in the kingdom of heaven: but whosoever shall do and teach them, the same shall be called great in the kingdom of heaven.

20. For I say unto you that unless your righteousness shall exceed the righteousness of the Scribes and Pharisees, ye shall in no wise enter into the kingdom of heaven.

Judas the holy said, "Be as careful to obey a trifling command as a great one."—Pirké-Abot, 2–4.

This verse shows that so far from inculcating contempt of the Mosaic law, the author of these chapters intended it to be observed with more strictness than the Scribes and Pharisees did. The word $\delta\iota\kappa\alpha\iota\sigma\sigma\nu\nu\eta$ means justice, not righteousness, and appears to be used in this place in the sense of merit, which is obtained, according to the Talmud, by works of piety, by the study of the law, and by the imputed merits of a person's ancestors.

21. Ye have heard that it hath been said by them of old time, Thou shalt not kill, and whoever shall kill shall be in danger of the judgment.

22. But I say unto you that whosoever is angry with his brother without a cause shall be in danger of the judgment, and whosoever shall say to his brother, Raca, shall be in danger of the council, but whosoever shall say Thou fool shall be in danger of the Gehenna of fire.

Thou shalt not kill.—Exod. xx. 15.
Thou shalt not kill.—Deut. v. 17.

R. Chiskias said, Whoever calleth his neighbour resho (wicked) he is thrust into Gehenna.
He who shall cause his brother to be ashamed in public, shall have no place in the future life.—Talmud, Treatise Aboth, iii. 13.
Be not hasty in thy spirit to be angry, for anger resteth in the bosom of fools.—Eccl. vii. 4.
It is better for a man to throw himself into a furnace than to make his brother ashamed in public.—R. Simon ben Johaï, Treatise Sota, f. 10.
Bear not hatred to thy neighbour for every wrong, and do nothing at all by injurious practices.—Eccl. x. 6.
Be slow to anger and be quick to be reconciled. — Talmud, Pirké-Abot, ii. 10.

23. Therefore if thou bring thy gift to the altar, and there rememberest that thy brother hath aught against thee;

24. Leave there thy gift before the altar: first be reconciled to thy brother, and then come and offer thy gift.

25. Agree with thine adversary quickly, whiles thou art in the way with him, lest at any time the adversary deliver thee to the judge, and the judge deliver thee to the officer, and thou be cast into prison.

26. Verily I say unto thee, Thou shalt by no means come out thence, till thou hast paid the uttermost farthing.

The Jom-Kipour (the Day of Atonement) does not expiate sins unless there has been reconciliation. —Treatise Yoma, Mischna.

Whose sins does God forgive? His who himself forgives injuries.— Treatise Meghilla, f. 28.

If the offender should offer in sacrifice all the sheep in Arabia, he would not be absolved until he had asked pardon of him whom he had injured.—Talmud, B. Kamma, f. 92.

He is the friend of God who does not become angry, and who sets an example of humility.—Treatise Pesachin, 113.

Whoso is quick in forgiving, his sins also shall be forgiven him.— Talmud, F. Meghilla, f. 25.

The beginning of strife is as when one letteth out water: therefore leave off contention before it be meddled with.—Prov. xvii. 14.

The discretion of a man deferreth his anger, and it is his glory to pass over a transgression.—Prov. xix. 11.

This verse is connected with the doctrine of purgatory, which the Jews held. In Treatise Rosch Haschanah, c. I., it is said, "There will be three divisions on the day of the last judgment; one consisting of the perfectly just, the other of the perfectly wicked, and the third of those who are neither the one nor the other. The just are inscribed and sealed immediately for eternal life; the wicked are also immediately inscribed and sealed for hell, for it is written, 'And many of them that sleep in the dust of the earth shall awake, some to everlasting life, and some to shame and everlasting contempt.' Dan. xii. 2. The middle class descend into hell, where they groan, where they moan, and whence they ascend afterwards, for it is written 'And I will bring the third part through the fire, and will refine them as silver is refined, and will try them as gold is tried: they shall call upon my name, and I will hear them.' Zech. xiii. 9. Hamah also says on this subject, 'Jehovah killeth and maketh alive, he bringeth down to school, and bringeth up again.'" As it would be too much to expect agreement upon this or any other subject, we find that the school of

Hillel taught that grace would predominate—that is, that souls would not go to purgatory at all.

27. Ye have heard that it was said by them of old time, Thou shalt not commit adultery:

28. But I say unto you that whoever looketh on a woman to lust after her, hath committed adultery with her already in his heart.

Thou shalt not commit adultery.—Exod. xi. 14.
Thou shalt not commit adultery.—Deut. v. 18.
In every act it is especially the thought, the intention, which God looks at and judges.—Treatise Yoma, f. 20, a.
Thou shalt not covet thy neighbour's wife.—Exod. xx. 17.
Thou shalt not covet thy neighbour's wife.—Deut. v. 21.
He who looks upon a woman with an evil intention, has already, so to speak, committed adultery.—Talmud, Treatise Kollah.

29. And if thy right eye offend thee, pluck it out and cast it from thee, for it is profitable for thee that one of thy members should perish, and not that thy whole body should be cast into Gehenna.

30. And if thy right hand offend thee, cut it off, and cast it from thee, for it is profitable for thee that one of thy members should perish, and not that thy whole body should be cast into Gehenna.

These verses refer to those ascetic practices which existed among the Jews as among all other nations, and which were literally carried out. Rabbi Matthia ben Hanas plucked out his eyes in order that he might not be led into temptation, and this incident has given rise to a very curious midrasch or parable (Jalcout. Sect. Wayechi, No. 16) in which Satan assumes the form of a beautiful woman. Rabbi Matthia, fearing that the temptation would be too much for him, tells his favourite disciple to heat a nail in the fire, with which he puts out his eyes. Satan being thus defeated, God sends Raphael to cure him, but Rabbi Matthia, fearing to be tempted again, refuses to be cured, and it is not till God pledges his word that Satan shall have no more power over him that he allows himself to be cured.

31. It hath been said, Whosoever shall put away his wife, let him give her a writing of divorcement.

When a man hath taken a wife, and married her, and it come to pass that she find no favour in his eyes because he hath found some uncleanness in her, let him write her a bill of divorcement

32. But I say unto you, That whosoever shall put away his wife, saving for the cause of fornication, causeth her to commit adultery, and whosoever shall marry her that is divorced committeth adultery.

33. Again ye have heard that it hath been said by them of old time, Thou shalt not forswear thyself, but shalt perform unto the Lord thine oaths.

34. But I say unto you, swear not at all, neither by heaven, for it is God's throne, nor by the earth, for it is his footstool, neither by Jerusalem, for it is the city of the Great King. Neither shalt thou swear by thy head, because thou canst not make one hair white or black.

37. But let your communication be Yea, yea, Nay, nay, for whatsoever is more than these cometh of evil.

38. Ye have heard that it hath been said, An eye for an eye and a tooth for a tooth.

and give it in her hand, and send her out of his house.—Deut. xxiv. 1.

A wife must not be put away except for adultery.—Schammaï in the Talmud, Treatise Quittin, p. 90.

The altar itself sheds tears over him who puts away his wife.—R. Eliezer, Talmud, ib.

Thou shalt not take the name of the Lord thy God in vain.—Exod. xx. 7.

Ye shall not swear by my name falsely, neither shalt thou profane the name of thy God: I am the Lord.—Lev. xix. 13.

Thou shalt not take the name of thy God in vain.—Deut. v. 11.

Accustom not thy mouth to swearing, neither use thyself to the naming of the Holy One. For as a servant that is continually beaten shall not be without a blue mark, so he that sweareth and nameth God continually shall not be faultless. A man that useth much swearing shall be filled with iniquity . . . . and if he swear in vain, he shall not be innocent, but his house shall be full of calamities.—Eccl. xxiv. 9–11.

Let thy nay be nay. Let thy yea be yea.—Treatise Baba-Mezia, f. 49.

Life for life, eye for eye, tooth for tooth, hand for hand, foot for foot, burning for burning, wound for wound, stripe for stripe.—Exod. xxi. 24.

Give to every man as his right, as far as possible, the equivalent of the evil you have done. Every one ought, as far as possible, to repair the evil he has caused.—Talmud, Baba Kama, 84.

In this same treatise the Talmud, speaking of the above law, says that the proof that only a compensation was intended is that the literal interpretation would have the effect of rendering a one-eyed man blind because he had put out one of the eyes of some one else who had two eyes. All the doctors of the second Temple agreed in interpreting this verse as signifying that pecuniary compensation was to be made, which was only forbidden to be taken in the case of murder, "Ye shall take no satisfaction for the life of a murderer." Numb. xxxv. 31.

39. But I say unto you, That ye resist not evil: but whosoever shall smite thee on thy right cheek, turn to him the other also.

40. And if any man will sue thee at the law, and take away thy coat, let him have thy cloak also. And whosoever shall compel thee to go a mile, go with him twain.

42. Give to him that asketh thee, and from him that would borrow of thee turn thou not away.

43. Ye have heard that it hath been said, Thou shalt love thy neighbour and hate thine enemy.

He giveth his cheek to him that smiteth him.—Lam. iii. 30.
Say not thou, I will recompense evil, but wait on the Lord, and he shall save thee.—Prov. xx. 22.
They who submit to injury without repaying it; they who hear themselves disparaged and do not reply; they whose only motive is love, who joyfully submit to the ills of life, these are they of whom the prophet speaks when he says, The friends of God shall one day shine like the sun in all his splendour.— Talmud, Yoma, p. 23.
He is ever merciful, and lendeth, and his seed is blessed.—Ps. xxxvii. 26.
Thou shalt open thine heart wide unto thy brother, to thy poor, and to thy needy in thy land.—Deut. xv. 11.
Thou shalt NOT hate thy brother in thine heart. . . . Thou shalt NOT avenge nor bear any grudge against the children of thy people, but thou shalt love thy neighbour as thyself. I am the Lord.—Lev. xix. 17, 18.
If thou meet thine enemy's ox or his ass going astray, thou shalt surely bring it back to him again. If thou see the ass of him that hateth thee lying under his burden, and wouldst forbear to help him, thou shalt surely help him.—Exod. xxiii. 4, 5.

This verse shows that whoever wrote this chapter did not hesitate to alter the Scriptures when it suited him; for there is no sentence in the Bible which enjoins hatred to an enemy, and the whole of the Jewish teaching was entirely opposed to it. It is evident from the commencement of the next verse "But I say unto you," that it was intended to make the teaching of Christ appear superior to that of the Jews.

44. But I say unto you, Love your enemies, bless them that curse you, do good to them that hate you, and pray for them which despitefully use you, and persecute you.

45. That ye may be the children of your Father which is in heaven, for he maketh his sun to rise on the

If thine enemy be hungry, give him bread to eat, and if he be thirsty, give him water to drink.— Prov. xxv. 21.
Rejoice not when thine enemy faileth, and let not thine heart be glad when he stumbleth.—Prov. xxiv. 17.
We must not hate the wicked, but wickedness.—Treatise Berachoth.

evil and on the good [and sendeth rain on the just and the unjust]. (The words in brackets are not in the Codex Sinaiticus.)

46. For if ye love them which love you, what reward have ye? do not even the publicans the same?

47. And if ye salute your brethren only, what do ye more than others? do not even the publicans so?

48. Be ye therefore perfect, even as your heavenly Father is perfect. [Cod. Sin.]

MATTHEW, CHAPTER VI.

1. Take heed that ye do not your alms before men, to be seen of them: otherwise ye have no reward of your Father which is in heaven.
2. Therefore when thou doest thine alms, do not sound a trumpet before, as the hypocrites do in the synagogues and in the streets, that they may be seen of men. Verily I say unto you, They have their reward.
3. But when thou doest alms, let not thy left hand know what thy right hand doeth:
4. That thine alms may be in secret, and thy Father which seeth in secret himself shall reward thee [openly]. (Not in Cod. Sin.)

Hatred stirreth up strife, but love covereth all sins.—Prov. x. 12.
All things come alike to all: there is one event to the righteous and to the wicked: to the good, and to the clean, and the unclean; to him that sacrificeth and to him that sacrificeth not: as is the good, so is the sinner; and he that sweareth as he that feareth an oath.—Eccles. ix. 2.
If I have rewarded evil unto him that was at peace with me; (yea I have delivered him that without cause is mine enemy).—Ps. vii. 4.
Whose sins does God forgive? His who himself forgives injuries. Talmud, Treatise Meghilla, f. 28.
If I rejoiced at the destruction of him that hated me, or lifted up myself when evil found him.—Job xxxi. 29.
Rejoice not over thy greatest enemy being dead.—Eccl. vii. 7.
We must neither rejoice at the misfortunes of an enemy, nor rejoice at his fall.—Pirké-Abot, iv. 21.
Be compassionate and merciful like God: make thyself equal to God.—Treatise Sabbat.

Lay up thy treasure according to the commandments of the Most High, and it shall bring thee more profit than gold.—Eccl. xxix. 11.
It is as good not to give at all as to give ostentatiously, and in public. —Treatise Chaguiga, f. 5.

Shut up alms in thy storehouses: and it shall deliver thee from all affliction.—Eccl. xxix. 12.
He that doeth alms in secret is greater than Moses himself.—Treatise Buta Bitra.

Maimonides (Hilchet-Matanot-Amyîm, X.) has found eight degrees of charity in the Talmud. The first, and highest, is that of the man who supports the poor before their fall either by gifts, or by loans, or by means of an association, so as to prevent them from becoming poor. The second is that of him who gives to the poor without knowing or being known. The third is that of him who knows the poor to whom he gives, but does not make himself known, &c. The exhortations to charity in the Old Testament are very numerous, and they had so great an effect on the Jewish nation that about A.D. 120 the doctors of the law assembled at Ouscha, under the presidency of R. Ismaël, and drew up a law by which persons were prohibited from giving more than a fifth part of their income to the poor.

5. And when thou prayest thou shalt not be as the hypocrites are, for they love to pray standing in the synagogues and in the corners of the streets, that they may be seen of men. Verily I say unto you, They have their reward.

6. But thou, when thou prayest, enter into thy closet, and when thou hast shut thy door, pray to thy Father which is in secret, and thy Father which seeth in secret shall reward thee [openly]. (Not in Cod. Sin.)

7. But when ye pray, use not vain repetitions as the heathen do; for they think that they shall be heard for their much speaking.

8. Be ye not therefore like them, for [God] your Father knoweth what things ye have need of before ye ask him. (Cod. Sin.)

9. After this manner therefore pray ye:

Our Father which art in heaven, hallowed be thy name. Thy kingdom come. Thy will be done in earth as it is in heaven. Give us this day our daily bread. And forgive us our debts as we forgive [have forgiven, Cod. Sin. and Vat] our debtors. And lead us not into temptation, but deliver us from evil [for thine is the kingdom, and the power, and the glory, for ever. Amen.] (Not in the Sinaitic or Vatican Codex.)

Who is it that will not see the face of God? The hypocrites, and next to them the liars.—Treatise Sota, p. 41.

The doctor whose mind does not resemble his outward practice does not deserve the name of doctor.—Treatise Yoma, f. 72.

Such a man only feareth the eyes of men, and knoweth not that the eyes of the Lord are ten thousand times brighter than the sun, beholding all the ways of men, and considering their most secret parts.—Eccl. xxiii. 19.

It is better to make a short prayer with reflection than a long prayer without fervour.—Treatise Menachoth, 110.

Our Father which art in heaven, be gracious to us, O Lord our God; *hallowed be thy name*; and let the remembrance of thee be glorified *in heaven* above, *and upon earth* here below. Let *thy kingdom* reign over us, now and for ever. Thy holy men of old said, Remit and *forgive* unto all men whatsoever they have done against me. *And lead us not into temptation, but deliver us from* the *evil* thing. *For thine is the kingdom*, and thou shalt reign in *glory, for ever* and for evermore. The Kadish, a Jewish prayer.

" Our Father which art in heaven " is a Jewish expression, and occurs not only in the above prayer, but repeatedly in the Jewish compositions which preceded the Christian era. In the most ancient prayers used in the synagogues the words " Our

Father" and "Our Father in heaven," in Hebrew שבשמים אבינו, are stereotyped forms of expression. In the Mischna Rosch-Haschana it is said, "The Israelites have always been great in raising their thoughts, and submitting their hearts to *their Father who is in heaven.*" See also Isa. lxiii. 16, "Thou, O Lord, art our father, our redeemer," and Jer. xxx. 20, xxxi. 9, Deut. xiv. 1, Ps. ciii. 13, &c.

"Give us this day our daily bread" is an expression which is found in the Talmud, Treatise Yom-Tob. p. 16A, "May God be blessed each day for the daily bread which he gives us," and was uttered by Hillel. "And forgive us our debts, as we forgive our debtors" is also in Treatise Meghilla, f. 28: "whoever is ready to forgive, his sins also are forgiven him."

In Luke this prayer is said to have been taught the disciples on a totally different occasion, and it would seem from this passage that Jesus had never taught his disciples any form of prayer until he was on his last journey. The disciples are represented as knowing that John taught his disciples to pray, and as asking Jesus for a form of prayer on that account. The prayer is much shorter than that in Matthew, and is as follows (Luke xi. 2–4, Cod. Sin.).

"Father, Hallowed be thy name. Thy kingdom come. Thy will be done, as in heaven, so in earth. Give us day by day our daily bread. And forgive us our sins, for we also forgive every one that is indebted to us. And lead us not into temptation."

14. For if ye forgive men their trespasses, your heavenly Father will also forgive you.

15. But if ye forgive not men their trespasses, neither will your Father forgive your trespasses.

16. Moreover, when ye fast, be not as the hypocrites, of a sad countenance: for they disfigure their faces, that they may appear unto men to fast. Verily I say unto you, They have their reward.

17. But thou, when thou fastest, anoint thine head, and wash thy face;

Forgive thy neighbour the hurt that he hath done unto thee, so shall thy sins also be forgiven when thou prayest.—Eccl. xxviii. 2.

The discretion of a man deferreth his anger, and it is his glory to pass over a transgression.—Prov. xix. 11.

One man beareth hatred against another, and doth he seek pardon from the Lord? He showeth no mercy to a man, which is like himself, and doth he ask forgiveness of his own sins?—Eccl. xxviii. 3, 4.

He who captivates public opinion by feigned virtue, by imposture, is a thief. Whoever steals the esteem, the good opinion, of his fellow-creatures, it is the same as if he stole the favour of God.—Treatise Chinim, p. 92; Josifta, Baba-Mezia, m.

CONTEMPT OF WEALTH ENJOINED. 111

18. That thou appear not unto men to fast, but unto thy Father which is in secret, and thy [the] Father which seeth in secret shall reward thee [openly]. (Not in Cod. Sin.)

19. Lay not up for yourselves treasure upon earth, where moth and rust doth corrupt, and where thieves break through and steal:

20. But lay up for yourselves treasures in heaven, where neither moth nor rust doth corrupt, and where thieves do not break through nor [and] steal:

21. For where your [thy] treasure is, there will your [thine] heart be also.

Lay up thy treasure according to the commandments of the Most High, and it shall bring thee more profit than gold.—Eccl. xxix. 11.

I wish to amass inexhaustible treasures while my ancestors have only sought for perishable wealth in this world. Baba-Bathra, p. 11.

I will only teach my son the law, for we live on its fruits in this world. and the capital is preserved for us for the life to come.—R. Nehoraï, Mischna, Kiduschin, f. 82.

Be not as servants who serve their master for a salary, but be rather as servants who serve their master without hope of reward.—Talmud, Antigone of Socho (n.c. 200), Pirké-Abot, 1.

22. The light of the body is the eye: if [therefore] thine eye be single, thy whole body shall be full of light.

23. But if thine eye be evil, thy whole body shall be full of darkness. If therefore the light that is in thee be darkness, how great is that darkness!

24. No man can serve two masters: for either he will hate the one, and love the other; or else he will hold to the one, and despise the other. Ye cannot serve God and Mammon.

The wise man's eyes are in his head; but the fool walketh in darkness.—Eccles. ii. 14.

Give me neither poverty nor riches.—Prov. xxx. 8.

Riches are good unto him that hath no sin, and poverty is evil in the mouth of the ungodly.—Eccl.xiii.24.

He that loveth gold shall not be justified, and he that followeth corruption shall have enough thereof.—Eccl. xxxi. 5.

Contempt of mammon or wealth was never taught among the Jews until the Essenes arose. Before that it was taught that it was not right to seek for excessive wealth, only for a sufficiency.

25. Therefore I say unto you, Take no thought for your life, what ye shall eat [or what ye shall drink], nor yet for your [the] body, what ye shall put on. Is not the life more than meat, and the body than raiment?

Commit thy way unto the Lord; trust also in him, and he shall bring it to pass.—Ps. xxxvii. 5.

Cast thy burden upon the Lord, and he shall sustain thee.—Ps. lv. 22.

The young lions do lack, and suf-

26. Behold the fowls of the air: for they sow not, neither do they reap, nor gather into barns: yet your heavenly Father feedeth them. Are ye not much better than they?

27. Which of you by taking thought can add one cubit to his stature? [can add to his life one span, literally one cubit.—Cod. Sin.].

28. And why take ye thought for raiment? Consider the lilies of the field, how they grow; they toil not, neither do they spin:

29. And yet I say unto you, That even Solomon in all his glory was not arrayed like one of these.

fer hunger, but they that seek the Lord shall not want any good thing.—Ps. xxxiv. 10.

The young lions roar after their prey, and seek their meat from God. These all wait upon thee that thou mayest give them their meat in due season.—Ps. civ. 21, 27.

In whose hand is the soul of every living thing, and the breath of all mankind?—Job xiii. 10.

Yet their lives were prolonged for a season and time.—Dan. viii. 12.

Thou openest thine hand, and satisfiest the desire of every living thing.

The magnificence of Solomon's dress was proverbial in Israel.

30. Wherefore, if God so clothe the grass of the field, which to-day is, and to-morrow is cast into the oven, shall he not much more clothe you, O ye of little faith?

31. Therefore take no thought, saying, What shall we eat? or, What shall we drink, or, Wherewithal shall we be clothed?

32. (For after all these things do the Gentiles seek:) for your heavenly Father [for God your Father] knoweth that ye have need of all these things.

33. But seek ye first the kingdom of God and his righteousness [his kingdom and righteousness] and all these things shall be added unto you.

34. Take therefore no thought for the morrow: for the morrow shall take thought for the things of itself [shall take thought for itself]. Sufficient unto the day is the evil thereof.

MATTHEW, CHAPTER VII.

1. Judge not, that ye be not judged.

2. For with what judgment ye judge ye shall be judged: and with what measure ye mete it shall be measured to you again.

Who giveth food to all flesh.—Ps. cxxxvi. 25.

He giveth to the beast his food, and to the young ravens which cry.—Ps. cxlvii. 9.

O fear the Lord, ye his saints, for there is no want to them that fear him.—Ps. xxxiv. 9.

What should a man do to live? Let him die. What should he do to die? Let him live.—Talmud, Treatise Tamid, p. 32. The Legend of Alexander the Great.

He who has but a morsel of bread in his basket, and who asks himself, What shall I eat to-morrow? is a man of little faith.—Talmud, Treatise Sota.

Trouble suffices for each hour.—Treatise Berachoth, f. 9.

Judge not thy neighbour so long as thou art not thyself in his place.—Treatise Aboth.

Man is measured by the measure he hath made use of.—Treatise Sota.

He who judges his neighbour charitably will be judged charitably by God.—Treatise Schabbath, i. 27.

3. And why beholdest thou the mote that is in thy brother's eye, but considerest not the beam that is in thine own eye?

4. Or how wilt thou say [or how sayest thou] to thy brother, [Brother,] let me pull out the beam out of thine eye; and behold, a beam is in thine own eye?

5. Thou hypocrite, first cast the beam out of thine own eye [cast out of thine own eye the beam]; and then shalt thou see clearly to cast out the mote out of thy brother's eye.

6. Give not that which is holy unto the dogs, neither cast ye your pearls before swine, lest they trample them under their feet, and turn again and rend you.

7. Ask, and it shall be given unto you: seek, and ye shall find; knock, and it shall be opened unto you:

8. For every one that asketh receiveth; and he that seeketh findeth: and to him that knocketh it shall be opened.

9. Or what man is there among you, whom if his son ask [of whom his son shall ask] bread, will he give him a stone?

10. Or if he ask a fish, will he give him a serpent?

11. If ye then, being evil, know how to give good gifts unto your children, how much more shall your Father which is in heaven give good things to them that ask him?

12. [Therefore] all things whatsoever ye would that men should do unto you, do ye even so to them, for this is the law and the prophets.

13. Enter ye in at the strait gate, for wide is the gate and broad is the way [for wide and broad is the way] that leadeth to destruction, and many there be which go in thereat.

14. Because strait is the gate, and narrow is the way which leadeth unto life, and few there be that find it.

15. Beware of false prophets, which come to you in sheep's clothing, but inwardly they are ravening wolves.

Physician, first heal thine own wound. — Midrasch - Rabba-Bereschit, xxiii.

Who knows how to retrace his steps? says R. Tryphon; who knows how to profit by remonstrances?— Alas! if one says to any one, Take out that mote which is in thine eye, one is answered, Take out that beam which is in thine.—Treatise Araklin, f. 16.

Speak not in the ears of a fool, for he will despise the wisdom of thy words.—Prov. xxiii. 9.

The gates of prayer are never shut. —Treatise Sota, p. 49A.
Then shall ye call upon me, and ye shall go and pray unto me, and I will hearken unto you, and ye shall seek me and find me, when ye shall search for me with all your heart.— Jer. xxix. 12, 13.

Thou shalt love thy neighbour as thyself.—Lev. xix. 18.
Do not unto others that which it would be disagreeable to thee to experience thyself. This is the chief commandment—all the rest is but the commentary upon it.—Hillel, Talmud-Sabbat, 306.

The way of sinners is made plain with stones.

Thus saith the Lord concerning the prophets that make my people err, that bite with their teeth, and cry Peace.—Micah iii. 5.

This verse and the following are not in Luke, and v. 18 is connected with v. 5 respecting the mote and the beam. The epithets false prophet in sheep's clothing, ravening wolf, worker of iniquity, caster-out of devils, doer of wonderful works, he who says, Lord, Lord, and does not the will of God, are all used of Paul. The corrupt tree is faith, the good tree represents works. Luke vi. 45 is in quite a different connection in Matthew, where it is found in c. xii. 35.

16. Ye shall know them by their fruits. Do men gather grapes of thorns, or figs of thistles?

17. Even so every good tree bringeth forth good fruit, but a corrupt tree bringeth forth evil fruit.

18. A good tree cannot bring forth evil fruit, neither can a corrupt tree bring forth good fruit.

19. Every tree that bringeth not forth good fruit is hewn down, and cast into the fire.

20. Wherefore by their fruits ye shall know them.

21. Not every one that saith unto me, Lord, Lord, shall enter into the kingdom of heaven, but he that doeth the will of my Father which is in heaven.

22. Many will say to me in that day, Lord, Lord, have we not prophesied in thy name? and in thy name have cast out [many] devils? and in thy name done many wonderful works?

23. And then will I profess unto thee, I never knew you: depart from me, ye that work iniquity.

24. Therefore whosoever heareth these sayings of mine, and doeth them, I will liken him [shall be

For the works of a man shall he render unto him, and cause every man to find according to his ways. —Job xxxii. 11.

Therefore will I judge you, O house of Israel, each one according to his ways.—Ezek. xviii. 30.

Thou renderest to man according to his work.—Ps. lxxii. 3.

Providence sees all: liberty is granted: the world is judged by goodness, and everything is recompensed according to works.—Pirké-Abot, III. 19.

If thou sayest, Behold we know it not, doth not he that pondereth the heart consider it? And he that keepeth thy soul, doth he not know it? And shall not he render to every man according to his works? —Prov. xxiv. 12.

Trust ye not in lying words, saying, The temple of the Lord, the temple of the Lord, the temple of the Lord are these. For if ye thoroughly amend your ways and your doings . . . then will I cause you to dwell in this place, in the land that I gave to your fathers, for ever and ever.—Jeremiah vii. 4-7.

Israel shall cry unto me, My God, we know thee.—Hos. viii. 2.

Depart from me, all ye workers of iniquity.—Ps. vi. 8.

My son, gather thou instruction from thy youth up: so shalt thou find wisdom till thine old age. Come likened] unto a wise man, which built his house upon a rock:

25. And the rain descended, and the floods came, and the winds blew, and beat upon that house: and it fell not, for it was founded upon a rock.

26. And every one that heareth these sayings of mine, and doeth them not, shall be likened unto a foolish man which built his house upon the sand:

27. And the rain descended, and the floods came, and the winds blew, and beat upon that house; and it fell: and great was the fall thereof.

to her as one that ploweth and soweth, and wait for her good fruits: for thou shalt not toil much in labouring about her, but thou shalt eat of her fruits right soon.—Eccl. vi. 18, 19.

As timber girt and bound together in a building cannot be loosed without shaking, so the heart that is stablished by advised counsel shall fear at no time. A heart settled upon a thought of understanding is as a fair plaistering in the wall of a gallery. Pales set on an high place will never stand against the wind: so a fearful heart in the imagination of a fool cannot stand against any fear.—Eccl. xxii. 16-18.

CHAPTER IV.

THE teaching contained in the Sermon on the Mount and in the Old Testament is by no means exclusively of Jewish origin. We find it in existence in countries far remote from Judæa at a period when it was certainly not incorporated with Jewish teaching. In the Lun-Tu, or Philosophical Conversations of Confucius (who died B.C. 478), is the following passage: "The philosopher said, 'San!' (the name of his disciple Thsing-tsen) 'my doctrine is easy and simple to be understood.' Thsing-tsen replied, 'That is certain.' The philosopher having gone out, his disciples asked what their master had meant to say. Thsing-tsen replied, 'The doctrine of our master consists solely in possessing rectitude of heart, and in loving one's neighbour as oneself.'" This passed about half a century later into that portion of Leviticus which was composed in the reign of Nehemiah. But the doctrine is in reality of much greater antiquity, for Zoroaster says in gate the 71st of his Sadder, "Offer up thy grateful praises to the Lord, the most just and pure Ormuzd, the supreme and adorable God, who thus declared to his prophet Zardusht (Zoroaster), 'Hold it not meet to do unto others what thou wouldest not have done to thyself: do that unto thy people, which, when done to thyself, proves not disagreeable to thyself.'"

There is also the beautiful A'rya couplet, which pronounces the duty of a good man, even at the instant of his destruction, to consist, "not only in forgiving, but even in a desire to benefit his destroyer, as the sandal tree at the moment of its overthrow sheds perfume on the axe which fells it." Sadi, the Persian, has also written verses in which he says, "The virtuous man confers benefits on him who has injured him," using an Arabic sentence, and apparently adopting an ancient Arabic maxim. Hafiz, too, who cannot be suspected of having borrowed this doctrine, says:—

> "Learn from yon orient shell to love thy foe,
> And store with pearls the hand that brings thee woe.
> Free like yon rock from base vindictive pride,
> Imblaze with gems the wrist that rends thy side.
> Mark, when yon tree rewards the stormy shower
> With fruit nectareous, or the balmy flower,
> All Nature calls aloud, shall man do less
> Than heal the smiter, and the railer bless?"

It would be easy to multiply instances, but we must return to the consideration of the immediate origin of the Gospel narratives.

The sect known as the Ebionites or Essenes had obtained considerable influence among the lower orders of the Jews at the period immediately preceding the Christian era. Calmet has observed that neither Jesus, nor the evangelists, nor the authors of the Epistles have mentioned this sect, and this silence shows that the Judæo-Christians were either a branch of this sect, or were themselves Essenes. These Essenes, who seem to be mentioned by Epiphanius and Eusebius by the name of 'Ιέσσαιοι, or Jessæans, a name which they say was given to the first Christians, became afterwards known as Nazarites, a name taken from Gen. xlix. 26, where it is said that Joseph was a Nazarite (בור) among his brethren, for he was separated from them by his rank.

There were Essenean settlements at Rome, Corinth, and in Galatia, and it is from them that the learned Manichæan Christians say that the collection of traditions or histories was made by Papias, Hegesippus, &c., or their informants, they having formed part of their Scriptures. Eusebius, as has already been shown, says in the most positive manner, speaking of the Therapeutæ, who were the same sect as the Ebionites, Essenes, &c., that "the ancient writings made use of by this sect were in all probability none other than our gospels and apostolic writings, and that certain Diegeses, after the manner of allegorical interpretations of the ancient prophets, were the epistles." Τάχα δ' εἰκὸς ἅ φησιν ἀρχαίων παρ'αὐτοῖς εἶναι· συγγράμματα, εὐαγγελία, καὶ τὰς τῶν ἀποστόλων γραφάς. Διηγήσεις τέ τινες κατὰ τὸ εἰκὸς τῶν πάλαι προφητῶν ἑρμηνευτικὰς, ἐπιστολὰς ταῦτα εἶναι. (H. E., l. ii. c. 16.) He then gives an account of them from Philo, who must have written this description when Jesus was not more than ten years old, and at least fifty years before the existence of any of our epistles or gospels, and in the whole of whose writings there is not the least allusion to Christ, although he was at Jerusalem during the period of his ministry.

According to this account, as soon as they entered upon the prophetic life, they divested themselves of all the revenues of their estates, "as it is recorded in the accredited Acts of the Apostles that all the associates of the apostles, after selling all their possessions and substance, distributed to all according to the necessity of each one, so that there was none in want among them." Persons resorted to Lake Maria, where the Therapeutæ had founded a colony, from all parts of the world. Philo says, "in every house there is a sacred shrine which is called the holy place, and the monastery in which they retire by themselves and perform all the mysteries of a holy life, bringing in nothing, neither meat, nor drink, nor anything else which is indispensable towards supplying the necessities of the body, but studying in that place the laws and the sacred oracles of God." He also says that "the explanations of the sacred Scriptures are delivered by mystic expressions in allegories, for the whole of the law appears to these men to resemble a living animal, and its express commandments seem to be the body, and the invisible meaning concealed under and lying beneath the plain words resembles the soul in which the rational soul begins most excellently to contemplate what belongs to itself, as in a mirror, beholding in these very words the exceeding beauty of the sentiments, and unfolding and explaining the symbols, and bringing the secret meaning naked to the light to all who are able, by the light of a slight intimation, to perceive what is unseen by what is visible." A striking proof of resemblance to the Judæo-Christians is that they would not eat anything that had blood in it (Conf. Acts xvi. 29).

The Ebionites, or Nazarites, obeyed the laws of Moses most scrupulously, and had the greatest confidence in the prophecies of the Old Testament. Hence the character of Jesus is made to resemble that of Joshua, who is called Jesus in the New Testament (Philo also calls him Ἰησοῦς, that is one who came not to destroy the law, but to fulfil it). This is exactly the character which tradition gave to Joshua, who, as the successor of Moses, fulfilled the mission of that legislator by establishing the people of God in the promised land (see Philo, Περὶ Φιλανθρωπίας). The Jews consider that the sect of the Ebionites originated at the period when the

Cohanim, or sons of Aaron, claimed a superiority over the rest of the Levites, which appears to have been in the reign of Jehoshaphat, or perhaps earlier. The usual results followed, and while the dominant caste allowed the Jewish religion to fall into abeyance, and did not oppose the worship of idols, the Levites continued poor and attached to their primitive faith.

Before the final defeat and death of Judas Maccabæus at Eleasa, when the whole Jewish nation went into mourning (1 Macc. ix. 18–21), he had endeavoured to procure the assistance of the Romans, and the Asmonean princes had also endeavoured to obtain the assistance of Mithridates I., the king of Parthia. This displeased a powerful party called the Assideans, who were originally only distinguished by their exemplary piety from the rest of the people. The word 'Hassid means a perfectly pious man. It is derived from המר, grace, charity, and signifies a person whose love embraces all that exists. This party placed all their confidence in God, and held that he would do unto their enemies as he did unto the Midianites, to Sisera, and to the other enemies of Israel (Ps. lxxxiii. 9, 10). Besides these two parties there was a third, the Hellenists, who were in favour of the enemy.

The Assideans were the ancestors of the Pharisees and of the Ebionites or Essenes. They not only observed in the most scrupulous manner the Mosaic law and the ordinances of the sopherim, or scribes, but subjected themselves to voluntary mortifications, abstained from wine temporarily or for life, and submitted to the rules of Levitical purity. Jose ben Joeser of Zeuda, one of the Assideans who were put to death by Bacchides, preserved the same degree of purity with regard to garments and other particulars as the priests (Haguiga, 18b).

This party considered every engagement which was not regulated by the law as a sin. The Mischna (Aboth, VI. 4) gives an idea of the asceticism which they practised: "This is what the law teacheth thee to do: eat bread and salt, drink water in moderation, sleep on the ground, lead a life of mortification, and study the law." Jose ben Johanan of Jerusalem, who was a colleague of Jose ben Joeser in the chief council or Council of the Elders (Sikne beth-din), used to exhort to the most unlimited charity, following the maxim of the Assideans, "Mine is thine, as thine is mine" (Aboth, V. 13). He used to say, "Consider the poor as members of thy family," and at the same time recommended austerity, saying, "Do not talk much to women" (ib. I. 5). The principal occupation of the Assideans was the study of the law, and the transmission of oral tradition to posterity. Jose ben Joeser used to say, "Let thy house be a place of meeting for the doctors of the law; sit at their feet, and quench thy thirst with their words." It was on this account that the men who belonged to this party were also called scribes (γραμματεῖς). The words Scribe and Assidean are always synonymous (1 Macc. vii. 12, 13; 2 Macc. vi. 18). In their capacity of scribes they filled the functions of magistrates and doctors of the law, and thus exerted a great influence over the education of youth and over the people generally.

The Hellenistic party were diametrically opposed to the Assideans. This party dates from the time of Jason, who obtained the dignity of high priest from Antiochus Epiphanes by means of bribes, and promised the king 150 talents of silver more if he would allow him to establish a gymnasium for Greek sports, which he actually set up in the outer court of the Temple, and made the young men wear hats. The Greek fashions and religion became so prevalent that the priests deserted the Temple, neglected the sacrifices, and resorted to the gymnasium (2 Macc. iv. 7–15). This party naturally excited the indignation of the stricter Jews.

The three surviving sons of Mattathias were at the head of the patriotic party, and after many struggles Jonathan succeeded in obtaining an honourable peace. During the nine years of his government (B.C. 152-154) he succeeded in increasing the power of the Jewish nation to so great an extent that he laid the foundation of an independent state. His brother Simon, who succeeded him, enlarged the frontiers of Judæa, raised numerous fortresses, and freed the people entirely from the domination of Syria. In his time "the ancient men sat in all the streets communing together of great things, and the young men put on glorious and warlike apparel. . . . He made peace in the land, and Israel rejoiced with great joy, for every man sat under his vine and his fig-tree, and there were none to fray them" (1 Macc. xiv. 9–12). He also annihilated the remainder of the Hellenists, who were entrenched in Gazara, Bethsura, and the Acra or Citadel of Jerusalem. The latter fortress, which had held out for twenty-three years, was taken on the 23rd of May, B.C. 141, and the Jewish soldiers entered it, preceded by a band of music, and singing religious songs. From this date the Jewish nation became more than ever exclusive and devoted to their peculiar faith.

From the time when the Asmonean princes first became victorious, the more pious among the Assideans had given themselves up more and more to religious study and practices. After the final victory, those who were the allies of the patriotic party became divided, some taking to public affairs, war, and diplomacy, while the greater number gave themselves up to the study of the law, to legislation, to administration, and to internal government. Hence arose two parties, the Sadducees, or aristocratic party, and the Pharisees, or scribes, who formed the democratic party, which befriended or was hostile to the Asmonean dynasty according as the latter favoured the Mosaic law or otherwise. The people of course always favoured the democratic party.

Simon had the confidence of the people and of the Pharisees during the whole of his life. He, however, committed the fatal error of sending an ambassador, Munenius, to Rome, with a present of a great shield of a thousand pounds weight, to confirm the league with the Romans, thus placing Judæa under the protection of that empire, which, less than two centuries later, required that one of its emperors should receive divine honours in the Temple of Jerusalem; and which, thirty years afterwards, destroyed Jerusalem, and finally dispersed the nation.

Some years later the Assideans were composed of the Assideans proper, who were afterwards called the Essenes, and of the Pharisees, or Separatists, so called because, like the Essenes, they abstained from all illegal pleasures. They had nothing in common with the sacerdotal class. Unlike the Sadducees, who thought that in temporal affairs the maxims of worldly policy were to be followed, the Pharisees held that the laws and customs of their ancestors ought to be the sole rule of conduct for the state as well as for individuals. They appear to have been men who united to great personal austerity and indifference to wealth, great mildness in their magisterial functions. One of their principal men, Joshua ben Perachia, used to say to his disciples, "When you deliver sentence, always look for extenuating circumstances." No doubt many of them were hypocrites, but the Pharisees themselves held these up to public contempt, calling them "the painted ones" and "the sore of the Pharisees." Even those whose devotion only resulted from the fear of God were not held to be true brothers; they only allowed those who obeyed the commandments of the law through love of God to be really Pharisees. (Babl. Sotah, 23^b; Jerus. Sotah, iv.)

The Sadducees differed from the Pharisees more in a political than a religious point of view. They held that if God has gifted man with free-will it is because he has made him master of his destiny, and that men receive here below the rewards and punishments of their evil actions. As legislators and magistrates they were inexorably severe, and interpreted the Mosaic law literally. This is the origin of their name, which is Zadouquim in Hebrew, derived from Zadig, the Just.

The sect of the Essenes originated from the custom of making Nazarites recorded in the story of Samson, who is represented as being a Nazarite for life (Judges xiii. 7). Samuel also was vowed by his mother to be a Nazarite for life (1 Sam. i. et sqq.). This sort of Nazarite is called Nazir olam. There was, however, another sort of Nazarites who only took temporary vows, and these are the only ones spoken of in the Pentateuch (see Numbers vi.), but after the return from the Captivity, the Assideans, or men of distinguished piety, were not satisfied with observing the law as laid down in the Pentateuch, but became Nazarites for life. Thus they were obliged to give up all social intercourse in order to preserve that Levitical purity which it was incumbent on them to do. Some even renounced marriage, not because they considered it as a sin, for there were married Essenes, but because according to the Mosaic law women stood frequently in need of purifications. The wars which took place during the reign of the Asmonean princes ultimately drove them into the desert, for the soldiers who returned from the field of battle might have been in contact with corpses, and this was sufficient to render the Nazir olam impure. They therefore settled in the oasis of Engadi in the desert which is situated to the west of the Dead Sea, and lived on the dates which grew there in abundance. They had their meals in common, and found a precedent for this in the Passover, which was eaten in common by the guests. From this to communism was but a step. Private property was useless to them, and each one gave up his possessions to the treasury of the Order, which provided for the general wants.

Some of the Essenes who lived in the desert wore white linen dresses as an external symbol of the sacerdotal state which they had chosen (Lev. xvi. 4). Josephus, who was an eye-witness, and had lived amongst them, says that they put on these dresses for their meals, and that if any guests arrived they caused them to partake of their repasts. They wore aprons (keraphaim) in order to dry themselves after their ablutions. It is from this practice that their name of Baptists, Toblè schacharith, 'Ημέρο-Βαπτισταί, is derived. They believed in the unity of God, in the immortality of the soul, and in a future life. Josephus says, "They do not speak until sunrise, except when they utter certain prayers which they have received from their fathers as if to invite that planet to rise." He also says, "They make use of frequent purifications, and fear to pollute the rays of the sun, the image of God. They alone offer no bloody sacrifices at the temple of Jerusalem. Symbols, parables, and allegories are familiar to them: in this they imitate the ancients. Skilled in the use of minerals and simples, they cure gratuitously any sick persons who are brought to them." At sunrise they recited the Schemah, after which they used to assemble and continue their prayers in silence, for they had no other settled forms of prayer at that time. They abstained from speaking for some time before prayer, and observed the same silence at their meals, which they considered as a sort of worship, the table representing the altar, and the food the sacrifices. These habits of silence naturally led them to those mystic speculations for which they were remarkable.

They had several names for God besides those in the Old Testament, and they endeavoured by meditating on them to discover their hidden meaning, and those speculations, according to them, gave them the Holy Spirit, and the gift of prophecy. They in fact laid the foundation of Gnostic theosophy, which aimed at discovering the influence of God on the creation of the world and on the development of the human mind. They contemplated in a similar manner the names of the angels. These mysteries were disclosed to the initiated accompanied by certain ceremonies. Josephus says, " When a candidate for admission presents himself, they try him for three years, one of which is passed outside the house, and two inside. Before admitting him they make him promise with terrible oaths to serve God, to love mankind, to avoid wicked persons, to protect the wealthy, to keep faith with every one, and especially with the Prince; they also make him swear that he will never betray the secrets of the association to others ; that he will keep them secret at the peril of his life, and will teach nothing but what he has learnt from his masters; that he will preserve the mystical books of the Order, and the traditional names of the angels." Those who were initiated in the first degree were called Zenniïm. There were three degrees of initiation altogether, preparation for which was made in the lower degrees by the practice of austerity and the acquisition of knowledge.

The great aim of the Essenes was to revive the pretended prophetic power of the earlier Nazarites. The prophets had long ceased to be heard, and they believe that by their mode of life they might be enabled again to hear the voice of God. The less they seemed likely to hear it the greater the austerities they subjected themselves to, in order that the Holy Spirit, the Rouah-ha-Kadesch, might descend upon them. They were convinced that on the day that they should again behold the celestial vision the kingdom of heaven (Malcouth-Schamaïm), or the Messianic period, would have arrived, and would put an end to all evil. One of their number has stated clearly and concisely how these expectations were connected with the basis of their belief: " Step by step zeal for the law and Pharisaic purity lead to Hassidouth (to humility and hatred of sin); thence we arrive at the gift of the Holy Spirit, which will at last bring about the resurrection of the dead by Elias, the forerunner of the Messiah " (see Mischna Sotah, fin.; Aboda Sara, 206 ; Jerus. Sabbat, I. p. 3 ; Schekalim, III., p. 47 ; Midrasch canticum, p. 3).

The common people admired and revered the Essenes. Besides their piety, frugality, and readiness to succour others, a certain air of mystery which has always been captivating to the vulgar surrounded them, added to which they were said to be able to perform miraculous cures. Some of them, such as Judas Manahem, and Simeon, were said to be able to predict future events and to interpret dreams. Onias, another Essene, was said to be able to bring down rain from heaven in times of drought. Their medical skill was also a subject of wonder among an ignorant and credulous race. Since the Jews had been brought into contact with the Persians they believed in the existence of evil spirits or demons (Schédim, Mazihim). Any one whose mind was in any degree affected was said to be possessed by a demon, who must be exorcised before the patient could be relieved. All uncommon diseases, such as palsy, leprosy, excessive issues of blood, &c., were attributed to demoniacal agency. The Essenes pretended to excel in exorcism. They studied medicine in a book called Sépher-rephorioth, which was attributed to Solomon. They frequently made use of verses from the Old Testament and other formulas, which they recited in a low voice (Le'hischa); at other times they made use of roots or stones, to which they attributed a magic power, and it is probable that they also understood something of what is termed animal magnetism. The Pharisees regarded them with the utmost contempt, and there is no doubt that the expression "pious fool" (Hassid Schota) which is applied in the Talmud to those who withdraw themselves from the society of even the most pious persons is intended for them. Their system of exorcising by means of verses from the Old Testament excited, however, not their contempt, but their indignation, for they held it to be a profanation of the Scriptures, and considered exorcism to be a species of sorcery which was forbidden by the law of Moses. They therefore declared that those who practised exorcism were unworthy of the life to come. This explains the antagonism which is represented in the Gospels as existing between the Nazarites or Judæo-Christians and the Pharisees, while it also shows how false such representations are as those in Matt. xii. 27, where the disciples of the Pharisees are represented as casting out devils. It explains also the blasphemy against the Holy Spirit mentioned in Mark iii. 29, 30 and Matt. xii. 32, and shows how impossible it was for Jews who were not Essenes to believe in miracles which the law of

Moses taught them to look upon as witchcraft and sorcery. It would seem from Irenæus (l. II. c. 5), however, that some similar belief afterwards spread among the Jews, for he says, "The Jews even now by this same invocation of the name of God drive out devils," and Origen (Contra Cels. l. V.) says, "If a man invoke by the name of the God of Abraham, Isaac, and Jacob, the devils will try and do what they are commanded, but if he translates these names according to their meaning into any other language, they will have no force at all!"

The Ebionites, that is the poor people, the name being derived from Ebjion, poor, were not looked upon as heretics by the early Fathers. Justin (Dial. cum Tryph., 48) says, "There are among the members of our creed some who acknowledge that Jesus is the Christ, but who consider him to be a man begotten by men." Tertullian says, "Ebion holds that Jesus Christ is only a man of the seed of David, that is to say, a man who is not the Son of God." Origen (Contra Cels. v. 61) says, "There are some among us who say that they are Christians, because they admit Jesus to be the Messiah, and who nevertheless, like the greater number of the Jews, observe steadfastly the law of Moses. Such are the Ebionites, both those who acknowledge with us that Jesus was born of a virgin, and those who refuse to believe it, and say that he was engendered in the same way as other men." This shows that in Origen's time (circa A.D. 250) there were two sorts of Ebionites. Eusebius (H. E. III. 27) says, "The Ebionites believe that Christ was only an ordinary man, born of a father and mother in the same way as other people, and was only distinguished from others by his virtue. They held that it was necessary to follow the Mosaic law. Others, who are also called Ebionites, admit that the Lord was born of the Virgin by the operation of the Holy Spirit, but they do not admit that he has been the Logos and the wisdom of his Father from all eternity. They pay as much respect as the others to the Mosaic rites. They reject all the epistles of the apostle (Paul), whom they call a renegade. They only use the Gospel according to the Hebrews, and hold the rest in no estimation at all."

The Nazarites and Ebionites were neither considered to be different sects nor heretical, till Epiphanius and Jerome, in the fourth century, described them as such. Jerome says the

Nazarites were those who believed that Jesus was born of the Virgin Mary, but this distinction has been erroneously referred to the first century, for Theodoret, who wrote long after Jerome, says "The Nazarites are Jews who honour Jesus as being a just man." The Ebionites recognised Jesus as a Saviour, not in the sense of Wisdom xvi. 7, where God is called the Saviour of all, nor as their redeemer from the consequences of the sin of Adam, but merely as one who at the last judgment would acknowledge all who had recognised him as the Messiah in this world. In Epiphanius and in the Clementine Homilies certain Ebionites are spoken of who only recognised such pious men as had existed up to the time of Joshua as being true prophets, and who detested all the prophets of later date, especially David and Solomon (Epiph. Hæres. 30, 18). David, as being a sanguinary conqueror, was an object of special aversion to them, for they looked upon bloodshed as one of the greatest of sins, and David's adultery and Solomon's harem were objects of even greater abomination to them.

The appearance of the Messiah was expected by many of the Jews to be attended by signs and miracles. Expressions such as Is. xxxv. 5 et sqq., which are merely metaphorical, and are a species of song of rejoicing over the fall of Babylon, were applied to the miracles which he was to perform. According to this passage the eyes of the blind were to be opened, the ears of the deaf to be unstopped, the lame were to leap, and the tongue of the dumb was to sing. This portion of the book of Isaiah is not written by Isaiah, but by a later writer, who quotes from another portion of Isaiah (c. xiii.), which he calls the Book of Jehovah. Notwithstanding this, Jesus himself is represented (Matt. ii. 5) as referring to it. The same remark applies to another passage (Isa. xlix. 7), which was also applied to the Messiah, and which is a song of rejoicing for the return from Babylon written in the time of Zerubbabel. .

One of the chief passages relied on was Deut. xviii. 15, in which Moses is represented as saying, "The Lord thy God will raise up unto thee a prophet from the midst of thy brethren like unto me; unto him shall ye hearken." This passage, which is applied to the Messiah in Acts iii. 22 and vii. 37, was written, as was the greater part of the book of Deuteronomy, in the reign of Josiah, and differs essentially from the earlier books, in that Moses, not Jehovah, is represented as uttering the commands. It also ignores the second chapter of Genesis, by ordering the Sabbath to be kept holy, not because God rested on that day, but because God had brought the Jews out of Egypt (Deut. v. 15). Some of the Rabbis, however, said that the second God, or Redeemer, was to be similar to the first. Thus in Midrasch Kobeleth, f. 75, 3, it is said, "R. Berechias nomine R. Isaaci dixit: Quemadmodum Goel primus (Moses) sic etiam postremus (Messias) comparatus est. De Goele primo quidnam Scriptura dixit, Exod. iv. 20 : Et sumpsit Moses uxorem et filios, eosque asino imprimit. Sic Goel postremus, Zach. ix. 9 : ' Pauper et insidens asino. Quidnam de Goele primo nôsti? is descendere fecit Man. q. d. Exod. xvi. 14: Ecce ego pluere faciam vobis panem de cœlo. Sic etiam Goel postremus Manna descendere faciet, q. d. Ps. lxxii. 16 : Erit multitudo fermenti in terrâ. Quomodo Goel primus comparatus fuit? is ascendere fecit puteum : sic quoque Goel postremus ascendere faciet aquas, q. d. Joel iv. 18: Et fons e domo Domini egredietur, et torrentem Sittim irrigabit." According to this mode of prophetic interpretation Moses setting his wife and sons upon an ass is a type of the triumphal entry into Jerusalem ! Christ, however, did not bring down manna from heaven, nor did he make a fountain come out of the house of the Lord to water the valley of Shittim, neither did he, as is said in Tauchuma, f. 54, 4, cause the sea to dry up as Moses did.

Although the miracles which Jesus is represented as performing are of the most astonishing description, the people seem to be scarcely surprised at them. In John vii. 31 [Cod. Sin.] they do manifest some surprise however, but no conviction, for they ask, "When Christ cometh will he do more miracles than these which this man doeth?" Their state of mind is probably correctly represented, for not only were they much influenced by the pretended miracles wrought by the Essenes, but the priests of the second temple themselves performed miracles, and imposed upon the people with as great success as Christian priests have in later times. In Treatise Rosch Haschanah we are told that on the Day of Atonement a scarlet thread used to be fastened on the great interior door of the temple. As soon as the scape-goat which was loaded with the sins of the people attained the desert, this scarlet thread became white, in order to fulfil the supposed prophecy in Isa. i. 18. This miracle was brought about by the prayer of the high priest. Besides this miracle there were ten standing miracles, one of which was that no woman was ever inconvenienced by the bad smell of the meat offered in sacrifice; another, that no fly was ever seen in the sacred slaughter-house; another, that no serpent or viper ever bit anybody in Jerusalem; another, that rain never extinguished the sacred fire, &c. It must be admitted that though the priests refused to admit the miracles of the Essenes, they had plenty of their own.

There are absolutely no limits to human credulity on this subject. Eusebius assures us on the authority of the elders of the Churches of Lyons and Vienne, that the bodies of some of the martyred saints of those churches were found alive and uninjured in the stomachs of the wild beasts who had devoured them. Tertullian (De An. c. 51) says that the body of a Christian which had been some time buried moved itself to one side of the grave in order to make room for another corpse which was going to be laid beside it. St. Jerome (Epist. l. III. De vitâ Hilarionis) says that St. Hilarion, who was a disciple of St. Anthony, used to heal those who were possessed, the palsied, and the blind in the same way as Christ and the Emperor Vespasian did, that is, by touching them, by words, and by saliva : while legions of devils were unable to hold their own for an hour against this holy personage. Eusebius says that when the Emperor Marcus Aurelius was about to engage in battle with the Germans and Sarmatians, he and his army were suffering from thirst. Upon this the Christian soldiers that belonged to the Melitine legion fell on their knees and began to pray, whereupon lightning came down from heaven and dispersed and destroyed the enemy, and a shower came down and refreshed the Roman army. On this account, he adds, this legion was called the fulminea, or thundering legion. Tertullian (who is quoted by Eusebius) tells this lie with a circumstance, for he says, "There are epistles of the most learned Emperor Marcus still extant, in which he himself bears testimony that when his army was ready to perish for want of water, it was saved by the prayers of the Christians." These statements sink into nothingness beside the account of a Christian dog, who used to slide along on his haunches to receive the Sacrament. This dog was canonized by the Pope, and many miracles have been wrought at his shrine in the parish church of San Andres, near Valladolid.

Eusebius objects to the miracles attributed to Apollonius Tyanæus in much the same way as the Jews are said to have objected to those attributed to Jesus. In his answer to Hierocles (c. 35), after enumerating the miracles which Apollonius in the fourth book of his Life, by Philostratus, is said to have performed, he says, " Such are the miracles which Apollonius is said to have worked. It would be well to examine the circumstances attending them, in order to show that, even if these deeds should be true, they ought only to be attributed to the assistance Apollonius may have received from the devil." The early Christians accused Apollonius of sorcery, and their writers termed him an impostor and a worker of false miracles, which however they did not deny that he performed. St. Chrysostom says, " that miracles are only proper to excite sluggish and vulgar minds, that men of sense have no occasion for them, and that they frequently carry some untoward suspicions along with them." This is true, for not only are miracles, according to the Bible itself, insufficient to prove the divine mission of any one, but they are also insufficient to prove any doctrine, and are thus entirely useless. The following illustration of the inutility of miracles to prove any doctrinal statement is abridged from the Talmud (Treatise Baba-Mezia) :—

" On that day R. Eliezer ben Orcanaz replied to all the questions that were put to him, but his arguments having been found to be inferior to his pretensions, the doctors who were present condemned his answers, and refused to admit his conclusions. Then R. Eliezer said to them, ' My doctrine is true, and this karoub tree which is near us will show how true my conclusions are.' Immediately the tree, obeying the voice of R. Eliezer, arose out of the ground and planted itself a hundred cubits farther off. But the Rabbis shook their heads, and answered, ' The karoub tree proves nothing.' ' What!' cried Eliezer, ' you resist so great a testimony of my power! Then let this rivulet flow backwards, and at length attest the truth of my teaching.' Immediately the rivulet, obeying the command of Eliezer, flowed backwards towards its source. But the Rabbis continued to shake their heads, and said, 'The rivulet proves nothing.' 'How!' said Eliezer, 'you do not understand the power I make use of, and yet you do not believe the doctrine I teach!' The Rabbis, shaking their heads, answered, 'The Rabbis wish to understand before they believe.' 'Will you believe me,' said Eliezer, 'if the walls of this house of study fall down at my command?' And the walls, obeying him, began to fall, when R. Joshua exclaimed, 'By what right do the walls interfere in our debates?' And the walls stopped in their fall in honour of R. Joshua, but did not recover their upright position in honour of R. Eliezer, and the Talmud says ironically that they are still leaning. Then R. Eliezer, mad with rage, cried out, 'Then, in order to confound you, and since you compel me to it, let a voice from heaven be heard.' And immediately the Bath-kol (the voice from heaven) was heard at a great height in the air, and it said, ' However numerous ye may be, what are ye compared to R. Eliezer? What are all your opinions together against his opinions? When he has spoken, his opinion ought to prevail.' Hereupon R. Joshua rose and said, 'It is written, The law is not in heaven (Deut. xxx. 12), it is in thy mouth and in thy heart (ib. v. 16). It is also in your reason, for it is written, 'I have left you free to choose between life and death and good and evil' (ib. v. 15 and 19), and it is in your conscience; for if ye love the Lord and obey his voice (v. 19), that is the voice by which he speaks within ye, ye will find happiness and truth. Wherefore then does Rabbi Eliezer bring in a karoub tree, a rivulet, a wall, and a voice to settle such questions? And what is the only conclusion which can be drawn from their introduction but that they who have studied the laws of nature have been mistaken, and that we must now admit that in certain cases a karoub tree can unroot itself and move a hundred cubits off; that in certain cases rivulets flow backwards towards their sources; that in certain cases walls obey a command as iron does the magnet, and that in certain cases voices from heaven teach doctrines? But what connection is there between the observations which relate to natural history and the teaching of Rabbi Eliezer? What connection is there between the roots of the karoub tree, the rivulets, the stones of the walls, the voices from on high, and logic? No doubt these miracles were very extraordinary, and they have filled us with astonishment, but to wonder is not to answer, and it is arguments, not phenomena, that we require. When, therefore, Rabbi Eliezer shall have proved to us that the karoub trees, the rivulets, the walls, and the unknown voices afford us, by their unusual movements, reasonings equal in value to those which the eternal God has placed within us in order to serve as guides to our free-will, then alone will we make use of such testimonies, and estimate their number and the value of their assertions. Till then, Rabbi Eliezer, we will keep to the teaching of the law. No, Eliezer, it is in vain that, in such matters, you address yourself to our senses. Our senses may deceive us, and when they affirm what our reason denies, and what our conscience disapproves, we must reject the evidence of our senses, and only listen to reason, aided by conscience.'" This teaching is identical with that of Maimonides, who says, "When thy senses affirm that which thy reason denies, reject the perceptions of thy senses, and believe only in thy reason."

CHAPTER V.

In Mark viii. 31 Jesus is represented as teaching his disciples that he must "suffer many things, and be rejected of the elders, and of the chief priests, and scribes, and be killed, and the third day rise again." This is repeated in almost the same words in Luke ix. 22, but in Matt. xvi. 21 it has been altered into "must suffer many things of the elders, and chief priests, and scribes," which he never did, and which is contradicted by the subsequent narrative. Six or eight days after this the Transfiguration is said to have taken place (Mark ix. 2–8, and parallel passages). The original passage [Cod. Sin.] states that he took Peter, James, and John into "an exceeding high mountain." In Matthew (xvii. i.) this has diminished into a "high mountain," and in Luke (ix. 26) is simply "a mountain." The fourth gospel, which is supposed to have been written by John, who was present, makes no mention of the Transfiguration whatever. Mark says that Jesus was transfigured, and that "his raiment became shining, exceeding white ['as snow' is an addition], so as no fuller on earth can white them." In Matthew it is added that "his face did shine as the sun." Luke merely says that "the fashion of his countenance was altered." This is quite in accordance with Jewish traditions. Adam, Moses, and Joshua had all either shining garments or shining faces. Thus in Bereschith Rabba, 20, 29, it is said, "Vestes lucis vestes Adami primi," and "Fulgida fuit facies Mosis instar solis (the very expression applied to Jesus in Matthew), Josuæ instar lunæ; quod idem affirmarunt veteres de Adamo." In Exod. xxxiv. 29 it is said that "the skin of Moses' face shone." It is evident from a Jewish writing (Nizzachon vetus, p. 40) in which it is objected that Jesus could not be the Messiah because he did not resemble Moses in this respect, that the one narrative must have been founded on the other. This Jew knew nothing of the Transfiguration scene mentioned in the gospels, nor would it have satisfied him, for he says that the Messiah's face ought to have been visible from one end of the earth to the other. The expressions in the gospels are identical with those in the LXX. in many places, especially the νεφέλη φωτεινὴ (νεφέλη φωτὸς, LXX.), the φωνὴ ἐκ τῆς νεφέλης, and the εἰσελθεῖν εἰς τὴν νεφέλην (Luke ix. 34). This seems to show that the narrative was compiled and inserted in order to meet the Jewish objection above stated. The voice out of the cloud is represented as quoting from Ps. ii. 7 and Isa. xlii. 1, as on the occasion of the baptism, and from Deut. xviii. 15, as to the second or concluding portion. The words are identical in Mark and Luke, but Matthew has added the words from Isaiah, so that it is impossible to know what the voice is really supposed to have said. The six days are imitated from Exod. xxiv. 16, where Moses is said to have been six days on Mount Sinai before the Lord called to him. Luke (ix. 28) says it was the eighth day, but the other gospels do not warrant this assertion. If Jesus were the Messiah, who was only to establish the kingdom of God after great struggles and sufferings, and for whom his disciples had to expect contests and danger of their lives (Matt. xvi. 21 et sqq.), it is difficult to see how this agrees with what the Scribes said (Matt. xvii. 10 et sqq.) that the restoration of all things by Elias should *precede* the coming of the Messiah, which Jesus himself confirms (ib. 11, 12). Moreover, the enquiry about Elias, and the answer of Jesus that Elias is indeed come in the person of John, cannot possibly agree with the statement that the original Elias appeared upon the mountain, which must be the original statement, to which the scene on the mountain must have been added.

Some time after the Transfiguration Jesus, according to Mark (x. 1), leaves Galilee and comes by the farther side of Jordan into "the coasts" of Judæa, and in v. 46 we find him at Jericho. In Matt. xix. 1 this wonderful piece of geographical information is made still more extraordinary, for we are told that he departed from Galilee and came into "the coasts of Judæa beyond Jordan." The word "coasts" is applied in such passages as Matt. xv. 21 to towns on the sea-coast, and we must suppose the writer's ignorance of geography to have been so great as to suppose that Jericho was on the sea, or that the Mediterranean was on the other side of Jordan. Luke (ix. 51) contradicts both the other gospels by saying that he went to Jerusalem through Samaria. John (x. 40) makes him go "beyond Jordan into the place where John at first baptized." He then goes to Bethany, thence to Ephraim, a city about ten miles distant, whence he returns to Bethany, and thence goes to Jerusalem (c. xii. 1). Thus two apostles, Matthew and John, the reputed authors of the gospels which bear their name, contradict each other in the most unequivocal manner on a simple matter of fact as to how Jesus reached Jerusalem on so memorable an occasion as his last journey to that place, and as all the apostles were with him (Matt. xxi. 1), it is quite impossible to reconcile such a contradiction. Mark (xi. 1) says that when Jesus came nigh to Bethphage and Bethany, at the Mount of Olives, he sent two of his disciples into "the village over against them" with orders to take a colt upon which no man had ever sat and bring him. Matthew (xxi. 1) omits all mention of Bethany, and only speaks of Bethphage. Probably it was felt that the other statement did not admit of the "village over against you," which Bethany might supply the place of. Matthew (xxi. 2) says that there was an ass as well as a colt, and John (xii. 14), who, if he wrote the gospel attributed to him, must have been an eye-witness as well as Matthew, contradicts all three gospels by saying that Jesus himself "found a young ass," and thus the very objectionable proceeding of taking the animal is transferred from the apostles to Jesus himself. What proves this narrative to be unhistorical is that Jesus is represented as entering Jerusalem for the first time, which it is not possible that as a Jew it can have been. The result of this triumphal entry is represented to have been his condemnation and death.

Mark (xiv. 1, Cod. Sin.) says, "After two days was the feast of the passover and of unleavened bread: and the chief priests and the scribes sought how they might take him by craft, and put him to death. For they said, Not on the feast day, lest there be an uproar of the people." In Matthew this statement is altered into a prediction of Jesus that he should be crucified, and instead of a fresh narrative commencing as in Mark, this prediction is joined to the preceding discourses. On this occasion we are told that "the chief priests and the elders of the people" assembled at "the palace of the high priest, who was called Caiaphas." Luke omits this assembling at the palace of Caiaphas, and the hesitation the priests felt at killing Jesus on the feast-day, and merely says that "the chief priests and scribes sought how they might kill him, for they feared the people." He then goes on to state how the devil entered into Judas, and omits the story of the woman with an alabaster box of ointment, which is so abruptly introduced in Mark and Matthew, and which in the Gospel of the Infancy is connected with the circumcision of Christ (ii. 1–4).

Mark says that Judas went to the chief priests to betray Jesus to them, and that they promised to give him money. Matthew says that it was thirty pieces of silver. Luke says that Satan entered into Judas at this time, but makes no mention of the sum agreed upon, which he must therefore have considered as unimportant.

Mark says that on the first day of unleavened bread, when they killed the passover, his disciples asked him where they should prepare for him to eat it. Jesus sends two of his disciples with instructions to go into the city where they would meet a man bearing a pitcher of water, who would conduct them to an upper room, where they could make ready. Matthew (xxvi. 17–19) has altered this by specifying the man, but says nothing about the pitcher of water. Luke (xxiv. 7–13) has almost the same narrative as Mark, but has altered the two disciples into Peter and John, the latter of whom says nothing about this remarkable prediction. The synoptical gospels make Jesus eat the passover with his disciples on the 14th Nisan, the day preceding his death. The fourth gospel speaks of a mere ordinary supper ($\delta\epsilon\hat{\iota}\pi\nu o\nu$) which took place on the 13th Nisan, and could have no connection with the passover at all.

The agony of Jesus at Gethsemane consists in Mark of a prayer that the "cup" might be taken from him—in other words, that he might not be crucified, and, consequently, that this (supposed) expiatory sacrifice might not be accomplished. And he tells Peter that "the spirit truly is ready, but the flesh is weak." This is already sufficiently improbable conduct for the Son of God, but Luke adds to it by informing us that "an angel appeared unto him from heaven strengthening him," and that a bloody sweat accompanied his earnest prayer. This alone would settle the question as to Matthew and John being the authors of the gospels attributed to them, for Matthew was in the garden at the time, and says nothing about the angel, and John was one of the three disciples who were near to Jesus, and is equally silent on the subject. If it is said that they were overcome with sleep, how did Luke learn that such an appearance took place? Again, a bloody sweat is one of the rarest of phenomena, and is only a symptom of particular diseases. It can only be regarded in this place as a poetical expression or a mythical insertion. We cannot regard the account of what took place in the Garden of Gethsemane as historical, for it assumes that Jesus was divinely forewarned of what was going to happen to him, which is impossible, for if it had been so, he could not have made use of false interpretations of prophecies.

While Jesus was exhorting the disciples to arise and go because he was about to be betrayed, Judas, it is said (Mark xiv. 43), comes with a great multitude armed with swords and staves, whom the chief priests, scribes, and elders had sent to apprehend him. Matthew and Luke have substantially the same narrative, but in John the kiss of Judas is omitted, and Jesus himself declares "I am he," upon which all the men and officers fall to the ground (John xviii. 6). Mark says that they led Jesus away to the high-priest, who is specified as Caiaphas in Matthew. In John xviii. 13, on the contrary, Jesus is led to Annas, the father-in-law of Caiaphas, first, and in v. 24 Annas sends him bound to Caiaphas. In v. 14 it is said, "Now Caiaphas was he which gave counsel to the Jews that it was expedient that one man should die for the people." The fact is, that though Annas was the father-in-law of Caiaphas, Annas possessed the confidence of the Jews, and there was no participation of power between them whatever. Pilate, who was violent against the Jews, deposed Annas because he refused to submit to him, and named Caiaphas in his place in A.D. 26. Eleven years afterwards Vitellius, the successor of Pilate, who wished to please the Jews, nominated Jonathan, the son of Annas, to fill the office of high-priest.

Luke (iii. 2) makes Annas and Caiaphas to be both high-priests, being evidently unaware that the Jews had but one high-priest, and that Annas had been deposed, and in Acts iv. 24 Annas is represented as being high-priest after the death of Jesus, whereas it was Jonathan the son of Annas who succeeded Caiaphas!

Caiaphas and the chief priests, and the elders, and scribes (Mark xiv. 53 et sqq.) endeavoured to get false witnesses against Jesus, but their testimony did not agree. This most improbable statement, which represents the chief men of Jerusalem as resorting to the meanest devices to entrap Jesus, and failing in doing so, is omitted by Luke and John. Caiaphas, having failed in this attempt himself, asks Jesus, "Answerest thou nothing?" and again, "Art thou the Christ, the Son of God?" [Cod. Sin.]. Jesus answers, "I am, and ye shall see the Son of man sitting at the right hand of power, and coming in the clouds of heaven." This is taken from Dan. vii. 13, a portion of Daniel which belongs to the reign of Antiochus Epiphanes, circa B.C. 170. The present quotation follows the LXX. and the Chaldee original. Matthew (xxvi. 64) has altered "with the clouds" into "in the clouds," referring to Jesus, whose coming in the clouds was expected (conf. Matt. xxiv. 30 and Mark xiii. 26). The high-priest then rends his clothes, and pronounces Jesus to be guilty of blasphemy.

In the morning the priests having consulted with the elders and scribes and the whole council, bound Jesus and took him to Pilate (Mark xv. 1). In Luke they again ask him whether he is the Christ. Jesus says to them, "If I tell you, ye will not believe, and if I also ask you, ye will not answer" (xxii. 67, Cod. Sin.). Upon their asking him whether he is the Son of God, he returns an evasive answer, and is then taken to Pilate. Pilate asks him, "Art thou the king of the Jews?" and Jesus returns the same answer as he does in Luke (supra). The chief priests repeated their accusation, but Jesus made no reply to Pilate's question, "Answerest thou nothing?" and ultimately Pilate, willing to content the people, releases a robber named Barabbas to them, scourges Jesus, whom, however, he had not found guilty (Matt. xxvii. 23, 24, Luke xxiii. 14-16), and delivers him to be crucified.

The Pilate of history is the exact opposite of the Pilate of the gospels. Philo (Leg. ad Caium) says of him, "Pilate was of a violent and obstinate disposition, which could not lend itself to please the Jews. . . . . . One day some remonstrances were addressed to him, but as he was of a violent and severe character, he resisted them. Then the Jews exclaimed, 'Cease to provoke seditions and wars, cease to render peace impossible. The will of Tiberius is that our laws shall be respected. If thou hast received any new edict or letter, let us know, that we may send a deputation immediately." These words only exasperated the procurator, who feared lest an appeal to Rome might disclose his crimes, the venality of his sentences, his robberies, his ruin of families, and the outrages of which he was the author, such as the punishment of persons who had never been tried, and excesses of cruelty of every description.

Josephus says, "Between the people and the procurator there existed on either side nothing but hatred, contempt, menaces, and insults. One of the coercive measures which Pilate put in practice redoubled the animosity of the Jews. In order, as he said, to repair the aqueducts which brought water into Jerusalem, and to make other buildings, the Roman deputy wished, on his own authority, to take possession of a reserve fund which was kept in the temple. Every fresh act of foreign usurpation, however it might be disguised, added to the fermentation. The procurator saw assemblies of the people form and increase in numbers. He ordered a portion of his troops and his agents to adopt the costume of the country, and to conceal large sticks under their cloaks. These men, thus disguised, mingled with the multitude, and on a preconcerted signal being given, fell both on the promoters of the tumult and on the peaceable inhabitants." (Bell. Jud. l. ii. c. 9 ; Ant. Jud.)

This tyrant, whose reign of terror lasted ten years, was appointed by Sejanus, the astute and powerful minister of Tiberius, and it was during his ministry that the first persecution of the Jews at Rome was commenced. "This," says Josephus, "was the reason why the Jews said that it was a settled design of Pontius Pilate to abolish the Jewish law." Such is the man who is represented in the gospels as sacrificing his own convictions and the honour of the Roman name, and allowing a judicial murder to take place in order "to content the people."

Josephus tells us (Ant. Jud. xviii. ii. 2, xix. vi. 4, xviii. ii. 1) that Annas, Ismaël, Eleazar, and Simeon were successively deprived of the high priesthood by Valerius Gratus, the Governor of Judæa, on account of their hostility to the Romans. Josephus, surnamed Caiaphas (Ant. xviii. 4), that is, "the support" (of the Romans), held the office of high-priest for eleven years in succession, from A.D. 26 to A.D. 37, from which we may certainly conclude that his policy was different to that of his predecessors. The history of his fall as given by Josephus proves this to have been the case, for he says that he was deposed in A.D. 37 because Vitellius, who was prefect of Syria, wished to render himself popular with the Jews, and that this deposition was one of a series of measures intended to bring this about. His successor in fact was Jonathan, son of Annas, the former high-priest, who had been deposed for favouring the Jews.

The Caiaphas of the Gospels resembles the Caiaphas of history as little as Pilate does. In the Gospels he is represented as acting in concert with his father-in-law Annas, and with the chief priests and scribes, and never as acting under the orders of Pilate. The fact, however, is, that at this period the authority of the high-priest had been all but abolished in consequence of the action of the Roman procurator. Matters had come to such a pass that the room in the temple to which the high-priest retired on the Day of Atonement, and which was formerly called the Council Chamber, was then called the servant's cell. The Talmud (Talmud Baba, treatise Yoma) says, "The reason of this was that the dignity of high-priest was conferred for money."

The object of the writers of the Gospels was to throw the whole blame of the illegal trial, condemnation, and crucifixion of Jesus on the Jews. With this object Caiaphas is made in Matt. xxvi. 62, 63 [Cod. Sin.] to address Jesus as follows: "And the high-priest arose and said unto him, I adjure thee by the living God that thou tell us whether thou be the Christ, the Son of God." Upon his answering that he was, Caiaphas rends his clothes, and proclaims that he has spoken blasphemy. The Council, consisting of the chief priests, elders, and all the council, then pronounce Jesus guilty of death. In Mark (xiv. 65) it is said, "some of them began to spit on him, and to cover his face, and to buffet him, and to say unto him, Prophesy; and the servants did strike him with the palms of their hands." In Matthew (xxvi. 67, 68) this is extended to the whole council, and we are required to believe that the highest dignitaries in the nation, having first pronounced a sentence which they had no power to do, joined in this extraordinary treatment of an untried prisoner. Yet in Luke xiii. 31, we are told that some of the Pharisees warned Jesus to depart, because he was in danger from Herod, and in the next chapter we find him eating bread on the Sabbath-day in the house of one of the chief Pharisees. In the third gospel all is altered, and the men that held Jesus are represented as reviling and smiting him, and striking him on the face, &c., *before* he is taken to the Council (Luke xxii. 65, 66). John (xviii. 22) says that it was one of the officers who struck Jesus with the palm of his hand when he was before Annas, not before Caiaphas. Thus we have three, if not four, distinct statements, all contradicting each other respecting a simple matter of fact.

The Council before which Jesus is said to have been brought cannot have been the Grand Sanhedrim, for that was presided over by one of the descendants of Hillel, and Caiaphas was the president on this occasion. The trial is represented as turning, in reality, not on the saying imputed to Jesus that he could destroy the Temple of God and build it up in three days, which could not expose him to any punishment, but on his blasphemous pretension (quiddouf) to be the Son of God. In Mark (xiv. 60) Jesus answers the question of Caiaphas boldly, "I am," but in Matthew (xxvi. 64) he only says "Thou hast said," which might mean a denial. In Luke (xxii. 66–70) there is no high-priest at all, and Jesus answers the elders and the chief priests and scribes in the same evasive way, "Ye say that I am." In John (xviii. 13, 19–23) Jesus is interrogated by Annas, and no reference whatever is made to his being the Son of God. Jesus himself in this Gospel contradicts in the most explicit manner the statements in the other Gospels by saying that his doctrine was perfectly orthodox and open. He tells Annas "I spake openly to the world; I ever taught in the synagogue, and in the temple, whither all the Jews resort; *and in secret have I said nothing.* Why askest thou me? ask them which heard me what I have said unto them: behold, they know what I said." (John xviii. 20, 21, Cod. Sin.) The Jews accuse him of being a "malefactor" (v. 30), but there is no accusation of blasphemy, and Pilate finds no fault in him at all (v. 38). In Mark and Matthew the high-priest rends his clothes, which the traditional law among the Jews ordered should be done in cases of blasphemy (Sanhedr. VIII. 10, 11). This mass of contradictions is completed by the omission of this ceremony in

Luke and John, and Jesus in Luke (xxiii. 2) is taken before Pilate, not for blasphemy, but for forbidding to pay tribute to Cæsar!

The punishment for blasphemy, of which crime alone a Jewish council could have found Jesus guilty, was stoning. "He that blasphemeth the name of the Lord, he shall surely be put to death, and all the congregation shall certainly stone him" (Lev. xxiv. 16). If Jesus had been condemned for blasphemy, he would have been tried in the daytime, not at night, and by the Sanhedrim, not by Caiaphas, and he would then have been stoned in accordance with the above law. According to the Mischna (Sanhedr. v. 7) blasphemy and idolatry were punished with stoning, and after the culprit was dead his body was to be "hanged on a tree" (Deut. xxi. 21, 22).

The Jews, being subject to the Romans, had no longer, at this time, the power of pronouncing judgment in capital cases, and consequently could not condemn Jesus to be guilty of an offence punishable with death by the Roman law. Their powers were limited to the punishment of heresies by the synagogues, which consisted of corporal punishments, usually inflicted by the hazzan, Ὑπηρέτης, or apparitor (Luke v. 29), who belonged to each synagogue. Examples of the punishments inflicted by them are to be found in Matt. v. 25, x. 17, xxiii. 34; Mark xiii. 9; Luke xii. 11, xxi. 12; Acts xxii. 19, xxvi. 11, and 2 Cor. xi. 24, in none of which cases is there any mention of capital punishment, though death, of course, sometimes resulted from stoning. When it was intended that death should be the penalty, the sentence was carried out by the principal witnesses throwing large stones at the criminal's head (Deut. xvii. 7), and it was only after he had thus been slain that the people were allowed to throw stones at him. This is the origin of the expression "Let him that is without sin among you, let him first cast a stone at her," which is an adaptation of a proverbial expression among the Jews.

The form of criminal punishment is set forth in the Mischna: "When it is a question of life and death, the accused may be acquitted on the first day. But if he is found guilty, *it is absolutely necessary that the trial should be deferred till the next day*" (Sanhedr., 32). It is also perfectly certain that no trial could take place, either on the eve of the Sabbath, or on the eve of a feast day, and that it could not take place at night.

In John xi. 47 et sqq. it is said that the chief priests and Pharisees gathered a council together, and said, "What do we? for this man doeth many miracles. If we let him alone, all men will believe on him, and the Romans shall come and take away both our place and nation." Caiaphas answers that it was expedient "that one man should die for the people, and that the whole nation perish not." This, we are told, he spake not of himself, but, being high-priest that year (the fact that he was high-priest for eleven years in succession being apparently unknown to the writer), he "prophesied." Prophesying, however, was no part of the duty of a Jewish high-priest at any time, the "prophets" having always formed a distinct body, and, if he prophesied, he prophesied wrongly, for, notwithstanding the crucifixion of Jesus, the Romans did come and take away both the place and the nation.

Even if this were the true version, however, Jesus would not have been guilty of any blasphemy, for all that could be brought against him was that he performed miracles. It was a general belief at the time the gospels were written that miracles could be performed by any one. St. Justin (Dial. cum Tryph., 7) says that false prophets and false apostles perform miracles just as easily as the true ones, and that there is no difference between them except that the first teach error and the worship of the gods, and that the others teach the worship of God and of Christ!

The real trial of Jesus took place before Pilate, according to the Gospels, for he alone had the power of life and death (John xviii. 31). In the next verse we are told that this was done "that the saying of Jesus might be fulfilled, signifying what death he should die;" a saying which, however, is not recorded in this gospel. Matthew alone has this saying, the other gospels merely saying that he predicted his death; and the words in Mark x. 34, which in the Codex Sinaiticus are, "And they shall mock him, and shall spit upon him, and shall scourge him, and shall kill him," and which are almost identical in Luke (xviii. 32, 33), appear in Matthew (xx. 19) with the important alteration of "kill" into "crucify."

Jesus is represented as being taken before Pilate on a

charge that he said he was the King of the Jews, for no Roman governor would have interfered in any religious questions, universal toleration being the rule. Mark xv. 2, in which Jesus admits to Pilate that he is the King of the Jews, is an interpolation, which contradicts v. 5, in which it is said that Jesus answered nothing, and v. 14, in which Pilate asks, "What evil hath he done?"

We are next informed, on the authority of the evangelists only, of a custom which existed of releasing a prisoner to the Jews, whomsoever they desired, at the feast of the Passover. This custom existed among the Romans and Athenians on the occasion of certain great festivals; but Pilate would never have done so on the occasion of a Jewish festival, nor would he have risked the censure of the authorities at Rome for releasing a seditious person in order to content the Jews, whom he oppressed and hated. In John xi. 50 (conf. c. xviii. 14) the whole complexion of this transaction is changed, for it is there said that Caiaphas represented to the chief priests and Pharisees that "it was expedient that one man should die for the people, and that the whole nation perish not." What is meant by this extraordinary statement it is impossible to conceive; but we are told a few verses further on that the intended victim did his best to avoid his fate by retiring to Ephraim.

In the synoptical gospels (Mark xiv. 14–17, Matt. xxvi. 18–20, Luke xxii. 11–15) Jesus ate the Passover on the first day of the feast of unleavened bread—that is, on the day when they killed the passover (Mark xiv. 12, Luke xxii. 7), and was crucified the next day (Mark xv. 1, Matt. xxvii. 1, Luke xxii. 66). This has been shown to be impossible, for if he were condemned to death he was entitled to two days' trial [see ante]. According to the fourth gospel, the last meal of Jesus took place "before the feast of the passover" (John xiii. 1, conf. v. 29); and the following day, which was the day of the crucifixion, was "the preparation of the passover" (xix. 14, 31), which prevented the Jews from entering the prætorium lest they should be defiled (xviii. 28). This gospel is therefore in contradiction not only with the synoptical gospels, but with the epistles, in which the last supper is said to have taken place on the same night in which Jesus was betrayed (1 Cor. xi. 23), and in which the cup is called "the cup of blessing," which was the name given to the third cup at the passover feast by the Jews. The epistle asserts that this communication respecting the Last Supper was "from the Lord" (xi. 22), and we are thus prevented from accepting the Johannine statement. The Churches of Asia Minor, as we have seen, observed the 14th Nisan, and said that they followed the example of Christ, who had eaten the passover before his death. Justin Martyr (Dial. cum Tryph., c. 111) says that "Jesus was arrested, as it is written, on the day of the Passover, and was also crucified during the Passover." In the Archiepiscopal Palace at Bourges, now burnt, was long preserved what pretended to be the order for the execution of Jesus Christ, which is interesting as showing the belief of the Church on this subject. It is as follows:—

"Jesus of Nazareth, of the Jewish tribe of Juda, convicted of imposture and rebellion against the divine authority of Tiberius Augustus, Emperor of the Romans, having for this sacrilege been condemned to die on the cross by sentence of the judge, Pontius Pilate, on the prosecution of our lord Herod, lieutenant of the Emperor in Judæa, shall be taken to-morrow morning, the 23rd day of the Ides of March, to the usual place of punishment, under the escort of a company of the Prætorian Guard. The so-called King of the Jews shall be taken out by the Strumean Gate. All the public officers and the subjects of the Emperor are directed to lend their aid to the execution of this sentence.

"(Signed)   CAPEL.

"Jerusalem, 23rd day of the Ides of March, year of Rome 783."

Whoever forged this extraordinary document (which was the personal property of the family De la Tour d'Auvergne, and is about as authentic as the correspondence of Ignatius with the Virgin Mary) has completely exonerated the Jews from all participation in the death of Jesus, and has established as far as in him lay that it was a strictly political offence for which he suffered. In fact, if Jesus was really executed by Pilate, this must have been the case. Nothing can be more distinct than the refusal of Gallio, the Roman deputy of Achaia (Acts xviii. 12–17), to have anything to do with the insurrection of the Jews against Paul. He says to them, "If it were a matter of wrong, or wicked lewdness, O ye Jews, reason would that I should bear with you: but

L

if it be a question of words and names, *and of your law, look ye to it, for I will be no judge of such matters.*"

This document gives us to understand that the crucifixion took place in A.D. 30. Eusebius states (H. E., i. 10) that the ministry of Jesus lasted nearly four years, thus making it commence A.D. 26, which he calls the fourth year of Pilate's procuratorship, Pilate having been appointed in A.D. 25. Not content with this, he says that Jesus began his ministry when Annas was high-priest, and continued it under his successors until the time of Caiaphas. This, however, is the year in which Caiaphas was appointed; and to have begun his ministry under Annas, Jesus must have commenced in A.D. 22, and it must have lasted eight years, there being four priests in the four years preceding the appointment of Caiaphas. Valerius Gratus, who deposed Annas, was appointed by Tiberius immediately after the death of Augustus in A.D. 14.

The circumstances which followed the trial and condemnation of Jesus, the purple robe, the crown of thorns, &c., would never have disgraced the judicial administration of a Roman magistrate. In Mark, Pilate delivers Jesus to be crucified after scourging him, and the Roman soldiers lead him to the Prætorium—that is, to Herod's palace—which was at that time the residence of Pilate, and having called together the whole band (about 600 men), clothe him with purple, plat a crown of thorns, which they put on his head, salute him as King of the Jews (thus showing the nature of his supposed offence), smite him on the head with a reed, spit upon him, and worship him in mockery (Mark xv. 15–20). In Matthew, they also take him into the Prætorium, and after gathering the whole band together, put upon him a *scarlet* robe instead of a purple one, plat a crown of thorns, which they put on his head, put a reed in his right hand instead of smiting him with it, salute him as King of the Jews, and spit upon and smite him with the reed afterwards (Matt. xxvii. 29, 30). In Luke, Pilate finding that the man was a Galilæan, and belonged to Herod's jurisdiction, sends him to Herod Antipas, the tetrarch of Galilee, who was at Jerusalem at that time. Herod, we are told, was exceeding glad to see him, for he hoped to have seen a miracle done by him; but Jesus did not answer his questions, and the chief priests and scribes stood and vehemently accused him. According to this gospel, therefore, it was Herod with his men of war who "set him at nought, and mocked him, and arrayed him in a gorgeous robe, and sent him again to Pilate" (Luke xxiii. 11), to whose jurisdiction we had just before been told he did not belong. In the fourth gospel we have yet another version. Pilate takes Jesus (xix. 1–7) and scourges him; the soldiers plat a crown of thorns and put it on his head, and put on him a purple robe, as in Mark; but while both Mark (xv. 20) and Matthew (xxvii. 30) state that Jesus was led forth to execution in his own clothes, this gospel states that he came forth "wearing the crown of thorns and the purple robe." It is then stated that the chief priests and officers cried out as soon as they saw him, "Crucify, crucify him!" and that ultimately Pilate gave Jesus up to the chief priests (v. 16) to carry out an exclusively Roman punishment for an offence against Cæsar!

Philo—who was constantly at Jerusalem during the lifetime of Jesus, and who, though he did not die till twenty-five years after the date assigned to his crucifixion, never so much as alludes to the extraordinary events narrated in the gospels—mentions the mocking and reviling of Herod Agrippa, the King of the Jews, at Alexandria, when he was on his way to Palestine in A.D. 38. This was effected by the substitution for him of a certain wretch named Carabbas, and the account of this transaction (Phil. contra Flacc., c. 6) closely resembles the gospel narratives. He says, "There was a certain poor wretch named Carabbas, . . . who spent all his days and nights naked in the roads, . . . the sport of idle children and wanton youths; and they, driving the poor wretch as far as the public gymnasium, and setting him up there on high that he might be seen by everybody, flattened out a leaf of papyrus and put it on his head instead of a diadem, and clothed the rest of his body with a common door mat instead of a cloak, and instead of a sceptre they put into his hand a small stick of the native papyrus, which they found lying by the wayside, and gave to him; and when, like actors in theatrical spectacles, he had received all the insignia of royal authority, and had been dressed and adorned like a king, the young men bearing sticks on their shoulders stood on each side of him instead of spear-bearers, in imitation of the body-guards of the king; and then others came up, some as if to salute him, and others making as though they wished to plead their causes before him, and others pretending to wish to consult with him about the affairs of the State." The names Carabbas and Barabbas are almost identical; but while Philo's account is historical and intelligible, it is wholly unintelligible how the substitution of an innocent victim for a guilty one should have saved the people from perishing, even admitting that the custom of releasing a prisoner existed, and that Pilate would have been willing to jeopardise his position in order to content the Jews.

Mark (xv. 21) says that the Roman soldiers compelled one Simon, a Cyrenian, the father of Alexander and Rufus, to bear the cross of Christ. Matthew (xxvii. 32) says, also, that it was a man of Cyrene, Simon by name; and Luke (xxiii. 26) adds that he was coming out of the country. John (xix. 17) contradicts all these statements by saying that Christ bore his own cross, and does not mention Simon at all. On this occasion Luke represents Jesus as uttering words to the people which cannot have been written until after the siege of Jerusalem. Verse 30 is taken from Hosea x. 8, refers to the destruction of the high places of Aven, and cannot possibly refer to Jerusalem in her latter days. In Matthew xvi. 21, and Luke xiii. 33, it is stated that Jesus must suffer at Jerusalem, because "it cannot be that a prophet perish out of Jerusalem;" thus putting an historical untruth into the mouth of Jesus himself. This is not the only one, however, for in Mark ii. 26 Jesus is made to mistake Abiathar, the son of the high-priest, for Ahimelech, concerning whom the story is told (1 Sam. xxi. 1)!

Jesus, surrounded by the Roman soldiers, was taken "unto the Golgotha" (Mark xv. 22, Cod. Sin.), which was situated to the north or north-west of Jerusalem. Luke (xxiii. 33) calls it Κρανίον, "which is called a skull" (Cod. Sin.) This word has been translated "Calvaria" in the Vulgate, and probably took its name from its being the place of execution; not, as has been supposed, from being a hill which resembled a skull.

Mark states (xv. 22) that when they arrived at the place of execution they offered Jesus wine mingled with myrrh, which was an intoxicating beverage intended to allay pain. In Matthew (xxvii. 34) this has been altered into "wine mingled with gall" (Cod. Sin.), and ultimately into "vinegar mingled with gall;" because in Psalm lxix. 21 it is said, "They gave me also gall for my meat, and in my thirst they gave me vinegar to drink," which the writers wished to represent as a fulfilment of prophecy. In John xix. 29 we have a spunge filled with vinegar only, and put upon hyssop, which appears to be derived from Exodus xii. 22; and in direct contradiction to the synoptical gospels, it is offered him *after* the execution instead of before. In Luke xxiii. 36 vinegar only is offered in mockery by the soldiers, and, as in the fourth gospel, after the crucifixion. Nothing is said of this drink being offered to those who were crucified with him, which it would naturally have been, the object being apparently to show that Jesus was above receiving such aid.

The Jewish practice was that when a person had been condemned to any of the four capital punishments, viz.—stoning, burning, beheading, or strangulation—an intoxicating drink was presented to him in order to take away the pain of the punishment, which used to be prepared by charitable ladies (Sanhedr. 43a), who often brought it themselves to the condemned persons in order to stupefy them. This humane practice has been represented in the gospels as a cruel act, in order to make out that a supposed prophecy has been fulfilled. It is evident, moreover, that an intoxicating beverage which might operate in deadening the pain of an ordinary execution could be of no use for the slow, lingering death of a punishment like crucifixion, nor is it probable that Roman soldiers would be allowed to adopt a Jewish practice.

The criminals were then stripped, and the Roman soldiers, who were the executioners, and who usually kept such of the clothes (pannicularia) of the condemned as were of little value (Dig. xlvii., xx.; De Bonis Damnat., 6, a custom which was limited by Adrian), cast lots for his garments. John (xix. 24) alters the passage by representing the soldiers as casting lots "for" instead of "upon" the vesture, which he also represents as a single garment ($\chi\iota\tau\grave{\omega}\nu$), because it was "without seam" ($\ddot{\alpha}\rho\rho\alpha\phi\sigma$), and "woven from the top throughout" ($\dot{\upsilon}\phi\alpha\nu\tau\grave{o}\varsigma\ \delta\iota'\ \ddot{o}\lambda\sigma\upsilon$). This was no doubt intended to make Jesus appear as a high-priest, for the dress of the Jewish high-priest was made in this fashion (Joseph. Ant. III. vii.

4) : "The high-priest, indeed, is adorned with the same garment that we have described, without abating one; only over these he puts a vesture of a blue colour. . . . Now this vesture was not composed of two pieces, nor was it sewed together upon the shoulders and the sides, but it was one long vestment so woven as to leave an aperture for the neck." Philo says that the dress of the high-priest, taken as a whole as well as in its parts, represented the whole and the parts of the universe; and that when he entered the temple he was considered to invest himself with a small world, the image of that great one which was animated by the Deity, and which was his first temple. It is against all probability that anyone would have been allowed to assume or imitate the dress of the high-priest. At nine o'clock in the morning, according to Matthew and Mark, but at midday, according to Luke and John, the cross was erected, and Jesus, having been crucified, gave up the ghost about three o'clock in the afternoon. As has already been pointed out, this could by no possibility have been a Jewish punishment. The Mischna (Sanhedr. v. 7) lays it down expressly that the crimes of blasphemy and idolatry were punished by stoning, and after the culprit was dead, the body was to remain exposed on a tree or gibbet for a whole day, in order that the people might fear (Deut. xiii. 11; xxi. 22, 23). Yet in Acts v. 30, Peter and the other apostles are represented as accusing the Jews of themselves putting Jesus to death in this very manner. The cross, on the contrary, was a Roman punishment, reserved for slaves, and for cases where the aggravation of ignominy was intended to be added to that of death. It was a suitable punishment for murderers and robbers, but was quite inapplicable to a man of blameless life, in whom the Roman Governor could see no fault. If his crime had been of a political nature, death by the sword would have been his punishment, rather than the ignominious death of a highwayman, for crucifixion was reserved for criminals of the latter description. Neither of the Jewish historians, neither Justus of Tiberias nor Josephus, make any mention of Jesus, or of his crucifixion, though they both enter into every detail of what took place during Pilate's government.

The cross on which criminals suffered was formed of two beams bound together in the shape of a T, and was so low that the feet of the criminal nearly touched the ground. He was fastened to it by driving nails through the hands; the feet were frequently nailed, but were sometimes only bound with ropes. A piece of wood, a sort of horn, was attached to the shaft of the cross, and passed between the legs of the criminal, who rested upon it. Without this the hands would have been torn, and the body would have sunk down. At other times a horizontal piece of wood was fixed where the feet came, and supported them.

Mark (xv. 27) says that two robbers (λησταί) were executed with Jesus. These robbers are supposed to fulfil a prophecy of Isaiah (liii. 12) in which the words "He shall be numbered with the transgressors" appear; and Jesus is represented (Luke xxiv. 37) as quoting this verse with reference to himself. Independently, however, of the fact that this portion of Isaiah is not written by that prophet, but by an unknown writer, Mark xv. 28, in which this verse is applied to the crucifixion, is not in the Codex Sinaiticus, neither is it quoted in Matthew, and it appears for the first time in Luke; but it is not mentioned in the fourth gospel, where it is merely said that "two others" were crucified with Jesus. Mark says nothing about their conduct on the cross, but Matthew (xxvii. 44) says that, besides the mockery of the passers by, both the thieves also mocked Jesus on the cross. In Luke (xxiii. 39-43) this is completely altered, for while one of the thieves rails on Jesus, the other rebukes him, and afterwards asks Jesus to remember him, upon which Jesus promises him that he shall be with him that day in Paradise, which, if he was to be three days in the bowels of the earth, he could not do.

It was customary to place over the cross an inscription stating the crime for which the criminal suffered. Mark says that on this occasion "the superscription of the accusation" which was written over was Ὁ βασιλεὺς τῶν Ἰουδαίων, "The King of the Jews," and we find elsewhere that this superscription is said to have been written by Pilate himself, who, however, had *not* found Jesus guilty on that account, but is represented (Mark xv. 35) as giving him up in order "to content the people." How is it possible then to suppose that he should have written an accusation of a crime of which he had not found the accused guilty? In Matthew it is the soldiers who set up over his head an accusation quite differently worded—Οὗτός ἐστιν Ἰησοῦς ὁ βασιλεὺς τῶν Ἰουδαίων, " This is Jesus the King of the Jews" (Matt. xxvii. 37)—and no mention is made of Pilate's having written it. In Luke (xxiii. 38) we have a third superscription, differing from the two preceding ones : Οὗτός ἐστιν ὁ βασιλεὺς τῶν Ἰουδαίων, " This is the King of the Jews," and this time it is in Greek, in Latin, and in Hebrew letters, though in the Vatican Codex the words " in letters of Greek, and Latin, and Hebrew " are omitted ; and in it and in the Codex Sinaiticus the inscription runs, " The King of the Jews is this." In John xix. 19, however, both the Codices have, " And the writing was in Hebrew and Latin and Greek, JESUS THE NAZARITE, THE KING OF THE JEWS," thus altering the text of all the inscriptions, for none of which is there any authority, and the whole exhibits traces of a made-up narrative.

Mark xv. 29, " And they that passed by," &c., is taken from Ps. xxii. 7, which is in the LXX., πάντες οἱ θεωροῦντές με ἐξεμυκτήρισάν με, ἐλάλησαν ἐν χείλεσιν, ἐκίνησαν κεφαλήν. In v. 31 the high-priests (οἱ ἀρχιερεῖς) are represented as mocking. This is a gross blunder, for there was but one high-priest among the Jews; and it is evident that the author knew the difference between priests and high-priests from c. ii. 26, where ἱερεῦσι is correctly used for priests. Matthew (xxvii. 41) has fallen into the same error, which Luke has avoided by calling them " the rulers " (xxiii. 33), and John has omitted the incident altogether.

At three o'clock in the afternoon Jesus, according to Mark and Matthew, " cried with a loud voice," saying, " Eloi, Eloi, lama sabacthani," according to Mark; but " Eli, Eli, lama sabacthani," according to Matthew. Neither Luke nor John mention those words, which is very remarkable. There can be little doubt that they were intentionally omitted by Luke, for he mentions (xxiii. 46) that " Jesus cried out with a loud voice," and he inserts the words, " Father, into thy hands I commend my spirit," from Ps. xxxi. 5.

The disciples had all fled. There were only present Mary of Magdala (near Tiberias), Mary the mother of James the Less and of Joses, and Salome, with many other women who had followed and ministered to Jesus when he was in Galilee, according to Mark. In Matthew (xxvii. 56, Cod. Sin.) they are enumerated as follows : " Among whom was Mary the mother of James, and the Mary of Joseph, and the Mary of the sons of Zebedee: Joses." In Luke (viii. 2) we have an addition to these women in the shape of Joanna, the wife of Chuza, Herod's steward, and Susanna, who, with many others, "ministered unto him of their substance." Mark (xv. 40) speaks of a person called Joses, of whom we know nothing; but the original reading of Mark vi. 3 is Joseph, not Joses, and Jesus is said [Cod. Sin.] to be the son of Mary, and "the brother of James and Joseph, and of Juda and Simon;" and the corrected reading of Mark xv. 40, in the Codex Sinaiticus, gives Joseph instead of Joses, thus agreeing with Mark vi. 3, and showing that Joses is a clerical error. Matt. x. 3 contradicts this by saying that James was the son of Zebedee, substitutes John for Joseph, and makes Simon to be the brother of Andrew. In John xix. 25, three women, and three only, are represented, not as "looking on afar off" (Mark xv. 40), but as standing by the cross, thus contradicting Luke xxiii. 49, which says that all his acquaintance ($\pi\acute{a}\nu\tau\epsilon s$ $o\acute{i}$ $\gamma\nu\omega\sigma\tau o\grave{\iota}$ $a\grave{v}\tau o\hat{v}$) were present, as well as all the women that followed him from Galilee. These women are Mary the mother of Jesus, Mary her sister, the wife of Cleophas, and Mary of Magdala; and whereas Matthew and Mark give us to understand that none but women were present, this gospel says that "the disciple whom Jesus loved" was also there. It is perfectly hopeless to attempt to reconcile these contradictions.

In Mark viii. 31, Jesus tells his disciples that he must rise again "after three days," which agrees with Matt. xxvii. 63, " Sir, we remember that that deceiver said, while he was yet alive, After three days I will rise again." In Matt. xii. 39, 40; xvi. 1-4, however, he says that he must be "three days and three nights in the heart of the earth." There is not the slightest intimation in the Old Testament that the Messiah was to be raised the third day, and therefore this is a mere arbitrary assumption. In Matthew Jesus addresses these words to the Scribes and Pharisees; in Luke he addresses them to the people on a totally different occasion (Luke xi. 16, 29–32), but says nothing about his being three days in the earth.

It is evident that the story about Jonah is an insertion, for Matt. xii. 43 is naturally connected with v. 37 or v. 30. Compare Luke xi., in which vv. 24, 25, which are the parallel passage to Matt. xiii. 43–45, join Luke xi. 23, which corresponds to Matt. xii. 30. This interpretation of the sign of Jonas is not found elsewhere, and contradicts Matt. xvi. 4 (conf. Mark viii. 12 and Luke xi. 30) as it does Matt. xii. 41, 42. The Book of Jonah was written some three hundred years later than the time of that prophet, who lived in the time of Jeroboam II., B.C. 804–764. The whole of Jonah's prayer in c. ii. 2-9 is to be found in the Psalms. Verse 2 is from Ps. cxx. 1; v. 3 from Ps. xlii. 7, &c. Tzetes in his commentary on the lines written by Lycophron respecting Hercules, says that he passed three nights in the belly of a whale; and it was said that the bones of this whale were discovered at Joppa, the very place where Jonah is said to have been swallowed up. St. Cyril, in his commentary on Jonah xi., mentions this tradition. He says Hercules came out of the whale with the loss of all his hair, and refers to the passage in Lycophron. Theophylact, in his commentary on this same chapter of Jonah, marvels that the Greeks will not believe in the miracle of Jonah when they believe in a similar occurrence which befel Hercules.

The prophecy of Jesus that he should be three days and three nights in the heart of the earth was not accomplished according to the Gospels. He was alive on the cross at the ninth hour of the Jewish Saturday, or three o'clock in the afternoon of our Friday (Mark xv. 34, Matt. xxvii. 46), and died shortly afterwards (Mark xv. 37, Matt. xxvii. 50, Luke xxiii. 46). Joseph of Arimathæa went to Pilate to ask permission to cut down the body and prepare it for burial, "when even" was come, i.e., about six o'clock (Mark xv. 42, Matt. xxvii. 57, Luke xxiii. 54, John xix. 31, 42). Some time elapsed before he obtained permission, for Pilate had to send a centurion to see whether Jesus was really dead. When permission was at last obtained, some time was required to prepare the body for burial (John xix. 40), so that it could not have been buried earlier than ten o'clock that night, but this would have been against the law, for it was unlawful to allow the bodies of malefactors to remain all night upon the tree, or to bury them on the Sabbath. Being, however, entombed after the commencement of the Sabbath, Jesus was found to have risen, according to Mark, very early in the morning of the next day; according to Matthew, *in the end* of the same Sabbath, when it drew towards the next day; according to Luke, on the first day of the week, very early; and, according to John, on the first day of the week, while it was yet dark. Mark says that certain women went to the sepulchre "very early in the morning of the first day of the week" (xvi. 2); and Matthew says (xxviii. 1) that they came "in the end of the Sabbath," and found that he had risen. According to Matthew, therefore, he rose on the very same day he was buried, and, according to Mark, he rose a few hours later. Thus, according to the one, he was not in the tomb twenty-four hours; according to the other, about thirty hours; and in either case he is represented as having falsified his own prediction.

Jesus is represented as hanging *three* hours on the cross, and he was to rise again in *three* days. The shortness of the time, however, gave rise to many doubts as to the reality of his death. A few hours of hanging on the cross appeared to persons who were in the habit of witnessing crucifixions, quite inadequate to produce such a result. Many cases were cited of crucified persons who, after being taken down sufficiently soon, had been recalled to life by energetic remedies. Josephus (Vita, 75) says, "Having been sent by Titus Cæsar with Cerealis and a thousand horsemen to a certain village called Thecoa, to examine whether the place was capable of being fortified, I saw, as I came back, several prisoners crucified; and having recognised three with whom I had been acquainted, I was distressed at it, and I told Titus of it, weeping. He immediately ordered them to be taken down, and that all possible care should be taken of them. Two died, notwithstanding the treatment, but the third survived." (See also Herod. vii. 194.) Victorinus, who was crucified under Nerva with his head downwards, lived three days. The martyrs Timotheus and Maura lived nine days. Persons of strong constitution were able to sleep on the cross, and only died of hunger. Origen (In Matt. Comment.) was obliged to call in the aid of a miracle to account for it.

In John xix. 31, it is said that the Jews asked Pilate that the legs of the criminals might be broken, in order that they might take them away before the Sabbath day. This circumstance is not mentioned in any of the other gospels, and is an error, for the crucifragium had nothing to do with crucifixion among the Romans. It was a separate punishment for slaves, prisoners of war, &c. It has been inserted here to represent the resemblance of Christ to the Passover Lamb (Exod. xii. 46; Numb. ix. 12). The same is the case with the piercing of his side, in this gospel, by a soldier (who is called Longinus in the Gospel of Nicodemus, c. vii. 8), which has been inserted to correspond with Zech. xii. 10, a book which from the prominence it gives to horses, upon which the angels are represented as riding, is evidently of post-Captivity origin. In John xix. 37, there is a quotation from Zech. xii. 10: "They shall look upon him whom they pierced." This is according to the Hebrew version, for the LXX. Ἐπιβλέψονται πρός με, ἀνθ' ὧν κατωχρήσαντο, would not have suited the writer's purpose. The same is the case with the quotation from Isaiah in Matt. viii. 17, which is in the LXX. Οὗτος τὰς ἁμαρτίας ἡμῶν φέρει, καὶ περὶ ἡμῶν ὀδύναται. Here also the Greek version would not have suited the writer's purpose, which was to represent Isaiah as prophesying that Jesus would heal physical infirmities.

CHAPTER VI.

The synoptical gospels say that Jesus died soon after three o'clock in the afternoon, but that from twelve to three there was darkness over the whole land according to Matthew and Mark, and "over all the earth" according to Luke (xxiii. 44-5), "the sun being eclipsed" [Cod. Sin.] Darkness of this description is of frequent occurrence in Pagan as well as Jewish writers. The sun was eclipsed at the assumption of Romulus; and when Cæsar died, Servius (Ad Virg. Georg. I., 165 sqq.) says, " Constat, occiso Cæsare in senatu pridie Idus Martias, solis fuisse defectum ab lunâ sextâ usque ad noctem." The darkness therefore commenced on this occasion at the same hour (mid-day) as it is said to have done in the gospels. The darkening of the sun is represented in several passages of the Old Testament as the mourning of the Deity for the sins of mankind. In R. Bechai Cod. Hakkema the death of an illustrious Rabbi is said to resemble the setting of the sun at mid-day, and in Succa f. 29, 1, it is said that when persons of high rank in the priesthood die the sun becomes darkened if the last honours are not paid to them. In Megillath Taanith, p. 50, col. 1, it is said that there was darkness over the world for three days when the Septuagint version of the Scriptures was published. This is interpreted by R. Gedalia to signify a three days' fast, such as is recorded in Esther iv. 16.

In the Anaphora or Relation of Pilate to Tiberius, which relates the miracles of Christ as recorded in the Gospels, with one or two additional ones, it is said respecting the darkness on this occasion, "There was darkness over the whole earth, the sun in the middle of the day being darkened, and the stars appearing, among whose lights the moon appeared not, but, as if turned to blood, it left its shining." This exactly agrees with what Peter is represented as quoting from Joel (Acts ii. 20) : " The sun shall be turned into darkness, and the moon into blood, before that great [and notable] day of the Lord come." The words " and notable," and the next verse, " And it shall come to pass that whoever shall call upon the name of the Lord shall be saved," are not in the Codex Sinaiticus. This portion of Joel is an insertion, in which a return from captivity is promised to Judah and Jerusalem (Joel iii. 1), and has no prophetic meaning whatever. Arnobius, who is quoted by Lardner as evidence of the "uncommon darkness and other surprising events at the time of our Lord's passion and death" (vol. II., p. 255), says that " When he had put off his body, which he carried about in a little part of himself, after he suffered himself to be seen, and that it should be known of what size he was, all the elements of the world, terrified at the strangeness of what had happened, were put out of order; the earth shook and trembled ; the sea was completely poured out from its lowest bottom ; the whole atmosphere was rolled up into *balls* of darkness (globis tenebrarum); the fiery orb of the sun itself caught cold and shivered."

Gibbon asks, very reasonably, " How shall we excuse the supine inattention of the Pagan and philosophic world to these evidences which were presented by the hand of Omnipotence, not to their reason, but to their senses? This miraculous event, which ought to have excited the wonder, the curiosity, and the devotion of mankind, passed without notice in an age of science and history. It happened during the lifetime of Seneca and the elder Pliny, who must have experienced the immediate effects or received the earliest intelligence of the prodigy. Each of these philosophers, in a laborious work, has recorded all the great phenomena of nature—earthquakes, meteors, comets, and eclipses, which his indefatigable curiosity could collect; both the one and the other have omitted to mention the greatest phenomenon to which the mortal eye has been witness since the creation of the globe."

Eusebius (Chron. ad Olymp. 202, 203) has endeavoured to make out the darkness at the Crucifixion to have been real by quoting Phlegon of Tralles, who speaks of an eclipse of the sun as having occurred in the fourth year of the 202nd Olympiad (A.D. 30), and who says that at the sixth hour of the day the stars were distinctly visible. Unfortunately Kepler has shown that this eclipse really took place on the

24th of November, at two o'clock in the afternoon, thus being rather more than six months too late, besides which, the Crucifixion having taken place at the season of full moon, no eclipse of the sun was possible at that time, and this is no doubt why the original reading of Luke xxiii. 45, "The sun being eclipsed" [Cod. Sin. and Vat.], has been altered into "And the sun was darkened."

In Mark xv. 38, the rending of the veil of the temple is placed after the death of Jesus, and the verse in which it is mentioned breaks the connection between v. 37 and v. 39, showing that it is an insertion. In the Gospel of Nicodemus this event is placed before the death of Jesus, and is connected with the eclipse of the sun, and c. viii. 4, 5 read exactly as Mark xv. 37–39 would if this verse were omitted. Jerome says that in the Gospel to the Hebrews it was not stated that the veil of the temple was rent, but that an immense beam broke in two.

Eusebius, who is determined to have a miracle on this occasion, has quoted Josephus, who says that on the day of Pentecost the priests perceived a motion and noise, and afterwards heard a voice in the inmost parts of the temple, uttering the words, "Let us depart hence." He says that this occurrence took place about the time of the Crucifixion, though he must have been well aware that the date given by Josephus is A.D. 66, or thirty-six years after the date he himself assigns to that event!

Matt. xxvii. 51ᵇ–53 are unhistorical traditions, which are not found in the other Gospels. Like the rending of the veil of the temple, they are represented in the Gospel of Nicodemus (viii. 2) as taking place before the death of Jesus. The word ἔγερσις in v. 53 is found nowhere else in the New Testament, and ἐμφανίζεσθαι, spoken of a supernatural occurrence, is also peculiar to this passage. "And the graves were opened" is not in the Codex Sinaiticus. This passage appears to be a substitution for that in the Gospel of Nicodemus (xii. 14) where Joseph says to Annas and Caiaphas respecting Jesus, "It is, indeed, a thing really surprising that he should not only himself arise from the dead, but also raise others from their graves, who have been seen by many in Jerusalem," and these persons are represented to be Charinus and Lenthius, the sons of Simeon the high-priest, who were spending their time in devotional exercises in the city of Arimathœa. This passage was probably inserted into Matthew because without it there is no allusion in the Gospels to the existence of Christ between his crucifixion and ascension, nor is this subject touched upon in any part of the New Testament except in the first epistle of Peter, which few persons now believe to be genuine, and all that is said in it is that Christ preached to the antediluvians at that time. It is now, however, part of what is termed the Apostles' Creed that Jesus descended into hell. Mr. Justice Bayly says of this Creed in his Common Prayer Book, " It is not to be understood that this creed was framed by the Apostles, or indeed that it existed in their time." He then gives this Creed as it existed in A.D. 600, which is as follows:—

" I believe in God the Father Almighty, and in Jesus Christ his only begotten son our Lord, who was born of the Holy Ghost and Virgin Mary, and was crucified under Pontius Pilate, and was buried: and the third day rose again from the dead, ascended into heaven, sitteth on the right hand of the Father, whence he shall come to judge the quick and the dead; and in the Holy Ghost, the Holy Church, the remission of sins, and the resurrection of the flesh. Amen."

The origin of this Creed's being attributed to the Apostles appears to be an assertion by Ambrose (Serm. 38) that " the twelve Apostles, as skilful artificers, assembled together, and made a key by their common advice, that is, the Creed, by which the darkness of the devil is disclosed, that the light of Christ may appear." Du Pin, Archbishop Ussher, and many others have admitted that this Creed is not authentic. The words "he descended into hell" have been inserted since A.D. 600. Bishop Parsons says that these words were not to be found in the ancient creeds or rules of faith. They are not in the Nicene Creed, or in others which, like it, were made by the Councils as fuller explanations of the Apostles' Creed, nor in the rules of faith delivered by Irenæus, Origen, Tertullian, or Eusebius. They are not in the Creed expounded by St. Augustine, nor in those of St. Basil, Epiphanius, or Gelasius. Ruffinus (Exposit. in Symbol. Apost. § 20) says that in his time it was neither in the Roman nor in the Oriental Creeds.

In the Gospel of Nicodemus (xiii. 3) the coming of Jesus into hell is thus described by Charinus and Lenthius: " When we were placed with our fathers in the depth of hell, in the blackness of darkness, on a sudden there appeared the colour of the sun like gold, and a substantial purple-coloured light enlightening the place." This is quite the Jewish idea. Scheol שׁאול, the Jewish hell, signifies a cavern, and also demand, prayer (petitio, rogatio, preces), and is derived from the radical Chaldæan, signifying "he has asked, he has interrogated." It is synonymous with the Hebrew "he has proposed, asked, enquired." The hieroglyph of this word is the warrior who receives the crown, and departs victorious to conquer again. Scheol therefore means the place of desire, and resembles the Greek "Ἀδης. This place is also called Abadon or Abeda (abyss, Ps. lxxxviii. 12, Prov. xxviii. 17), Doruna, the kingdom of silence (Ps. lxxiv. 7), and Erez Neschia, the country of oblivion (Ps. lxxxviii. 12), the same as the Greek Lethe. To get there it was necessary, as in the Egyptian, Persian, and Greek mythology, to traverse infernal rivers (Nachle B'liaal) (Ps. xviii. 5), and to pass through a gate of hell (Isa. xviii. 10). There were also the depths of Scheol (Prov. ix. 18), the lowest Scheol (Deut. xxxii. 22), and the lowest country (Ezek. xxxi. 16). There were also chambers of the dead (Prov. vii. 27). The empire of the dead was looked upon as a dark place at a great depth below the earth, and at the antipodes of heaven (Job xi. 8, v. 21, 22). This is similar to the idea of the Pagans, who called the concave which surrounds the South Pole the pit, while the other concave was called the mountain. Hence Helion and Acheron, Heli-on being the sun at his highest, while Achar-on is On or the sun in Achar, his last stage or condition. This is the bottomless pit.

The primitive belief respecting the resurrection is that set forth in 1 Cor. xv. 3–11, that the crucified Jesus had returned from Hades, not however invested with his former body of flesh and blood, which remained in the grave, but with a new and heavenly body. The Scheol he returned from was the kingdom of the dead, not the kingdom of souls, like hell, Tartarus, &c. Scheol may be considered in fact as an ideal representation of the tomb. Even after the return from captivity, when the Jews had very generally adopted the ideas of their neighbours, belief in the immortality of the soul was neither clear nor well reasoned, for they refused all participation in a future life to those who denied the resurrection and the Last Judgment, which was equivalent to total annihilation for unbelievers. Eternal life was looked upon as a recompense for good principles, and for having faith in them, not as the universal destiny of mankind. The Sadducees were the faithful preservers of the ancient faith and the pure tradition of the sons of Israel.

In Isa. xxvi. 19 it is said, " Thy dead men shall live, together with my dead body shall they arise. Awake and sing, ye that dwell in the dust, for thy dew is as the dew of herbs, and the earth shall cast out the dead." This verse, which occurs in a triumphal song written to celebrate the fall of Babylon, and which is merely allegorical, has been interpreted by the Jews, in the book Zohar, to signify that at the last day a kind of plastic dew shall fall upon the dead, and engender with a little bone called Luz, and that out of this little bone all the rest of the bones and the whole man shall be restored. This word לז Luz is a Chaldee word, which signifies an almond, an almond-tree, and the hazel, and is used by the Rabbis to signify a certain bone in the human body, which they say is incorruptible, and out of which the resurrection body will be formed. The Rabbinical Lexicon, called Baal Aruch, says that Luz is a small bone at the end of the eighteenth vertebra. In Bereshith Rabba, sect. 28 (which is a voluminous commentary on the book of Genesis), the same thing is stated. The bone is evidently the os coccygis. Luz is the Assyrian goddess Ishtar, the personification of the female, called "the almond-shaped one," and is the wife of Nergal, the solar light. Hence the idea of resurrection or new birth became associated with it.

When this transformation has taken place, the soul, armed with a glorified body, an ethereal Nephesch, becomes reunited, according to the Hebrews, to its ancestors, to the people of God. It is to the bosom of Abraham that the souls of Sarah, Jacob, Aaron, and Moses himself fly from the different parts of the world in which they died. The Jews still address the following prayer to God at the Feast of Tabernacles:—" May his soul (in answer to this) be bound up in the bundle of life with the souls of Abraham, of Sarah, of Rebecca, and of Leah, and of the other just persons of both sexes who are in Paradise." This virtuous soul finds its reward in the development of its love, its intelligence, and its activity, and in studying the divine laws and commandments. The soul, which has dwelt apart from its heavenly Father, and in which the Ronab (the divine breath) of Jehovah has slept, and remained like an useless sword, becomes regenerated by repentance, by the aid of fraternal souls, and by that of the physician of souls. This is why Scheol, or the place of departed souls, signifies also prayer, or aspiration to Him who said I am the sovereign Good. The celestial life might begin on earth, as in the cases of Enoch and Elijah. The lower Scheol was the abode of the Rephaim, erroneously translated "giants" in our version, but which really signifies "the weak," those who are destined to pardon, penitence, healing, and regeneration. In the higher Scheol, under the guard of Raphaël, the physician of souls, the works of the righteous shine like divine fruits on the tree of eternal life, and these fruits heal nations.

The Zohar, which contains the traditions and mysteries of the Hebrew faith, and which was edited, about A.D. 121, by R. Simon-ben-Jochaï, and has been added to by his disciples, sets forth our origin, our future destiny, and our relations to God from the Jewish point of view. "Man," it says, " is both the summary and the highest expression of creation : this is why he was not created till the sixth day. As soon as man appeared all was finished, both the higher and the lower world; for everything reappears in man, who unites all forms in himself. But he is not only the image of the world, and of the universality of beings, including the Absolute Being; he is also, he is above all, the image of God considered solely in the aggregate of his infinite attributes."

In the first of these two aspects, that is as a microcosm, or representation of the world on a small scale, man is represented as follows : " Do not believe that man consists merely of flesh, skin, bones, and veins. Far from this being so, that which really constitutes man is his soul, and what we have mentioned, his skin, his flesh, his bones, and his veins, are but a covering, a shell, an integument; they are not man, and cannot make man. When man leaves this vile earth he gradually loses all the vices which he is full of."

The microcosm is alluded to by Plato in his "Timæus," and signified that everything had been created in the image of God, who was androgynous. Thus all animated nature was believed to be of both sexes. The celestial Adam being thus the result of a male and female principle, this must likewise be the case with the terrestrial Adam, and must apply, not only to his body, but to his soul. The Zohar says, " Every form in which the male and female principle is not found, is not a superior and complete form. The Holy One (blessed be He !) does not dwell where these two principles are not perfectly united: his blessings are only showered down when this union exists, as we learn from these words: 'He blessed them, and called their name Adam on the day that he created them;' for even the very name of man can only be given to a man and a woman, who are but one and the same being." The duality of the souls is thus explained : " Before coming into this world, every soul and every spirit is composed of a man and a woman, who form one being; when they appear on earth, these two halves separate, and animate different bodies. When the time for marriage comes, the Holy One (blessed be He !), who knows all souls and all spirits, joins them as before, and then they form, as before, one body and one soul."

The teaching in the epistles respecting the resurrection of Christ is in accordance with these doctrines. The old abandoned body of flesh and blood, which is subject to corruption and death, is as it were put off, and the spirit, rising from Hades, during its stay in which it had been without any corporeal covering, is to be clothed with a new body, which is prepared in heaven for them that believe; and this body has nothing in common with the body of flesh and blood which has been put off. The 37th verse of 1 Cor. xv. is, in the Codex Sinaiticus, "That which thou sowest is not that body that shall be ;" and this is evidently the teaching of that epistle, and also that of the Apostles (see v. 3), for men were able, when Jesus was yet alive, even when the body lay in the grave, or when, as was the case with the Baptist, the head was divided from the trunk, and the body was buried without its head (Mark vi., 28, 29), to believe, without troubling themselves about the corpse, that Jesus was John, who had risen from Hades, as the place of departed spirits is called in the New Testament (Mark vi., 14-16). The Pharisees did not teach that the *same* body would rise again, but that the souls of the pious would go at the conclusion of their sojourn in Hades, εἰς ἕτερον σῶμα, into another or glorified body (Josephus, Bell. Jud. ii. 8, 14). Conf. Mark xii. 25, ix. 2, and Luke xx. 35, 36, ix. 31.

On the day before the Sabbath, according to Mark (xv. 42), Joseph of Arimathæa went in the evening to Pilate and craved the body of Jesus. Having received the body from Pilate, he brought fine linen, and wrapped him in it, and laid him in a sepulchre which was hewn out of a rock, and rolled a stone to the door of the sepulchre. In Matthew (xxvii. 60) this is converted into "his own new tomb, which he had hewn out in the rock." In Luke (xxiii. 53) it is merely "a sepulchre that was hewn in stone," but it is added that no man had ever before been laid in it. In John all these statements are contradicted, for it is there said (xix. 41) that he was buried where he was crucified—that is, in Golgotha—where there was a garden, and in the garden there was a new sepulchre, and not a word is said about its being hewn out of a rock, or belonging to Joseph. We have also here a new person, Nicodemus, who is not mentioned in the other gospels, and who brings a hundred pound weight of myrrh and aloes, and assists Joseph to bury him. This is nearly identical with the Gospel of Nicodemus (viii. 14, 15): "And Nicodemus came, bringing with him a mixture of myrrh and aloes, about a hundred pound weight; and they took down Jesus from the cross with tears, and bound him with linen cloths, with spices, according to the custom of burying among the Jews, and placed him in a new tomb which Joseph had built and caused to be cut out of a rock, in which never any man had been put; and they rolled a great stone to the door of the sepulchre." Mark and Luke, however, say that it was the women, who had seen "how his body was laid," who returned and prepared spices and ointments, when the body had already been embalmed, "as the manner of the Jews is to bury." The most extraordinary thing of all is that Paul in Acts xiii. 29 accuses those that dwell at Jerusalem, and their rulers, of taking Jesus down from the tree and laying him in a sepulchre, and has evidently never heard of Joseph of Arimathæa, the disciple of Jesus (Matt. xxvii. 57), who laid him in his own tomb out of reverence. In 1 Cor. xv. 4, this subject is dismissed in even a more summary manner, for it is merely said that Jesus was buried and rose again, and no mention is made of the women, or the angel, or the earthquake, or any one of the incidents enumerated by the evangelists.

Mark (xv. 47) says that Mary of Magdala and Mary the mother of Joseph saw where he was laid. As Joseph (vi. 3) is one of the brothers of Jesus, this is a most remarkable expression, for it surely ought to have been the mother of Jesus. In c. xv. 1 we have another change: "And when the sabbath was past, Mary Magdalene, and Mary the mother of James, and Salome, had brought sweet spices that they might come and anoint him." In this gospel, therefore, three women pay the last rites to the dead. In Matthew (xxvii. 61; xxviii. 1) there are only two women; but the statement in Mark has been altered, in c. xxvii. 56, by making Mary the mother of James and Joseph. Salome is altogether omitted in Matthew. In Luke (xxiii. 55) all the women that came with Jesus from Galilee follow Joseph to the sepulchre, and then go to prepare the spices and ointments. In c. xxiv. 10 we are told who these women were, viz., "Mary Magdalene, and Joanna, and Mary the mother of James, and other women which were with them." We have thus three women in Mark, two in Matthew, and in Luke a number of women who had followed Jesus from Galilee. In all these Mary the mother of James appears. What is our surprise, therefore, in the fourth gospel (John xx. 1) to find only one woman, and that woman Mary of Magdala! In the Gospel of Nicodemus all mention of the names of the women is avoided, and the Jews, who call together the soldiers who guarded the sepulchre of Jesus, say (c. x. 8) "We know not who the women were."

The three women came to the sepulchre very early in the morning, at sun-rise, on the first day of the week (Mark xvi. 2 et sqq.), and found the stone rolled away from the door of the sepulchre, inside which they saw "a young man, sitting on the right side, clothed in a long white garment." He tells them that Jesus of Nazareth, who was crucified, had risen, and charges them to tell Peter and the apostles that he would precede them into Galilee, where they should see him. The women, however, fled from the sepulchre in trepidation, and said nothing to any man, for they were afraid (v. 8).

In Matthew the two women come to the sepulchre "as it began to dawn toward the first day of the week," and instead of a young man sitting inside the sepulchre, we have an angel of the Lord, who descends from heaven, a great earthquake accompanying his descent; and instead of the women finding the stone rolled away, the angel himself rolls it back from the door, and sits upon it. We also learn, for the first time, that there were keepers of the sepulchre (xxviii. 4), who became as dead men. The angel gives much the same message to the women as in Mark, but in this gospel they depart from the sepulchre "with fear and great joy," and run to bring the apostles word (v. 8).

In Luke all the women who accompanied Jesus from Galilee came "upon the first day of the week, very early in the morning," bringing the spices which they had prepared, and, as in Mark, find the stone rolled away from the sepulchre, upon which they enter in, and find that the body of Jesus is not there (xxiv. 1–3). We find now, however, no angel, but "*two* men in shining garments" [raiment, Cod. Sin.], who deliver a totally different address to the women, and say nothing about Jesus appearing to the disciples in Galilee, which would be inconsistent with the remainder of this gospel.

In John, as has been before observed, Mary of Magdala comes alone to the sepulchre, on the first day of the week, "early, while it was yet dark" (xx. 1), and finds the stone taken away from the sepulchre. There is no earthquake, no young man, no angel; but Mary runs and finds, not "the apostles," but Simon Peter and "the other disciple whom Jesus loved," who outruns Peter, and is consequently the first witness of the empty state of the tomb. Here, therefore, we are supposed to have the evidence of the author of the fourth gospel, who was an eye-witness of what took place, and who contradicts, in the most unequivocal manner, the assertions of the other evangelists. It is no wonder that Bishop Marsh is obliged to confess that, after all his attempts to reconcile the contradictions of St. John's account of the resurrection of Christ with those of Mark and Luke, "he has not been able to do it in a manner satisfactory to himself, or to any other impartial inquirer after truth."

The contradictions do not stop here. After the two apostles had returned to their own home, Mary looked into the sepulchre and saw two angels in white standing, one at the head and one at the feet, where the body had lain. Immediately afterwards she sees Jesus himself standing by her, who tells her that he is about to ascend to heaven. In this gospel, therefore, as in the added portion of Mark's Gospel (xvi. 9), Jesus first appears to Mary Magdalene; but it is impossible to conceive why she should be selected for so distinguished an honour. In the added portion of Mark it is said that the apostles did not believe her, but nothing is said of this in John.

In the Gospel of Nicodemus all this narrative is put into the mouth of one of the soldiers who kept the sepulchre of Jesus, and who stated in the assembly, which "the rulers, Annas and Caiaphas" had just left, that " while they were guarding the sepulchre of Jesus there was an earthquake; and we saw an angel of God roll away the stone of the sepulchre and sit upon it ; and his countenance was like lightning and his garment like snow; and we became through fear like persons dead. And we heard an angel saying to the women at the sepulchre of Jesus, Do not fear; I know that you seek Jesus who was crucified; he is risen as he foretold. Come and see the place where he was laid; and go presently and tell his disciples that he is risen from the dead; and he will go before you into Galilee ; there ye shall see him as he told you." (x. 3-6.)

Justin Martyr, Tertullian, Eusebius, Epiphanius, Chrysostom, and Orosius all agree in stating that Pilate sent to the Emperor Tiberius to inform him of the unjust sentence he had pronounced against an innocent and divine person. Tiberius (who believed in no religion whatever) is said upon the receipt of this letter to have thought of placing Christ among the gods of Rome, but the senate having disobeyed his commands, Tiberius contented himself with protecting the Christians. Justin says that the memory of this transaction was preserved in the most public and authentic records, which, however, have unfortunately not been seen by any one but himself. Eusebius (H. E. ii. 2) assures us on the testimony of Tertullian, that Tiberius was so convinced by the account Pilate had sent him of the resurrection of Christ that he threatened death to any one who should accuse the Christians. Tertullian also says " that it was an ancient decree that no one should be consecrated a god by the emperor before it had been approved by the senate. Marcus Aurelius has done this in reference to a certain idol, Alburnus, so that this evidence has been given in favour of our doctrine, that divine dignity is conferred among you by the decrees of men. *Unless a god pleases men, he is not made a god*, and thus, according to this procedure, it is necessary that man should be propitious to the god."

Pilate, according to this account, informed the emperor that " early in the morning of the first of the Sabbaths the resurrection of Christ was announced by a display of the most astonishing and surprising feats of Divine Omnipotence ever performed. At the third hour of the night the sun broke forth into such splendour as was never before seen, and the heavens became enlightened seven times more than on any other day. And the light ceased not to shine all that night." This is sufficiently startling, but it is nothing to what follows, for we are told that " an instantaneous chasm took place, and the earth opened and swallowed up all the unbelieving Jews." The Jewish temple and synagogues all vanished away, not a single synagogue being left in all Jerusalem, and the Roman soldiers who had kept the sepulchre went mad! Such is the veracious statement of Pontius Pilate as certified by Tertullian and Eusebius.

The Gospel of Matthew mentions the appearance of Jesus to the whole of the apostles after the crucifixion, and says that it took place in Galilee, on a mountain where Jesus had appointed them to meet him. This, however, is not mentioned in c. xxvi. 32, which merely states that after he was risen he would go before them into Galilee. In Luke the apostles never leave Judæa, and Jesus appears first to them at Emmaus. John (xx. 19) contradicts both gospels by saying that the appearance took place at Jerusalem.

The ascension is not mentioned in any of the original gospels. Luke xxiv. 50, 51 is in the original: "And he led them out unto Bethany, and he lifted up his hands, and blessed them. And it came to pass, while he blessed them, he was parted from them," " and carried up to heaven," not being in the Codex Sinaiticus. There is therefore no authority in the gospels for the ascension having taken place, nor for Jesus " sitting at the right hand of God." In Acts i. 12 it is said that it took place on " the mount called Olivet." In the Gospel of Nicodemus (x. 18–21) we have this statement confirmed by three witnesses, for " a certain priest Phinees, Ada a schoolmaster, and a Levite named Ageus, they three came from Galilee to Jerusalem, and told the chief priests and all who were in the synagogues, saying,

We have seen Jesus whom ye crucified talking with his eleven disciples, and sitting in the midst of them in Mount Olivet, and saying to them, Go forth into the whole world, preach the gospel to all nations, baptizing them in the name of the Father, and the Son, and the Holy Ghost, and whosoever shall believe, and be baptized, shall be saved. And when he had said these things to his disciples, we saw him ascending into heaven." This resembles the conclusion of Matthew's Gospel, except that Jesus is represented there as being on a mountain in Galilee, and that there is no account of the ascension. In the Acts Jesus tells the apostles that they shall only receive power after the Holy Ghost had come upon them (i. 8), and says nothing about their preaching the gospel or baptizing. A circumstantial account of the ascension is then given, to the effect that Jesus was taken up, that a cloud received him out of their sight, and that two men in white apparel stood by them as he went up. In the third gospel, and also in the added portion of Mark, the ascension is represented as taking place on the same day that Jesus left the tomb: in the Acts, on the contrary, it is expressly stated (i. 3) that he was forty days on earth between his resurrection and ascension. Paul (1 Cor. xv. 5, 6) renders all these accounts impossible by distinctly stating that, after he had been seen of Cephas, *then of the twelve* (not the eleven), he was seen of above five hundred brethren at once, afterwards of James, then of all the apostles, and lastly by himself; and does not mention a visible ascension at all. A distinction is made in this account, which we are told Paul had "received," between the Twelve and James and the apostles. Cephas, as will be shown subsequently, was not Peter, but one of the seventy disciples.

The account of the ascension is imitated from the traditional account of the disappearance of Moses, which is given by Josephus (Ant. IV. viii. 48) : " Now as soon as they (i. e., the Senate, Eleazar the high priest, and Joshua) were come unto the mountain called Abarim (which is a very high mountain, situate over against Jericho, and one that affords, to such as are upon it, a prospect of the greatest part of the excellent land of Canaan), he dismissed the Senate, and as he was going to embrace Eleazar and Joshua, and was still discoursing with them, a cloud stood over him on the sudden, and he disappeared in a certain valley, *although he wrote in the holy books that he died*, which was done out of fear, lest any one should venture to say that, because of his extraordinary virtue, he went to God." Philo, however, gives a different account of this occurrence (Vita Moys. c. 39) and one more in accordance with Jewish belief, for he says that, "when he was about to depart from hence to heaven, to take up his abode there, and, leaving this mortal life to become immortal, having been summoned by the Father, who now changed him, having previously been a double being, composed of soul and body, into the nature of a single body, transforming him wholly and entirely into a most sun-like mind; he then," &c. To this he adds that " he prophesied admirably what should happen to himself after his death, relating, that is, how he had died when he was not as yet dead, and how he was buried without any one being present so as to know of his tomb, because, in fact, he was entombed not by mortal hands, but by immortal powers, so that he was not placed in the tomb of his forefathers," &c. It is evident that this tradition would be inconsistent with a corporeal resurrection and ascension, and, consequently, the other tradition was followed.

If the crucifixion of Jesus took place in the manner it is stated to have done, it must have been a political execution on the part of the Roman governor. Tacitus (Annal. xv. 44) says that the Christians "had their denomination from Christus, who, in the reign of Tiberius, was put to death (supplicio adfectus erat) by the procurator, Pontius Pilate." This passage of Tacitus, which, since the forged passage in Josephus has been given up, is the only external evidence of this event, is not quoted by any of the Fathers. Tertullian, who has quoted largely from Tacitus, has not alluded to it, and, if he had known of it, he could not have called Tacitus " the most prating of all liars," " mendaciorum loquacissimus." Eusebius would gladly have availed himself of it if he had known of its existence. Clemens Alexandrinus, who brought together all that Pagan authors had admitted respecting the existence of Christ or Christians, is silent respecting it. The statement that Nero inflicted the most exquisite punishments upon the Christians is explicitly contradicted by the statement of Melito, who was Bishop of Sardis, and who states, in his Apology, the date of which Eusebius fixes at A.D. 170, that, up to his time, the Christians had never been persecuted; and Tertullian, in his Apology, addressed to the Emperor and Senate of Rome in A.D. 198, says, " The Christian persecutors have always been men divested of justice, piety, and common shame, upon whose government you yourselves have put a brand, and rescinded their acts by restoring those whom they condemned. But of all the emperors, down to this present reign, who understood anything of justice or humanity, name me ONE who ever persecuted the Christians. On the contrary, we show you the excellent Marcus Aurelius for our protector and patron, who, though he could not publicly set aside the laws, yet he did as well, he publicly rendered them ineffectual in another way, by discouraging our accusers with the last punishment, viz., burning alive." When it is added that the Annals of Tacitus were first published by Johannes de Spire, at Venice, in the year 1468, from a single manuscript which was in his own possession, and from which all other manuscripts and printed copies are taken, it becomes evident that this passage also is a forgery, either by Johannes de Spire himself, or by the transcriber of the manuscript, which was said to date from the eighth century.

Tacitus was born in A.D. 62, and wrote his Annals towards the close of his life, probably about A.D. 107. Irenæus, who wrote about A.D. 182, and was accounted one of the most eminent and illustrious early writers of the Church, not only ignores this passage, but accuses the Gospel writers of forgery. In Dr. Grabe's Irenæus (l. II. c. 39), which is entitled " A demonstration that the Lord preached after his baptism, not merely for one year, but that he employed in preaching the whole term of his life," the following passage occurs : " For he came to save all through himself—all, I say, who through him are born to God—infants, little children, boys, youths, and old people. Therefore he preached in every stage of life, and became an infant with infants, sanctifying infants; a child among children, sanctifying those of the same age as himself, and at the same time supplying an example to them of piety, of justice, and of submission ; a youth among youths, becoming an example to youths, and sanctifying them to the Lord. So, also, an elder among elders, that the teacher might be perfect in all things, not only according to the exposition (law or rule) of truth, but also according to the period of life ; and sanctifying at the same time the elders, becoming an example even to them. After that he came to death, that he might be the first-born from the dead, he himself having pre-eminence in all things, the Prince of Life, above all, and excelling all. *But to establish their own forgery*, that it is written of him, *to call* (it ?) *the acceptable year of the Lord*, they say against themselves that he preached (during) one year (only ?), and suffered on the twelfth month (of it ?). They have forgotten—giving up every (important ?) affair of his, and taking away the more necessary, the more honourable, and, I say, that advanced period of his in which, teaching diligently, he presided over all. For how did he obtain disciples if he did not teach ? And how did he teach —not having attained the age of a master (or doctor ?) ? For he came to baptism who had not yet completed thirty years of age (for thus Luke, who indicates his years, lays it down, and Jesus was, as it were, entering on thirty years when he came to baptism) : and after (his ?) baptism he preached only one year—on completing his thirtieth year he suffered (death), being as yet only a young man, who had not attained maturity. But as the chief part of thirty years belongs to youth (or, as a person of thirty may be considered as a young man ?), and every one will confess him to be such until the fortieth year; but from the fortieth to the fiftieth year he declines into old age, *which our Lord having attained he taught*, "as the gospel and all the elders who in Asia assembled with John the disciple of the Lord *testify*, and as John himself had taught them. And he (John ?) remained with them till the time of Trajan. And some of them saw not only John, but other apostles, and heard the same things from them, and bear the same testimony to this revelation."

This passage shows that Jesus cannot have died till A.D. 47, for Irenæus expressly adopts the statement of Luke that he was thirty years of age in the fifteenth year of Tiberius. Pontius Pilate succeeded Valerius Gratus in A.D. 28 and ceased to govern in A.D. 37, therefore Jesus must have outlived his supposed execution some eighteen years, and have died peaceably in the bosom of his family at the end of that time. Irenæus was the disciple of Papias, who also ignored the Crucifixion, and the Pauline epistles admit that the doctrine of a crucified Christ was "unto the Jews a stumbling-block, and unto the Gentiles foolishness," thus showing that even at the time they were written Christians were not agreed respecting the Crucifixion. It was a stumbling-block because there is no prediction whatever of a crucified Messiah in the Old Testament. Dan. ix. 26 really refers to the Romans establishing an aristocracy in the place of a monarchy, and Zech. xii. 10 belongs apparently to the reign of Jehoahaz, and refers to the conquest of Jerusalem by some nation which is not mentioned, and speaks of the great mourning in the city for one who is lamented as an only son, who seems to be king Josiah. Ezek. xxxvi. 25 and xxxvii. 23 were written during the Captivity, refer to the deliverance of the Jewish people from the idolatrous nations which surrounded them, and strike at the root of the doctrine of vicarious sacrifice by declaring that every man is to be punished for his own sins only. Josephus does not say a word respecting the Messianic hopes of his countrymen, and Philo, who does speak of a hero similar to the Messiah, says not a word of his crucifixion or death. Isa. liii. is by an unknown author who wrote after the return from Captivity, and refers to the writer himself. All the passages in the New Testament which refer to the accomplishment of prophecy were written *after* the event, and are consequently valueless.

Origen (Contra Cels., c. 10) admits that blind belief was all that was required of the people. He says, "Since our adversaries are continually making such a stir about our taking things on trust, I answer that we who see plainly and have found the vast advantage that the common people, who make up by far the greater number, do manifestly and frequently reap thereby, I say we, who are well advised of these things, *do professedly teach them to believe without examination.*" This is very different from the injunction of St. Chrysostom, who says, "Examine, examine the Scriptures. What! when we receive money, we desire to count it over ourselves, and when Divine knowledge is in question, shall we accept blindly the opinions of others? Examine, examine the Scriptures."

Irenæus bases his accusation against the evangelists upon Luke iv. 19, where Jesus is represented as saying that he had been appointed "to preach the acceptable year of the Lord." This refers to Lev. xxv. 10, a passage which belongs undoubtedly to a late period of Jewish legislation, the chapters in which it occurs having the commands addressed to the children of Israel instead of to Aaron and his sons. In the following verses it is directed that there shall be neither sowing nor reaping, planting, pruning, nor gathering for that whole year, which is so manifestly impossible that it cannot be supposed that it was ever acted upon, still less that it was ever a Divine command. Irenæus appears to be endeavouring to substitute a figurative year of fifty years' duration as the "acceptable year." However this may be, it is certain that he did not believe in the Crucifixion of Jesus, and he makes John live till the time of Trajan, who began to reign A.D. 98. This agrees with Eusebius's statement that John was present at the Council of Ephesus in A.D. 99. It is evident that there were two parties in the Church, the one believing with the Paulinists in the Crucifixion, the other disbelieving that such an event had ever taken place.

We have already seen that Paul recognised the Sibyls as inspired, according to Clemens Alexandrinus, who quotes his very words, and the Sibyl speaks plainly of the crucifixion and also of other events narrated in the Gospels. The Erythræan Sibyl, from whom we are about to quote, informs us (l. 287 et sqq.) that she was one of Noah's daughters-in-law, and was on board the ark. The book opens with God speaking to Noah from heaven. After commanding him to make the ark, &c., God continues,—

"My name has nine letters and four syllables: consider who I am. The three first syllables have each two letters, the other has the rest, and there are five consonants. The hundreds of all this number are twice eight, and thrice three decads, with their sevens. He that knows who I am shall not be ignorant of that divine wisdom which is from me."

These verses are in Greek, but no Greek name of God has these letters, and the original must have been written in some Eastern language. In the account of the Deluge the Sibyl places Ararat in Phrygia, near a city called Celœnes, while the Jewish Ararat was situated to the east of the Caspian Sea, and certainly not in Asia Minor. The Samaritan version calls Ararat Serendib, which is the name of Ceylon, the island where the Hindoos place Paradise. There are several other differences from the Jewish account, such as there being a key to the ark, Noah's sending forth a dove first instead of a raven, and his only remaining forty-one days in the ark. These differences are only mentioned here to show that these verses were not written by either a Jew or a Christian. What is to the purpose is that it was here that the worship of Atys, who, as Martianus Capella informs us, was identical with Osiris, Ammon, Adonis, Apollo, &c., and who was *suspensus a ligno* and restored to life again on the 25th of March, more particularly prevailed, while the death of Apollo after he had been killed by Python was bewailed by three women, just as that of Christ is in Mark's gospel.

After describing the golden age after the Deluge, which is the sixth generation according to the Sibyl (Josephus makes seven generations before that event), and the second generation of terrestrial men, the Titans, who are the seventh, she proceeds as follows:—

" Then the son of the Great God shall come amongst men, being clothed with flesh, being like mortal men on the earth. His name shall have four vowels and two consonants which are double, and I will declare and interpret what number may be made by the numeral letters in that name. First, there are eight monads or units, as many tens, and eight hundred, in all 888." This makes Ἰησοῦς, thus:—

Ἰ	=	10
η	=	8
σ	=	200
ο	=	70
υ	=	400
ς	=	200
		888

This name and number refer to the higher branches of astrology, and form part of what is termed the sacred language, upon which it is not necessary to dwell here. The Sibyl indicates this by saying " The numbers above mentioned will signify Christ's name to the men who are infidels," showing that the allusion was well known. The period when Christ was to come is fixed in the third book as follows:—

Αὐτὰρ ἐπεὶ 'Ρώμη καὶ Αἴγυπτον βασιλεύσει,
Εἰς ἓν ἰθύνουσα, τότε δὴ βασιλεία μεγίστη
Ἀθανάτου βασιλῆος ἐπ' ἀνθρώποισι φανεῖται.
"Ηξει δ' ἁγνὸς ἄναξ, πάσης γῆς σκῆπτρα κρατητῶν
Εἰς αἰῶνας πάντας, ἐπειγομένοιο χρόνοιο.

Christ was therefore to come after Rome had annexed Egypt to the empire. Returning to the first book we find it predicted that priests shall offer to Christ gold, myrrh, and frankincense; that there shall be a voice crying through the desert to mortals to make their paths straight, and that a barbarous man, being enticed by dancing, shall cut off the speaker's head and give it as a reward. The beautiful stone shall then come out of the land of Egypt, and the Hebrew nation shall stumble against it; but the Gentiles shall be gathered together by his conduct, for he shall show eternal life to the elect; but for the wicked he shall prepare eternal fire. The miracles Christ is to perform are then predicted, especially the feeding the five thousand, only in the Sibyl there is only one fish, and the twelve baskets-full are given to the Virgin. Israel is then represented as striking and spitting venom upon the Son of God, and as giving him gall for meat and vinegar for drink. This, however, is done in the gospels by the Roman soldiers, as it would have been impossible to represent the Jews, who had no legal power to do so, as crucifying Christ. We have then the crown of thorns and the piercing of Christ's side by a spear, to which the author of the fourth gospel has added the pouring forth of blood and water. The Sibyl says that, *in consequence* of the piercing of the side, there should be three hours of monstrous dark night in the middle of the day. In the gospels this darkness precedes the death of Jesus.

The Sibyl concludes by saying that Solomon's temple shall give a wonderful sign to men. This anachronism is avoided in the gospels by saying that the veil of "the" temple was rent in twain. The old temple had at this time been pulled down by Herod, and a new one had been built, which was inaugurated in A.D. 14 with great splendour, and it was placed under the protection of Rome. To the scandal of the faithful, a Roman eagle, made of gold, was placed over the principal entrance. Herod acquired so much popularity among the Jews by this act, that many held him to be the promised Messiah, and the sect of the Herodians continued to exist even after his death. The Sibyl represents a connection as existing between the sign given by the temple and the descent of Christ to Hades to preach the resurrection to the dead. She represents him as rising on the third day, demonstrating to men that death resembles a slumber, and as then being taken up in the clouds to a heavenly habitation. After this there are to be no more prophets; but the Σόλοι, a word of which the meaning is unknown, are to be the guides. The sixth book treats of "the great and celebrated son of the immortal God," whom it calls "the first God, of the first fire [a Hindu expression], and his Son begotten by a dove, the Spirit, which appeared like a dove with white wings." After speaking of the miracles, &c., the Sibyl exclaims, "O thou happy wood on which God was extended, the earth shall not keep thee, but thou shalt see the heavenly mansion, where the near fiery countenance of God shall shine like lightning." This book is important because it is quoted both by Lactantius and Sozomen, who says "Ipsi Gentiles fatuntur hoc esse Sibyllæ carmen, 'O Lignum felix!'" &c. Lactantius mentions the complaint against Judæa in the verses which precede it.

Before such predictions as these could be credited by men of sense and learning, there must have been some system, however erroneous, to which they corresponded. We find this system set forth and accredited by the eminent astronomer Cassini. He bases it on the assertion of Josephus (Ant. Jud. l. i. c. 3) that "God prolonged the life (of the patriarchs who lived before the Deluge) as well by reason of their virtue as to afford them the means to perfect the sciences of geometry and astronomy, which they had invented; which they could not possibly do, if they had lived less than six hundred years, because that it is not till after the revolution of six ages that the great year is accomplished." He considers this great year to be a period of lunisolar years, and proceeds to say that "the second lunisolar period composed of ages is that of 2,300 years, which, being joined to one of 600, makes a more exact period of 2,900 years; and two periods of 2,300 years, joined to a period of 600 years, do make a lunisolar period of 5,200 years, which is the interval of the time which is reckoned, according to Eusebius's chronology, from the creation of the world to the vulgar epocha of the years of Jesus Christ. . . . Thus the year of Jesus Christ (which is that of his incarnation and birth, according to the tradition of the Church, and as Father Grandamy justifies it in his Christian Chronology, and Father Ricciolus in his Reformed Astronomy) is also an astronomical epocha, in which, according to the modern tables, the middle conjunction of the Moon with the Sun happened the 24th of

March, according to the Julian form, re-established a little after by Augustus, at one o'clock and a half in the morning, at the meridian of Jerusalem, the very day of the middle Equinox, a Wednesday, *which is the day of creation of these two planets.*

"The day following, March 25th, which, according to the ancient tradition of the Church, reported by St. Augustine (De Trin. l. iv. c. 5), was the day of our Lord's incarnation, was likewise the day of the first phasis of the moon; and, consequently, it was the first day of the month, according to the usage of the Hebrews, and the first day of the sacred year, which, *by the divine institution*, must begin with the first month of the spring, and the first day of a great year, the natural epocha of which is the concourse of the middle equinox, and of the middle conjunction of the Moon with the Sun.

"This concourse terminates, therefore, the lunisolar periods of the preceding ages, and was an epocha from whence began a new order of ages, according to the oracle of the Sibyl, related by Virgil in these words (Eclog. IV.):—

'Magnus ab integro sæclorum nascitur ordo:
Jam nova progenies cœlo dimittitur alto.'

"This oracle seems to answer the prophecy of Isaiah, Parvulus natus est nobis (c. ix. 6, 7), where this new-born is called God and father of future ages: Deus fortis, pater futuri sæculi."

Here we have the origin of the system adopted by Constantine, Eusebius, and the Church. Boullanger (Exam. Critiq. de St. Paul, c. 3) has observed on this whole subject:

"The learned Dodwell admits that the books which compose the New Testament were not made public till at least a century after the death of Christ. His words are as follows (Dissert. in Irenæum, c. 38, p. 66): 'Latitabant enim usque ad recentiora illa, seu Trajani, seu etiam fortasse Adriani, tempora in privatarum ecclesiarum, seu etiam hominum, scriniis scripta illa canonica, ne ad Ecclesiæ Catholicæ notitiam pervenirent.' If this is certain, how can we be sure that these books existed at all before that time? These works were therefore entirely in the hands of churchmen down to the third and fourth centuries, that is to say, they were at the mercy of certain men with whom self-interest and the spirit of party have always been the rule of conduct, and who never had either the honesty or the knowledge which are necessary for the discovery of truth and for its transmission in its original purity. Thus each doctor was enabled to make the sacred books be what he chose; and when, in the reign of Constantine, the Christians found themselves supported by the emperor, their leaders were enabled to adopt or to cause to be adopted as authentic such books as would suit their own interests best, and to reject as apocryphal those which did not agree with the dominant sect. But, in fact, even if we were certain of the authenticity of the books which are now adopted by the Church, we should have no guarantee of the authority of these writings except the writings themselves, and what history can pretend to prove itself by itself? Can one listen to witnesses who give no proof of what they state except their own word? We must remember, however, that the first Christians were famous for their lies, their fictions, and those frauds which are termed 'pious' when they tend to advance the cause of religion. Have not these pious forgers attributed works to Jesus Christ himself, and to his successors, the apostles? Have we not from them Sibylline verses, which are evidently Christian prophecies made after the events, and often copied word for word from the Old and New Testaments? If the Nicene Fathers had chosen to regard these prophecies as divinely inspired, who could have prevented them from inserting them among the canonical writings? and then the Christians would certainly have looked upon them as indubitable proofs of the truth of their religion. If the Christians, at the very beginning of Christianity, believed in works full of lying dreams, such as the Shepherd of Hermas, the Gospel of the Infancy, and the letter of Jesus Christ to Abgarus, what reliance can we place on the books which remain to us from them? Can we even suppose that we have the books as they were originally written? How can we now distinguish between what is true and what is false in works in which we see enthusiasm, knavery, and credulity appear in every page? .... If a body of men in possession of power, and able to take advantage of the credulity of mankind, were to find their interest concerned in doing so, they would make men believe at the end of a few centuries that the adventures of Don Quixote are prefectly true, and that the prophecies of Nostradamus have been inspired by God Himself. By dint of glosses, of commentaries, and of allegories, it is easy to discover and to prove what one pleases; however glaring an imposture may be, it can be made at last, by the aid of time, cunning, and power, to pass for truth, which no one must doubt. Deceivers who are obstinate, and who are supported by public authority, can make ignorant people, who are always credulous, believe anything, *especially if they can persuade them that there is merit in not noticing inconsistencies, contradictions, and palpable absurdities, and that there is danger in making use of their reason.*"

So confidently did the compilers of the Gospels rely upon the ignorance of their readers that they have not hesitated to put a false quotation from the Old Testament into the mouth of Jesus himself in John vii. 38, for there is no such passage to be found as "Out of his belly shall flow rivers of living water." This is on a par with the mistake of the divinely-inspired Stephen, who, in Acts vii. 37, mistakes Jehovah, who in Exodus is represented as speaking to Moses on Mount Sinai, for an angel, and with that of Paul, who speaks in Gal. iii. 19 of a promise "ordained by angels in the hand of a mediator," which "angels" are nowhere to be found. It is also on a par with the unscrupulous perversion of history in Acts xii. 23, where we are told that "the angel of the Lord" smote Herod, because he gave not God the glory. The story as given by Josephus (Ant. XIX., viii. 2) is as follows: "Having now reigned over Judæa three years, he entered the town of Cæsarea, which was formerly called the Tower of Strabo. Here he celebrated some shows in honour of Cæsar. . . . On the second day of these shows he came into the theatre in the early part of the day, dressed in a robe of silver, of most beautiful workmanship. The rays of the sun, just then rising, made his dress glitter so as to give him a majestic and awful appearance. The flatterers soon began in several parts of the theatre to utter acclamations which proved injurious to him, calling him a god, and saying, 'Be propitious to us, and as we have hitherto respected you as a man, now we acknowledge you to be more than mortal.' The king neither reproved these persons, nor rejected their impious flattery. Presently, however, casting his eyes upwards, he saw an owl sitting upon a rope over his head. He perceived it to be a messenger of evil to him, as it had been before of his prosperity, and immediately was grieved at heart. Violent pains in his bowels also began to affect him, which caused him the greatest agony from the first. Turning to his friends, he said, 'I, your god, am required to depart this life. Fate has immediately confuted the false applauses you have bestowed on me, and I who have been called immortal by you am hurried away to death. But the will of Destiny must be submitted to, since it is God's will, and I have not lived by any means a bad and mean life (οὐδαμῇ φαύλως), but in that splendour which men consider to be the greatest of happiness.'" Josephus adds that he died after five days of suffering, and that the whole population, with their wives and children, were imploring God to save their king, and that every place was full of weeping and lamentation, so that Herod himself could not abstain from weeping. Not content with misrepresenting this occurrence as a Divine judgment, the author of the Acts has taken advantage of the ambiguous meaning of the word ἄγγελος, which means messenger and angel, to represent the owl as "an angel of the Lord." Eusebius (H. E. l. II., c. 10) has deliberately mistranslated the passage as follows: "After a little while, raising himself, he saw an angel sitting above his head on a rope:" Ἀνακύψας δὲ τῆς ἑαυτοῦ κεφαλῆς ὑπερκαθιζόμενον εἶδεν ἄγγελον ἐπὶ σχοινίου τινὸς. For this he is justly reprehended by Lardner, but what are we to think of the "inspired" author of the Acts, whom Eusebius has done little more than follow?

M. Boullanger, in the above passage, accuses the Christians of having forged the Sibylline verses. But Cicero (De Div., l. I.) says, "We take notice of the verses of the Sibyl, which she is said to have penned in a fury or prophetic frenzy, the interpretation whereof was lately thought to have been about to declare in the Senate House that, if we would be safe, we should acknowledge him for a king who really was so. If there be any such thing contained in the Sibylline books, then, we demand, concerning what man is it spoken, and of what time? For whoever framed these Sibylline verses, craftily contrived that, whatsoever should come to pass, might seem to have been predicted by them, by taking away all distinctions of persons and times. He also purposely affected obscurity, that the same verses might be accommodated, sometimes to one thing, sometimes to another. But that they proceeded, not from fury and prophetic frenzy, but rather from art and contrivance, doth no less appear otherwise than from the Acrostic in them. This shows that the Acrostic was in the Sibylline books in Cicero's time, and Eusebius says that Cicero quoted the very verses which contained the Acrostic, which has been translated by Wye Saltonstall as follows:—

I n that time, when the Great Judge shall come,
E arth shall sweat; the Eternal King, from 's throne,
S hall judge the world, and all that in it be;
U nrighteous men and righteous shall God see
S eated on high with saints eternally

C ompassed, which in the last age have been,
H ence shall the earth grow desolate again;
R egardless statues and gold shall be held vain;
I n greedy flames shall burn earth, seas and skies,
S tand up again dead bodies shall, and rise,
T hat they may see all these with their eyes.

C leansing the faithful in twelve fountains, He
R eign shall for ever unto eternity;
V ery God that he is, and our Saviour too,
X hrist that did suffer for us—and I trust that will do.

CHAPTER VII.

ALTHOUGH Eusebius adopted the remarkable period of 5200 years, which has the peculiarity of including several systems besides the one in which it originates, the authorities are by no means agreed upon the subject. According to Josephus the period from the Creation to Christ is 5088 years. According to the Œcumenical Council held at Constantinople in A.D. 381, which has been followed by the Greek and Armenian Churches, the world was created in B.C. 5509. The Church Council held at Alexandria in A.D. 362, fixes it in B.C. 5439, while the English Church follows Archbishop Ussher in placing it in B.C. 4004, or, as it should be, in B.C. 4000. It was also settled at a council held at Jerusalem in A.D. 200 that the Creation took place on Sunday the 8th of April, at the vernal equinox, and at the fall of the moon, and all the cosmogonies are agreed that the Creation took place at this period of the year. This is the case with the Mithraic system also, the resemblance between which and Christianity was so strong that the Pagans accused the early Christians of being merely a sect who worshipped the sun under the name of Christ: "Alii planè humaniùs et verisimiliùs solem credunt Deum nostrum" (Tertull. Apologet.). The Fathers of the Church, unable to deny the resemblance, attributed it to the Devil, who, they said, foreseeing what was about to happen, and wishing to deprive the mystery of Redemption of its novelty, hastened to forestal God in order to set forth this ineffable mystery under the name of Mithra (Tertull. Apolog. et De Coronâ; Justin, Apolog., l. II. et Dial. cum Tryph.).

The Mithraic Zodiacs represented the vernal equinox as corresponding to the commencement of Cancer (Porphyr. de antro) in what they held to be the primæval state of the heavens, and as the birth of Mithra took place when this equinox corresponded with the commencement of Taurus, the followers of Mithra said that their Redeemer was born

4000 years after the Creation, for they, like the Egyptians, allowed 2000 years for the passage of the sun through a sign. The same is the case among the Hindus. Vishnu, the Mediator God, who became incarnate as a green shepherd, and took the name of Chris-en, delivered the world from the serpent Calengam at the very same period that Mithra regenerated it. This is why the sacred paintings of India represent Chris-en sometimes as a green child held in the arms of the Virgin, who is seated on Taurus, and sometimes as a green warrior, who is seated on the celestial elephant—a figure composed of the elect arranged in such a way as to represent that animal—and pointing his divine arrow at the serpent Calengam, the symbol of evil, thus resembling the Grecian Apollo who kills the serpent Python with his arrows.

The proof of the connection between Mithraism and Christianity is that on several churches, some of as late date as the eleventh century, are still to be seen the Mithraic emblems *adapted to the Christian astrology*, which differs both from the Mithraic system and from the astronomical systems adopted by Eusebius and others. The religious monuments of the Middle Ages have their symbolical hieroglyphics, just as the Egyptian temples had. The grotesque figures which adorn them had a meaning for those who erected these buildings which is now lost, but it is only our ignorance of their meaning which makes us suppose them to be the result of architectural caprice. We might as well believe that the Egyptian hieroglyphs were the result of the extravagant fancies of their priests, for if we admit that the Zodiacs of Denderah and Esne are astrological representations, we must in common consistency look upon the Zodiacs of the Byzantine churches as having also a hidden meaning.

The title of the gospels, Εὐαγγελία, or "glad tidings," is usually supposed to refer to the redemption of mankind by the death of Christ from the penalties attached to the sin of Adam, but the "glad tidings" really were the near approach of the kingdom of God and of the end of the world, which, according to the Christian astrological system, was to begin at that period. The end of the world is announced in the most explicit terms in Matt. xxiv. and parallel passages, and also in the Epistles (Phil. iv. 4, 5, James v. 7–9). The early Christians expected with the greatest impatience the coming of the celestial Redeemer who was to place them on his right hand, and as war, famine, and pestilence were supposed to be the forerunners of the great catastrophe, they wished for and predicted nothing but calamities. This was why the Pagans looked upon them as men to be avoided, and why it was considered extremely unlucky to meet one (Lucian, Philopatris). Although it had been predicted by certain Alexandrian astrologers long before the Christian era that this event was near at hand (for the end of the world, the rising of the Sun of Judgment, and the general resurrection of the dead were Egyptian beliefs), little attention was paid to their predictions until the Roman Empire began to extend its iron sway over the whole of the East. The Jews, seeing their temple profaned, Jerusalem subjected to a foreign and intolerable yoke, and the impossibility of averting the ruin of their country, began then to think that nothing but a miracle could save the house of Jacob from ruin, and those who still had faith in the God of their fathers thought that their Messiah had come, and that the kingdom of God was really at hand. This was the origin of their contempt for worldly things. " The Christians despise every thing," says Lucian (De morte Peregrini); " they consider all goods as common to them all." It is so evident that the gospels are mistaken on this point that Christian writers have been forced to admit it (Baron. vol. I., p. 656; Mills, Proleg. to the New Testament, p. 146). This admission is, of course, fatal to the prophetic nature of the discourses on this subject attributed to Jesus.

In Mark xiii. 14 and Matt. xxiv. 15, there is an indication of the signs which are to precede the final catastrophe: "When ye shall see the abomination of desolation spoken of by Daniel the Prophet, standing where it ought not (let him that readeth understand), then let them that be in Judæa flee to the mountains," &c. (Mark xiii. 14). In Matthew this is altered into "stand in the holy place," ἐν ἱερῷ τόπῳ, thus agreeing with the LXX., καὶ ἐπὶ τὸ ἱερὸν βδέλυγμα τῶν ἐρημώσεων, but differing from the Hebrew, which is " *Upon the battlements* shall be the abominations of desolation." This refers to the conquest of Jerusalem by the Romans under Gabinius (B.C. 51), when the Jewish monarchy was declared to be at an end, and the idolatrous ensigns of the Romans stood upon the battlements; but this would not have suited the writer's purpose. It is very remarkable that in

Luke (xxi. 20) there is no allusion to Daniel's prophecy, and the passage contains only the trite announcement, "When ye shall see Jerusalem encompassed with armies, then know that the desolation thereof is nigh."

A clue to the date when these passages were written may be found in 1 Macc. i. 54, where an "abomination of desolation" is also spoken of, which consisted in the setting up of a statue of Jupiter on the altar at Jerusalem by Antiochus Epiphanes: "Now the fifteenth day of the month Casleu, in the hundred forty and fifth year, they set up the abomination of desolation upon the altar, and builded idol altars throughout the cities of Juda on every side." It is certain that no Pagan ruler profaned the temple again until the time of Adrian. Dio Cassius says that the emperor, after transforming Jerusalem into Ælia Capitolina, raised a temple to Jupiter on the site of that of Jehovah (Hist. Rom. l. lix. 12). Jerome (Ad Is. ii.) says, "Ubi quondam erat templum et religio Dei, ibi Hadriani statua est, et Jovis Idolium collocatum est." There was, therefore, a statue of Adrian as well as one of Jupiter. Moreover, Jerome (Ad Matt. xxiv. 15) says positively that that passage referred to the times of Adrian. In the terrible insurrection which followed, Bar-Chozeba, who received the name of Bar-Cochba, or the Son of the Star, and to whom the prophecy of Balaam, "There shall come a star of Jacob," and of Haggai, "I will shake the heavens and the earth," was applied, was looked upon as the Messiah; but after gaining wonderful victories over the Romans, he was finally defeated and killed.

One of the most singular episodes in the history of the Church is the recognition of a new gospel called the Evangelium Eternum by the Romish Church in the twelfth century. This gospel was first published (after having been preached for some time) by Joachim, the Abbot of Sora, in Calabria. It was called the Covenant of Peace, and was intended to unite the Mohammedan and all other sects. Nearly all the monkish orders, including the Dominicans and Franciscans, received it. This gospel was also called the Gospel of the Holy Ghost. It taught that the two imperfect ages, that of the Father and of the Son, represented by the Old and New Testaments, were past, and that that of the Holy Ghost, the perfect one, was at hand. Mosheim says that this gospel was not only preached, but actively supported by the Roman See for upwards of thirty years. In A.D. 1250 Gerhard, a Franciscan friar, published an introduction to this gospel, in which he prophesied the destruction of the Roman See, and said that the Gospel of Christ was to be abrogated in the year 1260. This referred to the Millennium which was expected by the Pope and the faithful in that year, but upon which Gerhard, instead of predicting the destruction of all things prior to the reign of Christ on earth, put a different construction. The Pope caused the book to be burned, and banished the author to his house in the country. The year 1260 having passed without the moon and stars falling from heaven, the "infallible" Pope found himself in the wrong, and the whole matter was quietly allowed to drop.

The idea of vicarious punishment is so plainly contrary to all those notions of justice which are universally received and acted upon, that nothing but the existence of a system in which the sacrifices of unoffending animals were believed to have been ordained by God to appease his wrath at human wickedness from time immemorial can have reconciled the human mind to so extravagant an absurdity. The Jewish institution of the Day of Atonement, on which occasion two goats were brought to the tabernacle, one of which was slain as a sin-offering, is universally considered to be typical of the sacrifice of Christ. The goat which bore the sins of the people was however not sacrificed, but was taken into the wilderness, where Azazel was supposed to be waiting for it. This institution is evidently contrary to the teaching of other parts of Scripture, as has already been shown, and is the result of the contact of the Jews with Pagan nations during the Captivity. It is after that event that the doctrine "every man shall be put to death for his own sin" (Deut. xxiv. 16) disappears to give place to the belief in Azazel, which is affirmed in Lev. xvi.

Azazel, whose name in its later sense signifies "defiance to God," and the first portion of whose name is identical with Typhon, who had his home in the desert, was the Evil Spirit, and corresponded to the Persian Ahriman. A Midrasch of the Talmud says on this subject, "The people offered sacrifices to demons, and to evil spirits, for they liked to offer sacrifices, and would not dispense with them. But the Lord said, 'Offer your sacrifices unto ME: then it will at any rate be to the only God that you will have sacrificed them.'"

Azazel is not mentioned in any canonical or apocryphal book of the Old Testament. In the book of Enoch he is represented to be one of the fallen angels, and the name also occurs in Jewish traditions, but he was never a subject of Jewish belief until popular superstition, aided by priestly influence, eventually made him such. The Mischna says that the liberality of Joshua ben Gamalia was such that he caused the two wooden tablets in the urn in the Temple, on one of which was the inscription "To Jehovah" and on the other "To Azazel," to be replaced by two golden ones (Mischna, Joma, III., 8).

It is evident from Deut. xvi. 16, a portion of the Pentateuch which is of pre-Captivity date, that the Day of Atonement was not then observed as a festival. The Feast of Unleavened Bread, the Feast of Weeks, and Feast of Tabernacles are enjoined in it; but not a word is said of that festival the neglect of which was punished by being cut off from the nation. The Jewish name for this day is Jom Kipour. The word Kipour, however, does not signify pardon. In the same book (Leviticus) in which the Day of Atonement is ordered to be kept, it is said (xii. 8) respecting the woman who brings a sacrifice of turtles, "vekipour aleah hakohen," "and the priest shall purify her," for it is evident that the priest has nothing to pardon in a woman who has been confined. The same word is applied (xiv. 20) to a leper who has been cleansed; and in v. 53, to a house which has been tainted by leprosy. It would evidently be absurd to say that the priest had pardoned a house, and the word really means "to purify." The Day of Atonement only preceded the Feast of Tabernacles by four days. It is inconceivable, therefore, that the people should not have been ordered in the above cited chapter of Deuteronomy to repair to Jerusalem four days before that festival if it had been then in existence. Another festival is omitted in Deuteronomy— that of the New Year, or the Rosch Haschanah. This festival is also connected with the Day of Atonement, for it is said (Treatise Rosch Haschanah, 1. I.), "God only judges men during the twelve days which elapse between New Year's Day and the Day of Atonement." R. Jachonon says, "Three books are open on the day of Rosch Haschanah, one inscribed with the names of the perfectly wicked, another with those of the perfectly just, and the third with those of persons who are neither the one nor the other. The just are immediately inscribed and sealed for life; the wicked for death; while the others remain in a state of suspense from New Year's Day till the Day of Atonement. If they repent, they are inscribed for life; if not, for death."

Satan, according to the Talmud (Treatise Jouma, Jom Hakipourim), has no power on the day of Jom Kipour, though he is all powerful on other days. The Talmud asks why? and gives the following highly satisfactory reply: "Rami, the son of Hami, has said, 'The numeral letters of Satan (written Sadan, as it was occasionally spelt) make three hundred and sixty-four days. During these three hundred and sixty-four days he has power to do evil, but on the three hundred and sixty-fifth, which is the day of Kipour, he has no power at all.'"

Origen (Contra Cels., l. II.) praises Jesus for having lived a Jew, attached to the letter as well as the spirit of the Mosaic teaching. It is evident, therefore, that he must have been supposed to teach one or other of the opposing doctrines which have been spoken of. We find, however, that in the very earliest period of Christianity two parties—known as that of Peter and James, and that of Paul—were in existence. In Galatians i. 19 Paul says that he saw James, the brother of Jesus. Clement (Const. Apost., i. 8, c. 35), or the author of that work, calls him "James, the brother of Christ according to the flesh, his servant as the son of God, Bishop of Jerusalem, ordained by Christ himself and by the apostles." Ignatius (Adscript. Epist. ad S. Joann., apost. et evang.) says, "James strongly resembled Jesus in his personal appearance, as well as in his mode of speaking, and his manner of living, so that one would have taken him for his twin brother"—"ac si ejusdem uteri frater esset gemellus." The only description of Christ's personal appearance extant is contained in the forged letter of Publius Lentulus, on which the pictorial representations of Christ are founded. It being a well-known custom for the provincial authorities to transmit information respecting anything of moment which occurred in their provinces to the Emperor and Senate at Rome, it was felt that inconvenient questions might be asked as to why the existence of Christ—who went about accompanied by twelve apostles, seventy disciples, and a number of women and other followers, and performing the most wonderful miracles—should not have been reported. Accordingly, the following letter, purporting to be written by Publius Lentulus, the supposed predecessor of Pontius Pilate, containing a description of his personal appearance, was forged, and first appeared in the History of Christ by Hieronymus Xavier, a cousin of the celebrated Francis Xavier. It is preceded in some parchment MSS. of the Gospels—which were written about 370 years ago, and are preserved in the library at Jena—by the following inscription :—

"In the time of Octavius Cæsar, Publius Lentulus, proconsul in the parts of Judea and the territory of Herod the king, is said to have written this letter to the Roman senate, which was afterwards found by Eutropius in the annals of the Romans."

It is not many years since the great libraries of England, France, and Germany pretended to possess authentic copies of this epistle, which is as follows :—

"Lentulus, Præfect of Jerusalem, to the Senate and People of Rome, greeting :

"At this time there hath appeared, and still lives, a man endued with great powers, whose name is Jesus Christ. Men say that he is a mighty prophet: his disciples call him the Son of God. He restores the dead to life, and heals the sick of all sorts of ailments and diseases. He is a man of stature proportionately tall, and his cast of countenance has a certain severity in it, so full of effect as to induce beholders to love and yet to fear him. His hair is of the colour of wine as far as to the bottom of his ears, without radiation, and straight, and from the lower part of his ears it is crooked down to his shoulders; at the top of his head it is parted *after the fashion of the Nazarites.* His forehead is smooth and clean, and his face without a pimple, adorned by a certain temperate redness : his countenance gentlemanlike and agreeable, his nose and mouth nothing amiss, his beard thick and divided into two bunches, of the same colour as his hair: his eyes blue and uncommonly bright. In reproving and rebuking he is formidable; in teaching and exhorting of a bland and agreeable tongue. He has a wonderful grace of person united with seriousness. No one hath ever seen him smile, but weeping indeed they have. He hath a lengthened stature of body; his hands are straight and turned up; his arms are delectable; in speaking, deliberate and slow, and sparing of his conversation—the most beautiful of countenances among the sons of men."

It is unfortunate that this portrait contradicts not only Tertullian, Clemens Alexandrinus, Origen, and Augustine, who all say that Jesus was rather ugly than handsome, and was unpleasant to look at, but also the supposed prophecy in Isa. liii. 14, " His visage was so marred more than any man, and his form more than the sons of men." Several other impositions of the same description as the letter of Publius Lentulus have been sanctioned by the Church. Towards the end of the sixth century it was proclaimed that a letter from Jesus Christ had fallen from heaven on the altar dedicated to him in St. Peter's at Rome, which ordered the faithful not to work on Sundays, or to prepare meals, or to travel on that day. Another letter was said to have been brought to Jerusalem by Michael the archangel, towards the end of the eighth century, in which the faithful were ordered to pay their tithes regularly, and to go to church with liberal offerings. The most important of these celestial letters was the one which Peter the Hermit carried about in 1096 to excite the Christians to join in the Crusades. Xavier also inserted in his History of Jesus Christ a pretended letter from Pontius Pilate to the Emperor—" A man hath appeared in these days in this country whom his disciples call God, and who performed sundry miracles. He has been seen by a great number of persons, *and went up to heaven alive*. His disciples are now doing many wonderful things, and say that he is God, and has brought the true way of salvation." This is on a par with the forged testimony to Christ fathered on Josephus by Eusebius, who has the insolence to exult as follows over it (H. E. i. 11): " When such testimony as this is transmitted to us by an historian who sprang from the Hebrews themselves, both respecting John the Baptist and our Saviour, what subterfuge can be left to prevent these from being considered as shameless deceivers, who have forged the acts against them?" In the above passage he has adroitly contrived to slip in the forged passage respecting Christ with the passage respecting John the Baptist which is in Josephus.

James, the brother of Jesus, who must certainly have followed the teaching of his brother and of the chief of the apostles (if Peter were such), was martyred according to St. Epiphanius (Hær. 28, 50, Antidic. No. 1, 7, 13) at the age of ninety-six years. He says, "He was still a virgin; he had never had his hair cut, had never bathed, had never eaten anything that had lived, and had always worn a single tunic." Hegesippus, who is quoted by Eusebius, says, "James, the brother of the Lord, surnamed the Just, was charged with the other apostles with the government of the Church. He was holy from his mother's womb; he never drank wine or anything that could impair his reason; he never ate flesh, never cut his hair, and never made use of baths or perfumes." He used, we are told, to enter the sanctuary alone, and was clothed not with wool but with linen. Entering in this fashion into the temple, he prayed on his knees, and was so assiduous in prayer that they became like the knees of a camel. The authorities are not agreed as to the time and circumstances of his martyrdom. Eusebius says that "the Scribes and Pharisees" put him on a wing of the temple, but that upon his testifying in favour of Jesus instead of against him, they began to stone him, and that one of them, a fuller, beat out his brains with the club with which he used to beat clothes. Dorotheus, Bishop of Tyrus, who wrote the Lives of the Apostles, says that he was killed by St. Paul; that the Jews set him on a pinnacle of the temple; and that Saul, who was afterwards called Paul, thrust him off, and while he yet breathed after his fall some one came with a fuller's club and despatched him.

The Nazarenes, Nazarites, or Ebionites, were nothing but reformed Jews; "Nec disciplina illa apud illos alia quam Judaismus reformatus, seu cum fide in Messiam seu Christum rite conjunctus" (Selden in Synedr. L. I. c. 5). Jerome (in Isa. v. 15) says that the Jews used to curse them three times a day in their synagogues, which they would certainly not have done if they had not considered them to be dissenting Jews. The Acts (iii. 1) represent Peter and John as praying at the appointed hours, and as observing all the precepts of the law. They also observed the Sabbath day, and so entirely cœnobitic was their mode of life that Lucian (De morte Peregrini, 13) represents them two centuries later as a sect of communists. He says that Peregrinus (who was a cynical philosopher) got himself initiated into the Christian mysteries when he was in Judæa. He adds, however, that "Peregrinus soon showed them that they were mere children in comparison with him, for he became not only a prophet, but the head of their sect. He interpreted their writings, and composed some himself, so that the Christians at last looked upon him not only as their legislator, but as a saint."

The Ebionites generally considered Jesus to be nothing but a man who was superior to other men (Iren. i. 26; Euseb. H. E. iii. 27; Epiph. Hæres. vii. n. 2; Theodor. Hæret. fab. ii. 1 and 2.) In the Acts (ii. 22) Peter calls him merely a man: "Jesus the Nazarite, a man approved of God among you by miracles and wonders and signs which God did by him in the midst of you." Origen (Contra Cels.) speaks of two sorts of Ebionites, to the earlier belief of whom such passages as Matt. v. 17, "Think not that I am come to destroy the law or the prophets: I am not come to destroy, but to fulfil," refer. The first Christians, as we have seen, were all circumcised, but when the Gospel began to spread among the Gentiles, who were unwilling to submit to this painful operation, the imposition of hands, fasting, and prayer, as practised by the Egyptians, were substituted in Christian initiation. The Christians at Rome were always looked upon as Jews. It is Jews whom Horace banters on their stupidity, and Martial on their fasts. They are spoken of in the same way by Ammianus Marcellinus and by Persius. If these authors had known that there were any differences between the Jews and that portion of them who called themselves Christians, they would not have been silent on the subject. Even in the Apocalypse Christians are spoken of as being Jews in reality, for it says (ii. 9), "I know the blasphemy of them which say they are Jews, and are not, but are the synagogue of Satan."

In Luke iv. 8 Jesus tells Satan "It is written, Thou shalt worship the Lord thy God, and HIM ONLY shalt thou serve." Jesus as an orthodox Jew could hold no other language on this subject. This was the distinctive dogma of Judaism, and the Talmud curiously illustrates this as follows: "A Rabbi once said, 'The daughter of Pharaoh (who adopted Moses) was an Israelite.' 'How can that be?' 'Because she believed in the unity of God.'" Spinoza has observed in one of his letters, "As to what is alleged by certain churches, that God has assumed our nature, I have expressly stated that I did not know what they meant, and, to speak plainly, I will confess that they appear to me to speak as absurdly as a person who should say that a circle has assumed the form of a square."

Jesus the Nazarite, Ἰησοῦς ὁ Ναζωραῖος, that name which our translators have so singularly avoided mentioning, is the term which conveys to us what the brother of James was really supposed to be. In Mark's gospel Jesus nowhere gives the title of Son of God to himself, and even in c. xiii. 32, which is a later insertion, and which is omitted in several MSS., he is only represented as an intermediate being between the angels and God. In Matthew, however, he is represented as using it very often. See c. x. 32, 33, xv. 13, xvi. 17, xviii. 10, 14, 19, xxv. 34, xxvi. 53, in none of the parallel passages to which is there any similar expression in Mark. Conf. also Matt. xii. 50, ὁ πατήρ μου ὁ ἐν οὐρανοῖς, with Mark iii. 35, ὁ Θεός: Matt. xx. 23, ἡτοίμασται ὑπὸ τοῦ πατρός μου, in which passage Mark has only ἡτοίμασται: Matt. xxiv. 36, εἰ μὴ ὁ πατήρ μου, while Mark xiii. 32 has only ὁ πατήρ; Matt. xxvi. 29, ἡ βασιλεία τοῦ πατρός μου, while Mark xiii. 25 has ἡ βασιλεία τοῦ Θεοῦ; and Matt. xxvi. 39, 42, πάτερ μου, while Mark xiv. 36 has Ἀββᾶ ὁ πατήρ.

Even where the term Son of God is used it has no such meaning as has been given to it in later times. In Matt. v. 9, 45 and Luke vi. 35 the "sons of God" are spoken of in a metaphorical sense: and in Hos. xi. 1, and Exod. iv. 22, Israel, and in 2 Sam. vii. 14, and Ps. ii. 7 (conf. Ps. lxxix. 27) kings, are called sons and first-born of God. Angels and men are also called sons of God in Gen. vii. 2, Job i. 6, ii. 1, Hos. i. 16, Luke xx. 36, and Gal. iii. 26. It was a generic title, like that of Christ, which is applied to the heathen king Cyrus in Isa. xlv. 1, and to the whole Jewish nation in Ps. cv. 15, רועו אל רוחי בטשירוי ולבביאי אל, Μὴ ἅψησθε τῶν Χριστῶν μου, καὶ ἐν τοῖς προφήταις μου μὴ πονηρεύεσθε (LXX.), "Touch not my Christs, and do my prophets no harm" (Conf. 1 Chron. xvi. 22). The following is the teaching of the Koran, which inculcates the primitive belief in the unity of God, on this subject. It must be remembered that the Mohammedans believe Jesus to have been the "Word of God," and the "Spirit of God," but that they do not believe that either he or their own prophet was the Son of God in the sense in which that term is generally used. They believe that Christ re-established the worship of the Unity of the Godhead (upon which Jewish theologians had begun to make inroads), and that the doctrine of the Trinity crept into Christianity after the time of the apostles. The Koran says:—

"After the prophets we sent Jesus to establish the Pentateuch; we gave him the Gospel, which is the torch of faith, and which sets a seal on the ancient writings. The Christians will be judged according to the Gospel. The faithful, the Jews, and the Sabæans, who believe in God, and who have led virtuous lives, shall not be tormented; the same will be the case with a small number of Christians; but those who say that the son of Mary is God are impious men. They who maintain the doctrine of the Trinity are blasphemous; there is but one God."

Sir W. Jones (Diss. VI. on the Persians) says, "The primeval religion of Iran, if we may rely on the authorities adduced by Monsani Fárú, was that which Newton calls the oldest (and it may justly be called the noblest) of all religions; a firm belief that 'one supreme God made the world by his power, and continually governed it by his providence; a pious fear, love, and adoration of him; and due reverence for parents and aged persons; a fraternal affection for the whole human species; and a compassionate tenderness even for the brute creation.'"

Augustine, who had been a Manichæan, makes Faustus admit the Triune God most clearly in the following words:— "Igitur nos Patris quidem Dei omnipotentis, et Christi Filii ejus, et Spiritûs Sancti, unum idemque sub triplici appellatur colimus numen." "We therefore worship one and the same Deity under the triple appellation of the Father, the Almighty God, and of Christ his Son, and of the Holy Ghost." The Manichæans therefore were Trinitarians, and the only *important* heretical opinion which they held was directed against the supremacy of the Holy See. It was not till the latter end of the second century that the word Trinity was made use of by Theophilus, the bishop of Antioch. Christianity had been introduced into France in A.D. 250, yet Gregory of Tours (Hist. l. IX., c. 39) attributes the introduction of this dogma into that country to St. Martin, who lived as late as the middle of the fourth century, for he says, "He it was who caused the first germs of our venerable faith to burst forth, for the ineffable mysteries of the Trinity were at that time known only to a very small number of persons."

In the Shepherd of Hermas, which was composed by Hermas, the brother of Pius I. (A.D. 142), and which was considered to be divinely inspired by Irenæus and Origen, it is laid down that the Son, anterior to the creation, was not Christ, but the Holy Spirit (III. Hermas, Simil. v. 54), that is a kind of archangel, but not the Holy Ghost. Jesus was the servant of this being, and owed it to his more than perfect obedience that he was invested with his dignity and prerogatives. In the Clementine Homilies, which belong to the middle of the second century, Jesus is represented as the original man who appeared as the prophet of the truth in Adam, Enoch, Noah, Abraham, Isaac, and Moses successively, and finally in Christ; and the author speaks in terms of reprobation of those who should apply to Jesus the name of God. Justin (Dial. cum Tryph.), and Lactantius (l. ii. c. 8 and l. iv. c. 16), who lived in the time of Constantine, looked upon Jesus as a person sent by God to teach men. They held that there was but one God, Jehovah; that the faithfulness of Christ was rewarded by God, who invested him with the dignity of Priest for ever, with the honours of Supreme King, and the power of Judge; that Jesus had preserved the name of God; and that it was by this name that the ancient Fathers of the Church agree in saying that he performed his miracles. The meaning of this is, that the word Jehovah when read with points is multiplied by the Jewish doctors into 12, 42, and 72 letters, of which words are composed that are thought to possess miraculous powers. By them Moses slew the Egyptians, Israel was preserved from the destroying angel of the wilderness, Elijah separated the waters of the river to open a passage for himself and Elisha, &c. In the Masonic mummeries the search after the sacred word pronounced by Jesus is still kept up. The Talmud will not admit that the ineffable word is Jehovah, or even Adonai, but says it is Sem Hamphorasch, from which the compilers of the French masonic rite called it Sem-Hame-Phoras, which signifies "the name well pronounced."

The General Epistle of James, which is omitted by Origen in his catalogue of the canonical writings, and admitted by Eusebius to be considered spurious, and which, by its being addressed to "the twelve tribes which are scattered abroad," seems to refer to the final dispersion of the Jews under Vespasian, can only be considered as embodying the views of that party which was opposed to the Pauline teaching. This it does in very express terms: "What doth it profit, my brethren, though a man say that he hath faith, and have not works? Can faith save him?" (ii. 14, see also vv. 17, 18). In the Judæo-Christian literature however, Peter, not James, is represented as the antagonist of Paul. There is an allusion to this antagonism in Gal. ii. 7, 8, but it is there represented merely as the result of the differences which arose respecting circumcision. It is generally supposed that in this epistle Paul speaks of having abode with Peter fifteen days (i. 18). But the original reading in the principal MSS. is "to acquaint myself with Cephas." This Cephas, whom Paul reprehended at Antioch (Gal. ii. 11), was, as appears from the catalogue of Dorotheus, one of the seventy disciples, and not one of the apostles, and was bishop of Caunia, in Caria. Yet in this epistle, which purports to be written by Paul himself, we have the extraordinary blunder made of calling him one of the apostles (v. 19). That he was not one of them is certain, and Eusebius distinctly states (H. E. I., 12) that he was not, for he says, "Clemens, in the fifth of his Hypotyposes, or Institutions, in which he also mentions Cephas, of whom Paul also says that he came to Antioch, and that he 'withstood him to his face'—says that one who had the same name with Peter was one of the seventy." Clemens Alexandrinus also says that Cephas and Peter were two distinct persons. The Recognitions, the three first chapters of which are believed to be the "Preaching of Peter" mentioned by Clemens Alexandrinus, Eusebius, and others, in a revised form, and the Clementine Homilies, from which the following discussion between Peter and Paul is taken, are therefore correct in representing the antagonism between Peter and Paul as being between rival teachers, not fellow-apostles, though we must suppose Peter to be a representative name in this instance, as Simon avowedly is for Paul.

Simon (that is, Paul) says to Peter (Clem. Homil. xvii. 13, 19), "Thou boastest that thou hast thoroughly understood thy Master, because thou hast seen and heard him, and thou hast added that no one can arrive at the same result by means of visions. I am going to demonstrate to thee that this is not the case. He who converses with any one is not on that account completely convinced by his words: he ought to ask himself whether he who appears to be a man does not lie. But a vision gives of itself to him who beholds it the assurance that it is divine."

Peter answers, "Thou pretendest that one attains to a better understanding of things by means of visions than by direct communication, and that thou art better informed than I am of all that regards Jesus. But a prophet, by the mere fact of his being a prophet, and of its being known beforehand that he proclaims the truth, may be believed in with confidence; he replies to all questions that may be put to him. On the contrary, he who puts faith in visions or in dreams, remains in uncertainty, for he does not know what he believes in; in fact, it might be a demon, or a deceiving spirit, who pretended to be that which he was not. In any case, the being with whom one holds communication in this manner does not remain longer than he wishes, and he disappears like a flash of lightning without giving to him who interrogates him the answer he wishes for. Besides, it is not possible during sleep to investigate the things we would wish to; the thoughts of the sleeper are not in his power."

After distinguishing between true and false visions, and showing by examples from Scripture that the first have no value, and that the second are only sent to the wicked, Peter continues:—

"If, therefore, our Jesus has appeared to thee also, and has spoken to thee in a vision, he has only manifested himself to thee by these visions, these dreams, or even by these external revelations, as he would to an adversary with whom he was justly angry. Can any one, however, be rendered capable of teaching by means of visions? If thou sayest that he can, how is it that the Master continued for a whole year in constant communication with people who were wide awake? Besides, why should we believe thee when thou pretendest that he manifested himself to thee? How can Jesus have appeared to thee, since thy opinions are contrary to his teaching? If, after having been visited and instructed by him for an hour, thou hast really been made an apostle, in that case do thou preach his doctrine, explain his word, love his apostles, and cease to contend against me, his faithful companion. But although I am the solid stone, and the foundation of the Church, thou hast openly resisted me. If thou wert not an enemy, wouldst thou have calumniated me, and despised my preaching? Wouldst thou have been the cause that some refuse to believe in me when I repeat what I have heard said by the Lord himself, and that I am blamed when I ought to be praised? In saying that I am to be blamed, thou accusest God Himself, who has revealed Jesus Christ to me, and thou attackest him who has called me happy on account of this revelation. If thou desirest to co-operate really and sincerely in the work of truth, begin by learning from us what he himself has taught us, and render us thy aid by becoming a disciple of the truth."

We are not told whether the hardened apostle of the Gentiles was converted by this address, but it is evident that the doctrine taught by him was considered to be diametrically opposed to that taught in the gospels. This, in fact, is plain from the first chapter of the Epistle to the Galatians, where Paul says expressly that the gospel he preached was " not after man "; and he adds, that he " neither received of man, nor was I taught it but by the revelation of Jesus Christ." He claims the priority for his own gospel (vv. 6-9), and is so confident that it is the true one that he would not go to Jerusalem to them that were apostles before him, nor confer with flesh and blood, but went straightway, $\varepsilon \vec{v} \theta \acute{\varepsilon} \omega s$, into Arabia (why we are not told), and never saw any of the apostles for three years after his conversion. He does not, however, speak of any miraculous conversions, such as those recorded in the Acts (for there are no fewer than three accounts of it in that work which differ from one another in many particulars), but merely says that it pleased God to reveal His Son in him.

The Acts contradict the Epistle to the Galatians in every possible respect. So far from not conferring with flesh and blood and retiring to Arabia, Paul remains certain days at Damascus "with the disciples" after his conversion (Acts ix. 19), and immediately ($\varepsilon \vec{v} \theta \acute{\varepsilon} \omega s$) preaches Christ in the synagogues, no doubt in accordance with the instructions he had received from the disciples, and when, "after many days," he comes to Jerusalem (v. 23), instead of seeing "James, the Lord's brother," we are told that all the disciples were afraid of him, and when they became reconciled to him, " he was with them coming in and going out of Jerusalem," and "disputed against the Grecians," though in Gal. i. 32 he says that he was "unknown by face unto the Churches of Judæa."

The Acts of the Apostles are the only authority for saying that Paul was a Roman citizen and a native of Tarsus. Lucian, however, in his dialogue entitled "Philopatris," speaks of him as a Galilæan with a bald forehead and a crooked nose, who pretended that he had been raised to the third heaven, and describes his followers as a set of tatterdemalions, almost naked, with fierce looks, and the gait of madmen, who predicted a thousand misfortunes to the empire, and cursed the Emperor. The Acts of Paul and Thecla, which were held to be genuine by the primitive Christians and many of the Fathers, and which Baronius and others consider as belonging to a very early period, confirm this description, for it is said in them that Onesiphorus and his family, having waited for him at Lystra, at length "saw a man coming (namely Paul), of a low stature, bald on the head, crooked though handsome legs, hollow-eyed, and who had a crooked nose." (Paul and Thecla, i. 7.) Similar descriptions of him are given in the epistles attributed to him, such as 2 Cor. v. 13; x. 10; xii. 7. The assertion of Lucian that he was a Galilæan is not only probable in itself, but is confirmed by a passage in Gittin 34[b], which speaks of the practice of having two names, one in Judah, and the other in Galilee (which for the Jews was a country which might be called semi-heathen, as so many foreigners lived in it), as well-known. These names, which Zenz (Namen der Juden S. 27 ff.) says were added to the Jewish names after the period of the Chaldæan and Persian supremacy, were always chosen on account of some resemblance in sound to the Jewish ones—as, for example, Jose-Jason. The same is the case in modern times—e.g., Mose-Moritz, Gerson-Gustav, &c.—the foreign name remaining unaltered.

It is impossible to reconcile the statements in the Acts respecting Paul's conversion, &c. with those in the Galatians, but the mode in which they arose will be explained presently. Paul's own statement (Gal. i. 10) is that, like Jeremiah, he was "separated" from his mother's womb, and having thus been specially selected for some great purpose, it pleased God to reveal His Son in him. As Peter is represented as observing in the Clementine Homilies, we have only Paul's word for this "revelation" having been made to him; but as not only in this passage, but also in 2 Cor. xii. 1, he speaks of visions and revelations, ὀπτασίας καὶ ἀποκαλύψεις, as having been made to him, it may be as well to consider what meaning was really attached to these words by educated men.

The highest aim of man was held to be the knowledge of God—that is, of truth—and especially of truth concerning God. The Valentinians called initiation "light." The enjoyment of this light was the most valuable result of epopty (ἐποπτεία). Psellus (Ad Orac. Zoroast.) says that epopty was attained when the initiated person was allowed to behold the Divine Light. One of the precepts given by Zoroaster to the Archimagi was to obtain manifestations of the "Divine glory." Porphyry says that the Gnostics boasted that they had revelations or Apocalypses from Zoroaster. Er of Pamphylia, whom Plato speaks of in his Republic, and to whom the destiny of souls after death was revealed, is, according to some, no other than Zoroaster himself. Clemens Alexandrinus (Protrept. p. 74), imitating the language of a person who had been initiated into the mysteries of Bacchus, and inviting this initiated person, whom he calls a blind man, like Tiresias, to come and enjoy the vision of Christ which is about to shine before his eyes with more dazzling brightness than the sun, exclaims, " O truly holy mysteries! O pure light! By the light of the torch of the torch-bearer the heavens and the Deity appear to me in this epopty. I am initiated; I have become holy." "The Lord," continues Clemens, " acts as hierophant in these mysteries. He marks with his seal the initiated person whom he has illumined with his light, and to reward his faith he recommends him to his Father as a precious treasure which he is to keep for ever. These are my mysteries and my orgies. Become initiated, and you will form with the angels the retinue of that God who has never been born, and who will never die—the only true God." The initiated person who had attained to the epopty was a *seer*—that is, a person who sees or beholds. Eusebius (Præp. Evang.) explains the word Heber (Hebrew) to mean "him who passes beyond," and says that it was given to those whose religious philosophy or knowledge passed beyond the limits of the visible world, and obtained access into the spiritual world, and into the Divine Light in which the invisible and hidden beings reside. An Israelite also was a *seer* (Isid. Orig., Firm. de Error. Prof. Rel.) Philo says that Israel is a Chaldee word, and signifies "the seeing nation." Those who were initiated into the higher mysteries were therefore called epopts, or seers, or beholders, while those who had only been admitted to the lesser mysteries were called "initiated," like the Catechumens of Christian initiation. A period varying from one to five years was required to elapse between the initiatory ceremony and the epopty.

Religion and philosophy united with abstinence were held to free the soul from the corruptions of matter, and to render it fit to hold intercourse with spiritual beings, for it was said that that which was impure must not come into contact with that which was pure. In proportion as it was necessary that the soul should be adorned by knowledge and by virtue so as to be able to unite itself with immortal beings, it was also necessary that the Ochema or luminous medium should be pure, and detached from matter, so that it might hold communication with ethereal beings. Augustine (De Civ. Dei, l. x. c. 9) follows Porphyry in speaking of the effect produced upon what he terms the animal portion of the soul by the theurgic operations called teletes, which rendered it fit to communicate with spirits and with angels, and to become capable of beholding the gods.

It is evident from Paul's reference to the Sibyl that he was well acquainted with the prevalent systems, and it has been thought that he was an epopt in the Christian mysteries, which were founded on the Pagan ones. The words in the epistle, however, do not imply anything more than an ordinary conversion, probably brought about by the study of the same books which converted Constantine, but the following considerations seem to show that the practice of assigning to persons of celebrity books they had never written, which was very common in ancient times, as Origen (Contra Cels.) informs us, and which was frequently done without waiting for the death of the supposed author, has been adopted with respect to the Pauline epistles. This was especially the practice among the Jews, who have composed books which they attribute to almost all the persons in Genesis. Thus we have a Gospel of Eve, a Testament of Adam, a book by Seth on the star which is to announce the coming of the Messiah, prophecies by Enoch and Ham, a

Testament of Noah, Psalms by Melchizedek and Isaac, a Prayer by Joseph, &c. In early Christian times, when any particular doctrine was wished to be established, books were fabricated which, under the imposing names of Peter, Matthew, Dionysius the Areopagite, &c., came to be regarded as of authority.

Paul, we are told, was brought up at the feet of Gamaliel (Acts xxii. 3), and was taught according to the perfect manner of the law of the fathers; and in c. xxvii. 5 he is represented as saying himself that "after the most straitest sect of our religion I lived a Pharisee." Yet out of the eighty-four quotations from the Old Testament in the Pauline epistles thirty-four are taken from the LXX., thirty-six differ from it to some extent, and ten differ from it to a considerable extent. This, however, was the version which, as we have seen, the orthodox Jews had the greatest horror of; and they used to call out on the day of mourning for it, "The king compelled me to write the law in Greek; ploughing the field on my back, they made long furrows." It is evident that in the epistles as in the gospels these versions are used to suit the purpose of the writer. Thus, in Rom. ix. 17 the Hebrew text is followed in "Even for this purpose have I raised thee up;" the LXX. having "Ενεκεν τούτου διετηρήθης, "On this account hast thou been preserved." In 1 Cor. x. 8 the number of Israelites who fell is put at twenty-three thousand, thus differing from both the Hebrew and the LXX., which both have twenty-four thousand. In Rom. xi. 8 the passage referred to (Isaiah xxix. 10) has been completely altered, while the quotation from Psalm lxix. in the next verse is taken partly from the LXX. and partly from the Hebrew. Gal. iii. 11, "The just shall live by faith," is in the LXX. Ὁ δὲ δίκαιος ἐκ πίστεώς μου ζήσεται, "But the just shall live by *my* faith." The next quotation, however (v. 13), is from the LXX., because the words ἐπὶ ξύλου, "on a tree," are not in the Hebrew version.

In Gal. iii. 17 the statement in the LXX. version of Exod. xii., 40, that the children of Israel dwelt four hundred and thirty years in Canaan and Egypt, is adopted. This does not agree with Gen. xv. 13, in which God tells them that the period during which they should be afflicted in a foreign land is four hundred years, which again is itself contradicted by the subsequent history; for as Joseph was only thirty-nine years old when the descent into Egypt took place, the Israelites must have been protected by the Pharaohs for at least seventy years of that period, and probably much longer, thus reducing the actual period of servitude to about three hundred years. The LXX. in endeavouring to reconcile the contradictions and incongruities in the narrative have reduced it to 215 years, thus contradicting God's own words; but it is evident from the narrative in Exodus that the oppression of the Israelites is supposed to have begun not long before the birth of Moses, who was eighty years of age at the time of the Exodus. This would make the total period of oppression to be some hundred years or so, and makes all the statements in both versions hopelessly wrong. When it is added that Moses is the grandson of Levi (who accompanied Jacob to Egypt) through his mother Jochebed, it becomes evident that we have here to do with an unhistorical statement which the "inspired" apostle nevertheless adopts as true.

The Acts of the Apostles had not gained general acceptance as late as A.D. 407; for Chrysostom, who was Bishop of Constantinople at that time, says in his first homily on the title and beginning of this work, "To many this book is unknown; by others it is despised, because it is clear and easy." The first of his homilies upon the whole book begins with the following sentence:—" By many this book is not at all known, neither the book itself, nor who wrote it and put it together." This book, the title of which in the Codex Sinaiticus is simply "Acts," has been shown by modern critics—such as Baur, Schwegler, and Zeller—to be the work of a Pauline Christian, who, in order to conciliate the two hostile Christian parties, endeavoured to make Paul resemble Peter and Peter resemble Paul as much as possible. This is shown by the contents of the book. Peter, the apostle of the Circumcision, is represented in it as inaugurating the mission to the Gentiles, and as embracing the most liberal Pauline views. He even speaks of faith and grace (Acts xv. 7, 11), and says that circumcision was a yoke too hard to be borne. The Clementine Homilies, on the contrary, say (ii. 17)—" If Peter travels all over the world, it is in pursuit of his rival, represented by Simon: if he preaches the doctrine of Jesus, it is by combating in all his discourses the false gospel of the impostor." In another place it is said, "If he (Peter) calls upon the Pagans to take part in the Messianic kingdom, it is by imposing upon them the observances to which Judaism subjects its proselytes, and by proclaiming with the true prophet that the law will last for ever." Baur has well described the two parties as follows :—" According to the Judæo-Christians, it was necessary to be a Jew first, and then a Christian; according to Paul, it was necessary to renounce Judaism in order to become a Christian."

CHAPTER VIII.

WITH the final victory of Adrian over Barchocab and his followers in A.D. 135, during whose revolt the Judæo-Christians had established themselves at Pella, and with the appointment of uncircumcised bishops at Jerusalem, the Pauline teaching gained the ascendant; and those who held the opposite opinions retired to Peræa, and established themselves there. Although the term Pauline is applied to the doctrines taught in the Epistles, it is a mistake to suppose that they are of Christian origin. Philo taught before any Christian work was in existence that not even our best works are acceptable to God; but that faith in a Redeemer, who is the Word, and who is also a ransom for sin, is the first requisite, the next being repentance through faith, and good works as the result of that repentance. The priest of Mithra, as Tertullian (De præscript. Hær., l. xl.) informs us, used to promise the initiated person whom he had dipped in the water that all the stains of guilt would be effaced by that act. Socrates has described the unjust man who considers himself safe against the punishments of Tartarus, because he knows how to escape from them by means of initiation. Plutarch, in his answer to the Epicureans, also says that true believers know that they can be delivered from the pains of hell by lustrations and initiations, by means of which men attain to the abodes of happiness. Not only private individuals, but whole towns were allowed to offer expiatory sacrifices; and the priests used to beg at the doors of the great and the rich, and engage to deliver them from the wrath of the gods by means of certain sacrifices and enchantments. Theophrastus (Caract.) describes one of these superstitious people, who, he says, never fails to go every month to the Orpheotelestai to get purified, taking his wife and children with him.

Most of the Fathers represent the death of Christ as a

ransom paid to the devil, who is our legitimate owner, and to whom Christ, in order to get men away from him, is obliged to pay an equivalent. Augustine says, "Parvulus trahit peccatum originale ab Adam," and "Deus prædestinat ad æternam mortem propter originale peccatum." Jerome enquires, "Quare infantuli baptizantur?" and answers, "Ut eis peccata dimittantur." In another place Augustine says, "Non est ulli ullus medius locus ut possit esse nisi cum diabolo qui non est cum Christo," because "*certum est* apud orthodoxos, pueros decedentes in originali peccato sine baptismo descendere in locum quemdam infernum et subterraneum qui nominatur Limbus"—all little children who are not baptized go to limbo. In his letter to Jerome he says that even newborn infants cannot escape eternal damnation except by being baptized. Yet in this same letter he asks continually why God should inflict so dreadful a calamity upon innocent children—"Tantum ergo malorum, quæ fiant in parvulis, causa dicatur." He concludes, however (De peccatorum meritis et remiss.), that they would not be damned if they had not sinned: "Non autem damnari possent si peccatum ubique non haberent;" and he says in this same treatise that it is impossible for God to damn anyone unjustly: "Nec Divino judicio injuste posse aliquem damnari." He ends by saying that as it is impossible they can have sinned before they attained the age of reason, they must have inherited the sin of Adam *by the mere fact of their being born*, and that it is this sin of Adam which renders the whole human race liable to damnation, and explains this statement by saying that all the souls of men have been, as he expresses it, one in Adam—"Omnes illæ unus homo fuerunt"—and that they are all derived from the sinful substance of his soul, like branches which grow from a single diseased stem, sin being transmitted to children by the vice of their birth, in the same way as the sap is transmitted from the trunk into all the branches of a tree!

In A.D. 418 the General Council of Africa excommunicated all who refused to believe that grace is neither an effect of divine mercy which grants us pardon for our sins, nor a celestial inspiration which makes us love what is good, nor something sent us from on high to aid us to act rightly; but an act of God which is really performed within us, in consequence of which we do good, or rather which renders it impossible for us not to do good. This is somewhat different from Prov. xvii. 15: "He that justifieth the wicked and he that condemneth the just, even they are both an abomination unto the Lord"; but it is in accordance with the teaching of Philo, who says (De Morte Abeli et Caini): "The just man is the expiatory victim of the wicked man." Philo has even invested his goddess, Grace, with personal existence. "Grace," he says, "is that celestial virgin who serves as mediatrix between God and the soul—between God who offers and the soul which receives. All the written law is but a symbol of grace." He speaks of the Word as the "image of God," and "the shepherd of his holy flock." In his treatise on Creation he speaks of the Word as superior to the angels and to all created beings, and says that man stands in need of redemption, and that the soul must obtain its freedom by a ransom and price of redemption being given for it. It pleased God, therefore, to appoint his Logos to be a medium or intercessor between the Creator and the created, and he is accordingly the advocate for all mortals. The Word of God, being the image of God, is seated immediately next to the one God, without any interval of separation. Philo calls the Word the High Priest, the Holy Word, the firstborn of God. He also lays it down (De Serm.) that "we must by no means think that we of ourselves are able without the grace of God to wash and cleanse our mortal frame from the stains with which it abounds."

The opposition between the two schools of doctrine is shown plainly in the fact that while in the Gospels Jesus is never represented as using the word "sacrifice" with reference to either his life or his death, this word is so used in the Epistles repeatedly. It is impossible, however, to find language directed more plainly against the ideas of sacrifice and atonement than is to be found in the very prophets who are supposed to have predicted the coming of the Messiah. Thus Micah (vi..7, 8) says, "Will the Lord be pleased with thousands of rams or with thousands of rivers of oil? Shall I give my firstborn for my transgression, the fruit of my body for the sin of my soul? He hath shewed thee, O man, what is good, and what doth the Lord require of thee but to do justly, to have mercy, and to walk humbly with thy God?"

Unfortunately the Reformation has brought the Pauline doctrines into greater prominence than before. Luther declared against Melancthon that good works were mortal sins, and this declaration was approved by the Diet of Worms. Calvin declared that God pays no attention to good works; and the Church of England lays it down in her Articles of Faith that works done before the grace of Christ are not only not pleasant to God, but have the nature of sin. In A.D. 1618 the Calvinist synod went so far as to say that morality had nothing to do with justification; and this teaching culminates in the Westminster Confession of Faith, in which it is said that God has chosen those of mankind that are predestinated unto life before the foundation of the world was laid, "*without any foresight of faith or good works, or perseverance in either of them,*" and that the rest of mankind God was pleased "to pass by, and *to ordain them to dishonour and wrath* for their sins, to the praise of his glorious justice."

These doctrines would never have prevailed had there not been something in them which was acceptable to the mass of mankind. Nature has implanted in the heart of man principles which he cannot deviate from without feeling remorse and pain, but these natural feelings are obliterated when plenary absolution is held forth as the result of repentance, or of confession to a priest. So dangerous to morality were these doctrines considered to be by those who had the control over the ancient initiations that certain crimes were declared to be incapable of expiation. Nero (Sueton. Vit. Neron., c. 34) dared not present himself at the Temple of Eleusis; his crimes were too great to allow him even to enter it. The Pythoness of Delphi also heaped reproaches on him, and compared him to Orestes the matricide. This, however, was too much for Nero. He caused several persons to be put to death, and let their blood flow into the opening of the sacred cave, after which he had it filled up. The blood-stained Constantine also vainly sought for absolution from the Pagan priests; and David, the man after God's own heart, would probably have sought for it with just as little success. The expiatory ceremonies in Greece are, however, of comparatively recent date, for their institution is recorded in the marbles of Paros (Marsham, Chronic. Sæcul., ii.).

This system was adopted by the Christians. Mosheim, speaking of the Church in the second century, says, "It is here to be attentively observed that the form used in the exclusion of heinous offenders from the society of Christians was at first extremely simple, but was, however, imperceptibly altered, enlarged by the addition of a vast multitude of rites, and new modelled according to the discipline used in the ancient mysteries." In another place he says, "The profound respect that was paid to the Greek and Roman mysteries, and the extraordinary sanctity that was attributed to them, induced the Christians (of the second century) to give their religion a mystic air, in order to put it upon an equal footing in point of dignity with that of the Pagans. For this purpose they gave the name of mysteries to the institutions of the Gospel, and decorated particularly the holy sacrament with that solemn title. They used in that sacred institution, as also in that of baptism, several of the terms employed in the heathen mysteries, and proceeded so far at length as even to adopt some of the rites and ceremonies of which those renowned mysteries consisted."

Photius quotes some fragments of John Stobœus (who lived in the fifth century), in which, speaking of initiation into the Christian mysteries, he represents it as being the end of the profane life, and the death of vice. The neophyte who had reached the end of the profane life found at the gates of initiation nothing but fear, and obstacles which stood in the way of his painful and laborious progress; but these toils once endured, celestial light shone before him; he beheld around him an enchanting prospect, and beautiful scenery; choirs, accompanied by melodious instruments, struck pleasingly on his ears; sacred visions appeared to him; he became initiated, he became one of the elect by his admission; no longer the slave of fear, he was crowned, and triumphed. Then he was admitted to the sublime knowledge of the sacred doctrines (that is, of the reproduction of beings, which was allegorically taught) of the Resurrection.

Minutius Felix says, "You observe that the philosophers have maintained precisely the same things as we Christians, but this is not on account of our having copied from them, but because they, from the divine teaching of the prophets, have imitated the shadow of truth interpolated; thus the more illustrious of their wise men, Pythagoras first, and especially Plato, with a corrupted and half-faith, have handed down the doctrine of regeneration." Tertullian (Apolog. c. 46, 47) calls the Pagan philosophers the thieves, the interpolators, and adulterators of divine truth, and says that " from a design of curiosity they put our doctrines in their works, not sufficiently believing them to be divine to be restrained from interpolating them, and that they mixed that which was uncertain with that which they found certain." Theodoret (Therap. l. II.) says that Plato purposely mixed muddy and earthy filth with the pure fountain from which he drew the arguments of his theology. Eusebius says that the fable of Phaeton falling from the chariot of his father the Sun was a wicked corruption of the account in 2 Kings ii. of Elijah being taken up to heaven, the ancients being so ignorant as to confound Elias with Helios (the sun)! Justin (Apol. 2) explains the matter in a most satisfactory manner. He says that " it having reached the Devil's ears that the prophets had foretold that Christ would come for the purpose of tormenting the wicked in fire, he set the heathen poets to bring forward a great many who should be called (and were called) sons of Jove: the devil laying his scheme in this to get them to imagine that the true history of Christ was of the same character as those prodigious fables and poetic stories."

These and similar passages are attempted refutations of the charges brought by the Pagans against the Christians, such as that attributed to Cæcilius by Minutius Felix in his Octavius (circa A.D. 211): "All these figments of crack-brained belief, and silly solaces, played off in the sweetness of song by deceitful poets, have been shamefully dressed up again by you over credulous creatures, and applied to your own God." Porphyry charged Origen with being a Pagan, brought up in the school of the Gentiles, who in order to serve his own ambitious purposes had contrived to turn the whole Pagan system into the new-fangled Christian theology. Celsus, in his treatise on the True Logos, charges the Christians with recoining the ancient doctrine of the Logos. The Emperor Julian (Apud Cyrill. l. II.) tells them, " If any one should wish to know the truth with respect to you Christians, he will find your impiety to be made up partly of the Jewish audacity, and partly of the indifference and confusion of the Gentiles, and that ye have put together, not the best, but the worst characteristics of them both."

Middleton says in his Free Inquiry, "In the performance of their miracles the primitive Christians were always charged with fraud and imposture by their adversaries. Lucian tells us that when any crafty juggler, expert in his trade, and who knew how to make a right use of things, went over to the Christians, he was sure to grow rich immediately by making a prey of their simplicity; and Celsus represents all the Christian wonder-workers as mere vagabonds and common cheats, who rambled about to play their tricks at fairs and markets, not in the circles of the wiser and better sort (for among such they never ventured to appear), but whenever they observed a set of raw young fellows, slaves or fools, there they took care to intrude themselves and to display their arts.

Some idea of the means by which Christianity was propagated may be formed from the following oration delivered by Julius Firmicius Maternus to the Emperors Constantius and Constans, the sons and successors of Constantine the Great, calling upon them to seize all the property of the Pagan priesthood which their father had spared: " Take away, take away, in perfect security, O most holy emperors, take away all the ornaments of their temples. Let the fire of the mint, or the flames of the mines, melt down their gods. Seize upon all their wealthy endowments, and turn them to your own use and property. And, O most sacred emperors, it is absolutely necessary for you to revenge and punish this evil. You are commanded by the law of the Most High God to persecute all sorts of idolatry with the utmost severity: hear and commend to your own sacred understandings what God himself commands. He commands you not to spare your son, or your brother; he bids you plunge the avenging knife even into the heart of the wife that sleeps in your bosom; to persecute your dearest friend with a sublime severity, and to arm your whole people against these sacrilegious Pagans, *and tear them limb from limb.* Yea! even whole cities, if you should find this guilt in them, must be cut off. O most holy emperors! God promises you the reward of his mercy upon condition of your thus acting. Do therefore what he commands—complete what he prescribes." This charitable recommendation was carried out in part by Gratian, who seized all the lands and endowments which had been set apart to maintain the priests and sacrifices of Paganism, and appropriated them to his own use. In the reigns of Valentinian and Theodosius any one who apostatised from Christianity was rendered incapable of bequeathing property by will, and the profession of Paganism was finally suppressed by condemning all who professed it to death, and thousands of Pagan martyrs underwent that penalty. Theodosius carried out the advice of Julius Firmicius to the letter by putting the whole of the heterodox citizens of Thessalonica to the sword, and utterly destroying everything that breathed. On the other hand, Symmachus, a Pagan high priest, ventured to present the following petition, for which he was condemned by Theodosius to go into exile :—

"Does not the religion of the Romans come under the protection of the Roman laws? By what name shall we call an alienation of rights which no laws or circumstances of things ever justified? Freed men receive legacies, nor are even slaves deprived of the privilege of receiving what is left to them by will; it is only the noble vestals, and the attendants on the sacred rites upon which the public welfare depends, who are deprived of the privilege of receiving estates legally bequeathed to them. The Treasury detains the lands which were given to the vestals and their officers by our dying progenitors. Do but consult your own generous minds, and you will not think that those things belong to the public which you have already appropriated to the use of others. If length of time be of weight in matters of religion, surely we ought to preserve that faith which has subsisted for so many ages, and to follow our parents, who have so happily followed theirs. We ask for no other state of religion than that which secured the empire to your blessed father, and gave him the happiness of a legitimate issue to succeed him. That blessed prince now looks down from heaven, and beholds the tears of the priests, and considers the breach of their privileges as a reflection on himself."

In their anxiety to prove that everything was of Jewish or Christian origin, the Fathers have endeavoured to show that Pythagoras was a Jew, and was a disciple of Ezekiel, and that he, as well as Plato and others, had learned the doctrine of the true God from the Jews!

The Jews themselves said that Pythagoras had travelled in Judæa, and that he had been initiated into the sect of the Essenes. Ammonius, Jamblichus, and Plotinus consider the birth of Pythagoras to have been supernatural, and compare it to that of Jesus. They say that he was the son of Apollo; that an oracle had proclaimed his nativity; that the soul of God had come down to earth to give him life; that he was the Mediator between God and man; that he knew what passed in the Universe; that he commanded the elements, preached the loftiest virtue to men, and was at last slain like Jesus by ferocious assassins. Constantine (Orat. c. 9) in his oration to the clergy, says, with a marvellous disregard of chronology, that Pythagoras was an impostor, for " he delivered those things which the prophets had foretold to the Romans as if God had particularly revealed them to him." Lactantius however (Divin. Inst., l. IV., c. 2) admits that all these statements are erroneous, for he expresses his wonder " that when Pythagoras, and afterwards Plato, incited by the love of seeking truth, had travelled as far as to the Egyptians, the Magi, and the Persians, to learn the rites and ceremonies of those nations, they should never have consulted the Jews, with whom alone the true wisdom was to be found, and to whom they might have gone more readily."

In 1682 the Carmelites of Beziers maintained in public theses that Pythagoras had been a monk and a member of their order. The fact is, all orders of this description were more or less connected. The historian of the Carmelites (Hist. Carmel. Ordin., I., 4) calls the Druids "the holy Druids, the sons of Elias, our brothers and predecessors." In order to understand the nature of this connection we must remember that Pythagoras had been initiated in Egypt, and that the doctrine of one God in the double personality of the Father and the Son was taught both at Thebes and Memphis. On a pillar of the XIXth dynasty at Berlin the Supreme Being is called " God making himself God, existing by himself, the double being, the Begetter from the beginning." The same idea is expressed respecting Ammon on a Theban papyrus: "The double Being, Begotten from the beginning, God making himself God, begetting himself." The special action attributed to the Son did not destroy the Unity. It is in this sense that this god is called Ua en Ua, the one of one, πρῶτος τοῦ πρώτου Θεοῦ. which is the mode in which the second Divine Essence is expressed. This second God is the visible manifestation of the Invisible God. Sometimes this character is attributed to the sun, which creates living beings as the Father creates the ideal essences. On another pillar in the Berlin Museum, the sun is called " the firstborn, the Son of God, the Word." On one of the walls of the temple at Philæ and on the door of the temple of Medinet Aboo is written " It is the sun who has made all that exists, and without him nothing has ever been made." The third god in the Hermetic books is man, who is analogous to Osiris, who is sometimes taken as the ideal type of humanity. In the Funeral Ritual the soul which presents itself to be judged is called " Osiris such a one."

Orpheus, who was one of the first sages who was allowed to borrow the principles of morals and theology from Egypt, says in his verses on the Orgyas (mysteries), " Consider the Λόγος or Divine Word : never cease to contemplate it. Direct your heart and mind in the right way, and look up to the Ruler of the Universe, who alone is immortal, and who alone has engendered from himself. All things proceed from Him alone, and He dwells in them. Invisible to all mortals, He nevertheless sees all that goes on." Eusebius (Præp. Ev., l. xiii. 12) has handed down to us entire the hymn of Orpheus called the 'Palinode,' of which Justin, Clemens Alexandrinus, Cyril, the patriarch of Alexandria, and Theodoret have quoted certain portions. In this hymn Orpheus declares the unity of God, a dogma which is also recognised in the commencement of the invocation of the funeral ritual, which has been translated by Lepsius, and which the Egyptians used to deposit in the sarcophagi of all who died. When the soul had come into the presence of the supreme tribunal, where God himself sits surrounded by the forty-two celestial judges, it expresses itself in the following manner :—

" O great God ! Lord of Truth ! I have come to thee, O Lord ! I have come myself to receive Thy favour. I know Thee. I know Thy name. I know the names of the forty-two deities who are seated with Thee at the tribunal of the two truths, which is instituted for the punishment of the wicked, who were brought up at a distance from it, on the day when an account must be given of all words that have been uttered in the presence of the good, the purified being, ruler of hearts, Lord of truth—that is Thy name ! "

The metaphysical triad belonged to the later period of the

teaching of Orpheus, and to the worshippers of light under the name of Phanes. Then the dogma of the Λόγος, or the Νοῦς, its incarnation, death and resurrection, or the transfiguration of its union with matter, of its dispersion into the visible world, and of its return to the original Unity was taught, and all this theory related to the origin of the soul, and its destiny, that is, to the great aim of the mysteries. The philosophers, says Eusebius (Præp. Ev., l. III. c. 9), compared the Universe to a great man, and man himself to a small Universe. They saw in both the Universe and man a single being, but they thought that, without injury to the unity of that being, they might draw a distinction between the principle of intellect and the principle of life and motion, and they held that in this respect man exactly resembled the Universe, or rather that man is only endowed with life and intelligence because the Universe, of which he forms a portion, and out of which he was made, is itself endowed with these qualities. Proclus (Comm. in Tim., l. I., c. 123) says, "The elements which enter into the composition of our bodies form a portion of those which exist in the universe on a large scale. It would be very strange if all that is lowest in our nature should exist in the universe, and what is most excellent and divine in it should not be found still more universally therein, and that as there is a universal elementary matter, there should not also be a universal intellect and soul."

Virgil (Æn. vi.) represents Anchises as teaching this doctrine of a universal spiritus, or life-giving breath, to which is joined a soul which regulates its movements, and maintains the harmony of the immense body throughout which it is spread. It was from this intellectual fire, as Orpheus declared it to be, that those souls endowed with reason had emanated, which at death returned to that other principle of fire endowed with reason of which the stars are formed. Eusebius (Præp. Ev., l. ix. c. 3) tells us that the Essenes among the Jews attributed this same origin to our souls, which they held to be an emanation from the ethereal fire. The spiritus was God, for the spiritus, or universal soul, was spoken of as God diffused throughout nature (Manil. l. ii.).

The question which lies at the bottom of all speculations on the great question of man's destiny here and hereafter, and without which theology would be a mere mass of arid speculations, the origin of evil, did not fail to engage the attention of the philosophers. Maximus of Tyre (Orat. xxv.) ridicules Alexander, who went to consult the oracle of Jupiter Ammon to know where the sources of the Nile were situated, and of what description they were. "Was nothing else wanting to complete the happiness of that king but to comprehend a natural phenomenon which was of so little consequence? He should have asked Jupiter a question, the answer to which would have interested the whole human race. He need not, however, have inquired whence blessings come. There is no occasion to interrogate the gods on that subject. The cause of them cannot be unknown, and is patent to all mortals. The cause is the Father and the Creator of all things. It is he who has instituted in the heavens that order which we see prevail there; it is he who holds the reins of the sun and the moon; who directs the course of the stars; and who appoints to the brilliant chorus of the stars the movements they are to go through. It is he who has divided the seasons, who rules the winds, who has brought the seas together, and laid the foundations of the earth; who makes the rivers flow, and gives fertility to plants and animals. It is that pure and immortal Spirit which can undergo no change, and which, with incredible swiftness, and in the twinkling of an eye ($\tau\acute{a}\chi\epsilon\iota$, $\dot{\omega}s$ $\pi\rho o\sigma\beta o\lambda\hat{\eta}$ $\ddot{o}\psi\epsilon\omega s$), sets in motion, gives light to, and adorns all nature. I cannot explain how it brings so many marvels to pass, but Homer intimates it in these words, 'He spake, and the black-eyed daughter of Saturn (Nature) obeyed immediately.' At the first signal that Jupiter gave, the earth and all that it produces were formed; the sea and all that it contains in its abysses; the air and all that it contains; the heavens and all that moves therein. The will of Jupiter brought all these into existence in a moment. On this subject I require no oracle. I believe Homer on the subject; I put faith in Plato; I pity Epicurus. But if I turn to contemplate evil I cannot help asking, what can be its origin? Did it come from Ethiopia with the plague, or from Babylon with Xerxes, or from Macedonia with Philip? For most assuredly it does not come from heaven. Envy is banished for ever from that abode of happiness. This is where I stand in need of an oracle? Let us inquire of the gods."

Arnobius (Adv. Gent. l. II.) suggests that God must be

the cause of evil, because nothing can happen without his permission. This appears to him to be incontestable, yet so dreadful are the consequences of this belief that he dares not adopt it. "Consider well what you are saying," he says as if replying to himself, "and let us take good care that we do not dishonour the majesty of the supreme God and Ruler while thinking to do him honour. Do ye ask why? Because if all things are done by God's will, and if nothing can happen except what he ordains, it follows that all evil is the effect or the result of his will. On the other hand, if we pretend to say that he is not the author of evil, and that evil exists without his sanction, will it not then appear either that it exists in spite of him, or that it exists without his knowing it? But it is impossible to say anything more ridiculous. If again we run the risk, in order to avoid these results, of saying, as some have done, that evil is non-existent, all the world will cry out against such a dogma, and will call the unnumbered woes which the human species has suffered from to witness against us. Since, therefore, we are unable to deny that the world is full of evil, it will be asked 'Why does not an Almighty God abolish it? Why does he endure it? Why does he allow it to subsist throughout all time?' Then, if we are enlightened by God's Spirit, and if we do not wish to be led away by foolish and impious conjectures, we shall be obliged to answer that it is better for us to remain in ignorance than to say that our will can do nothing without God's permission, for in that case it would be God who engendered the causes of evil, and who would be the creator of an infinite number of miseries."

It is unquestionably the difficulty of reconciling the existence of evil with the perfect nature attributed to God, which has led to the invention, through a religious motive, of a principle of evil. Plutarch (De Proc. Anim.) says expressly that the ancient philosophers who acknowledged a God and providence, only said "that evil was the produce of matter because they did not wish men to believe that God was the cause of it." Justin Martyr (Cohort. ad Gent.) also says that "Plato only taught that matter was self-existent in order to take away all pretext for saying that it made God to be the author of evil." Augustine (De Ord. l. ii. 1) says that he does not know any doctrine more detestable than that which makes God to be the author of evil: "Deum malorum auctorem detestabilius nihil mihi occurrit." And Plato (De Rep. l. ii.) says, "God is the only cause of good; but as for evil, he cannot be the cause of that; we must attribute that to anyone but to him." Hence it was that, as a learned modern author (Spenc. de Hirco Emis.) says, "The ancients, as Plutarch remarks, believed that there were two gods, who were opposed to each other, the first being the creator of good, the second of evil. They called the first God, and the second the Devil. The Egyptians called the good god Osiris, and the evil god Typhon. The superstitious Jews gave these two principles the name of Gad and Meni, and the Persians those of Oromasdes and Ahriman. The Greeks had also their good and evil spirits, and the Romans had their Joves and Vejoves, that is their beneficent and maleficent deities. Astrologers represent the same idea by favourable or malignant signs or constellations; philosophers by contrary principles; and the Pythagoreans, in particular, by their Monad and Dyad."

The words Gad and Meni occur in Is. lxv. 11, which are translated "that troop" and "that number" in the English version, and τῷ δαιμονίῳ and τῇ τύχῃ by the LXX. Meni was a Babylonian deity, and one of the names of the moon. Gad, according to the Rabbis, signifies a good angel, good fortune, a good spirit (Buxtorf, Dict. Hebr. Talm.).

Connected with this subject is the belief of the ancients respecting the eternity of matter. The modern Jews have believed for some five or six centuries at least that God created the universe out of nothing, and this is taught in their catechisms, and laid down as a fundamental article of belief (See Menass. B. Israël, Prob. I., De Creat.). This is not only opposed to scientific truth, but to the teaching of some of the most eminent among the Jews themselves. Philo praises Moses (De Opif. Mundi) " for having well comprehended, both by the light of philosophy, which he was thoroughly acquainted with, and also by means of divine revelation, that in order to form corporeal beings it is absolutely necessary to have two causes, one active, and the other passive, the agent and the subject. In the creation of the world this agent is the Spirit of the Universe ('O τῶν ὅλων Νοῦς), and the subject is a being which is dead, inanimate, incapable of self-motion, or at any rate of moving in an orderly manner, or of forming itself into shape, but capable of being moulded into that form which it may please God to give to it." Philo adds that "the Creator of the Universe being naturally good, and goodness not being invidious, but generous and liberal, he wished to extend his benefactions over a substance which, having nothing good in itself, might nevertheless become what the Creator wished to make of it." He is opposed to the belief of the Stoics, who thought that the world would be destroyed by fire, and gives among other reasons for rejecting it an ancient axiom of the philosophers that "As nothing can come from nothing, so nothing can be annihilated, and it is equally impossible for a thing to pass from existence to nothingness, and for a thing to pass from nothingness into existence." He says "The word corruption, or destruction, signifies in one respect a change for the worse, and in another, total destruction of what once existed, and which we may call annihilation. But this can never take place, because nothing can come of nothing, therefore neither can that which perishes be reduced to nothingness; and just as it is impossible that anything should be made of that which does not exist, so neither can it be believed that that which is should be totally destroyed, as the tragic poet says, 'Never does that which has been engendered perish, but, transmuted into other shapes, it becomes transformed in diverse manners.' It would be absurd, therefore, to suppose that the Universe can be destroyed."

Eliezer, surnamed the Great, asks, "Of what were the heavens made? God took some light from his garments, he spread out this light as a vesture, and the heavens were spread out and flowed, as it is said (Ps. civ. 2): 'Who coverest thyself with light as with a garment: who stretchest out the heavens like a curtain.' And of what was the earth made? God took some snow, which was under the throne of glory, and spread it on the waters, and they became frozen, according to that other saying (Job xxxvii. 6), 'He saith to the snow, Be thou on the earth.'" Eliezer also says that there were seven things which existed before the creation, which God had made, viz. the Law, Hell, Paradise, or the Garden of Eden, the Throne of Glory, the House of the Sanctuary, Repentance, and the Name of the Messiah. He says that God took man out of the House of the Sanctuary to place him in the garden of Eden, and that when he wished to adorn the earth with plants he opened a gate of this garden, and made the plants, which cover the face of the earth, go out at it.

The Jews have a cabalistic book which is called Jezirah, that is, formation, not creation as the modern Jews understand it. The Jews say that Abraham wrote this book; but whoever was the author of it, it is certain that it does not countenance the belief that the world was made out of nothing. It says that the three letters Aleph, Mem, and Tschin are the three mothers of all things, and that they begat the three fathers of all that exists in the Universe. The meaning of this is that these three letters are contained in the Jewish names for air, water, and fire, of which all things have been made. The souls, however, are not made of this substance, but of a subtle and spiritual body which the Jews called the Holy Ghost or Spirit, and they say that the angels are made of the same substance. Basnage (Hist. des Juifs, T. IV. c. 6) says "The Jews have had four different beliefs respecting the Creation. The first, who are the most numerous, follow Moses and the account in Genesis. The second have adopted the belief that another world existed before ours, which God had destroyed, and which had come to an end because each world ought only to last seven thousand years. The third class invented Spinozism, and the fourth conceive that all creatures emanated from God, but they have introduced many absurdities into this system." He also says that "in the time of Maimonides, in the twelfth century, a controversy arose respecting the age of the world, which was held to be eternal. Some, having embraced the Aristotelian philosophy, which was much in vogue at that time, adopted his opinions respecting the eternity of the world, while others said that matter was eternal," &c.

Photius says that Clemens Alexandrinus taught in his Hypotyposes that several worlds existed before Adam, Πολλοὺς πρὸ τοῦ 'Αδὰμ κόσμους τερατεύεται. St. Basil (In Hexam. Hom. I.) says "There existed before this world was created a world which was of a nature and a constitution which was totally different to ours: a world which was suitable to the celestial virtues, which existed before Time, and which is eternal and perpetual. The Creator formed in it an intellectual light (φῶς νοητὸν) such as is suitable for the happiness of reasonable and invisible natures which love the Lord."

Jerome in his Commentary on the Epistle to Titus is of the same opinion. "Our world," he says, "has not yet lasted six thousand years, but how many ages and how many eternities elapsed previously, during which time the angels, thrones, dominations, and other virtues (cæteræque virtutes) served the Lord, by whose command they existed when there was as yet neither measure nor vicissitudes of Time?" Origen, Chrysostom, Damascenus, Olympiodorus, and other Greek fathers, and Novatian, Ambrose, Isidore of Seville, Bede and others among the Latin fathers, have held the same opinion. In fact, those who believe in the existence of angels before the creation of the world must entertain it. It was held by all the Fathers that the angels had light, subtle bodies ($\sigma\omega\mu\alpha\tau\alpha$ $\lambda\eta\pi\tau\alpha$) made of fire or of ether, and therefore this igneous or ethereal substance must have been in existence even before the angels were created.

These speculations would possess little interest if they were not connected with psychological and other inquiries, but the whole fabric of theology as that term is usually understood rests upon them. The tradition of a war of the rebel angels with God, of which there is not a trace to be found in Genesis, was very generally spread throughout the East. Celsus, speaking of the Christians, says, "They have settled that God must have an adversary, whom they call the devil, which is an idea very insulting to the Deity, and which reduces him to the level of a mere mortal. The great God, therefore, when he wishes to do men good, finds an enemy who resists him, and prevents him from doing so." He also says, " The ancients speak enigmatically of a certain divine war; Heraclitus speaks of it as follows: '*If* we must admit that there has been a general war and dissension, and that everything is done and governed by this dissension.' Pherecides, who is a much more ancient author than Heraclitus, represents in a mystic fable two hostile armies, the leader of one of which is Saturn, and of the other Ophioneus. He narrates their mutual defiances and their combats, which were followed by a mutual agreement that whichever of the two parties should be driven into the ocean should confess itself conquered, and that the others, who had expelled their enemies, should remain, as conquerors, the masters of heaven. The story of the Titans and the giants who made war against the gods contains similar mysteries, as does also that of

Typhon, of Horus, and of Osiris among the Egyptians." Celsus goes on to mention what Jupiter says to Juno in Homer, namely, that she ought to remember that he suspended her one day in mid-air, and then says, " These are the words of God speaking to matter. This signifies that God in the beginning, finding matter in disorder and without form, gave it order and ornament by means of the justness of the bonds which he had joined the parts of, and that in order to punish the demons, who busied themselves in keeping matters in disorder, he had precipitated them into the infernal regions." The meaning of this is that the ancients considered Juno to be the emblem of matter, because she was the sister and wife of Jupiter; his sister because they believed her to be co-eternal with Jupiter, and his wife because she was the subject out of which he formed the world. Hierocles says that if matter is held to be uncreated, it is the equal of God and his sister, τὴν ἐπ' ἴσης αὐτῷ ἀγέννητον οὐσίαν . . . . καὶ ἀδελφήν.

The Magi, from whose traditions this fiction passed into the West, said that Ahriman, at the head of a powerful army, declared war against light, but that the angels, stepping in as mediators, made peace on certain conditions (Hyde de Vet. Pers. Rel., p. 296; see also Plutarch De Isid., who speaks of this war between Ormuzd and Ahriman). This is still the belief of those remnants of the ancient Persians who took refuge in India after the Arabian conquest. These people believe that God, having created the good angels, who are his ministers, ordered them to make heaven; but that as soon as heaven was created, hideous darkness appeared, which was distant nine thousand six hundred parasangs from God on all sides. As soon as God saw the darkness, he knew that it was Ahriman, and that he had a powerful army with him. Ahriman had already revolted, and had escaped from heaven, after breaking open the gates of his prison. God sent four of his strongest angels as soon as he could to fight with the devil and take him prisoner. These four angels were Erdibehist, that is the strongest angel in Paradise; Azur, or the angel who presides over fire; Somish, who is identical with Gabriel, his name having the same meaning, viz. the might of God; and Behram, or the angel who presides over war, and whose name indicates a red or fiery colour (Hyde, ib. p. 241, &c.). Ahriman was conquered and compelled to submit; but God would not destroy him and his angels, because if he did so the glory of his clemency would not shine forth so brightly, and because if everything were good in the world there would be no distinction between vice and virtue.

Plato, who took his system respecting the formation of the world and of the soul from Timæus of Locris, who in turn had taken it from Pythagoras, endeavours to explain in the Timæus how the First Cause formed the soul. "God," he says, "began by producing the soul, which has the advantage of being older than, as well as superior to the body. It is made to command the body, as the latter is made to obey it. God, therefore, took some of the indivisible substance, which is always the same, and always resembles itself, and some of that which is divisible, and divided amongst bodies (καὶ τῆς ἀν περὶ τὰ σώματα γιγνομένης μεριστής). Of these two substances he made one of a third species, which holds the middle place between the two others. This he placed between the indivisible and the divisible substance. Of these three substances united he made the human soul, which is composed of the same, of the different, and of essence (ἔκ τε ταύτου, καὶ θατέρου, καὶ τῆς οὐσίας)." Plato gave an arithmetical principle to the soul and a geometrical one to the body (Diog. Laert., l. iii.; Vit. Pythag.).

The most ancient and widely-spread belief was that the souls of men are pure and celestial substances, which existed before bodies were created, and which came down from heaven to animate the latter. R. Menasseh ben Israel (Probl. x. de Creat.) says that "this has always been the belief of his nation. Hermes, Pythagoras, Plato, and the other Pagans, took it from the Jews. It is taught in the Scriptures. All human souls were in existence when the world was created, and were present in the Garden of Eden when God entered into a compact with Adam." Lactantius (Inst. l. iii. 18) has observed that this was the belief of all the ancient philosophers: "They held that it was impossible that the soul should exist after the body if it had not existed before it." All the ablest of the Greek fathers embraced this opinion, and a portion of the Latin fathers followed them. Augustine (De Gen. ad liter. l. vii. 24) says that it is probable that God created all the souls of men in the beginning. St. Jerome is also said to have been of this opinion, and Philaster holds persons who do not believe that souls were created before bodies to be heretics.

Arnobius is much struck by the difficulty of the questions which arise from this supposition. After describing the miseries and vices of human nature, he asks, "How can one say, or rather think, that God tore peaceable and innocent souls from their abode of happiness in order to plunge them in a gulf of ills, by uniting them to matter, which is the inexhaustible source of them?" He finds himself compelled to believe that the soul is material and mortal; that the souls of the wicked are annihilated after being long punished; and that the souls of the just become immortal through the knowledge of the Saviour, "ejus enim cognitio fermentum quoddam est, vitæ ac rei dissociabilis glutinum."

The philosophers escaped from this difficulty by supposing that the souls had committed sin in their ante-natal state. Clemens Alexandrinus (Strom. l. iii.) says that Philolaus the Pythagorean taught that the soul is buried in the body as in a tomb in order to expiate certain sins, and adds that this belief was not peculiar to Philolaus, but that the most ancient theologians and prophets held the same belief. Plato supposed that the celestial souls are animated with a secret wish to unite themselves to bodies, and that this terrestrial longing is a weight which drags them down to this lower world. The Essenes also believed that "souls descend from the most subtle ether, attracted to bodies by the charms of matter." (Josephus, Bell. Jud. ii. 8.) The Cabalists developed this doctrine in their four worlds, the Azilutic, Briatic, Jeziratic, and Aziathic, through which souls descend. They held that virtuous souls return to the Azilutic world after once passing through the others; that to the rest, God allows them to make two more pilgrimages, and that if they are then unable to return to the Azilutic world, they are very severely punished.

Philo says, "The soul was not formed of anything that had been created. It came from the Father and Ruler of the Universe. For the words 'God breathed' mean nothing else than that this divine breath (or spirit) emanated from that happy Nature, and was sent here below, as into a foreign country, in order to be useful to Nature." The Jew Tryphon asks Justin Martyr, "What affinity, what connection is there between God and the soul? Is the soul divine, immortal, and a portion of the Royal Mind (τοῦ βασιλικοῦ Νοῦ), that is, of the Spirit which governs the world?" Justin answers, "It is so, beyond the possibility of contradiction." St. Augustine, however, has pointed out in his discussion with Fortunatus, the Manichæan bishop, that this involves the liability of a portion of the substance of God to error and sin. Notwithstanding this difficulty, which Augustine endeavours to remove by the absurd idea of distinguishing between the essence of God and the substance of his kingdom, that is, between the five good elements, air, light, good fire, good water, and good wind, as distinct from smoke, darkness, bad fire, &c. (Aug. de Hær., c. 46), Tatian, Justin's disciple, considers the soul to be material and mortal, but holds the spirit to be immortal, and to be a portion of the Father. The author of the Clementine Homilies (Hom. xv.) says that "the soul, proceeding from God, is of the same substance as God." Lactantius and Origen held the same opinion.

It was a maxim of ancient philosophy that God gave souls more or less perfect bodies to dwell in in proportion to their own merits. Porphyry says, "According to the dispositions of the soul it receives a body which is suitable to them. Perfectly pure souls receive bodies which approach as nearly as possible to the immateriality of ethereal bodies. Those souls which stoop from pure reason to the objects of sense receive a body of the same nature as the sun, but those which become effeminate, and which are captivated by the glitter of visible beauty, are compelled to dwell in bodies of the nature of the moon." It was also held that the spirits which dwelt in the stars were much more perfect than those which dwell in terrestrial bodies. Philo calls them very pure spirits, "perfectly just and holy, without any mixture, or any contagion of evil."

Plato held that there were three sorts of souls, differing in perfection and purity—the universal soul, the souls of the stars, and the human souls. He says that God mixed the indivisible substance with the divisible, and formed first the soul of the universe, which Synesius calls the Θεὸs ἐγκόσμιος, or the God who animates the world. As the composition of this soul did not exhaust all the substance that God had prepared, he poured the rest into a vase, and mingled them again in the same manner as he had done before, but the result of this mixture was not so pure as that of the former one. Souls appeared in it of a second and third rate description. After this, God having constructed the machine of the universe, selected the purest souls, and distributed them among the stars, showing them the world, the inspection and government of which he confided to them. He next took the most imperfect souls, and these were appointed to animate and rule human bodies. The reason of this, according to Chalcidius (in Tim.), is, that "souls made of the purest portion of the mingled substances would not have been able to fall into the vices of matter, nor to accommodate themselves to the fragile nature of mortal bodies."

CHAPTER IX.

THE Cabalists believed that as the soul is a portion of, and an emanation from, the Deity, it possessed the power of multiplying itself *ad infinitum*. Hence they concluded, first, that all human souls were included in the soul of Adam; and, secondly, that they have all sinned in Adam since they were all in him. Augustine says that he cannot decide whether Adam is only the father of our bodies, or of both our bodies and our souls, but he thinks that he must be the father of both, because when Eve was made out of Adam's rib, God did not breathe a fresh breath of life into her, and therefore the soul of Eve must have been a particle of or emanation from that of Adam, from which it follows that one soul can engender another soul without diminution of its substance. He applies this to the doctrine of Original Sin as follows (De Ani. et Orig. L. I. 17): "If it is true that man engenders man altogether—that is, that he engenders the body, the soul, and the spirit, the words of St. Paul, 'In whom all have sinned,' are spoken in their literal sense." This wonderful piece of reasoning was, however, looked upon in the Eastern Churches as not only very dangerous, but as being, as Methodius (In Symp.) calls it, "unworthy of any credence."

In John ix. 2, the disciples are represented as believing in the Metempsychosis, for they ask whether the man who was born blind had committed any sin in his ante-natal state. Josephus (De Bell. Jud. II. 7) says that the Pharisees only admitted the Metempsychosis for the souls of the just, but he has probably confounded it in this passage with the resurrection of the just. Sandius (De Orig. Animæ) gives the following account of what the belief really was: "R. Elias says that the doctrine of the Metempsychosis is received and approved by the doctors; they have no doubt that human souls pass at least three times from one body to another. They are positive that Adam's soul passed into David, and that it will one day animate the body of the Messiah. The Cabalistic proof of this mystery is the name of Adam, for A signifies Adam; D, David; and M, the Messiah. The Cabalists also say that the soul of an adulterer is sent into a camel, and that David would have undergone that penalty if he had not repented, and that this is what the prophet alludes to in the Psalms, ' I will praise the Lord on account of his goodness towards me, and because he has delivered my soul from the camel.'" Photius (Cod. 117) tells us that Origen held that the soul of Jesus Christ was the same as that of Adam, and there is no doubt that he, as well as Chalcidius, Synesius, and other eminent Christian divines and philosophers, believed in the transmigration of souls. The learned Rabbi Menasseh ben Israel (Prob. xvii. de Creat.) says, "God does not lose souls altogether, and never annihilates them, for he has not determined to banish them absolutely and for ever from his presence, but only for a time, until they are purified from their sins, after which he sends them back into the world by means of the Metempsychosis."

The teaching of the Fathers respecting the doctrines of the soul was exclusively founded on the belief that heaven was an immense vault extended above the earth. Synesius (Hym. III. vv. 618 et seq.) offers the following prayer to God: "Let my suppliant soul, marked with the seal of the Father, scare away the hostile demons, who, issuing forth from their subterranean caves, take possession of the loftier regions, and make impious efforts to prevent souls from attaining to heaven. Make a sign to thy servants, to the inhabitants of that glorious world, who hold the keys of the ethereal journey, to open to it the gates of light." Others held that souls, being on the earth, and united to bodies, necessarily acquired a certain degree of weight, which rendered it necessary for them to have some aid in order to enable them to get to heaven. The learned Windet (De vitâ functorum statu) says, "If we may believe the Samaritan interpolation, an angel took Enoch and transported him to heaven. St. Chrysostom represents the angels, whom he calls the guards of God, as carrying the soul of Lazarus into the bosom of Abraham. Euthymius Zigatenes says that the horses of fire which carried up Elijah were angels who had assumed that appearance, and we see in the Chaldee paraphrase of the Song of Songs that the souls of the saints are conveyed to Paradise by the angels."

The Emperor Julian (Orat. v.) has explained the Pagan belief: "Since the sun has the power of raising subtile and light bodies by means of corporeal heat, much more must he be able to raise virtuous souls by means of that secret, perfectly incorporeal, divine, and pure essence which dwells in his rays." This was a Chaldæan belief, for he adds, "If I wished to explain at greater length the secrets and mysteries which the Chaldæan has sung respecting the God who is illustrious by his rays, and who raises souls by his virtue, I should speak of things which are obscure and unknown, especially to the vulgar, but which are well known to those fortunate individuals who understand the mysteries of the Theurgy." St. Epiphanius says that the souls of the saved do not remain in the sun, but that the sun passes them on to the Æon of the happy. Tyrbonius says that "after the moon has remitted the souls she is full of to the Æons of the Father, they remain in the column of Glory, which is called the perfect air. This air is a column of light, because it is full of purified souls." The perfect air is that which is free from all admixture of matter, and is described in the verses attributed to Pythagoras as follows:

"Ἀν δ' ἀπόλειψας σῶμα, ἐς αἰθέρ' ἐλεύθερον ἔλθῃς,
Ἔσσεαι ἀθάνατος, Θεὸς ἄμβροτος, οὐκ ἔτι θνητός.

" When you have left this body, you will pass into the ether, which is free, and you will become an immortal god." The column of glory, or light, is the Milky Way.

These beliefs were modified by the supposed exigencies of Christian belief. Some of the Fathers held that as the faithful were to reign a thousand years on the earth with Christ, it would be necessary that they should rise with their bodies of flesh and blood, but that when they went to heaven they would leave their human and corruptible bodies behind them. St. Epiphanius (Hær. lxvi. § 35), however, thinks that the elect will eat and drink in heaven, but declines to mention the nature of the celestial aliments. St. Gregory of Nyssa, on the contrary, says with reference to Christ's body, and presumably with reference to all other bodies, that it has no longer the figure, or shape, or extent, or any internal or external parts of the human body. "I will never believe," he says, "that there is anything corporeal left of Jesus Christ."

The Essenes were of the same opinion as the Sadducees, who denied a corporeal resurrection. Josephus (De Bell. Jud. ii. 7) says that they considered that our bodies are corruptible, and that matter is not permanent, but that our souls, which are retained in our bodies as in a prison, gladly take their flight to heaven when they are delivered from the bonds of the flesh. Synesius (who was bishop of Ptolemais) believed that the soul was immortal, but could not believe in the resurrection of the body. He believed that souls were originally pure spirits, which had descended to the material world, and he says (Epist. 105), " You know that Philosophy is directly opposed to certain dogmas which are generally received. I can, therefore, never persuade myself that the soul was born after the formation of the body." In another place he says, " I will never believe that the world, or the other parts of the universe, will be destroyed." This was also in accordance with the teaching of those philosophers who held that it was impossible that God, who had created the universe, should ever destroy it. Such an act, they said, would show ignorance in the Creator, and imperfection in the work. Synesius adds that " as to that Resurrection which is preached, I am persuaded that it is a sacred and secret mystery, and I am very far from thinking about it as the common people do." As he held that matter is the cause of evil, it is easy to see that he cannot have believed in the resurrection of the body at all.

Modern divines not only believe in a bodily resurrection, but possess the most accurate information respecting the next world. Cardinal Bellarmine, in a treatise on Purgatory, says that there are four different places beneath the earth, or rather a place divided into four parts, the deepest of which is hell. This place contains all the souls of the damned, and also all the devils. The bodies of the damned will also be there after the resurrection. The nearest place to hell is Purgatory, where souls appease the anger of God by their sufferings. He says that there are the same fires and the same torments in both places, the only difference being in their duration. Next to Purgatory is the limbo of unbaptized infants. The fourth place is the limbo of those just men who died before the birth of Christ, but since that event this division is empty, like an apartment to let.

The celebrated theologian Tillemont condemns all the Pagans to the eternal torments of hell because they lived before the time of Jesus, and could not be benefited by his redemption.

The Fathers, however, are by no means agreed upon this subject. Besides Origen, Clemens Alexandrinus taught the universal redemption of mankind by Christ, and he is indignant with those who say that redemption is reserved for a few privileged persons (τῶν μέν· τῶν δ' οὐ). He says (Strom., l. VI.) that in creating man God has disposed everything in such a manner as to ensure the salvation of all: πρὸς μὲν γὰρ τὴν τοῦ ὅλου σωτηρίαν ταῦτά ἐστι διατεταγμένα, καὶ καθ' ὅλον, καὶ ἐπὶ μέρους. St. Gregory of Nyssa also says that there is a natural necessity why the immortal soul should be healed and purified, and that if it has not been so healed and purified during its life on earth, it must be so in the life to come.

Tatian, who was a disciple of Justin Martyr, taught (Contra Græc.) that "the devils are made of matter. Not only are their bodies made of it, but their souls also issued from it, which renders them dainty and luxurious. They have not flesh and blood as we have, but their substance is like fire and air. Being composed of what is most subtle and unconfined, as well as of what is most vicious in matter, they cannot be converted; their substance leaves no place for repentance, for they are the rays of matter and of wickedness. Some, however, whose nature is not so bad as that of the others, have become susceptible of repentance. They are, generally speaking, mortal, though they die with difficulty, because they are not made of flesh, but of a spiritual substance. Notwithstanding this they will rise again, and be subjected to much greater tortures than men, because, having lived for many ages, their sins are greater and more numerous." Arnobius (Adv. Gentes, l. I.) also says, "The devils dwell in the foulest part of the material world, which is their portion, and out of which they are made;" and Synesius (Hym. II. v. 50 et sqq.) explains that "God embellishes the universe from the highest heaven down to the lowest portion of matter (ὕλας) in which the dregs of nature produce the tumultuous and subtle troop of the devils."

The Fathers were sorely exercised by John viii. 44, for in Origen's time the reading of that passage was Ὑμεῖς ἐκ τοῦ πατρὸς τοῦ διαβόλου ἐστέ, "Ye are from the father of the devil;" and as in the same verse Jesus is represented as saying, "He is a liar, and the father of it," the difficulty of finding a father for Satan who was a liar was insuperable. Epiphanius, Archelaus, and Origen failed in the attempt. Cyril of Alexandria says that some Catholics thought that Satan had had a son after his fall from heaven, and that it was this son who tempted Adam and Eve. Others, according to Jerome, held that the father of the devil was the dragon, who rules the seas, and whom the Jews called Leviathan. The Fathers were still further pressed with difficulties by the heretics. They said that the devil could neither be the son of God nor created by him. He could not be his son, for in that case he would be consubstantial with God, which would be blasphemous. He could not be created by him, for he is the son of a father who is a liar, and God is truth. They also said that there was nothing in the Scriptures respecting the creation of the devil. Driven to desperation, the Fathers at length got from the LXX. the words in Job xl. 14 : Τουτέστιν ἀρχὴ πλάσματος Κυρίου. The dragon, or behemoth, "is the commencement of the creation of God." Origen (in Joan.) and others have actually been driven to this pitiable extremity.

In the Clementine Homilies (xix. § 4) there is a discussion on this subject between Simon Magus and no less a person than the Apostle Peter himself. Simon (who had been a disciple of John the Baptist, and who preached abstinence from all flesh and the most rigorous observance of the Sabbath) says to Peter, "Either the Evil One has been created, or he has not been created. If he has been created, he has been created by God who made all things, either as an animal formed by him, or as an emanation from his substance, which, being foreign to Nature, has come and mingled with her. Or else, perhaps, there was some animate or inanimate matter out of which the Evil One was generated spontaneously, or out of which God formed him. Or, lastly, God must have made him out of nothing, in which case he is no longer a real being, but a merely relative existence (ἢ καὶ ἐξ οὐκ ὄντων τῶν πρὸς τί ἐστιν). If, however, the Evil One has not been created, he must have always existed, and is therefore immortal." This series of dilemmas embarrasses the chief of the Apostles in no small degree. He has great doubts as to what he ought to say, and he ends ignominiously by endeavouring to show that the true God cannot be the cause of evil, but that Scripture has not chosen to explain the origin of the Devil. Simon is not satisfied with this evasive answer, and ends by informing Peter that "If matter is equal to God both in duration and in power, and is also hostile to God, it produces of itself powers which are hostile to the will of God."

All these speculations are founded on the literal interpretation of the allegory in Genesis, which Augustine, with all his ability, was unable to defend. He says that the verdure of the fields signifies the soul, and that when Moses says there was as yet no verdure on the ground, he means that souls had not felt any earthly affections. He admits that there are no means of preserving the literal meaning of the three first chapters of Genesis without attributing to God things which are unworthy of him. St. Basil and St. Gregory of Nyssa must have held the same opinion, for they collected the Philocalia, or book of chosen beauties, in which Origen, as we have seen, so mercilessly ridicules the literal interpretation. He also says (Philocal., c. 1) that "there are many simple persons who pride themselves upon being members of the Church, and on recognizing God as the Creator, in which they are right, but who also, being led astray by the letter of Scripture, attribute to Him opinions and acts which one would not attribute to the most unjust and barbarous of mankind." In his seventh Homily on Leviticus he goes if possible farther, for he says respecting the laws of Moses, "If we keep to the literal interpretation, and explain the things which were written in the law according to Jewish ideas, or according to the opinion entertained of them by the vulgar, I cannot admit that God gave such laws without blushing, for the laws of the Romans, for instance, and those of the Athenians, would be far more equitable." He even says that "amongst these laws there are many the observing of which appears to be impossible or unreasonable," Πολλοὶ τῶν νόμων . . . . τὸ ἄλογον ἐμφαίνουσι, ἕτεροι δὲ τὸ ἀδύνατον.

The ideas of heaven and hell which are prevalent in modern times are founded on that one of the numerous Apocalypses published in the early ages of the Church which is attributed to St. John. This composition is ignored by Papias, and St. Dionysius of Alexandria (quoted by Eusebius, H. E. VII. 25), who lived about the middle of the third century, says that those who lived before him held that " it had a false title, for it is not of John. Nay, that it is not even a revelation, for it is covered with such a dense and thick veil of ignorance that not one of the apostles, and not one of the holy men, or those of the Church, could be its author, but that Cerinthus, the founder of the sect of the Cerinthians, wishing to have reputable authority for his own fiction, prefixed the title." Dionysius himself, after examining the whole book, proved that it was impossible for it to be understood according to the obvious and literal sense, and also that, whoever was the author, it was certainly not John. The Council of Laodicæa, the first which framed a catalogue of the sacred books, and which was held in A.D. 364, does not include the Apocalypse in the list of canonical writings, though Laodicæa is one of the seven churches mentioned in it, and highly praised. In the Eastern churches neither Ebedjesu, the metropolitan bishop of Armenia, nor Gregory Barhebræus, nor James of Edessa have explained the book, because they did not consider it to be canonical, and because it is not in the ancient Syriac version of the New Testament. None of the Eastern churches, belonging to the Syrian rite, admitted it to be canonical, and Barhebræus said that it was written either by Cerinthus or by some one who was called John. St. Cyril of Jerusalem (A.D. 346) enumerates the sacred writings in his fourth Catechesis, but the Apocalypse is not among them. St. Gregory of Nazianzen also omits it, and, in modern times, Luther has declared it to be spurious.

The Apocalypse is in reality an astrological work, and is not an original fiction, but an abridged and deformed copy of the vision of Ezekiel, to which circumstance it probably owes its insertion into the canonical writings. The four animals of the Apocalypse are in Ezekiel, where they are represented as coming forth from the fire and from the most dazzling brightness. These animals moved in circles attached to wheels, and the Hebrews called the Zodiac " the wheel of the signs." Above these animals is the firmament of crystal (Ezek. i. 22), and the man that sat on the throne, who was like a jasper and a sardine stone, and round about whose throne was a rainbow (Rev. iv. 2), is taken from Ezek. i. 26 and Dan. x. 6. The prophet to whom the book was given to eat which became as sweet as honey in his mouth (Rev. x. 9, 10) is taken from Ezek. iii. 1–3. After this the most fearful calamities are announced as being about to fall on Jerusalem on account of the crimes of its inhabitants (Ezek. iv.). In the Apocalypse they are threatened against the universe. In both Rev. vii. and Ezek. ix. an angel goes about setting a mark upon those who were to be spared. In Ezek. x. 2 and Rev. viii. 5 an angel throws coals and fire upon the earth. War, famine, and pestilence and beasts, are the three great plagues which the avenging deity of the Apocalypse (c. vi.) makes use of, and the plagues in Ezek. vi. 11 and xii. 16 are identical. Both in Ezekiel and the Apocalypse the greater number perish, and only a few are allowed to escape. The whoredoms of Aholah and Aholibah (Ezek. xxiii.) have been copied in the Apocalypse under the emblem of the great whore of Babylon (c. xviii.), and these two myths represent the vices of the corrupt people, whose ruin the writer predicts. The ruin of Babylon is predicted in c. xvii. and xviii. of the Apocalypse in nearly the same terms as the fall of Tyre in Ezekiel (c. xxvii. et sqq.).

After the fall of Babylon the author of the Apocalypse describes the defeat of the great dragon (c. xx.). In the same way, after the destruction of the guilty generations of Palestine and of Tyre, Ezekiel sets forth the defeat of Pharaoh, whom he calls the great dragon (Ezek. xxix. 3), and in both works (Rev. xix. 17, 18, and Ezek. xxxii. 4) the birds of prey and the wild beasts eat the flesh of the conquered. In Ezek. xxxiv., after the defeat of the great dragon, Pharaoh, God says that he is about to come to the assistance of the oppressed sheep, to assemble them near him, to bring them out of a land of oppression, and to cause them to migrate into a land of plenty. He is going to abide with them, as being their Lord and their God. In the Apocalypse also (c. xx. 4) there is a judgment after the defeat of the great dragon, in which the faithful, who are about to reign with Christ, are set apart. In v. 8, however, Gog and Magog appear, who are in league with the great enemy of the faithful, and who make war with the saints and with the beloved city. Ezekiel also, after reassuring the chastised people (c. xxxvi.), makes Gog and Magog appear (c. xxxvii.), and, after the people have been gathered together and have enjoyed rest for some time, they come and trouble their happiness by forming a league of several nations against them (c. xxxviii. 14–16). They will fall upon the newly-assembled people, and they will appear in the last days before the re-establishment of all things, and before the new city is built, in a large body, and with powerful armies, but they will be destroyed by fire and brimstone (v. 21). God will send a fire on Magog (c. xxxix. 6), and they will be burnt with fire seven years (v. 9). This is exactly like the Apocalypse, in which, after the first resurrection and a reign of peace of a thousand years, the hosts of Gog and Magog, the number of whom is as the sands of the sea (Rev. xx. 7), are made to appear. They compass the camp of the saints about, but fire comes down from God out of heaven and devours them (v. 9). These fictions are identical. In Ezek. xxxviii. there is a resurrection which is followed by the defeat of Gog and Magog, and it is also after a resurrection that their defeat takes place in the Apocalypse (Rev. xx. 5).

In the same way that the author of the Apocalypse (c. xxi.) makes the new Jerusalem appear suddenly, glowing with light, and which is seen by the prophet from a lofty mountain on which he stands, Ezekiel (c. xl.) is also set on a high mountain, and sees a town and a temple which shadow forth the restoration of Jerusalem. The angel who speaks to John has a reed in his hand (Rev. xxi. 15) to measure the city, the dimensions of which he gives, and in which the duodecimal numbers are constantly repeated. Ezekiel also (c. xl. 3) sees a man or a spirit resembling brass, who holds a measuring reed in his hand, and who gives him the dimensions of the walls which he measures; three chambers to the east, and afterwards thirty chambers (a number equal to the degrees of a sign) formed the western front, in which there was a large door. Eight steps (v. 34) led up to it—a number equal to that of the eight spheres. The north, west, and south fronts were the same. Suddenly (c. xliii. 2) the glory of the God of Israel appeared, *coming from the East*. In the middle of the building rises an altar, called Harel, or the mountain [height] of God, the dimensions of which are twelve feet in every direction. The purification of the altar lasts seven days (v. 26), and on the eighth day offerings are made. No stranger or uncircumcised person is allowed to enter the sanctuary (c. xliv. 9). Those who were not inscribed in the sacred book of the Lamb were also excluded from the holy town. All these ceremonies relate to the sign Aries, or the Passover, as appears from c. xlv. 15, in which a lamb is ordered to be offered as an expiatory sacrifice.

Lastly, after a very detailed description of the new town and temple, all the dimensions of which are given to Ezekiel, the spirit makes him return to the door of the house (c. xlvii. 1), "and behold waters issued out from under the threshold of the house eastward . . . and the waters came down from under from the right side of the house, at the south side of the altar," like the river of Orion, which is under Aries in the constellations. A great many trees were planted on each side of the river (v. 7), whose leaves will never fade, and which will never be without fruit (v. 12), for they will bear fresh fruit every month. The fruit will be for meat, and the leaves for medicine. All that exist where the rivers come shall be healed and live (v. 9). This is identical with Rev. xxii. 1, 2, where the angel shows John the pure river of the water of life which proceeds out of the throne of the Lamb, and on the banks of which is the tree of life, which yields fruits twelve times, once every month, and the leaves of which possess the power of healing. Ezekiel concludes with the name of the holy city, Jehovah-shamma, "The Lord is there," and the Apocalypse concludes with "The grace of the Lord Jesus be with the saints." [Cod. Sin.]

Babylon, on whose forehead was written MYSTERY (Rev. xvii. 5), is an allegorical name intended to contrast with Jerusalem. Babylon, in which the Jews had been captives, and Jerusalem, were naturally hostile, and therefore the Jewish seer chose them as emblems of the two opposing principles. Babylon came to represent the world of darkness and corruption, which was to be destroyed together with the spirits or angels of darkness which ruled it, and Jerusalem represented the world of light which was to rise on the ruins of Babylon at the same time as the Lamb who was victorious over the dragon and darkness. This Lamb draws after him those who had been initiated into his mysteries, while the corrupt souls of the friends of the serpent are buried under the ruins of Babylon or of the dark world. Ezekiel (c. xxvi.) chose Tyre to represent the city which rejoiced over the misfortunes of Jerusalem. The author of the Apocalypse has borrowed the description of Aholah and Aholibah to describe the great whore, and that of Tyre to represent the destruction of Babylon and the terror of those who traded with her (conf. Rev. xvii., xviii. with Ezek. xxiii., xxvi., xxvii., and xxviii.). The expression in Rev. xvii. 1, "the great whore that sitteth upon many waters," agrees with the position of Tyre, but not with that of Babylon, and shows the source from which the description has been taken.

It is impossible for two fictions to resemble each other more strongly, either in the general plan, or in the succession of events, or in the similarity of the expressions, which are often identical. The names of the churches in the Apocalypse are Phrygian, but the names of Gog and Magog, of Babylon, and of the Euphrates, in which four angels are bound (Rev. ix. 14), all relate to the country in which Ezekiel was living, close to the Euphrates, during the Captivity. The author has even imitated (vii. 14, 17) the comparison of the shepherd (Ezek. xxxiv. 12-14) who will seek out his sheep, and bring them to their own land, and place them in a fat pasture on the high mountains of Israel by the rivers, and in the inhabited places of the country. In Ezekiel again guilty Jerusalem is replaced by the new Jerusalem: in the Apocalypse it is Babylon which is destroyed, and which is replaced by the new Jerusalem.

The same mystic idea pervades both works, namely, the return of the soul of the initiated person to the celestial country, when he has merited by initiation and repentance to be restored to his state of primitive innocence, and when he has been given up again to that immortal light which he had abandoned for this mortal life, the abode of darkness and misery, the wretchedness of which was bewailed in the mysteries of the Phrygian sectaries.

In c. i. 14, and vii. 10, the author of the Apocalypse has also taken the description of the ancient of days from Dan. vii. 9. In c. xiii., the beast with a lion's mouth, the feet of a bear, and the body of a leopard, has been made up from the four beasts in Daniel. In both works the beasts rise up out of the sea. In Dan. vii. 21, and Rev. xiii. 7, the same expression, "and it was given unto him to make war with the saints, and to overcome them," is made use of. The ten horns are also in Daniel, but are given to another beast (v. 7). The expression in the Apocalypse (xii. 14), "a time, and times, and half a time," is also in Dan. xii. 7. The ten horns which represent ten kings who are to arise in succession in the Apocalypse (xvii. 12) have the same meaning in Dan. vii. 24. In Rev. xvii. 13, 14, these horns aid the beast to make war with the Lamb, who overcomes them. In Dan. viii. 4, the beasts are also defeated by Aries, or the Ram. Lastly, in Dan. xii. 1, and in Rev. xxi. 27, it is said that every one that is written in the book of life shall be saved.

In John xvi. 34, the people are represented as saying to Jesus, "We have heard out of the law that Christ abideth for ever, and how sayest thou, The Son of Man must be lifted up? Who is this Son of Man?" The people were therefore ignorant that the Messiah was to be crucified, and the passages in the Old Testament which are supposed to speak of an expiation for the sins of the people which is to take place at the Messianic period (Ezek. xxxvi. 25, xxxvii. 23, Zech. xiii. 1, Dan. ix. 24), contain no indication that it was to be brought about by the sufferings and death of the Messiah. There are, indeed, passages in the Jewish writings which assert that a Messiah will die by a violent death, but they do not refer to the Messiah properly so called, the descendant of David, but to another, who descended from Joseph and Ephraim, and who occupied a subordinate position to the other. The Messiah ben Joseph, or son of Joseph, was to precede the Messiah ben David, or son of David. He was to re-unite the ten tribes of the old kingdom of Israel, and the two tribes of the kingdom of Judah, but was to perish in the battle against Gog and Magog, to which Zech. vii. 10 was held to refer. This belief is found in the Gemara of Babylon and in the Zohar.

When the religion spread, and it began to be believed that the Messiah had really come, genealogies were constructed which made Jesus (by omitting the inconvenient passage in Jer. xxii. 30) to be a lineal descendant of David, at least in appearance, and the expectation of the triumphant Messiah was abandoned. The general belief was that the one Messiah was to come from the tribe of Judah under the tropic of Capricorn, and the other from the tribe of Ephraim, which is the exactly opposite one in the camp of the Hebrews (the astrological nature of which has been explained by Kircher), that is under the tropic of Capricorn, as Sir William Drummond (Æd. Jud., plate 15) has shown. Sir William says, "Immediately on leaving the sign of Leo, the emblem of Judah, the sun passes into the sign where, as we have already seen, the ancient Persians, Arabians, and Syrians depicted Virgo with a male infant in her arms. Now, I observe that the Arabians make Messaiel the protecting genius in the sign of Virgo (see Kircher's Œdipus, vol. II. p. 245) . . . . Mesai El appears to be a corruption for משיח־אל (msih-al) Messaiah-El, the anointed of El, the male infant, who rises in the arms of Virgo, who was called Jesus by the Hebrews, that is, ישוע (iuso), the Saviour, and was hailed the anointed king or Messiah." In the Testament of Simeon it is said, " Now, dear brethren, obey Levi, and ye shall be delivered by Judah. Do not raise yourselves above these two tribes, because out of them shall proceed the salvation of God (ὅτι ἐξ αὐτῶν ἀνατέλει ὑμῖν τὸ σωτήριον τοῦ Θεοῦ). For God will raise the high priest out of Levi, and out of Judah he will raise the king, who is both God and man." In the Testament of Levi also, an angel is represented as saying to Levi, " It is through you and through Judah that the Lord will appear among men." These passages refer to the statement in the original Gospel of the Birth of Mary, that she was of the tribe of Levi, and which is adopted in the third Gospel, where she is made to be the cousin, or more properly the relative (συγγενὴς) of Elizabeth, who was of the tribe of Levi. The Testament of the Twelve Patriarchs, which is of very early date, also traces the descent of Mary to the tribe of Levi. The Fathers have endeavoured to get over this statement, which is fatal to the descent of Christ from David, by saying that Joachim, the father of Mary, married Anna, the daughter of Matthan, whom they suppose to have been a priest! It is unnecessary to say that there is not the slightest ground for this supposition.

The Fathers, however, went much beyond the limits of ingenious surmises: they did not hesitate to invent texts of Scripture when they thought the occasion required it. Thus Tertullian (De Carn. Christ. c. 23) says that the miraculous birth of Christ had been predicted by Ezekiel : " Legimus apud Ezechielem de vaccâ illâ quæ peperit et non peperit;" " We have read in Ezekiel of that cow which calved and yet did not calve." Clemens Alexandrinus (Strom. l. vii.) merely quotes from the Scripture generally : Τέτοκεν, καὶ οὐ τέτοκεν, λέγει ἡ γραφη. St. Epiphanius endeavours to fasten this supposed prophecy on Isaiah, for after quoting Isa. vii. 14, "Therefore the Lord himself shall give you a sign," &c., he says: "The young cow will calve, but they will say she has not calved," and he asserts this to be a prophetic indication of the heretics who did not believe in the miraculous birth of Christ! In later times the monks, in their eagerness to get, by fair or foul means, some confirmation of the story of the miraculous birth, forged some verses, which they attributed to Ovid, in which they pretended that the Sibyl of Tibur (Tivoli) showed Augustus the portrait of the Virgin and the infant Jesus. This production was printed at Lubeck in 1474. The following is an extract from l. iii. of this poem:

Et jam præcepit de quâdam Virgine, per quam
In mundum veniet: nobis erit hæc adeunda:
Hanc Mediatricem dabit humano generi Rex
Largiter veniæ, nostræque salutis amator.
O Virgo felix! O Virgo significata
Per stellas ubi spica nitet! &c.

The incorporeal nature of the Christ of the gospels is the natural result of his miraculous birth. The Manichæans objected that "If the son of Mary is really flesh and blood, she cannot have been a virgin; if she did continue a virgin, that which was born of her must have been a phantom." Augustine gives the following extraordinary answer: "Let the able Manichæus listen to another mystery. A ray of the sun passes through a glass: it penetrates the solid substance of it, and appears inside the room just as it does outside it: it has done no harm to the glass, either on its entrance or on its return: the glass remains entire. It is the same with the Virgin. God entered into her and returned without injury to her virginity." This, however, was merely an evasion of the difficulty. Manichæus spoke of flesh and blood, not of the Deity. He also relied on John i. 15, in which the Son is spoken of as being in the bosom of the Father, and on Matt. x. 40, and other passages, in which the Son is spoken of as having been sent. He also enquired whether the brethren of Jesus mentioned in Matt. xii. 47 were the children of Joseph, or had been miraculously born, and if they were not so born, he argued that Mary must have had Joseph for a husband after the miraculous birth of Christ.

Influenced by these considerations, Paschase Radbert, the celebrated monk of the ninth century, who either invented or propagated the doctrine of Transubstantiation in the West, said that Jesus Christ had never been born at all. He says: " Dicis turpem fuisse filio Dei per vulvam processisse : intorquet pars altera telum, NON EST NATUS DEUS PER NATURAM MULIERIS "—God was not born by means of a woman. Paschase and the monks who followed his teaching, said that Christ had emerged from the body of the Virgin by some aperture which he had made miraculously and closed immediately. Ratramne, his adversary, does not spare him either on the subject of the Real Presence or on this subject. He says, " We must then adopt the belief of the Brahmins, and say that Jesus Christ was born like Buddas, the founder of this sect, who came into the world through the side of a virgin." The orthodox Augustine has laid it down (In Joan. Tract., 221) that Jesus Christ never had any real body ; that his body passed through that of the Virgin without causing any alteration in it; and that this same body passed through the doors of the house where the disciples were when they were shut (John xx. 26). His words are, " Moli corporis ubi Divinitas erat ostia clausa non obstiterunt. Ille quippe, non eis apertis, intrare potuit, quo nascente virginitas matris inviolata permansit."

Plato, who was himself said to have been born of Parectonia without connection with his father Aristin, but by a connection with Apollo, and whom Origen quotes as an instance of the possibility of the miraculous birth, has the following remarks on the subject of incarnations in the second book of his Republic :—" If God were to metamorphose himself, he would assume a more or less perfect form. But it is ridiculous to say that he would change himself into a more perfect form, for then there would be something more perfect than he is, which is absurd. It is impious to admit that he would change himself into something less perfect, for God cannot degrade himself. Besides, if he were to appear in any other shape than his own, he would lie, because he would then appear to be that which he could not be. We must, therefore, conclude that he remains in his own simple form, which is beauty and perfection."

The reason why there is so much similarity between the

religious beliefs of the nations of antiquity is that studious men of all nations who aspired to become the legislators of their countries used to resort to Egypt to obtain instruction in legislation and in religion. Thus Plutarch tells us, for instance, that the hieroglyphs exactly resembled the precepts of Pythagoras, and Lycurgus, Solon, Plato, and many others drew their information from the abundant sources of Egyptian learning. The Egyptian astrologer-priests, however, only granted, generally speaking, a sort of half initiation to those foreigners who had the courage to submit to the formidable ordeals of the mysteries, and as these mysteries were always explained in allegorical language founded on the hieroglyphic writing, the initiated person was obliged to make himself acquainted with this language, which was a matter of extreme difficulty to those who had not been accustomed to it from childhood.

Zoroaster, which Hyde says is a name invented by the Greeks to translate the Persian name Zerdusht, and which is made up of the words Ζωρὸς and Ἀστήρ, that is, "pure star," has established in the Sad-der and the Zend-Avesta a religion which is exactly similar to the Egyptian, which seems to show that both must have had a common, though remote origin. We have Ormuzd and Ahriman, or the two principles which constituted the Deity in the early worship; we have the creation of the world during the six times of the six gâhans of the reign of God; we have the introduction of evil concurrent with the passage of the sun through Libra; we have the end of the world at the end of the six times or the six thousand of the reign of man; we have the redeeming Ram or Lamb; the unleavened bread; baptism; and the worship of that eternal fire which was to regenerate the world, the emblem of which was kept burning by the sacred virgins on the altar of Phtha at Memphis; we have, in short, all the dogmas and ritual of the astrological Egyptian religion.

Mihr, which signifies love, and heat, of which the Greeks, who were unable to pronounce it, made Mithra, was the sungod, or more strictly speaking, was the sun at the summer solstice, when he was represented as a grown-up man with a long beard, the sun at the winter solstice being represented as a child, at the vernal equinox as a young man without a beard, and at the autumnal equinox as an old man. The end of the world and the last judgment were to take place when the summer solstice had passed through the Ram or Aries. The Persians represented the end of the world allegorically by depicting Mithra seated on the ram or on a ram's head, as is shown on a votive bronze hand discovered at Herculaneum. The fingers of this hand express "Divine Justice" in mystic language, for the judgment of the living and the dead is to take place after the end of the world and the general resurrection. The Persian Mihr filled the functions of Virgo, who was the symbol of the summer solstice in Egypt when it was used to determine the different positions of the heavens. This is why in the time of Herodotus, when the Persians were in constant communication with the Egyptians, Mihr or Mithra was not represented by a bearded man, but by a young woman, the Celestial Virgin, whom Herodotus (Clio, c. 130) calls Venus Urania.

The religion of Mithra differs from that of Zoroaster in that according to the latter the end of the world will not take place until the summer solstice corresponds with the star *a* of Pisces, which will be some four thousand years hence, and therefore the disciples of Zoroaster were enabled to enjoy the goods of this world in security. Some of the Magi, however, probably from an erroneous interpretation of the hieroglyphs, thought that this event would take place when the vernal equinox had passed through the Ox, and corresponded to the Pleiades. The Ox, which is represented on the zodiacs of Denderah and Esne, is a different constellation to Taurus, and the stars which determine its position in the Egyptian zodiac are the Pleiades, and the brilliant star in the right shoulder of Orion, which was sacred to Horus, the conqueror of Typhon. They were, therefore, in constant expectation of the end of the world, and turned all their thoughts heavenward, practising self-abnegation, mortification, fasting, celibacy, isolation, and contempt of constituted authority (Tertull. de Præscript, 140). These antisocial ideas at length separated their sect altogether from that of Zoroaster, who formally condemns all these ascetic practices (see Hyde, Hist. Vet. Pers. p. 285; Fréret, Mém. de l'Acad. des Inscript., t. xvi. p. 283; and the Zend-Avesta, vol. iii. p. 601). This was why the Mithraic festival was held at the vernal equinox, while that of the Mirhagans of Persia only began at the winter solstice (Mém. de l'Acad.

ib.) The whole system is developed in the Mithraic monuments, but it is only necessary to observe here that the seven fires, stars, or flames which are on the bas-reliefs which represent this myth, and which are always placed between the sun and the moon, refer to the Pleiades, which correspond to the constellation of the Ox.

When Christianity arose, the Jews had thronged Alexandria, and had acquired by means of bribes many of the privileges reserved to the companions of Alexander (Jos. cont. Apion, l. ii. c. 4). The Ptolemies being patrons of literature and of science, learned men of all nations resorted to Alexandria, which soon became the theatre of religious disputes, and each party in turn appealed to the Egyptian monuments, on which the secrets of the mysteries were preserved in symbolic characters. Contact with Paganism produced the same effect on the Jews as it had done previously when the Asmonean princes had been compelled to issue an edict forbidding the Jews to read Greek books. Sects were formed, the Jewish sacred books were translated, and commentaries were written upon them. The Caraites wished to keep to the literal meaning of the Scriptures, but the majority addicted themselves to the allegorical interpretation of them, and Aristobulus went so far as to write a commentary on the Mosaic law in favour of Ptolemy Philometer.

At this time some of the Alexandrian astrologers ascertained that it was the blood of Aries, not that of the Ox, to the commencement of which the Iesou corresponded in the zodiacs. Iesou in the sacred language signifies the divine power of the heavens, or the winter solstice, because it is at that period that the sun resumes his strength in order to return towards the north.

The name of Jesus is always written ישו Ishυ, or Iesu, in the Talmud, while that of Joshua is written יהושע Ihυsho, or Jueso. The derivation of the name of Jesus given in Matt. i. 21 is erroneous, for in that case Samson would signify Saviour also, for he too was to save Israel (Judges xiii. 5). The Iesou, or winter solstice, always corresponded in the zodiacs to the first degree of Aries. This Iesou, which was symbolically represented by a child sucking its finger, was placed over the interval between Aries and Pisces, and as Virgo, the symbol of the summer solstice, had to come to the primitive Iesou, in order to determine when the reign of

God should commence, by means of the precession of the equinoxes, this Iesou was called the sacred, or anointed one, which the Greeks have correctly translated Χριστός, but which does not in the least correspond to the Jewish משיה (MS/IE) Messiah. All the great periods of antiquity are founded like this one upon the knowledge of the precession of the equinoxes. The Egyptians allowed 24,000 years for their great period, being at the rate of 66.66 years for a degree, or 666 years for a decan (ten degrees), omitting the fraction; 666 is an Apocalyptic number. The Chaldæans, who allowed a hundred years to a degree, allowed 36,000 years to their great period, and 18,000 years to the reign of man. These 18,000 years are identical with the Annus Magnus of Heraclitus. Even so late as the 17th century some learned men still believed in the Chaldæan period.

The Alexandrian astrologers saw the error into which the followers of Mithra had fallen, but either through ignorance or design they took Virgo, who marked the commencement of the year (Hor. Apollo, Hierog. iii.), for the symbol of the vernal equinox, at which period the Alexandrine year used to commence. They announced, therefore, that the end of the world would take place when the vernal equinox corresponded to the star *a* of Pisces. In the mystic language they would have said : "The blood of the Ram has just been shed; the union of Virgo and Aries has just been brought about; Virgo has just given birth to Aries; Virgo has just given birth to Iesou; Virgo has just crushed the head of the serpent [the spirit of death and darkness]; the reign of God is at hand."

We know that the names of Jesus, John, and Mary are found on monuments long anterior to Christianity. On the Zodiac of Denderah the Celestial Virgin holding Horus, symbols which the Egyptians called Marim and Iesou in the mystic language, have been so mutilated by the Christians that only the heads of them remain. This was probably done because there were hieroglyphs which might have revealed the mystery. Iesu, that is, "the divine power of the world," was the sacred name of the Word, or Demiurgus, and was therefore easily confounded with the Iesou of the Zodiacs. The Iesu whom the Virgin carried in her arms was to be put to death at the end of the world, in order to rise again, or give place to another Iesu. This mystery is represented in the sanctuary of the temple of Hermonthis (see

Atlas de la Commiss. d'Égypte, A, Vol. I.) The four virgins who represent the four ages of the world deliver Iesu up to the three virgins who represent the three ages of the reign of God, and Iesu is put to death by the first of the three virgins, in order to give place to the Iesu whom the last of them is suckling. The first Iesu has been mutilated by the Christians. Above this Iesu is the black Scarabæus, rolling in its claws the globe of the universe, so as to set forth the symbolic value of the incarnate Word, or Logos; for the Egyptians represented the Word by a black Scarabæus, as they did life by a green Scarabæus. The second Iesu was called Phtha at Memphis, and Uies (an anagram of Iesu) in the sacred language. In the Mysteries of Eleusis the future Word was also known by the name of Uies (Proclus, l. v.). Joan was the name of the sun from the summer to the winter solstice in the sacred language, after which it was called Iesou. Joan was also called the Baptizer, because the Nile overflows its banks at the summer solstice, and because the Egyptians held that the pure waters of the Abym, which were above the firmament, and from which the Nile was supplied, had the property of washing away the stains of the body and the soul.

Besides Herod the Great, there was another Messiah who preceded him, who was called Jesus (ישו), and who was the pupil of a member of the Sanhedrim called Joshua ben Perachja, with whom he went to Egypt to learn magic, (Sanhedr. f. 107, 2). This is the person alluded to by Celsus (Orig. cont. Cels. i. 28), who makes a Jew say that Jesus, having gone into service in Egypt, had there learnt some magical tricks, and on his return had given himself out to be God : Καὶ (λέγει) ὅτι οὗτος (ὁ Ἰησοῦς) διὰ πενίαν εἰς Αἴγυπτον μισθαρνήσας, κακεῖ δυναμέων τινων πειραθεὶς, ἀφ' αἷς Αἰγύπτιοι σεμνύνονται, ἐπανῆλθεν, ἐν ταῖς δυνάμεσι μέγα φρόνων, καὶ δι' αὐτὰς Θεὸν αὑτὸν ἀνηγόρευσε. The only passage in the gospels which speaks of Jesus as having been in Egypt is Matt. ii., 14, 15, in which, as has been already observed, the Hebrew text of Hos. xi. 2 has been adopted instead of that of the LXX., which has Ἐξ Αἰγύπτου μετακάλεσα τὰ τέκνα αὐτοῦ, "Out of Egypt have I called his [Israel's] children," which would not have suited the writer's purpose. An old MS. of the fourth gospel which is preserved in the archives of the Order of the Temple shows, however, that John vi. 41, 42, was originally, "The Jews then murmured at him because he said, I am the bread which came down from Heaven. And they said, Is not this Jesus, the son of Joseph, whose father and mother we know? how is it then he saith, I came down from heaven? Is it because he has dwelt with the Greeks that he comes thus to hold converse with us? What is there in common between what he has learnt from the Egyptians, and that which our fathers have taught us?" To say that he had dwelt among the Greeks to obtain instruction in Egypt, is to say that he came from Alexandria. Those Pagans who admitted the existence of Jesus, finding all the Egyptian ceremonies in the Christian ritual, said that the founder of Christianity had copied the mysteries of the Egyptian priests (Arnob. contr. Gentes, l. 1); and this passage was struck out in consequence.

The sacred Iesou, the symbol of the primitive winter solstice, would be proclaimed to be the offspring of Virgo, the symbol of the vernal equinox, according to the Alexandrian astrologers, when this equinox corresponded to the star *a* of Pisces. This would bring us to about a hundred years before the Christian era, and it has now been proved (Jost, Geschichte der Isr. 2, s. 80, ff. u. 142 der Anhänge) that Joshua ben Perachja, the instructor of the Jesus who went to Egypt, lived at that time. This Jesus was therefore in Egypt in the reign of Ptolemy VIII., who was despised by the Egyptians because he came to an understanding with the Jews to oppress his subjects, as is shown in a fragment of Porphyry preserved by Eusebius.

It is scarcely necessary to say that the gospels refer to the Zoroastrian prophecies. Sharistani gives the following oracle of Zerdusht or Zoroaster: "There will appear in the later times a man named Oshanderbegha—that is, the Man of the Universe, for he will re-establish justice and religion in it. Petiârch, that is, the Devil, will follow him closely, and use all his efforts to stop the spread of the doctrine of Oshanderbegha for twenty years; but at length another man, named Osiderbegha, will arise, who will cause justice to revive, and will re-establish the good ancient morality, which had been perverted. The kings will obey this man, because he will maintain the true religion, and make peace and prosperity flourish." Abulpharagius says, "Zoroaster, the teacher of the Maguseans, taught the Persians that our Lord Jesus Christ would be manifested, and ordered them to bring him presents when he should be born. He told them that in the last times a virgin should conceive, and that when her son was born a star would appear which would shine in the daytime, in the middle of which they would see the face of a young girl. 'It is you, my children,' added Zoroaster, 'who will see it before all other nations. As soon as ye see this star, go wherever it leads you. Worship this new-born child; offer your presents to him; for he is the lord who created heaven.'" Solomon, the Metropolitan of Bussora, gives a somewhat different account in his book called "Apis, or the Bee," in which there was a chapter on the prophecy of Zoroaster respecting Christ. He says that Zoroaster predicted the birth of Christ, but confided the secret to a certain Gusmazaph and to two other Persian magi, called Sasanes and Mahainades. The astrological character of all this is evident.

Lucian says that the Redeemer was expected by the early Christians in the month Mesin, which is the month in which the Egyptians celebrated the feast of Harpocrates, who is represented like the Iesou of the Zodiacs, as a child whom Isis was delivered of at the winter solstice (Plut. de Is. c. 11 and 12). The reason the Christian festivals were fixed on the same dates as the Egyptian ones was, that the bishops of Rome referred these matters to the patriarchs of Alexandria. Leo the Great admitted to the Emperor Marcian, that the Church of Alexandria had always had the privilege of appointing the moveable feasts. Speaking of the reform of the calendar he says: "This is why the Fathers of the Church have always *passed over errors*, and have delegated to the Bishop of Alexandria the task of appointing the festivals, because the Egyptians seem to have always had the gift of calculation."

The result of what has been said is that the Gospels, which lay no claim to Divine inspiration, cannot be regarded as historical documents, but as Origen observes, have incorporated with things which [may?] have happened, other things which have not happened. They are in all probability, as Philo (quoted by Eusebius, H. E. ii. 17) says, "the commentaries of ancient men, who, as the founders of the sect [of the Therapeutæ], have left many monuments of this doctrine in allegorical representations, which they use as certain models, imitating the manner of the original institution." "It is highly probable," continues Eusebius, "that the ancient commentaries which he says they have, are the very gospels and writings of the Apostles, and probably some expositions of the ancient prophets, such as are contained in the Epistle to the Hebrews, and many other of St. Paul's Epistles." He goes on to say that he considers the declarations of Philo to be spoken of men of his own religion only, and that their monastic and ascetic practices can only be found "in the religion of Christians, according to the Gospel." Conf. John xiv. 2. "In my Father's house are many cells ($\mu o \nu a i$)" as in a monastery. Eusebius also says that "they expound the sacred writings by obscure, allegorical, and figurative expressions. [Conf. Gal. iv. 24, 'which things are an allegory.'] For the whole law appears to these persons like an animal, of which the literal expressions are the body, but the invisible sense that lies enveloped in the expressions, the soul."

Basnage (Hist. des Juifs) has thoroughly examined the treatise of Philo on which Eusebius bases these statements, and has proved that the Therapeutæ were neither Christians nor monks, as indeed how could they be? Eusebius says, that though they were not Jews, nor inhabitants of Palestine, they were "very likely descended from Hebrews, and therefore were wont to observe very many of the customs of the ancients after a more Jewish fashion." The identity of the allegorical modes of interpretation may be seen in the following description of the Pagan mysteries by Julius Firmicus (De Error. Prof. Rel.), as compared with that of the Christian mysteries by the Fathers, as given by Beausobre. Firmicus says, "In those funerals and lamentations which are annually celebrated in honour of Osiris, their defenders wish to pretend a physical reason: they call the seeds of fruit Osiris, the earth Isis, *the natural heat* Typhon; and because the fruits are ripened by the natural heat, are collected for the life of man, and are separated from their matrimony to the earth, and are sown again when winter approaches, this they would have to be the death of Osiris; but when the fruits, by the genial fostering of the earth, begin again to be generated by a new procreation, this is the finding of Osiris." Beausobre says, "In one word, the suffering Jesus is nothing else than what the Manichæans called the members of God; that is to say, the celestial substance, or the souls which have descended from heaven. The earth is the Virgin; the heavenly substance which is in the earth is the substance of the Virgin, of which Jesus Christ was formed; the Holy Ghost is *the natural heat,* by whose virtue the earth conceived him; and he becomes an infant in being made to pass through the plants, and from thence again into heaven." The meaning of passing through the plants is explained, by St. Augustine, who says, in answer to Faustus, who asked him how many Christs there were, " The suffering Christ whom the earth conceives by the virtue of the Holy Ghost, and which it engenders, which not only hangs on all the trees, but which circulates through all plants, he whom the Jews crucified under Pontius Pilate, and he who dwells in the sun and in the moon, are they three Christs, or only one and the same Christ, who with reference to some of his parts is bound on all the trees, and who, being free as to his other parts, aids those which are bound and imprisoned." In another place he says, that according to the bodily presence there cannot be three Christs, one on the cross, another in the sun, and another in the moon.

It is impossible to understand how Christianity took such deep root among the civilized nations of the world without a full knowledge of the fabric of imposture by which it was sustained. Modern martyrs die in the most prosaic manner by the hands of the savage or the executioner, but the ancient ones seldom died like any one else. Polycarp, who was bishop of Smyrna, and who had been appointed, as we are informed, by the apostles, with whom he was personally acquainted, was surrounded by the flames like the sail of a vessel inflated by the wind, and when his persecutors saw that the flames would not injure him they ordered the executioner to plunge his sword into him, upon which such a quantity of blood gushed out that the fire was extinguished (Euseb., H. E., iv. 15). Eusebius also tells a story of a bull which tossed others that approached from without on his horns, but was not able even to approach the five saints who were cast before him (ib. viii. 5).

Miracles were in fact almost the rule, not the exception. Irenæus (quoted by Eusebius, H. E. v. 7) says, " Some must certainly and truly cast out devils . . . . others have the knowledge of things to come . . . . *and even the* dead have been raised, and continued with us for many years." Arnobius and Origen challenge the Pagans to cast out devils as was done daily by "the most simple and rustic Christians." Narcissus, finding the oil fail in the lamps while the deacons were keeping the vigils at the great watch of the Passover, prayed over some water from a neighbouring well, and it was turned into oil (Euseb., H. E., vi. 9). Eusebius says that some of this oil was preserved to his time. Fabianus was appointed bishop of Rome by a dove suddenly flying down from on high, like the Holy Spirit descending upon Christ (ib. vi. 29). At times an invisible hand restrains those who seek to rob the saints of their property, and even the dead were compelled to reveal where they had hidden it (Sozom. H. E., i. 11), and corpses used to cross their hands when the funeral service was read over them (Tertull. de Animâ, c. 51). The Pagans were invariably represented as men without faith or morals, guilty of every crime that could be mentioned, and exposed to the wrath of God. Some, however, whom God wished to convert, escaped by being lashed by holy angels throughout the night (Euseb., H. E., v. 28). Jerome (Comm. in Zech. xiv. 12) says, "Zechariah tells those who have fought against Jerusalem that their flesh shall consume away, and their eyes consume away in their holes, and their tongue consume in their mouth, and this prediction has been literally accomplished in the case of the oppressors of the Church, such as Valerian, Decius, Diocletian, Maximian, and Julian." It is needless to say that these assertions are totally false.

In conclusion, as the doctrine of original sin lies in reality at the root of all the doctrinal teaching of the present day, we shall briefly state what the Jews themselves believe respecting it, admitting, for the sake of argument, that the statement in Genesis is inspired, and is to be received literally. It is necessary, however, to observe that the Rabbis are greatly divided in opinion as to the nature of the sin of Adam. R. Eliezer (Pirké Eliezer, c. 21), speaking of the tree of knowledge, says, " This is what R. Zehira teaches on this subject. It is written, 'Ye shall not eat of the tree which is in the midst of the garden.' This does not refer to a tree, popularly so called, but to man, who resembles a tree, as it is said, 'Man is like a tree of the field.' As to the words 'The tree is in the midst of the garden,' they do not refer to the Garden of Eden, but are a metaphorical expression, videlicet in medio corporis, quod est medio horti, seu in medio fœminæ. The garden is the woman, as in Solomon's Song (iv. 12), 'A garden inclosed is my sister.'" Clemens Alexandrinus (Strom. l. III.) says that it consisted in Adam's marrying Eve before God had given his consent, and therefore they were justly condemned by God for not having obeyed his will (δικαία ἡ κρίσις τοῦ Θεοῦ ἐπὶ τοὺς οὐκ ἀναμείνοντας τὸ βούλημα). Philo (De Opif. Mund.) says that the serpent who tempted Adam and Eve was very probably nothing but pleasure.

The Jewish opinion to which we have alluded is that, even supposing that Adam sinned in the way described, the Deluge, which left only the just Noah and his descendants, did away with the consequences of it; for God (Gen. ix. 1) blessed Noah and his sons in the very same terms that he blessed Adam and Eve in Gen. i. 28. Enough has been said, however, to show that this absurd fable was not credited even by those who were most credulous in other matters, and that the ordinary representations of God as an inexorable creditor who will be paid, no matter how or by whom, are as false as they are irreligious. It is utterly false, too, to pretend that death is a penalty, or that there ever was a time when it did not exist. As Drummond asks in his "Cypress Grove," "Shall the heavens stay their ever-rolling wheels, and hold still time to prolong thy miserable days, as if the highest of their working were to do homage unto thee? Thy death is a part of the order of this *all*, a part of the life of this world; for while the world is a world, some creatures must die, and others take life. . . . And when the Lord of this universe hath showed us the amazing wonders of his various frame, should we take it to heart, when he thinketh time, to dislodge? This is his unalterable and inevitable decree: as we had no part of our will in our entrance into this life, we should not presume to any on our leaving it, but soberly learn to will that which he wills, whose very will giveth being to all that it wills; and, reverencing the orderer, not repine at the order and laws, which all-where and always are so perfectly established that who would assay to correct and amend any of them, he should either make them worse or desire things beyond the level of possibility."

LONDON: PRINTED BY
SPOTTISWOODE AND CO., NEW-STREET SQUARE
AND PARLIAMENT STREET

39 PATERNOSTER ROW, E.C.
LONDON: *November* 1872.

GENERAL LIST OF WORKS

PUBLISHED BY

Messrs. LONGMANS, GREEN, READER, and DYER.

ARTS, MANUFACTURES, &c............... 13
ASTRONOMY, METEOROLOGY, POPULAR
   GEOGRAPHY, &c. 8
BIOGRAPHICAL WORKS 4
CHEMISTRY, MEDICINE, SURGERY, and
   the ALLIED SCIENCES 11
CRITICISM, PHILOSOPHY, POLITY, &c.... 5
FINE ARTS and ILLUSTRATED EDITIONS 12
HISTORY, POLITICS, and HISTORICAL
   MEMOIRS 1
INDEX ....21—24
KNOWLEDGE for the YOUNG 20

MISCELLANEOUS WORKS and POPULAR
   METAPHYSICS 6
NATURAL HISTORY & POPULAR SCIENCE 9
PERIODICAL PUBLICATIONS 20
POETRY and THE DRAMA 18
RELIGIOUS and MORAL WORKS 14
RURAL SPORTS, &c...................... 19
TRAVELS, VOYAGES, &c. 16
WORKS OF FICTION 17
WORKS of UTILITY and GENERAL
   INFORMATION 19

History, Politics, Historical Memoirs, &c.

Estimates of the English Kings from William the Conqueror to George III. By J. LANGTON SANFORD, Author of 'Studies and Illustrations of the Great Rebellion' &c. Crown 8vo. price 12s. 6d.

The History of England from the Fall of Wolsey to the Defeat of the Spanish Armada. By JAMES ANTHONY FROUDE, M.A.

   CABINET EDITION, 12 vols. cr. 8vo. £3 12s.
   LIBRARY EDITION, 12 vols. 8vo. £8 18s.

The English in Ireland in the Eighteenth Century. By JAMES ANTHONY FROUDE, M.A. late Fellow of Exeter College, Oxford. In Two Volumes. VOL. I., 8vo. price 16s.

The History of England from the Accession of James II. By Lord MACAULAY:—

   STUDENT'S EDITION, 2 vols. crown 8vo. 12s.
   PEOPLE'S EDITION, 4 vols. crown 8vo. 16s.
   CABINET EDITION, 8 vols. post 8vo. 48s.
   LIBRARY EDITION, 5 vols. 8vo. £4.

Lord Macaulay's Works. Complete and uniform Library Edition. Edited by his Sister, Lady TREVELYAN. 8 vols. 8vo. with Portrait, price £5. 5s. cloth, or £8. 8s. bound in tree-calf by Rivière.

Memoirs of Baron Stockmar. By his Son, Baron E. VON STOCKMAR. Translated from the German by G. A. M. Edited by MAX MÜLLER, M.A. 2 vols. crown 8vo. price 21s.

Varieties of Vice-Regal Life. By Major-General Sir WILLIAM DENISON, K.C.B. late Governor-General of the Australian Colonies, and Governor of Madras. With Two Maps. 2 vols. 8vo. 28s.

On Parliamentary Government in England: its Origin, Development, and Practical Operation. By ALPHEUS TODD, Librarian of the Legislative Assembly of Canada. 2 vols. 8vo. price £1. 17s.

The Constitutional History of England since the Accession of George III. 1760—1860. By Sir THOMAS ERSKINE MAY, K.C.B. Cabinet Edition (the Third), thoroughly revised. 3 vols. crown 8vo. price 18s.

A Historical Account of the Neutrality of Great Britain during the American Civil War. By MOUNTAGUE BERNARD, M.A. Royal 8vo. price 16s.

The History of England, from the Earliest Times to the Year 1865. By C. D. YONGE, Regius Professor of Modern History in Queen's College, Belfast. New Edition. Crown 8vo. 7s. 6d.

A

Lectures on the History of England, from the Earliest Times to the Death of King Edward II. By WILLIAM LONGMAN. With Maps and Illustrations. 8vo. 15s.

The History of the Life and Times of Edward the Third. By WILLIAM LONGMAN. With 9 Maps, 8 Plates, and 16 Woodcuts. 2 vols. 8vo. 28s.

History of Civilization in England and France, Spain and Scotland. By HENRY THOMAS BUCKLE. New Edition of the entire work, with a complete INDEX. 3 vols. crown 8vo. 24s.

Realities of Irish Life. By W. STEUART TRENCH, Land Agent in Ireland to the Marquess of Lansdowne, the Marquess of Bath, and Lord Digby. Fifth Edition. Crown 8vo. 6s.

The Student's Manual of the History of Ireland. By M. F. CUSACK, Authoress of 'The Illustrated History of Ireland.' Crown 8vo. price 6s.

A Student's Manual of the History of India, from the Earliest Period to the Present. By Colonel MEADOWS TAYLOR, M.R.A.S. M.R.I.A. Crown 8vo. with Maps, 7s. 6d.

The History of India, from the Earliest Period to the close of Lord Dalhousie's Administration. By JOHN CLARK MARSHMAN. 3 vols. crown 8vo. 22s. 6d.

Indian Polity; a View of the System of Administration in India. By Lieut.-Col. GEORGE CHESNEY. Second Edition, revised, with Map. 8vo. 21s.

A Colonist on the Colonial Question. By JEHU MATHEWS, of Toronto, Canada. Post 8vo. price 6s.

An Historical View of Literature and Art in Great Britain from the Accession of the House of Hanover to the Reign of Queen Victoria. By J. MURRAY GRAHAM, M.A. 8vo. price 14s.

Waterloo Lectures: a Study of the Campaign of 1815. By Colonel CHARLES C. CHESNEY, R.E. late Professor of Military Art and History in the Staff College. Second Edition. 8vo. with Map, 10s. 6d.

Memoir and Correspondence relating to Political Occurrences in June and July 1834. By EDWARD JOHN LITTLETON, First Lord Hatherton. Edited, from the Original Manuscript, by HENRY REEVE, C.B. D.C.L. 8vo. price 7s. 6d.

Chapters from French History; St. Louis, Joan of Arc, Henri IV. with Sketches of the Intermediate Periods. By J. H. GURNEY, M.A. New Edition. Fcp. 8vo. 6s. 6d.

History of the Reformation in Europe in the Time of Calvin. By J. H. MERLE D'AUBIGNÉ, D.D. VOLS. I. and II. 8vo. 28s. VOL. III. 12s. VOL. IV. price 16s. and VOL. V. price 16s.

Royal and Republican France. A Series of Essays reprinted from the 'Edinburgh,' 'Quarterly,' and 'British and Foreign' Reviews. By HENRY REEVE, C.B. D.C.L. 2 vols. 8vo. price 21s.

The Imperial and Colonial Constitutions of the Britannic Empire, including Indian Institutions. By Sir EDWARD CREASY, M.A. &c. With Six Maps. 8vo price 15s.

Home Politics: being a Consideration of the Causes of the Growth of Trade in relation to Labour, Pauperism, and Emigration. By DANIEL GRANT. 8vo. 7s.

The Oxford Reformers—John Colet, Erasmus, and Thomas More; being a History of their Fellow-Work. By FREDERIC SEEBOHM. Second Edition. 8vo. 14s.

The History of Greece. By C. THIRLWALL, D.D. Lord Bishop of St. David's 8 vols. fcp. 28s.

The Tale of the Great Persian War, from the Histories of Herodotus. By GEORGE W. COX, M.A. late Scholar of Trin. Coll. Oxon. Fcp. 3s. 6d.

The Sixth Oriental Monarchy or, the History, Geography, and Antiquities of Parthia. Collected and Illustrated from Ancient and Modern sources. By GEORGE RAWLINSON, M.A. Camden Professor of Ancient History in the University of Oxford, and Canon of Canterbury. 8vo with Maps and Illustrations.
[*Nearly ready.*

Greek History from Themistocles to Alexander, in a Series of Lives from Plutarch. Revised and arranged by A. H CLOUGH. Fcp. with 44 Woodcuts, 6s.

Critical History of the Language and Literature of Ancient Greece By WILLIAM MURE, of Caldwell. 5 vols 8vo. £3 9s.

History of the Literature o Ancient Greece. By Professor K. O. MÜLLER Translated by LEWIS and DONALDSON 3 vols. 8vo. 21s.

The History of Rome. By WILHELM IHNE. English Edition, translated and revised by the Author. VOLS. I. and II. 8vo. 30s.

History of the City of Rome from its Foundation to the Sixteenth Century of the Christian Era. By THOMAS H. DYER, LL.D. 8vo. with 2 Maps, 15s.

History of the Romans under the Empire. By Very Rev. CHARLES MERIVALE, D.C.L. Dean of Ely. 8 vols. post 8vo. price 48s.

The Fall of the Roman Republic; a Short History of the Last Century of the Commonwealth. By the same Author. 12mo. 7s. 6d.

Encyclopædia of Chronology, Historical and Biographical: comprising the Dates of all the Great Events of History, including Treaties, Alliances, Wars, Battles, &c.; Incidents in the Lives of Eminent Men, Scientific and Geographical Discoveries, Mechanical Inventions, and Social, Domestic, and Economical Improvements. By B. B. WOODWARD, B.A. and W. L. R. CATES. 8vo. price 42s.

History of European Morals from Augustus to Charlemagne. By W. E. H. LECKY, M.A. 2 vols. 8vo. price 28s.

History of the Rise and Influence of the Spirit of Rationalism in Europe. By the same Author. Cabinet Edition (the Fourth). 2 vols. crown 8vo. price 16s.

God in History; or, the Progress of Man's Faith in the Moral Order of the World. By the late Baron BUNSEN. Translated from the German by SUSANNA WINKWORTH; with a Preface by Dean STANLEY. 3 vols. 8vo. 42s.

Socrates and the Socratic Schools. Translated from the German of Dr. E. ZELLER, with the Author's approval, by the Rev. OSWALD J. REICHEL, B.C.L. and M.A. Crown 8vo. 8s. 6d.

The Stoics, Epicureans, and Sceptics. Translated from the German of Dr. E. ZELLER, with the Author's approval, by OSWALD J. REICHEL, B.C.L. and M.A. Crown 8vo. 14s.

The English Reformation. By F. C. MASSINGBERD, M.A. Chancellor of Lincoln. 4th Edition, revised. Fcp. 7s. 6d.

Three Centuries of Modern History. By CHARLES DUKE YONGE, Regius Professor of Modern History and English Literature in Queen's College, Belfast. Crown 8vo. 7s. 6d.

Saint-Simon and Saint-Simonism; a Chapter in the History of Socialism in France. By ARTHUR J. BOOTH, M.A. Crown 8vo. price 7s. 6d.

The History of Philosophy, from Thales to Comte. By GEORGE HENRY LEWES. Fourth Edition, corrected, and partly rewritten. 2 vols. 8vo. 32s.

The Mythology of the Aryan Nations. By GEORGE W. COX, M.A. late Scholar of Trinity College, Oxford. 2 vols. 8vo. price 28s.

Maunder's Historical Treasury; comprising a General Introductory Outline of Universal History, and a Series of Separate Histories. Fcp. 8vo. price 6s.

Critical and Historical Essays contributed to the *Edinburgh Review* by the Right Hon. Lord MACAULAY:—
   STUDENT'S EDITION, crown 8vo. 6s.
   PEOPLE'S EDITION, 2 vols. crown 8vo. 8s.
   CABINET EDITION, 4 vols. 24s.
   LIBRARY EDITION, 3 vols. 8vo. 36s.

History of the Early Church, from the First Preaching of the Gospel to the Council of Nicæa, A.D. 325. By the Author of 'Amy Herbert.' New Edition. Fcp. 4s. 6d.

Sketch of the History of the Church of England to the Revolution of 1688. By the Right Rev. T. V. SHORT, D.D. Lord Bishop of St. Asaph. Eighth Edition. Crown 8vo. 7s. 6d.

History of the Christian Church, from the Ascension of Christ to the Conversion of Constantine. By E. BURTON, D.D. late Regius Prof. of Divinity in the University of Oxford. Fcp. 3s. 6d.

History of the Christian Church, from the Death of St. John to the Middle of the Second Century; comprising a full Account of the Primitive Organisation of Church Government, and the Growth of Episcopacy. By T. W. MOSSMAN, B.A. Rector of East and Vicar of West Torrington, Lincolnshire. 8vo. [*In the press.*

Biographical Works.

Life of Alexander von Humboldt.
Compiled, in Commemoration of the Centenary of his Birth, by JULIUS LÖWENBERG, ROBERT AVÉ-LALLEMANT, and ALFRED DOVE. Edited by Professor KARL BRUHNS, Director of the Observatory at Leipzig. Translated from the German by JANE and CAROLINE LASSELL. 2 vols. 8vo. with Three Portraits. [*Nearly ready.*

Autobiography of John Milton;
or, Milton's Life in his own Words. By the Rev. JAMES J. G. GRAHAM, M.A. Crown 8vo. with Vignette-Portrait, price 5s.

Recollections of Past Life. By Sir HENRY HOLLAND, Bart. M.D. F.R.S., &c. Physician-in-Ordinary to the Queen. Second Edition. Post 8vo. 10s. 6d.

Biographical and Critical Essays.
By A. HAYWARD, Esq., Q.C. A New Series. 2 vols. 8vo. [*In the press.*

The Life of Isambard Kingdom
Brunel, Civil Engineer. By ISAMBARD BRUNEL, B.C.L. of Lincoln's Inn, Chancellor of the Diocese of Ely. With Portrait, Plates, and Woodcuts. 8vo. 21s.

Lord George Bentinck; a Political Biography. By the Right Hon. B. DISRAELI, M.P. Eighth Edition, revised, with a new Preface. Crown 8vo. 6s.

The Life and Letters of the Rev.
Sydney Smith. Edited by his Daughter, Lady HOLLAND, and Mrs. AUSTIN. New Edition, complete in One Volume. Crown 8vo. price 6s.

Memoir of George Edward Lynch
Cotton, D.D. Bishop of Calcutta, and Metropolitan. With Selections from his Journals and Correspondence. Edited by Mrs. COTTON. New Edition. Crown 8vo.
[*Just ready.*

The Life and Travels of George
Whitefield, M.A. By JAMES PATERSON GLEDSTONE. 8vo. price 14s.

The Life and Times of Sixtus
the Fifth. By Baron HÜBNER. Translated from the Original French, with the Author's sanction, by HUBERT E. H. JERNINGHAM. 2 vols. 8vo. 24s.

Essays in Ecclesiastical Biography. By the Right Hon. Sir J. STEPHEN, LL.D. Cabinet Edition. Crown 8vo. 7s. 6d.

Father Mathew; a Biography.
By JOHN FRANCIS MAGUIRE, M.P. Popular Edition, with Portrait. Crown 8vo. 3s. 6d.

The Life and Letters of Faraday
By Dr. BENCE JONES, Secretary of the Royal Institution. Second Edition, with Portrait and Woodcuts. 2 vols. 8vo. 28s.

Faraday as a Discoverer. By JOHN TYNDALL, LL.D. F.R.S. New and Cheaper Edition, with Two Portraits. Fcp. 8vo price 3s. 6d.

The Royal Institution: its Founder and its First Professors. By Dr. BENCE JONES, Honorary Secretary. Post 8vo price 12s. 6d.

Leaders of Public Opinion in Ireland; Swift, Flood, Grattan, O'Connell By W. E. H. LECKY, M.A. New Edition revised and enlarged. Crown 8vo. 7s. 6d.

A Group of Englishmen (1795 to 1815); Records of the Younger Wedgwoods and their Friends, embracing the History of the Discovery of Photography. By ELIZA METEYARD. 8vo. 16s.

Life of the Duke of Wellington.
By the Rev. G. R. GLEIG, M.A. Popular Edition, carefully revised; with copious Additions. Crown 8vo. with Portrait, 5s.

Dictionary of General Biography;
containing Concise Memoirs and Notices of the most Eminent Persons of all Countries from the Earliest Ages to the Present Time Edited by WILLIAM L. R. CATES. 8vo price 21s.

Letters and Life of Francis
Bacon, including all his Occasional Works Collected and edited, with a Commentary by J. SPEDDING. VOLS. I. to VI. 8vo price £3. 12s. To be completed in One more Volume.

Felix Mendelssohn's Letters from
Italy and Switzerland, and *Letters* from 1833 to 1847, translated by Lady WALLACE With Portrait. 2 vols. crown 8vo. 5s. each

Musical Criticism and Biography.
Selected from the Published and Unpublished Writings of THOMAS DAMANT EATON, late President of the Norwich Choral Society. Edited by his SONS. Crown 8vo.

Lives of the Queens of England.
By AGNES STRICKLAND. Library Edition newly revised; with Portraits of every Queen, Autographs, and Vignettes. 8 vols post 8vo. 7s. 6d. each.

History of my Religious Opinions. By J. H. NEWMAN, D.D. Being the Substance of Apologia pro Vitâ Suâ. Post 8vo. price 6s.

Memoirs of Sir Henry Havelock, K.C.B. By JOHN CLARK MARSHMAN. People's Edition, with Portrait. Crown 8vo. price 3s. 6d.

Vicissitudes of Families. By Sir J. BERNARD BURKE, C.B. Ulster King of Arms. New Edition, remodelled and enlarged. 2 vols. crown 8vo. 21s.

Maunder's Biographical Treasury. Thirteenth Edition, reconstructed and partly re-written, with above 1,000 additional Memoirs, by W. L. R. CATES. Fcp. 8vo.6s.

Criticism, Philosophy, Polity, &c.

On Representative Government. By JOHN STUART MILL. Third Edition. 8vo. 9s. crown 8vo. 2s.

On Liberty. By the same Author. Fourth Edition. Post 8vo. 7s. 6d. Crown 8vo. 1s. 4d.

Principles of Political Economy. By the same. Seventh Edition. 2 vols. 8vo. 30s. or in 1 vol. crown 8vo. 5s.

Utilitarianism. By the same. 4th Edit.8vo.5s.

Dissertations and Discussions. By the same Author. Second Edition. 3 vols. 8vo. price 36s.

Examination of Sir W. Hamilton's Philosophy, and of the principal Philosophical Questions discussed in his Writings. By the same. Third Edition. 8vo. 16s.

The Subjection of Women. By JOHN STUART MILL. New Edition. Post 8vo. 5s.

Analysis of the Phenomena of the Human Mind. By JAMES MILL. A New Edition, with Notes, Illustrative and Critical, by ALEXANDER BAIN, ANDREW FINDLATER, and GEORGE GROTE. Edited, with additional Notes, by JOHN STUART MILL. 2 vols. 8vo. price 28s.

Principles of Political Philosophy; being the Second Edition, revised and extended, of 'The Elements of Political Economy.' By H. D. MACLEOD, M.A., Barrister-at-Law. In Two Volumes. VOL. I. 8vo. price 15s.

A Dictionary of Political Economy; Biographical, Bibliographical, Historical, and Practical. By the same Author. VOL. I. royal 8vo. 30s.

A Systematic View of the Science of Jurisprudence. By SHELDON AMOS, M.A. Professor of Jurisprudence, University College, London. 8vo. price 18s.

The Institutes of Justinian; with English Introduction, Translation, and Notes. By T. C. SANDARS, M.A. Barrister-at-Law. New Edition. 8vo. 15s.

Lord Bacon's Works, collected and edited by R. L. ELLIS, M.A. J. SPEDDING, M.A. and D. D. HEATH. New and Cheaper Edition. 7 vols. 8vo. price £3. 13s. 6d.

A System of Logic, Ratiocinative and Inductive. By JOHN STUART MILL. Eighth Edition. 2 vols. 8vo. 25s.

The Ethics of Aristotle; with Essays and Notes. By Sir A. GRANT, Bart. M.A. LL.D. Third Edition, revised and partly re-written. [In the press.

The Nicomachean Ethics of Aristotle. Newly translated into English. By R. WILLIAMS, B.A. Fellow and late Lecturer Merton College, Oxford. 8vo. 12s.

Bacon's Essays, with Annotations. By R. WHATELY, D.D. late Archbishop of Dublin. Sixth Edition. 8vo. 10s. 6d.

Elements of Logic. By R. WHATELY, D.D. late Archbishop of Dublin. New Edition. 8vo. 10s. 6d. crown 8vo. 4s. 6d.

Elements of Rhetoric. By the same Author. New Edition. 8vo. 10s. 6d. Crown 8vo. 4s. 6d.

English Synonymes. By E. JANE WHATELY. Edited by Archbishop WHATELY. 5th Edition. Fcp. 3s.

An Outline of the Necessary Laws of Thought: a Treatise on Pure and Applied Logic. By the Most Rev. W. THOMSON, D.D. Archbishop of York. Ninth Thousand. Crown 8vo. 5s. 6d.

Causality; or, the Philosophy of Law Investigated. By GEORGE JAMIESON, B.D. of Old Machar. Second Edition, greatly enlarged. 8vo. price 12s.

Speeches of the Right Hon. Lord MACAULAY, corrected by Himself. People's Edition, crown 8vo. 3s. 6d.

Lord Macaulay's Speeches on Parliamentary Reform in 1831 and 1832. 16mo. price ONE SHILLING.

A Dictionary of the English Language. By R. G. LATHAM, M.A. M.D. F.R.S. Founded on the Dictionary of Dr. S. JOHNSON, as edited by the Rev. H. J. TODD, with numerous Emendations and Additions. 4 vols. 4to. price £7.

Thesaurus of English Words and Phrases, classified and arranged so as to facilitate the expression of Ideas, and assist in Literary Composition. By P. M. ROGET, M.D. New Edition. Crown 8vo. 10s. 6d.

Three Centuries of English Literature. By CHARLES DUKE YONGE, Regius Professor of Modern History and English Literature in Queen's College, Belfast. Crown 8vo. 7s. 6d.

Lectures on the Science of Language. By F. MAX MÜLLER, M.A. &c. Foreign Member of the French Institute. Sixth Edition. 2 vols. crown 8vo. price 16s.

Chapters on Language. By F. W. FARRAR, M.A. F.R.S. Head Master of Marlborough College. Crown 8vo. 8s. 6d.

Southey's Doctor, complete in One Volume, edited by the Rev. J. W. WARTER, B.D. Square crown 8vo. 12s. 6d.

Manual of English Literature, Historical and Critical; with a Chapter on English Metres. By THOMAS ARNOLD, M.A. Second Edition. Crown 8vo. 7s. 6d.

A Latin-English Dictionary. By JOHN T. WHITE, D.D. Oxon. and J. E. RIDDLE, M.A. Oxon. Third Edition, revised. 2 vols. 4to. pp. 2,128, price 42s.

White's College Latin-English Dictionary (Intermediate Size), abridged from the Parent Work for the use of University Students. Medium 8vo. pp. 1,048, price 18s.

White's Junior Student's Complete Latin-English and English-Latin Dictionary. Revised Edition. Square 12mo. pp. 1,058, price 12s.

Separately { ENGLISH-LATIN, 5s. 6d.
{ LATIN-ENGLISH, 7s. 6d.

An English-Greek Lexicon, containing all the Greek Words used by Writers of good authority. By C. D. YONGE, B.A. New Edition. 4to. 21s.

Mr. Yonge's New Lexicon, English and Greek, abridged from his larger work (as above). Square 12mo. 8s. 6d.

A Greek-English Lexicon piled by H. G. LIDDELL, D.D. Christ Church, and R. SCOTT, D. of Rochester. Sixth Edition. C price 36s.

A Lexicon, Greek and E abridged for Schools from LIDI SCOTT'S *Greek-English Lexicon.* F Edition. Square 12mo. 7s. 6d.

The Mastery of Languag the Art of Speaking Foreign Idiomatically. By THOMAS PREN late of the Civil Service at Madras. Edition. 8vo. 6s.

A Practical Dictionary French and English Languages. fessor LÉON CONTANSEAU, ma French Examiner for Military Appointments, &c. New Edition, revised. Post 8vo. 10s. 6d.

Contanseau's Pocket Dicti French and English, abridged Practical Dictionary, by the Auth Edition. 18mo. price 3s. 6d.

A Sanskrit-English Dict The Sanskrit words printed bo original Devanagari and in Roma with References to the Best E Sanskrit Authors, and with Et and comparisons of Cognate Wor in Greek, Latin, Gothic, and An Compiled by T. BENFEY. 8vo. 5

New Practical Dictionary German Language; German-En English-German. By the Rev BLACKLEY, M.A. and Dr. CARI FRIEDLÄNDER. Post 8vo. 7s. 6d.

Historical and Critical Cc tary on the Old Testament; wi Translation. By M. M. KALIS Vol. I. *Genesis,* 8vo. 18s. or adap General Reader, 12s. Vol. II. *E:* or adapted for the General Re Vol III. *Leviticus,* Part I. 15s. o for the General Reader, 8s. Vol. *ticus,* Part II. 15s. or adaptec General Reader, 8s.

A Hebrew Grammar, with E By the same. Part I. *Outlines* cises, 8vo. 12s. 6d. KEY, 5s. Pa ceptional Forms and Construction

---

Miscellaneous Works and *Popular Metaphysics.*

An Introduction to Mental Philosophy, on the Inductive Method. By J. D. MORELL, M.A. LL.D. 8vo. 12s.

Elements of Psychology ing the Analysis of the Intellectu By J. D. MORELL, LL.D. Post 8

Recreations of a Country Parson.
By A. K. H. B. Two Series, 3s. 6d. each.

Seaside Musings on Sundays and Weekdays. By A. K. H. B. Crown 8vo. price 3s. 6d.

Present-Day Thoughts. By A. K. H. B. Crown 8vo. 3s. 6d.

Changed Aspects of Unchanged Truths; Memorials of St. Andrews Sundays. By A. K. H. B. Crown 8vo. 3s. 6d.

Counsel and Comfort from a City Pulpit. By A. K. H. B. Crown 8vo. 3s. 6d.

Lessons of Middle Age, with some Account of various Cities and Men. By A. K. H. B. Crown 8vo. 3s. 6d.

Leisure Hours in Town; Essays Consolatory, Æsthetical, Moral, Social, and Domestic. By A. K. H. B. Crown 8vo. 3s. 6d.

Sunday Afternoons at the Parish Church of a Scottish University City. By A. K. H. B. Crown 8vo. 3s. 6d.

The Commonplace Philosopher in Town and Country. By A. K. H. B. 3s. 6d.

The Autumn Holidays of a Country Parson. By A. K. H. B. Crown 8vo. 3s. 6d.

Critical Essays of a Country Parson. By A. K. H. B. Crown 8vo. 3s. 6d.

The Graver Thoughts of a Country Parson. By A. K. H. B. Two Series, 3s. 6d. each.

Miscellaneous and Posthumous Works of the late Henry Thomas Buckle. Edited, with a Biographical Notice by HELEN TAYLOR. 3 vols. 8vo. price 2l. 12s. 6d.

Short Studies on Great Subjects. By JAMES ANTHONY FROUDE, M.A. late Fellow of Exeter College, Oxford. 2 vols. crown 8vo. price 12s.

Miscellaneous Writings of John Conington, M.A. late Corpus Professor of Latin in the University of Oxford. Edited by J. A. SYMONDS, M.A. With a Memoir by H. J. S. SMITH, M.A. LL.D. F.R.S. 2 vols. 8vo. price 28s.

The Rev. Sydney Smith's Miscellaneous Works. 1 vol. crown 8vo. 6s.

The Wit and Wisdom of the Rev. SYDNEY SMITH; a Selection of the most memorable Passages in his Writings and Conversation. Crown 8vo. 3s. 6d.

The Eclipse of Faith; or, a Visit to a Religious Sceptic. By HENRY ROGERS. Twelfth Edition. Fcp. 8vo. 5s.

Defence of the Eclipse of Faith, by its Author. Third Edition. Fcp. 8vo. 3s. 6d.

Lord Macaulay's Miscellaneous Writings:—
LIBRARY EDITION, 2 vols. 8vo. Portrait, 21s.
PEOPLE'S EDITION, 1 vol. crown 8vo. 4s. 6d.

Lord Macaulay's Miscellaneous Writings and Speeches. Student's Edition, in One Volume, crown 8vo. price 6s.

Families of Speech, Four Lectures delivered at the Royal Institution of Great Britain. By the Rev. F. W. FARRAR, M.A. F.R.S. Post 8vo. with 2 Maps, 5s. 6d.

Chips from a German Workshop; being Essays on the Science of Religion, and on Mythology, Traditions, and Customs. By F. MAX MÜLLER, M.A. &c. Foreign Member of the French Institute. 3 vols. 8vo. £2.

A Budget of Paradoxes. By AUGUSTUS DE MORGAN, F.R.A.S. and C.P.S. of Trinity College, Cambridge. Reprinted, with the Author's Additions, from the *Athenæum*. 8vo. price 15s.

The Secret of Hegel: being the Hegelian System in Origin, Principle, Form, and Matter. By JAMES HUTCHISON STIRLING. 2 vols. 8vo. 28s.

Sir William Hamilton; being the Philosophy of Perception: an Analysis. By JAMES HUTCHISON STIRLING. 8vo. 5s.

As Regards Protoplasm. By J. H. STIRLING, LL.D. Second Edition, with Additions, in reference to Mr. Huxley's Second Issue and a new PREFACE in reply to Mr. Huxley in 'Yeast.' 8vo. price 2s.

Ueberweg's System of Logic, and History of Logical Doctrines. Translated, with Notes and Appendices, by T. M. LINDSAY, M.A. F.R.S.E. 8vo. price 16s.

The Philosophy of Necessity; or, Natural Law as applicable to Mental, Moral, and Social Science. By CHARLES BRAY. Second Edition. 8vo. 9s.

A Manual of Anthropology, or Science of Man, based on Modern Research. By the same Author. Crown 8vo. 6s.

On Force, its Mental and Moral Correlates. By the same Author. 8vo. 5s.

The Discovery of a New World of Being. By GEORGE THOMSON. Post 8vo. 6s.

Time and Space; a Metaphysical Essay. By SHADWORTH H. HODGSON. 8vo. price 16s.

The Theory of Practice; an Ethical Inquiry. By SHADWORTH H. HODGSON. 2 vols. 8vo. price 24s.

The Senses and the Intellect.
By ALEXANDER BAIN, LL.D. Prof. of Logic in the Univ. of Aberdeen. Third Edition. 8vo. 15s.

Mental and Moral Science: a Compendium of Psychology and Ethics. By ALEXANDER BAIN, LL.D. Third Edition. Crown 8vo. 10s. 6d. Or separately: PART I. *Mental Science*, 6s. 6d. PART II. *Moral Science*, 4s. 6d.

A Treatise on Human Nature; being an Attempt to Introduce the Experimental Method of Reasoning into Moral Subjects. By DAVID HUME. Edited, with Notes, &c. by T. H. GREEN, Fellow, and T. H. GROSE, late Scholar, of Balliol College, Oxford. 2 vols. 8vo. [*In the press.*

Essays Moral, Political, and Literary. By DAVID HUME. By the same Editors. 2 vols. 8vo. [*In the press.*

Astronomy, Meteorology, Popular Geography, &c.

Outlines of Astronomy. By Sir J. F. W. HERSCHEL, Bart. M.A. Eleventh Edition, with 9 Plates and numerous Diagrams. Square crown 8vo. 12s.

Essays on Astronomy. A Series of Papers on Planets and Meteors, the Sun and sun-surrounding Space, Stars and Star Cloudlets; and a Dissertation on the approaching Transit of Venus: preceded by a Sketch of the Life and Work of Sir J. Herschel. By R. A. PROCTOR, B.A. With 10 Plates and 24 Woodcuts. 8vo. price 12s.

Schellen's Spectrum Analysis, in its Application to Terrestrial Substances and the Physical Constitution of the Heavenly Bodies. Translated by JANE and C. LASSELL; edited, with Notes, by W. HUGGINS, LL.D. F.R.S. With 13 Plates (6 coloured) and 223 Woodcuts. 8vo. 28s.

The Sun; Ruler, Light, Fire, and Life of the Planetary System. By RICHARD A. PROCTOR, B.A. F.R.A.S. Second Edition; with 10 Plates (7 coloured) and 107 Woodcuts. Crown 8vo. price 14s.

Saturn and its System. By the same Author. 8vo. with 14 Plates, 14s.

Magnetism and Deviation of the Compass. For the use of Students in Navigation and Science Schools. By JOHN MERRIFIELD, LL.D. F.R.A.S. With Diagrams. 18mo. price 1s. 6d.

Navigation and Nautical Astronomy (Practical, Theoretical, Scientific) for the use of Students and Practical Men. By J. MERRIFIELD, F.R.A.S. and H. EVERS. 8vo. 14s.

Air and Rain; the Beginnings of a Chemical Climatology. By ROBERT ANGUS SMITH, Ph.D. F.R.S. F.C.S. Government Inspector of Alkali Works, with 8 Illustrations. 8vo. price 24s.

The Star Depths; or, other Suns than Ours; a Treatise on Stars, Star-Systems, and Star-Cloudlets. By R. A. PROCTOR, B.A. Crown 8vo. with numerous Illustrations. [*Nearly ready.*

The Orbs Around Us; a Series of Familiar Essays on the Moon and Planets, Meteors and Comets, the Sun and Coloured Pairs of Suns. By R. A. PROCTOR, B.A. Crown 8vo. price 7s. 6d.

Other Worlds than Ours; the Plurality of Worlds Studied under the Light of Recent Scientific Researches. By R. A. PROCTOR, B.A. Third Edition, revised and corrected; with 14 Illustrations. Crown 8vo. 10s. 6d.

Celestial Objects for Common Telescopes. By T. W. WEBB, M.A. F.R.A.S. New Edition, revised, with Map of the Moon and Woodcuts. [*In the press.*

A General Dictionary of Geography, Descriptive, Physical, Statistical, and Historical; forming a complete Gazetteer of the World. By A. KEITH JOHNSTON, F.R.S.E. New Edition. 8vo. price 31s. 6d.

The Public Schools Atlas of Modern Geography. In Thirty-one Maps, exhibiting clearly the more important Physical Features of the Countries delineated, and Noting all the Chief Places of Historical, Commercial, and Social Interest. Edited, with an Introduction, by the Rev. G. BUTLER, M.A. Imperial quarto, price 3s. 6d. sewed; 5s. cloth.

A New Star Atlas, for the Library, the School, and the Observatory, in Twelve Circular Maps (with Two Index Plates) Intended as a Companion to 'Webb's Celestial Objects for Common Telescopes.' With a Letterpress Introduction on the Study of the Stars, illustrated by 9 Diagrams. By RICHARD A. PROCTOR, B.A. Hon. Sec. R.A.S. Crown 8vo. 5s.

Nautical Surveying, an Introduction to the Practical and Theoretical Study of. By JOHN KNOX LAUGHTON, M.A. F.R.A.S. Small 8vo. price 6s.

Maunder's Treasury of Geography, Physical, Historical, Descriptive, and Political. Edited by W. HUGHES, F.R.G.S. With 7 Maps and 16 Plates. Fcp. 8vo. 6s.

Natural History and Popular Science.

Natural Philosophy for General Readers and Young Persons; a Course of Physics divested of Mathematical Formulæ and expressed in the language of daily life. Translated from Ganot's *Cours de Physique*, by E. ATKINSON, Ph.D. F.C.S. Crown 8vo. with 404 Woodcuts, price 7s. 6d.

Mrs. Marcet's Conversations on Natural Philosophy. Revised by the Author's SON, and augmented by Conversations on Spectrum Analysis and Solar Chemistry. With 36 Plates. Crown 8vo. price 7s. 6d.

Ganot's Elementary Treatise on Physics, Experimental and Applied, for the use of Colleges and Schools. Translated and Edited with the Author's sanction by E. ATKINSON, Ph.D. F.C.S. New Edition, revised and enlarged; with a Coloured Plate and 726 Woodcuts. Post 8vo. 15s.

Text-Books of Science, Mechanical and Physical. The following may now be had, price 3s. 6d. each :—
1. GOODEVE's Mechanism.
2. BLOXAM's Metals.
3. MILLER's Inorganic Chemistry.
4. GRIFFIN's Algebra and Trigonometry.
5. WATSON's Plane and Solid Geometry.
6. MAXWELL's Theory of Heat.
7. MERRIFIELD's Technical Arithmetic and Mensuration.
8. ANDERSON's Strength of Materials.

Dove's Law of Storms, considered in connexion with the ordinary Movements of the Atmosphere. Translated by R. H. SCOTT, M.A. T.C.D. 8vo. 10s. 6d.

The Correlation of Physical Forces. By W. R. GROVE, Q.C. V.P.R.S. Fifth Edition, revised, and Augmented by a Discourse on Continuity. 8vo. 10s. 6d. The *Discourse*, separately, price 2s. 6d.

Fragments of Science. By JOHN TYNDALL, LL.D. F.R.S. Third Edition. 8vo. price 14s.

Heat a Mode of Motion. By JOHN TYNDALL, LL.D. F.R.S. Fourth Edition. Crown 8vo. with Woodcuts, price 10s. 6d.

Sound; a Course of Eight Lectures delivered at the Royal Institution of Great Britain. By JOHN TYNDALL, LL.D. F.R.S. New Edition, with Portrait and Woodcuts. Crown 8vo. 9s.

Researches on Diamagnetism and Magne-Crystallic Action; including the Question of Diamagnetic Polarity. By JOHN TYNDALL, LL.D. F.R.S. With 6 Plates and many Woodcuts. 8vo. 14s.

Notes of a Course of Nine Lectures on Light, delivered at the Royal Institution, A.D. 1869. By J. TYNDALL, LL.D. F.R.S. Crown 8vo. 1s. sewed, or 1s. 6d. cloth.

Notes of a Course of Seven Lectures on Electrical Phenomena and Theories, delivered at the Royal Institution, A.D. 1870. By JOHN TYNDALL, LL.D. F.R.S. Crown 8vo. 1s. sewed, or 1s. 6d. cloth.

A Treatise on Electricity, in Theory and Practice. By A. DE LA RIVE, Prof. in the Academy of Geneva. Translated by C. V. WALKER, F.R.S. 3 vols 8vo. with Woodcuts, £3. 13s.

Light Science for Leisure Hours; a Series of Familiar Essays on Scientific Subjects, Natural Phenomena, &c. By R. A. PROCTOR, B.A. Crown 8vo. price 7s. 6d.

Light: its Influence on Life and Health. By FORBES WINSLOW, M.D. D.C.L. Oxon. (Hon.) Fcp. 8vo. 6s.

Professor Owen's Lectures on the Comparative Anatomy and Physiology of the Invertebrate Animals. Second Edition, with 235 Woodcuts. 8vo. 21s.

The Comparative Anatomy and Physiology of the Vertebrate Animals. By RICHARD OWEN, F.R.S. D.C.L. With 1,472 Woodcuts. 3 vols. 8vo. £3 13s. 6d.

Kirby and Spence's Introduction to Entomology, or Elements of the Natural History of Insects. Crown 8vo. 5s.

Homes without Hands; a Description of the Habitations of Animals, classed according to their Principle of Construction. By Rev. J. G. WOOD, M.A. F.L.S. With about 140 Vignettes on Wood. 8vo. 21s.

Strange Dwellings; a Description of the Habitations of Animals, abridged from 'Homes without Hands.' By J. G. WOOD, M.A. F.L.S. With a New Frontispiece and about 60 other Woodcut Illustrations. Crown 8vo. price 7s. 6d.

Van Der Hoeven's Handbook of ZOOLOGY. Translated from the Second Dutch Edition by the Rev. W. CLARK, M.D. F.R.S. 2 vols. 8vo. with 24 Plates of Figures, 60s.

The Harmonies of Nature and Unity of Creation. By Dr. G. HARTWIG. 8vo. with numerous Illustrations, 18s.

The Sea and its Living Wonders. By the same Author. Third Edition, enlarged. 8vo. with many Illustrations, 21s.

The Subterranean World. By the same Author. With 3 Maps and about 80 Woodcut Illustrations, including 8 full size of page. 8vo. price 21s.

The Polar World: a Popular Description of Man and Nature in the Arctic and Antarctic Regions of the Globe. By the same Author. With 8 Chromoxylographs, 3 Maps, and 85 Woodcuts. 8vo. 21s.

A Familiar History of Birds. By E. STANLEY, D.D. late Lord Bishop of Norwich. Fcp. with Woodcuts, 3s. 6d.

Insects at Home; a Popular Account of British Insects, their Structure, Habits, and Transformations. By the Rev. J. G. WOOD, M.A. F.L.S. With upwards of 700 Illustrations engraved on Wood. 8vo. price 21s.

Insects Abroad; being a Popular Account of Foreign Insects, their Structure, Habits, and Transformations. By J. G. WOOD, M.A. F.L.S. Author of 'Homes without Hands' &c. In One Volume, printed and illustrated uniformly with 'Insects at Home,' to which it will form a Sequel and Companion. [*In the press.*

The Primitive Inhabitants of Scandinavia. Containing a Description of the Implements, Dwellings, Tombs, and Mode of Living of the Savages in the North of Europe during the Stone Age. By SVEN NILSSON. 8vo. Plates and Woodcuts, 18s.

The Origin of Civilisation, and the Primitive Condition of Man; Mental and Social Condition of Savages. By Sir JOHN LUBBOCK, Bart. M.P. F.R.S. Second Edition, with 25 Woodcuts. 8vo. 16s.

The Ancient Stone Implements, Weapons, and Ornaments, of Great Britain. By JOHN EVANS, F.R.S. F.S.A. 8vo. with 2 Plates and 476 Woodcuts, price 28s.

Mankind, their Origin and Destiny. By an M.A. of Balliol College, Oxford. Containing a New Translation of the First Three Chapters of Genesis; a Critical Examination of the First Two Gospels; an Explanation of the Apocalypse; and the Origin and Secret Meaning of the Mythological and Mystical Teaching of the Ancients. With 31 Illustrations. 8vo. price 31s. 6d.

An Exposition of Fallacies in the Hypothesis of Mr. Darwin. By C. R. BREE, M.D. F.Z.S. Author of 'Birds of Europe not Observed in the British Isles' &c. With 36 Woodcuts. Crown 8vo. price 14s.

Bible Animals; a Description of every Living Creature mentioned in the Scriptures, from the Ape to the Coral. By the Rev. J. G. WOOD, M.A. F.L.S. With about 100 Vignettes on Wood. 8vo. 21s.

Maunder's Treasury of Natural History, or Popular Dictionary of Zoology. Revised and corrected by T. S. COBBOLD, M.D. Fcp. 8vo. with 900 Woodcuts, 6s.

The Elements of Botany for Families and Schools. Tenth Edition, revised by THOMAS MOORE, F.L.S. Fcp. with 154 Woodcuts, 2s. 6d.

The Treasury of Botany, or Popular Dictionary of the Vegetable Kingdom; with which is incorporated a Glossary of Botanical Terms. Edited by J. LINDLEY, F.R.S. and T. MOORE, F.L.S. Pp. 1,274, with 274 Woodcuts and 20 Steel Plates. Two PARTS, fcp. 8vo. 12s.

The Rose Amateur's Guide. By THOMAS RIVERS. New Edition. Fcp. 4s.

Loudon's Encyclopædia of Plants; comprising the Specific Character, Description, Culture, History, &c. of all the Plants found in Great Britain. With upwards of 12,000 Woodcuts. 8vo. 42s.

Maunder's Scientific and Literary Treasury; a Popular Encyclopædia of Science, Literature, and Art. New Edition, in part rewritten, with above 1,000 new articles, by J. Y. JOHNSON. Fcp. 6s.

A Dictionary of Science, Literature, and Art. Fourth Edition, re-edited by the late W. T. BRANDE (the Author) and GEORGE W. COX, M.A. 3 vols. medium 8vo. price 63s. cloth.

Chemistry, Medicine, Surgery, and the Allied Sciences.

A Dictionary of Chemistry and the Allied Branches of other Sciences. By HENRY WATTS, F.C.S. assisted by eminent Scientific and Practical Chemists. 5 vols. medium 8vo. price £7 3s.

Supplement, completing the Record of Discovery to the end of 1869. 8vo. 31s. 6d.

Contributions to Molecular Physics in the domain of Radiant Heat; a Series of Memoirs published in the Philosophical Transactions, &c. By JOHN TYNDALL, LL.D. F.R.S. With 2 Plates and 31 Woodcuts. 8vo. price 16s.

Elements of Chemistry, Theoretical and Practical. By WILLIAM A. MILLER, M.D. LL.D. Professor of Chemistry, King's College, London. New Edition. 3 vols. 8vo. £3.
PART I. CHEMICAL PHYSICS, 15s.
PART II. INORGANIC CHEMISTRY, 21s.
PART III. ORGANIC CHEMISTRY, 24s.

A Course of Practical Chemistry, for the use of Medical Students. By W. ODLING, M.B. F.R.S. New Edition, with 70 new Woodcuts. Crown 8vo. 7s. 6d.

Outlines of Chemistry; or, Brief Notes of Chemical Facts. By the same Author. Crown 8vo. 7s. 6d.

A Manual of Chemical Physiology, including its Points of Contact with Pathology. By J. L. W. THUDICHUM, M.D. 8vo. with Woodcuts, price 7s. 6d.

Select Methods in Chemical Analysis, chiefly Inorganic. By WILLIAM CROOKES, F.R.S. With 22 Woodcuts. Crown 8vo. price 12s. 6d.

Chemical Notes for the Lecture Room. By THOMAS WOOD, F.C.S. 2 vols. crown 8vo. I. on Heat, &c. price 5s. II. on the Metals, price 5s.

The Diagnosis, Pathology, and Treatment of Diseases of Women; including the Diagnosis of Pregnancy. By GRAILY HEWITT, M.D. &c. Third Edition, revised and for the most part re-written; with 132 Woodcuts. 8vo. 24s.

Lectures on the Diseases of Infancy and Childhood. By CHARLES WEST, M.D. &c. Fifth Edition. 8vo. 16s.

On Some Disorders of the Nervous System in Childhood. Being the Lumleian Lectures delivered before the Royal College of Physicians in March 1871. By CHARLES WEST, M.D. Crown 8vo. 5s.

On the Surgical Treatment of Children's Diseases. By T. HOLMES, M.A. &c. late Surgeon to the Hospital for Sick Children. Second Edition, with 9 Plates and 112 Woodcuts. 8vo. 21s.

Lectures on the Principles and Practice of Physic. By Sir THOMAS WATSON, Bart. M.D. Physician-in-Ordinary to the Queen. Fifth Edition, thoroughly revised. 2 vols. 8vo. price 36s.

Lectures on Surgical Pathology. By Sir JAMES PAGET, Bart. F.R.S. Third Edition, revised and re-edited by the Author and Professor W. TURNER, M.B. 8vo. with 131 Woodcuts, 21s.

Cooper's Dictionary of Practical Surgery and Encyclopædia of Surgical Science. New Edition, brought down to the present time. By S. A. LANE, Surgeon to St. Mary's Hospital, &c. assisted by various Eminent Surgeons. 2 vols. 8vo. price 25s. each.

Pulmonary Consumption; its Nature, Varieties, and Treatment: with an Analysis of One Thousand Cases to exemplify its Duration. By C. J. B. WILLIAMS, M.D. F.R.S. and C. T. WILLIAMS, M.A. M.D. Oxon. Post 8vo. price 10s. 6d.

Anatomy, Descriptive and Surgical. By HENRY GRAY, F.R.S. With about 410 Woodcuts from Dissections. Sixth Edition, by T. HOLMES, M.A. Cantab. With a New Introduction by the Editor. Royal 8vo. 28s.

The House I Live in; or, Popular Illustrations of the Structure and Functions of the Human Body. Edited by T. G. GIRTIN. New Edition, with 25 Woodcuts. 16mo. price 2s. 6d.

The Science and Art of Surgery; being a Treatise on Surgical Injuries, Diseases, and Operations. By JOHN ERIC ERICHSEN, Senior Surgeon to University College Hospital, and Holme Professor of Clinical Surgery in University College, London. A New Edition, being the Sixth, revised and enlarged; with 712 Woodcuts. 2 vols. 8vo. price 32s.

A System of Surgery, Theoretical and Practical, in Treatises by Various Authors. Edited by T. HOLMES, M.A. &c. Surgeon and Lecturer on Surgery at St. George's Hospital, and Surgeon-in-Chief to the Metropolitan Police. Second Edition, thoroughly revised, with numerous Illustrations. 5 vols. 8vo. £5 5s.

Clinical Lectures on Diseases of the Liver, Jaundice, and Abdominal Dropsy. By C. MURCHISON, M.D. Physician to the Middlesex Hospital. Post 8vo. with 25 Woodcuts, 10s. 6d.

Todd and Bowman's Physiological Anatomy and Physiology of Man. With numerous Illustrations. VOL. II. 8vo. price 25s.
VOL. I. New Edition by Dr. LIONEL S. BEALE, F.R.S. in course of publication, with numerous Illustrations. PARTS I. and II. price 7s. 6d. each.

Outlines of Physiology, Human and Comparative. By JOHN MARSHALL, F.R.C.S. Surgeon to the University College Hospital. 2 vols. crown 8vo. with 122 Woodcuts, 32s.

Copland's Dictionary of Practical Medicine, abridged from the larger work, and throughout brought down to the present state of Medical Science. 8vo. 36s.

Dr. Pereira's Elements of Materia Medica and Therapeutics, abridged and adapted for the use of Medical and Pharmaceutical Practitioners and Students. Edited by Professor BENTLEY, F.L.S. &c. and by Dr. REDWOOD, F.C.S. &c. With 125 Woodcut Illustrations. 8vo. price 25s.

The Essentials of Materia Medica and Therapeutics. By ALFRED BARING GARROD, M.D. F.R.S. &c. Physician to King's College Hospital. Third Edition, Sixth Impression, brought up to 1870. Crown 8vo. price 12s. 6d.

The Fine Arts, and *Illustrated Editions.*

Grotesque Animals, invented, described, and portrayed by E. W. COOKE, R.A. F.R.S. in Twenty-Four Plates, with Elucidatory Comments. Royal 4to. price 21s.

In Fairyland; Pictures from the Elf-World. By RICHARD DOYLE. With a Poem by W. ALLINGHAM. With Sixteen Plates, containing Thirty-six Designs printed in Colours. Folio, 31s. 6d.

Albert Durer, his Life and Works; including Autobiographical Papers and Complete Catalogues. By WILLIAM B. SCOTT. With Six Etchings by the Author and other Illustrations. 8vo. 16s.

Half-Hour Lectures on the History and Practice of the Fine and Ornamental Arts. By. W. B. SCOTT. Second Edition. Crown 8vo. with 50 Woodcut Illustrations, 8s. 6d.

The Chorale Book for England: the Hymns Translated by Miss C. WINKWORTH; the Tunes arranged by Prof. W. S. BENNETT and OTTO GOLDSCHMIDT. Fcp. 4to. 12s. 6d.

The New Testament, illustrated with Wood Engravings after the Early Masters, chiefly of the Italian School. Crown 4to. 63s. cloth, gilt top; or £5 5s. morocco.

The Life of Man Symbolised by the Months of the Year in their Seasons and Phases. Text selected by RICHARD PIGOT. 25 Illustrations on Wood from Original Designs by JOHN LEIGHTON, F.S.A. Quarto, 42s.

Cats and Farlie's Moral Emblems; with Aphorisms, Adages, and Proverbs of all Nations: comprising 121 Illustrations on Wood by J. LEIGHTON, F.S.A. with an appropriate Text by R. PIGOT. Imperial 8vo. 31s. 6d.

Sacred and Legendary Art. By Mrs. JAMESON. 6 vols. square crown 8vo. price £5 15s. 6d. as follows:—

Legends of the Saints and Martyrs. New Edition, with 19 Etchings and 187 Woodcuts. 2 vols. price 31s. 6d.

Legends of the Monastic Orders. New Edition, with 11 Etchings and 88 Woodcuts. 1 vol. price 21s.

Legends of the Madonna. New Edition, with 27 Etchings and 165 Woodcuts. 1 vol. price 21s.

The History of Our Lord, with that of His Types and Precursors. Completed by Lady EASTLAKE. Revised Edition, with 13 Etchings and 281 Woodcuts. 2 vols. price 42s.

Lyra Germanica, the Christian Year. Translated by CATHERINE WINKWORTH, with 125 Illustrations on Wood drawn by J. LEIGHTON, F.S.A. Quarto, 21s.

Lyra Germanica. the Christian Life. Translated by CATHERINE WINKWORTH; with about 200 Woodcut Illustrations by J. LEIGHTON, F.S.A. and other Artists. Quarto, 21s.

The Useful Arts, Manufactures, &c.

Gwilt's Encyclopædia of Architecture, with above 1,600 Woodcuts. Fifth Edition, with Alterations and considerable Additions, by WYATT PAPWORTH. 8vo. price 52s. 6d.

A Manual of Architecture: being a Concise History and Explanation of the principal Styles of European Architecture, Ancient, Mediæval, and Renaissance; with their Chief Variations and a Glossary of Technical Terms. By THOMAS MITCHELL. With 150 Woodcuts. Crown 8vo. 10s. 6d.

History of the Gothic Revival; an Attempt to shew how far the taste for Mediæval Architecture was retained in England during the last two centuries, and has been re-developed in the present. By C. L. EASTLAKE, Architect. With 48 Illustrations (36 full size of page). Imperial 8vo. price 31s. 6d.

Hints on Household Taste in Furniture, Upholstery, and other Details. By CHARLES L. EASTLAKE, Architect. New Edition, with about 90 Illustrations. Square crown 8vo. 18s.

Lathes and Turning, Simple, Mechanical, and Ornamental. By W. HENRY NORTHCOTT. With about 240 Illustrations on Steel and Wood. 8vo. 18s.

Perspective; or, the Art of Drawing what one Sees. Explained and adapted to the use of those Sketching from Nature. By Lieut. W. H. COLLINS, R.E. F.R.A.S. With 37 Woodcuts. Crown 8vo. price 5s.

Principles of Mechanism, designed for the use of Students in the Universities, and for Engineering Students generally. By R. WILLIS, M.A. F.R.S. &c. Jacksonian Professor in the Univ. of Cambridge. Second Edition; with 374 Woodcuts. 8vo. 18s.

Handbook of Practical Telegraphy. By R. S. CULLEY, Memb. Inst. C.E. Engineer-in-Chief of Telegraphs to the Post-Office. Fifth Edition, revised and enlarged; with 118 Woodcuts and 9 Plates. 8vo. price 14s.

Ure's Dictionary of Arts, Manufactures, and Mines. Sixth Edition, rewritten and greatly enlarged by ROBERT HUNT, F.R.S. assisted by numerous Contributors. With 2,000 Woodcuts. 3 vols. medium 8vo. £4 14s. 6d.

Encyclopædia of Civil Engineering, Historical, Theoretical, and Practical. By E. CRESY, C.E. With above 3,000 Woodcuts. 8vo. 42s.

Catechism of the Steam Engine, in its various Applications to Mines, Mills, Steam Navigation, Railways, and Agriculture. By JOHN BOURNE, C.E. New Edition, with 89 Woodcuts. Fcp. 8vo. 6s.

Handbook of the Steam Engine. By JOHN BOURNE, C.E. forming a KEY to the Author's Catechism of the Steam Engine. With 67 Woodcuts. Fcp. 8vo. price 9s.

Recent Improvements in the Steam-Engine. By JOHN BOURNE, C.E. New Edition, including many New Examples, with 124 Woodcuts. Fcp. 8vo. 6s.

A Treatise on the Steam Engine, in its various Applications to Mines, Mills, Steam Navigation, Railways, and Agriculture. By J. BOURNE, C.E. New Edition; with Portrait, 37 Plates, and 546 Woodcuts. 4to. 42s.

A Treatise on the Screw Propeller, Screw Vessels, and Screw Engines, as adapted for purposes of Peace and War. By JOHN BOURNE, C.E. Third Edition, with 54 Plates and 287 Woodcuts. Quarto, price 63s.

Bourne's Examples of Modern Steam, Air, and Gas Engines of the most Approved Types, as employed for Pumping, for Driving Machinery, for Locomotion, and for Agriculture, minutely and practically described. In course of publication, to be completed in Twenty-four Parts, price 2s. 6d. each, forming One Volume, with about 50 Plates and 400 Woodcuts.

Treatise on Mills and Millwork. By Sir W. FAIRBAIRN, Bart. F.R.S. New Edition, with 18 Plates and 322 Woodcuts. 2 vols. 8vo. 32s.

Useful Information for Engineers. By the same Author. FIRST, SECOND, and THIRD SERIES, with many Plates and Woodcuts. 3 vols. crown 8vo. 10s. 6d. each.

The Application of Cast and Wrought Iron to Building Purposes. By the same Author. Fourth Edition, with 6 Plates and 118 Woodcuts. 8vo. 16s.

Iron Ship Building, its History and Progress, as comprised in a Series of Experimental Researches. By Sir W. FAIRBAIRN, Bart. F.R.S. With 4 Plates and 130 Woodcuts, 8vo. 18s.

The Strains in Trusses Computed by means of Diagrams; with 20 Examples drawn to Scale. By F. A. RANKEN, M.A. C.E. Lecturer at the Hartley Institution, Southampton. With 35 Diagrams. Square crown 8vo. price 6s. 6d.

Mitchell's Manual of Practical Assaying. Third Edition for the most part re-written, with all the recent Discoveries incorporated. By W. CROOKES, F.R.S. With 188 Woodcuts. 8vo. 28s.

The Art of Perfumery ; the History and Theory of Odours, and the Methods of Extracting the Aromas of Plants. By Dr. PIESSE, F.C.S. Third Edition, with 53 Woodcuts. Crown 8vo. 10s. 6d.

Bayldon's Art of Valuing Rents and Tillages, and Claims of Tenants upon Quitting Farms, both at Michaelmas and Lady-Day. Eighth Edition, revised by J. C. MORTON. 8vo. 10s. 6d.

On the Manufacture of Beet-Root Sugar in England and Ireland. By WILLIAM CROOKES, F.R.S. With 11 Woodcuts. 8vo. 8s. 6d.

Practical Treatise on Metallurgy, adapted from the last German Edition of Professor KERL's *Metallurgy* by W. CROOKES, F.R.S. &c. and E. RÖHRIG, Ph.D. M.E. 3 vols. 8vo. with 625 Woodcuts, price £4 19s.

Loudon's Encyclopædia of Agriculture: comprising the Laying-out, Improvement, and Management of Landed Property, and the Cultivation and Economy of the Productions of Agriculture. With 1,100 Woodcuts. 8vo. 21s.

Loudon's Encyclopædia of Gardening : comprising the Theory and Practice of Horticulture, Floriculture, Arboriculture, and Landscape Gardening. With 1,000 Woodcuts. 8vo. 21s.

Religious and *Moral Works.*

The Outlines of the Christian Ministry Delineated, and brought to the Test of Reason, Holy Scripture, History, and Experience, with a view to the Reconciliation of Existing Differences concerning it, especially between Presbyterians and Episcopalians. By CHRISTOPHER WORDSWORTH, D.C.L. &c. Bishop of St. Andrew's, and Fellow of Winchester College. Crown 8vo. price 7s. 6d.

Christian Counsels, selected from the Devotional Works of Fénelon, Archbishop of Cambrai. Translated by A. M. JAMES. Crown 8vo. price 5s.

Ecclesiastical Reform. Nine Essays by various Writers. Edited by the Rev. ORBY SHIPLEY, M.A. Crown 8vo. [*Nearly ready.*

Authority and Conscience ; a Free Debate on the Tendency of Dogmatic Theology and on the Characteristics of Faith. Edited by CONWAY MOREL. Post 8vo. 7s. 6d.

Reasons of Faith ; or, the Order of the Christian Argument Developed and Explained. By the Rev. G. S. DREW, M.A. Second Edition, revised and enlarged. Fcp. 8vo. 6s.

Christ the Consoler ; a Book of Comfort for the Sick. With a Preface by the Right Rev. the Lord Bishop of Carlisle. Small 8vo. 6s.

The True Doctrine of the Eucharist. By THOMAS S. L. VOGAN, D.D. Canon and Prebendary of Chichester and Rural Dean. 8vo. 18s.

The Student's Compendium of the Book of Common Prayer ; being Notes Historical and Explanatory of the Liturgy of the Church of England. By the Rev. H. ALLDEN NASH. Fcp. 8vo. price 2s. 6d.

Synonyms of the Old Testament, their Bearing on Christian Faith and Practice. By the Rev. ROBERT B. GIRDLESTONE, M.A. 8vo. price 15s.

Fundamentals ; or, Bases of Belief concerning Man and God: a Handbook of Mental, Moral, and Religious Philosophy. By the Rev. T. GRIFFITH, M.A. 8vo. price 10s. 6d.

An Introduction to the Theology of the Church of England, in an Exposition of the Thirty-nine Articles. By the Rev. T. P. BOULTBEE, LL.D. Fcp. 8vo. price 6s.

Christian Sacerdotalism, viewed from a Layman's standpoint or tried by Holy Scripture and the Early Fathers ; with a short Sketch of the State of the Church from the end of the Third to the Reformation in the beginning of the Sixteenth Century. By JOHN JARDINE, M.A. LL.D. 8vo. 8s. 6d.

Prayers for the Family and for Private Use, selected from the Collection of the late Baron BUNSEN, and Translated by CATHERINE WINKWORTH. Fcp. 8vo. price 3s. 6d.

Churches and their Creeds. By the Rev. Sir PHILIP PERRING, Bart. late Scholar of Trin. Coll. Cambridge, and University Medallist. Crown 8vo. 10s. 6d.

The Truth of the Bible; Evidence from the Mosaic and other Records of Creation; the Origin and Antiquity of Man; the Science of Scripture; and from the Archæology of Different Nations of the Earth. By the Rev. B. W. SAVILE, M.A. Crown 8vo. 7s. 6d.

Considerations on the Revision of the English New Testament. By C. J. ELLICOTT, D.D. Lord Bishop of Gloucester and Bristol. Post 8vo. price 5s. 6d.

An Exposition of the 39 Articles, Historical and Doctrinal. By E. HAROLD BROWNE, D.D. Lord Bishop of Ely. Ninth Edition. 8vo. 16s.

The Voyage and Shipwreck of St. Paul; with Dissertations on the Ships and Navigation of the Ancients. By JAMES SMITH, F.R.S. Crown 8vo. Charts, 10s. 6d.

The Life and Epistles of St. Paul. By the Rev. W. J. CONYBEARE, M.A. and the Very Rev. J. S. HOWSON, D.D. Dean of Chester. Three Editions :—

LIBRARY EDITION, with all the Original Illustrations, Maps, Landscapes on Steel, Woodcuts, &c. 2 vols. 4to. 48s.

INTERMEDIATE EDITION, with a Selection of Maps, Plates, and Woodcuts. 2 vols. square crown 8vo. 21s.

STUDENT'S EDITION, revised and condensed, with 46 Illustrations and Maps. 1 vol. crown 8vo. 9s.

Evidence of the Truth of the Christian Religion derived from the Literal Fulfilment of Prophecy. By ALEXANDER KEITH, D.D. 37th Edition, with numerous Plates, in square 8vo. 12s. 6d.; also the 39th Edition, in post 8vo. with 5 Plates, 6s.

The History and Destiny of the World and of the Church, according to Scripture. By the same Author. Square 8vo. with 40 Illustrations, 10s.

The History and Literature of the Israelites, according to the Old Testament and the Apocrypha. By C. DE ROTHSCHILD and A. DE ROTHSCHILD. Second Edition. 2 vols. crown 8vo. 12s. 6d. Abridged Edition, in 1 vol. fcp. 8vo. 3s. 6d.

Ewald's History of Israel to the Death of Moses. Translated from the German. Edited, with a Preface and an Appendix, by RUSSELL MARTINEAU, M.A. Second Edition. 2 vols. 8vo. 24s. Vols. III. and IV. edited by J. E. CARPENTER, M.A. price 21s.

England and Christendom. By ARCHBISHOP MANNING, D.D. Post 8vo. price 10s 6d.

The Pontificate of Pius the Ninth; being the Third Edition, enlarged and continued, of 'Rome and its Ruler.' By J. F. MAGUIRE, M.P. Post 8vo. Portrait, price 12s. 6d.

Ignatius Loyola and the Early Jesuits. By STEWART ROSE. New Edition, revised. 8vo. with Portrait, 16s.

An Introduction to the Study of the New Testament, Critical, Exegetical, and Theological. By the Rev. S. DAVIDSON, D.D. LL.D. 2 vols. 8vo. 30s.

A Critical and Grammatical Commentary on St. Paul's Epistles. By C. J. ELLICOTT, D.D. Lord Bishop of Gloucester and Bristol. 8vo.

Galatians, Fourth Edition, 8s. 6d.
Ephesians, Fourth Edition, 8s. 6d.
Pastoral Epistles, Fourth Edition, 10s. 6d.
Philippians, Colossians, and Philemon, Third Edition, 10s. 6d.
Thessalonians, Third Edition, 7s. 6d.

Historical Lectures on the Life of Our Lord Jesus Christ : being the Hulsean Lectures for 1859. By C. J. ELLICOTT, D.D. Fifth Edition. 8vo. 12s.

The Greek Testament; with Notes, Grammatical and Exegetical. By the Rev. W. WEBSTER, M.A. and the Rev. W. F. WILKINSON, M.A. 2 vols. 8vo. £2. 4s.

Horne's Introduction to the Critical Study and Knowledge of the Holy Scriptures. Twelfth Edition; with 4 Maps and 22 Woodcuts. 4 vols. 8vo. 42s.

The Treasury of Bible Knowledge; being a Dictionary of the Books, Persons, Places, Events, and other Matters of which mention is made in Holy Scripture. By Rev. J. AYRE, M.A. With Maps, 15 Plates, and numerous Woodcuts. Fcp. 8vo. price 6s.

Every-day Scripture Difficulties explained and illustrated. By J. E. PRESCOTT, M.A. I. *Matthew* and *Mark*; II. *Luke* and *John*. 2 vols. 8vo. price 9s. each.

The Pentateuch and Book of Joshua Critically Examined. By the Right Rev. J. W. COLENSO, D.D. Lord Bishop of Natal. Crown 8vo. price 6s.

PART V. Genesis Analysed and Separated, and the Ages of its Writers determined 8vo. 18s.

PART VI. The Later Legislation of the Pentateuch. 8vo. 24s.

The Formation of Christendom. By T. W. ALLIES. PARTS I. and II. 8vo. price 12s. each.

Four Discourses of Chrysostom, chiefly on the parable of the Rich Man and Lazarus. Translated by F. ALLEN, B.A. Crown 8vo. 3s. 6d.

Thoughts for the Age. By ELIZABETH M. SEWELL, Author of 'Amy Herbert.' New Edition. Fcp. 8vo. price 5s.

Passing Thoughts on Religion. By the same Author. Fcp. 3s. 6d.

Self-examination before Confirmation. By the same Author. 32mo. 1s. 6d.

Thoughts for the Holy Week, for Young Persons. By the same Author. New Edition. Fcp. 8vo. 2s.

Readings for a Month Preparatory to Confirmation from Writers of the Early and English Church. By the same. Fcp. 4s.

Readings for Every Day in Lent, compiled from the Writings of Bishop JEREMY TAYLOR. By the same Author. Fcp. 5s.

Preparation for the Holy Communion; the Devotions chiefly from the works of JEREMY TAYLOR. By the same. 32mo. 3s.

Bishop Jeremy Taylor's Entire Works; with Life by BISHOP HEBER. Revised and corrected by the Rev. C. P EDEN. 10 vols. £5. 5s.

'Spiritual Songs' for the Sundays and Holidays throughout the Year. By J. S. B. MONSELL, LL.D. Vicar of Egham and Rural Dean. Fourth Edition, Sixth Thousand. Fcp. price 4s. 6d.

The Beatitudes. By the same Author. Third Edition, revised. Fcp. 3s. 6d.

His Presence not his Memory, 1855. By the same Author, in memory of his SON. Sixth Edition. 16mo. 1s.

Lyra Germanica, translated from the German by Miss C. WINKWORTH. FIRST SERIES, the *Christian Year*, Hymns for the Sundays and Chief Festivals of the Church; SECOND SERIES, the *Christian Life*. Fcp. 8vo. price 3s. 6d. each SERIES.

Endeavours after the Christian Life; Discourses. By JAMES MARTINEAU. Fourth Edition. Post 8vo. price 7s. 6d.

Travels, Voyages, &c.

Six Months in California. By J.G. PLAYER-FROWD. Post 8vo. price 6s.

The Japanese in America. By CHARLES LANMAN, American Secretary, Japanese Legation, Washington, U.S.A. Post 8vo. price 10s. 6d.

My Wife and I in Queensland; Eight Years' Experience in the Colony, with some account of Polynesian Labour. By CHARLES H. EDEN. With Map and Frontispiece. Crown 8vo. price 9s.

Life in India; a Series of Sketches shewing something of the Anglo-Indian, the Land he lives in, and the People among whom he lives. By EDWARD BRADDON. Post 8vo. price 9s.

How to See Norway. By Captain J. R. CAMPBELL. With Map and 5 Woodcuts. Fcp. 8vo. price 5s.

Pau and the Pyrenees. By Count HENRY RUSSELL, Member of the Alpine Club. With 2 Maps. Fcp. 8vo. price 5s.

Hours of Exercise in the Alps. By JOHN TYNDALL, LL.D., F.R S. Second Edition, with Seven Woodcuts by E. Whymper. Crown 8vo. price 12s. 6d.

Westward by Rail; the New Route to the East. By W. F. RAE. Second Edition. Post 8vo. with Map, price 10s. 6d.

Travels in the Central Caucasus and Bashan, including Visits to Ararat and Tabreez and Ascents of Kazbek and Elbruz. By DOUGLAS W. FRESHFIELD. Square crown 8vo. with Maps, &c., 18s.

Cadore or Titian's Country. By JOSIAH GILBERT, one of the Authors of the 'Dolomite Mountains.' With Map, Facsimile, and 40 Illustrations. Imp.8vo.31s.6d.

The Playground of Europe. By LESLIE STEPHEN, late President of the Alpine Club. With 4 Illustrations on Wood by E. Whymper. Crown 8vo. 10s. 6d.

Zigzagging amongst Dolomites; with more than 300 Illustrations by the Author. By the Author of 'How we Spent the Summer.' Oblong 4to. price 15s.

The Dolomite Mountains. Excursions through Tyrol, Carinthia, Carniola, and Friuli. By J. GILBERT and G. C. CHURCHILL, F.R.G.S. With numerous Illustrations. Square crown 8vo. 21s.

How we Spent the Summer; or, a Voyage en Zigzag in Switzerland, and Tyrol with some Members of the ALPINE CLUB. Third Edition, re-drawn. In oblong 4to. with about 300 Illustrations, 15s.

Pictures in Tyrol and Elsewhere. From a Family Sketch-Book. By the same Author. Second Edition. 4to. with many Illustrations, 21s.

Beaten Tracks; or, Pen and Pencil Sketches in Italy. By the Author of 'How we spent the Summer.' With 42 Plates of Sketches. 8vo. 16s.

The Alpine Club Map of the Chain of Mont Blanc, from an actual Survey in 1863—1864. By A. ADAMS-REILLY, F.R.G.S. M.A.C. In Chromolithography on extra stout drawing paper 28in. × 17in. price 10s. or mounted on canvas in a folding case, 12s. 6d.

History of Discovery in our Australasian Colonies, Australia, Tasmania, and New Zealand, from the Earliest Date to the Present Day. By WILLIAM HOWITT. 2 vols. 8vo. with 3 Maps, 20s.

Visits to Remarkable Places: Old Halls, Battle-Fields, and Scenes illustrative of striking Passages in English History and Poetry. By the same Author. 2 vols. square crown 8vo. with Wood Engravings, 25s.

Guide to the Pyrenees, for the use of Mountaineers. By CHARLES PACKE. Second Edition, with Maps, &c. and Appendix. Crown 8vo. 7s. 6d.

The Alpine Guide. By JOHN BALL M.R.I.A. late President of the Alpine Club. Post 8vo. with Maps and other Illustrations.

Guide to the Eastern Alps, price 10s. 6d.

Guide to the Western Alps, including Mont Blanc, Monte Rosa, Zermatt, &c. price 6s. 6d.

Guide to the Central Alps, including all the Oberland District, price 7s. 6d.

Introduction on Alpine Travelling in general, and on the Geology of the Alps, price 1s. Either of the Three Volumes or Parts of the *Alpine Guide* may be had with this INTRODUCTION prefixed, price 1s. extra.

The Rural Life of England. By WILLIAM HOWITT. Woodcuts by Bewick and Williams. Medium 8vo. 12s. 6d.

Works of Fiction.

Yarndale; a Story of Lancashire Life. By a Lancashire Man. 3 vols. post 8vo. price 21s.

The Burgomaster's Family; or, Weal and Woe in a Little World. By CHRISTINE MÜLLER. Translated from the Dutch by Sir J. G. SHAW LEFEVRE, K.C.B. F.R.S. Crown 8vo. price 6s.

Popular Romances of the Middle Ages. By the Rev. GEORGE W. COX, M.A. Author of 'The Mythology of the Aryan Nations' &c. and EUSTACE HINTON JONES. Crown 8vo. 10s. 6d.

Tales of the Teutonic Lands; a Sequel to 'Popular Romances of the Middle Ages.' By GEORGE W. COX, M.A. late Scholar of Trinity College, Oxford; and EUSTACE HINTON JONES. Crown 8vo. price 10s. 6d.

Hartland Forest; a Legend of North Devon. By Mrs. BRAY, Author of 'The White Hoods,' 'Life of Stothard,' &c. Post 8vo. with Frontispiece, 4s. 6d.

Novels and Tales. By the Right Hon. BENJAMIN DISRAELI, M.P. Cabinet Editions, complete in Ten Volumes, crown 8vo. price 6s. each, as follows:—

LOTHAIR, 6s.
CONINGSBY, 6s.
SYBIL, 6s.
TANCRED, 6s.
VENETIA, 6s.
ALROY, IXION, &c. 6s.
YOUNG DUKE, &c. 6s.
VIVIAN GREY, 6s.
CONTARINI FLEMING, &c. 6s.
HENRIETTA TEMPLE, 6s.

Stories and Tales. By E. M. SEWELL. Comprising *Amy Herbert*; *Gertrude*; the *Earl's Daughter*; the *Experience of Life*; *Cleve Hall*; *Ivors*; *Katharine Ashton*; *Margaret Percival*; *Laneton Parsonage*; and *Ursula*. The Ten Works complete in Eight Volumes, crown 8vo. bound in leather and contained in a Box, price TWO GUINEAS.

Cabinet Edition, in crown 8vo. of Stories and Tales by Miss SEWELL:—

AMY HERBERT, 2s. 6d.
GERTRUDE, 2s. 6d.
EARL'S DAUGHTER, 2s. 6d.
EXPERIENCE of LIFE, 2s. 6d.
CLEVE HALL, 2s. 6d.
IVORS, 2s. 6d.
KATHARINE ASHTON, 2s. 6d.
MARGARET PERCIVAL, 3s. 6d.
LANETON PARSONAGE, 3s. 6d.
URSULA, 3s. 6d.

A Glimpse of the World. Fcp. 7s. 6d.

Journal of a Home Life. Post 8vo. 9s. 6d.

After Life; a Sequel to the 'Journal of a Home Life.' Post 8vo. 10s. 6d.

The Giant; a Witch's Story for English Boys. Edited by Miss SEWELL, Author of 'Amy Herbert,' &c. Fcp. 8vo. price 5s.

Wonderful Stories from Norway, Sweden, and Iceland. Adapted and arranged by JULIA GODDARD. With an Introductory Essay by the Rev. G. W. COX, M.A. and Six Illustrations. Square post 8vo. 6s.

C

The Modern Novelist's Library. Each Work, in crown 8vo. complete in a Single Volume:—

MELVILLE'S DIGBY GRAND, 2s. boards; 2s. 6d. cloth.

———— GLADIATORS, 2s. boards; 2s. 6d. cloth.

———— GOOD FOR NOTHING, 2s. boards; 2s. 6d. cloth.

———— HOLMBY HOUSE, 2s. boards; 2s. 6d. cloth.

———— INTERPRETER, 2s. boards; 2s. 6d. cloth.

———— KATE COVENTRY, 2s. boards; 2s. 6d. cloth.

———— QUEEN'S MARIES, 2s. boards; 2s. 6d. cloth.

TROLLOPE'S WARDEN 1s. 6d. boards; 2s. cloth.

———— BARCHESTER TOWERS, 2s. boards; 2s. 6d. cloth.

BRAMLEY-MOORE'S SIX SISTERS OF THE VALLEYS, 2s. boards; 2s. 6d. cloth.

Becker's Gallus; or, Roman Scenes of the Time of Augustus. Post 8vo. 7s. 6d.

Becker's Charicles: Illustrative of Private Life of the Ancient Greeks. Post 8vo. 7s. 6d.

Tales of Ancient Greece. By the Rev. G. W. COX, M.A. late Scholar of Trin. Coll. Oxford. Crown 8vo. price 6s. 6d.

Poetry and The Drama.

Ballads and Lyrics of Old France; with other Poems. By A. LANG, Fellow of Merton College, Oxford. Square fcp. 8vo. price 5s.

Thomas Moore's Poetical Works, with the Author's last Copyright Additions :—
Shamrock Edition, price 3s. 6d.
People's Edition, square cr. 8vo. 10s. 6d.
Library Edition, Portrait & Vignette, 14s.

Moore's Lalla Rookh, Tenniel's Edition, with 68 Wood Engravings from Original Drawings and other Illustrations. Fcp. 4to. 21s.

Moore's Irish Melodies, Maclise's Edition, with 161 Steel Plates from Original Drawings. Super-royal 8vo. 31s. 6d.

Miniature Edition of Moore's Irish Melodies, with Maclise's Illustrations (as above), reduced in Lithography. Imp. 16mo. 10s. 6d.

Lays of Ancient Rome; with Ivry and the *Armada*. By the Right Hon. LORD MACAULAY. 16mo. 3s. 6d.

Lord Macaulay's Lays of Ancient Rome. With 90 Illustrations on Wood, Original and from the Antique, from Drawings by G. SCHARF. Fcp. 4to. 21s.

Miniature Edition of Lord Macaulay's Lays of Ancient Rome, with Scharf's Illustrations (as above) reduced in Lithography. Imp. 16mo. 10s. 6d.

Southey's Poetical Works, with the Author's last Corrections and copyright Additions. Library Edition. Medium 8vo. with Portrait and Vignette, 14s.

Goldsmith's Poetical Works, Illustrated with Wood Engravings from Designs by Members of the ETCHING CLUB. Imp. 16mo. 7s. 6d.

Poems. By JEAN INGELOW. Fifteenth Edition. Fcp. 8vo. 5s.

Poems by Jean Ingelow. With nearly 100 Illustrations by Eminent Artists, engraved on Wood by DALZIEL Brothers. Fcp. 4to. 21s.

A Story of Doom, and other Poems. By JEAN INGELOW. Third Edition. Fcp. price 5s.

Bowdler's Family Shakspeare, cheaper Genuine Edition, complete in 1 vol. large type, with 36 Woodcut Illustrations, price 14s. or in 6 pocket vols. 3s. 6d. each.

Horatii Opera, Library Edition, with Copious English Notes, Marginal References and Various Readings. Edited by the Rev. J. E. YONGE, M.A. 8vo. 21s.

The Odes and Epodes of Horace; a Metrical Translation into English, with Introduction and Commentaries. By Lord LYTTON. With Latin Text. New Edition. Post 8vo. price 10s. 6d.

The Æneid of Virgil Translated into English Verse. By JOHN CONINGTON, M.A. Corpus Professor of Latin in the University of Oxford. New Edition. Crown 8vo. 9s.

Rural Sports &c.

Encyclopædia of Rural Sports; a Complete Account, Historical, Practical, and Descriptive, of Hunting, Shooting, Fishing, Racing, &c. By D. P. BLAINE. With above 600 Woodcuts (20 from Designs by JOHN LEECH). 8vo. 21s.

The Dead Shot, or Sportsman's Complete Guide; a Treatise on the Use of the Gun, Dog-breaking, Pigeon-shooting, &c. By MARKSMAN. Fcp. with Plates, 5s.

A Book on Angling: being a Complete Treatise on the Art of Angling in every branch, including full Illustrated Lists of Salmon Flies. By FRANCIS FRANCIS. New Edition, with Portrait and 15 other Plates, plain and coloured. Post 8vo. 15s.

Wilcocks's Sea-Fisherman: comprising the Chief Methods of Hook and Line Fishing in the British and other Seas, a glance at Nets, and remarks on Boats and Boating. Second Edition, enlarged, with 80 Woodcuts. Post 8vo. 12s. 6d.

The Fly-Fisher's Entomology. By ALFRED RONALDS. With coloured Representations of the Natural and Artificial Insect. Sixth Edition, with 20 coloured Plates. 8vo. 14s.

The Ox, his Diseases and their Treatment; with an Essay on Parturition in the Cow. By J. R. DOBSON, M.R.C.V.S. Crown 8vo. with Illustrations, 7s. 6d.

A Treatise on Horse-shoeing and Lameness. By JOSEPH GAMGEE, Veterinary Surgeon, formerly Lecturer on the Principles and Practice of Farriery in the New Veterinary College, Edinburgh. 8vo. with 55 Woodcuts, 15s.

Blaine's Veterinary Art: a Treatise on the Anatomy, Physiology, and Curative Treatment of the Diseases of the Horse, Neat Cattle, and Sheep. Seventh Edition, revised and enlarged by C. STEEL. 8vo. with Plates and Woodcuts, 18s.

Youatt on the Horse. Revised and enlarged by W. WATSON, M.R.C.V.S. 8vo. with numerous Woodcuts, 12s. 6d.

Youatt on the Dog. (By the same Author.) 8vo. with numerous Woodcuts, 6s.

The Dog in Health and Disease. By STONEHENGE. With 73 Wood Engravings. New Edition, revised. Square crown 8vo. price 7s. 6d.

The Greyhound. By the same Author. Revised Edition, with 24 Portraits of Greyhounds. Square crown 8vo. 10s. 6d

The Setter; with Notices of the most Eminent Breeds now extant, Instructions how to Breed, Rear, and Break; Dog Shows, Field Trials, and General Management, &c. By EDWARD LAVERACK. With Two Portraits of Setters in Chromolithography. Crown 4to. price 7s. 6d.

Horses and Stables. By Colonel F. FITZWYGRAM, XV. the King's Hussars. With 24 Plates of Woodcut Illustrations, containing very numerous Figures. 8vo. 15s.

The Horse's Foot, and how to keep it Sound. By W. MILES, Esq. Ninth Edition, with Illustrations. Imp. 8vo. 12s. 6d.

A Plain Treatise on Horse-shoeing. By the same Author. Sixth Edition, post 8vo. with Illustrations, 2s. 6d.

Stables and Stable Fittings. By the same. Imp. 8vo. with 13 Plates, 15s.

Remarks on Horses' Teeth, addressed to Purchasers. By the same. Post 8vo. 1s. 6d.

Works of Utility and General Information.

Modern Cookery for Private Families, reduced to a System of Easy Practice in a Series of carefully-tested Receipts. By ELIZA ACTON. Newly revised and enlarged; with 8 Plates, Figures, and 150 Woodcuts. Fcp. 6s.

Maunder's Treasury of Knowledge and Library of Reference: comprising an English Dictionary and Grammar, Universal Gazetteer, Classical Dictionary, Chronology, Law Dictionary, Synopsis of the Peerage, Useful Tables, &c. Fcp. 8vo. 6s.

Collieries and Colliers: a Handbook of the Law and Leading Cases relating thereto. By J. C. FOWLER, Barrister. Second Edition. Fcp. 8vo. 7s. 6d.

The Theory and Practice of Banking. By HENRY DUNNING MACLEOD, M.A. Barrister-at-Law. Second Edition. entirely remodelled. 2 vols. 8vo. 30s.

M'Culloch's Dictionary, Practical, Theoretical, and Historical, of Commerce and Commercial Navigation. New Edition, revised throughout and corrected to the Present Time; with a Biographical Notice of the Author. Edited by H. G. REID, Secretary to Mr. M'Culloch for many years. 8vo. price 63s. cloth.

A Practical Treatise on Brewing; with Formulæ for Public Brewers, and Instructions for Private Families. By W. BLACK. Fifth Edition. 8vo. 10s. 6d.

Chess Openings. By F. W. LONGMAN, Balliol College, Oxford. Fcp. 8vo. 2s. 6d.

The Law of Nations Considered as Independent Political Communities. By Sir TRAVERS TWISS, D.C.L. 2 vols. 8vo. 30s. or separately, PART I *Peace*, 12s. PART II. *War*, 18s.

Hints to Mothers on the Management of their Health during the Period of Pregnancy and in the Lying-in Room. By THOMAS BULL, M.D. Fcp. 5s.

The Maternal Management of Children in Health and Disease. By THOMAS BULL, M.D. Fcp. 5s.

How to Nurse Sick Children; containing Directions which may be found of service to all who have charge of the Young. By CHARLES WEST, M.D. Second Edition. Fcp. 8vo. 1s. 6d.

Notes on Hospitals. By FLORENCE NIGHTINGALE. Third Edition, enlarged; with 13 Plans. Post 4to. 18s.

Notes on Lying-In Institutions; with a Proposal for Organising an Institution for Training Midwives and Midwifery Nurses. By FLORENCE NIGHTINGALE. With 5 Plans. Square crown 8vo. 7s. 6d.

The Cabinet Lawyer; a Popular Digest of the Laws of England, Civil, Criminal, and Constitutional. Twenty-third Edition, corrected and brought up to the Present Date. Fcp. 8vo. price 7s. 6d.

Willich's Popular Tables for Ascertaining the Value of Lifehold, Leasehold, and Church Property, Renewal Fines, &c.; the Public Funds; Annual Average Price and Interest on Consols from 1731 to 1867; Chemical, Geographical, Astronomical, Trigonometrical Tables, &c. Post 8vo. 10s.

Pewtner's Comprehensive Specifier; a Guide to the Practical Specification of every kind of Building-Artificer's Work: with Forms of Building Conditions and Agreements, an Appendix, Foot-Notes, and Index. Edited by W. YOUNG, Architect. Crown 8vo. 6s.

Periodical Publications.

The Edinburgh Review, or Critical Journal, published Quarterly in January, April, July, and October. 8vo. price 6s. each Number.

Notes on Books: An Analysis of the Works published during each Quarter by Messrs. LONGMANS & Co. The object is to enable Bookbuyers to obtain such information regarding the various works as is usually afforded by tables of contents and explanatory prefaces. 4to. Quarterly. *Gratis.*

Fraser's Magazine. Edited by JAMES ANTHONY FROUDE, M.A. New Series, published on the 1st of each Month. 8vo. price 2s. 6d. each Number.

The Alpine Journal; A Record of Mountain Adventure and Scientific Observation. By Members of the Alpine Club. Edited by LESLIE STEPHEN. Published Quarterly. May 31, Aug. 31, Nov. 30, Feb. 28. 8vo. price 1s. 6d. each Number.

Knowledge for the Young.

The Stepping Stone to Knowledge: Containing upwards of Seven Hundred Questions and Answers on Miscellaneous Subjects, adapted to the capacity of Infant Minds. By a MOTHER. New Edition, enlarged and improved. 18mo. price 1s.

The Stepping Stone to Geography: Containing several Hundred Questions and Answers on Geographical Subjects. 18mo. 1s.

The Stepping Stone to English History: Containing several Hundred Questions and Answers on the History of England. 1s.

The Stepping Stone to Bible Knowledge: Containing several Hundred Questions and Answers on the Old and New Testaments. 18mo. 1s.

The Stepping Stone to Biography: Containing several Hundred Questions and Answers on the Lives of Eminent Men and Women. 18mo. 1s.

Second Series of the Stepping Stone to Knowledge: containing upwards of Eight Hundred Questions and Answers on Miscellaneous Subjects not contained in the FIRST SERIES. 18mo. 1s.

The Stepping Stone to French Pronunciation and Conversation: Containing several Hundred Questions and Answers. By Mr. P. SADLER. 18mo. 1s.

The Stepping Stone to English Grammar: Containing several Hundred Questions and Answers on English Grammar. By Mr. P. SADLER. 18mo. 1s.

The Stepping Stone to Natural History: VERTEBRATE OR BACKBONED ANIMALS. PART I. *Mammalia*; PART II. *Birds, Reptiles, Fishes.* 18mo. 1s. each Part.

INDEX.

ACTON's Modern Cookery 19
ALLIES on Formation of Christendom 15
ALLEN's Discourses of Chrysostom 16
Alpine Guide (The) 17
—— Journal 20
AMOS's Jurisprudence 5
ANDERSON's Strength of Materials 9
ARNOLD's Manual of English Literature .. 6
Authority and Conscience 14
Autumn Holidays of a Country Parson 7
AYRE's Treasury of Bible Knowledge 15

BACON's Essays by WHATELY 5
—— Life and Letters, by SPEDDING .. 4
—— Works 5
BAIN's Mental and Moral Science 8
—— on the Senses and Intellect 8
BALL's Guide to the Central Alps 17
——Guide to the Western Alps 17
——Guide to the Eastern Alps 17
BAYLDON's Rents and Tillages 14
Beaten Tracks 17
BECKER's *Charicles* and *Gallus* 18
BENFEY's Sanskrit-English Dictionary 6
BERNARD on British Neutrality 1
BLACK's Treatise on Brewing 19
BLACKLEY's German-English Dictionary .. 6
BLAINE's Rural Sports 10
—— Veterinary Art 10
BLOXAM's Metals 9
BOOTH's Saint-Simon 8
BOULTBEE on 39 Articles 14
BOURNE on Screw Propeller 13
——'s Catechism of the Steam Engine .. 13
—— Examples of Modern Engines .. 13
—— Handbook of Steam Engine 13
—— Treatise on the Steam Engine.... 13
—— Improvements in the same 13
BOWDLER's Family SHAKSPEARE............. 18
BRADDON's Life in India 16
BRAMLEY-MOORE's Six Sisters of the Valley 18
BRANDE's Dictionary of Science, Literature,
  and Art 10
BRAY's Manual of Anthropology 7
—— Philosophy of Necessity 7
—— On Force 7
—— (Mrs.) Hartland Forest 17
BREE's Fallacies of Darwinism 10
BROWNE's Exposition of the 39 Articles.... 15
BRUNEL's Life of BRUNEL 4
BUCKLE's History of Civilisation 2
—— Posthumous Remains 7
BULL's Hints to Mothers 20
—— Maternal Management of Children.. 20
BUNSEN's God in History 3
—— Prayers 14

Burgomaster's Family (The) 17
BURKE's Vicissitudes of Families 5
BURTON's Christian Church 3

Cabinet Lawyer 20
CAMPBELL's Norway 16
CATES's Biographical Dictionary 4
—— and WOODWARD's Encyclopædia 3
CATS and FARLIE's Moral Emblems 12
Changed Aspects of Unchanged Truths 7
CHESNEY's Indian Polity 2
—— Waterloo Campaign 2
Chorale Book for England 12
Christ the Consoler 14
CLOUGH's Lives from Plutarch 2
COLENSO on Pentateuch and Book of Joshua 15
COLLINS's Perspective 13
Commonplace Philosopher in Town and
  Country, by A. K. H. B. 7
CONINGTON's Translation of Virgil's Æneid 18
—— Miscellaneous Writings 7
CONTANSEAU's Two French Dictionaries .. 6
CONYBEARE and HOWSON's Life and Epistles
  of St. Paul 14
COOKE's Grotesque Animals 12
COOPER's Surgical Dictionary 11
COPLAND's Dictionary of Practical Medicine 12
COTTON's Memoir and Correspondence 4
Counsel and Comfort from a City Pulpit .. 7
Cox's (G. W.) Aryan Mythology 3
—— Tale of the Great Persian War 2
—— Tales of Ancient Greece 17
—— and JONES's Romances 17
—— Teutonic Tales.. 17
CREASY on British Constitution 2
CRESY's Encyclopædia of Civil Engineering 13
Critical Essays of a Country Parson 7
CROOKES on Beet-Root Sugar 14
——'s Chemical Analysis 11
CULLEY's Handbook of Telegraphy 13
CUSACK's Student's History of Ireland 2

D'AUBIGNÉ's History of the Reformation in
  the time of CALVIN 2
DAVIDSON's Introduction to New Testament 15
Dead Shot (The), by MARKSMAN 19
DE LA RIVE's Treatise on Electricity 9
DE MORGAN's Paradoxes 7
DENISON's Vice-Regal Life 1
DISRAELI's Lord George Bentinck 4
—— Novels and Tales 17
DODSON on the Ox 19
DOVE's Law of Storms 9
DOYLE's Fairyland 12
DREW's Reasons for Faith 14
DYER's City of Rome 3

EASTLAKE's Gothic Revival 18
——— Hints on Household Taste 13
EATON's Musical Criticism and Biography 4
EDEN's Queensland...................... 16
Edinburgh Review 20
Elements of Botany 10
ELLICOTT on New Testament Revision.... 15
——————'s Commentary on Ephesians 15
——————————————— Galatians 15
——————————————— Pastoral Epist. 15
——————————————— Philippians,&c. 15
——————————————— Thessalonians 15
——————'s Lectures on Life of Christ 15
ERICHSEN's Surgery 11
EVANS's Ancient Stone Implements 10
EWALD's History of Israel 15

FAIRBAIRN'S Application of Cast and Wrought Iron to Building 13
——————— Information for Engineers ... 13
——————— Treatise on Mills and Millwork 13
——————— Iron Shipbuilding 13
FARADAY's Life and Letters 4
FARRAR's Chapters on Language 6
——————— Families of Speech 7
FITZWYGRAM on Horses and Stables 19
FOWLER's Collieries and Colliers 19
FRANCIS's Fishing Book 19
FRASER's Magazine..................... 20
FRESHFIELD's Travels in the Caucasus ... 16
FROUDE's English in Ireland 1
——————— History of England 1
——————— Short Studies 7

GAMGEE on Horse-Shoeing 19
GANOT's Elementary Physics 9
——————— Natural Philosophy 9
GARROD's Materia Medica 12
GIANT (The) 17
GILBERT'S Cadore 16
——— and CHURCHILL's Dolomites 16
GIRDLESTONE's Bible Synonyms 14
GIRTIN's House I Live In 11
GLEDSTONE's Life of WHITEFIELD 4
GODDARD's Wonderful Stories 17
GOLDSMITH's Poems, Illustrated 18
GOODEVE's Mechanism.................. 9
GRAHAM's Autobiography of MILTON..... 4
——————— View of Literature and Art 2
GRANT's Ethics of Aristotle........... 5
——————— Home Politics................. 2
Graver Thoughts of a Country Parson... 7
Gray's Anatomy....................... 11
GRIFFIN's Algebra and Trigonometry 9
GRIFFITH's Fundamentals 14
GROVE on Correlation of Physical Forces .. 9
GURNEY's Chapters of French History ... 2
GWILT's Encyclopædia of Architecture ... 13

HARTWIG's Harmonies of Nature......... 10
——————— Polar World 10
——————— Sea and its Living Wonders.... 10
——————— Subterranean World 10
HATHERTON's Memoir and Correspondence 2
HAYWARD's Biographical and Critical Essays 4
HERSCHEL's Outlines of Astronomy...... 7
HEWITT on the Diseases of Women 11

HODGSON's Time and Space.............. 7
——————— Theory of Practice 7
HOLLAND's Recollections................ 4
HOLMES's Surgical Treatment of Children.. 11
——————— System of Surgery 11
HORNE's Introduction to the Scriptures .. 15
How we Spent the Summer............... 16
HOWITT's Australian Discovery......... 17
——————— Rural Life of England 17
——————— Visits to Remarkable Places 17
HÜBNER's Pope Sixtus the Fifth 4
HUMBOLDT's Life....................... 4
HUME's Essays 8
——————— Treatise on Human Nature...... 8

IHNE's History of Rome 3
INGELOW's Poems 18
——————— Story of Doom 18

JAMES's Christian Counsels............ 14
JAMESON's Legends of Saints and Martyrs.. 12
——————— Legends of the Madonna 12
——————— Legends of the Monastic Orders 12
——————— Legends of the Saviour....... 12
JAMIESON on Causality................. 5
JARDINE's Christian Sacerdotalism 14
JOHNSTON's Geographical Dictionary ... 8
JONES's Royal Institution 4

KALISCH's Commentary on the Bible..... 6
——————— Hebrew Grammar............... 6
KEITH on Destiny of the World......... 15
——————— Fulfilment of Prophecy........ 15
KERL's Metallurgy, by CROOKES and RÖHRIG 14
KIRBY and SPENCE's Entomology........ 9

LANG's Ballads and Lyrics 18
LANMAN's Japanese in America 16
LATHAM's English Dictionary........... 6
LAUGHTON's Nautical Surveying........ 9
LAVERACK's Setters 19
LECKY's History of European Morals ... 3
——————— Rationalism 3
——————— Leaders of Public Opinion..... 4
Leisure Hours in Town, by A. K. H. B. ... 7
Lessons of Middle Age, by A. K. H. B. .. 7
LEWES's Biographical History of Philosophy 3
LIDDELL & SCOTT's Greek-English Lexicons 6
Life of Man Symbolised................ 12
LINDLEY and MOORE's Treasury of Botany 10
LONGMAN's Edward the Third 2
——————— Lectures on History of England 2
——————— Chess Openings............... 20
LOUDON's Encyclopædia of Agriculture ... 14
——————————————— Gardening 14
——————————————— Plants 10
LUBBOCK's Origin of Civilisation 10
LYTTON's Odes of Horace............... 18
Lyra Germanica 12, 16

MACAULAY's (Lord) Essays 3
——————— History of England 1
——————— Lays of Ancient Rome 18
——————— Miscellaneous Writings 7

MACAULAY'S (Lord) Speeches	5
———— Works	1
MACLEOD'S Principles of Political Philosophy	5
———— Dictionary of Political Economy	5
———— Theory and Practice of Banking	19
McCULLOCH'S Dictionary of Commerce	19
MAGUIRE'S Life of Father Mathew	4
———— PIUS IX.	15
Mankind, their Origin and Destiny	10
MANNING'S England and Christendom	15
MARCET'S Natural Philosophy	9
MARSHALL'S Physiology	12
MARSHMAN'S History of India	2
———— Life of Havelock	5
MARTINEAU'S Endeavours after the Christian Life	16
MASSINGBERD'S History of the Reformation	3
MATHEWS on Colonial Question	2
MAUNDER'S Biographical Treasury	5
———— Geographical Treasury	9
———— Historical Treasury	3
———— Scientific and Literary Treasury	10
———— Treasury of Knowledge	19
———— Treasury of Natural History	10
MAXWELL'S Theory of Heat	9
MAY'S Constitutional History of England	1
MELVILLE'S Digby Grand	18
———— General Bounce	18
———— Gladiators	18
———— Good for Nothing	18
———— Holmby House	18
———— Interpreter	18
———— Kate Coventry	18
———— Queen's Maries	18
MENDELSSOHN'S Letters	4
MERIVALE'S Fall of the Roman Republic	3
———— Romans under the Empire	3
MERRIFIELD'S Arithmetic and Mensuration	8
———— Magnetism	
———— and EVERS'S Navigation	8
METEYARD'S Group of Englishmen	4
MILES on Horse's Foot and Horse Shoeing	19
———— on Horses' Teeth and Stables	19
MILL (J.) on the Mind	5
MILL (J. S.) on Liberty	5
———— Subjection of Women	5
———— on Representative Government	5
———— on Utilitarianism	5
———— 's Dissertations and Discussions	5
———— Political Economy	5
———— System of Logic	5
———— Hamilton's Philosophy	5
MILLER'S Elements of Chemistry	11
———— Inorganic Chemistry	9
MITCHELL'S Manual of Architecture	13
———— Manual of Assaying	14
MONSELL'S Beatitudes	16
———— His Presence not his Memory	16
———— 'Spiritual Songs'	16
MOORE'S Irish Melodies	18
———— Lalla Rookh	18
———— Poetical Works	18
MORELL'S Elements of Psychology	6
———— Mental Philosophy	6
MOSSMAN'S Christian Church	3
MÜLLER'S (Max) Chips from a German Workshop	7
———— Lectures on the Science of Language	5
———— (K. O.) Literature of Ancient Greece	2
MURCHISON on Liver Complaints	12
MURE'S Language and Literature of Greece	2
NASH'S Compendium of the Prayer-Book	14
New Testament Illustrated with Wood Engravings from the Old Masters	12
NEWMAN'S History of his Religious Opinions	5
NIGHTINGALE on Hospitals	20
———— Lying-In Institutions	20
NILSSON'S Scandinavia	10
NORTHCOTT on Lathes and Turning	13
Notes on Books	20
ODLING'S Course of Practical Chemistry	11
———— Outlines of Chemistry	11
OWEN'S Comparative Anatomy and Physiology of Vertebrate Animals	9
———— Lectures on the Invertebrata	9
PACKE'S Guide to the Pyrenees	17
PAGET'S Lectures on Surgical Pathology	10
PEREIRA'S Elements of Materia Medica	12
PERRING'S Churches and Creeds	14
PEWTNER'S Comprehensive Specifier	20
Pictures in Tyrol	16
PIESSE'S Art of Perfumery	14
PLAYER-FROWD'S California	16
PRENDERGAST'S Mastery of Languages	6
PRESCOTT'S Scripture Difficulties	15
Present-Day Thoughts, by A. K. H. B.	7
PROCTOR'S Astromomical Essays	8
———— Orbs around Us	8
———— Plurality of Worlds	8
———— Saturn	8
———— Scientific Essays	9
———— Star Atlas	8
———— Star Depths	8
———— Sun	8
Public Schools Atlas	8
RAE'S Westward by Rail	16
RANKEN on Strains in Trusses	13
RAWLINSON'S Parthia	2
Recreations of a Country Parson, by A. K. H. B.	7
REEVE'S Royal and Republican France	2
REICHEL'S See of Rome	14
REILLY'S Map of Mont Blanc	17
RIVERS'S Rose Amateur's Guide	10
ROGERS'S Eclipse of Faith	7
———— Defence of Faith	7
ROGET'S Thesaurus of English Words and Phrases	6
RONALDS'S Fly-Fisher's Entomology	19
ROSE'S Loyola	15
ROTHSCHILD'S Israelites	15
RUSSELL'S Pau and the Pyrenees	16
SANDARS'S Justinian's Institutes	5
SANFORD'S English Kings	1
SAVILE on Truth of the Bible	15
SCHELLEN'S Spectrum Analysis	8
SCOTT'S Lectures on the Fine Arts	12
———— Albert Durer	12
Seaside Musing, by A. K. H. B.	7
SEEBOHM'S Oxford Reformers of 1498	2

SEWELL'S After Life	17
———— Glimpse of the World	17
———— History of the Early Church	3
———— Journal of a Home Life	16
———— Passing Thoughts on Religion	16
———— Preparation for Communion	16
———— Readings for Confirmation	16
———— Readings for Lent	16
———— Examination for Confirmation	16
———— Stories and Tales	17
———— Thoughts for the Age	16
———— Thoughts for the Holy Week	16
SHIPLEY's Essays on Ecclesiastical Reform	14
SHORT's Church History	3
SMITH's Paul's Voyage and Shipwreck	14
———— (SYDNEY) Life and Letters	4
———— Miscellaneous Works	7
———— Wit and Wisdom	7
———— (Dr. R. A.) Air and Rain	8
SOUTHEY's Doctor	6
———— Poetical Works	18
STANLEY's History of British Birds	9
STEPHEN's Ecclesiastical Biography	4
———— Playground of Europe	16
Stepping-Stone to Knowledge, &c.	20
STIRLING's Protoplasm	7
———— Secret of Hegel	7
———— Sir WILLIAM HAMILTON	7
STOCKMAR's Memoirs	1
STONEHENGE on the Dog	19
———— on the Greyhound	19
STRICKLAND's Queens of England	4
Sunday Afternoons at the Parish Church of a University City, by A. K. H. B.	7
TAYLOR's History of India	2
———— (Jeremy) Works, edited by EDEN	16
———— Text-Books of Science	8
TEXT-BOOKS OF SCIENCE	9
THIRLWALL's History of Greece	2
THOMSON's Laws of Thought	5
———— New World of Being	7
THUDICHUM's Chemical Physiology	11
TODD (A.) on Parliamentary Government	1
———— and BOWMAN's Anatomy and Physiology of Man	12
TRENCH's Realities of Irish Life	2
TROLLOPE's Barchester Towers	18
———— Warden	18
TWISS's Law of Nations	20
TYNDALL's Diamagnetism	9
———— Faraday as a Discoverer	4
———— Fragments of Science	9
———— Hours of Exercise in the Alps	16
TYNDALL's Lectures on Electricity	9
———— Lectures on Light	9
———— Lectures on Sound	9
———— Heat a Mode of Motion	9
———— Molecular Physics	11
UEBERWEG's System of Logic	
URE's Dictionary of Arts, Manufactures, and Mines	13
VAN DER HOEVEN's Handbook of Zoology	10
VOGAN's Doctrine of the Eucharist	14
WATSON's Geometry	9
———— Principles and Practice of Physic	11
WATTS's Dictionary of Chemistry	11
WEBB's Objects for Common Telescopes	8
WEBSTER & WILKINSON's Greek Testament	15
WELLINGTON's Life, by GLEIG	4
WEST on Children's Diseases	11
———— on Children's Nervous Disorders	11
———— on Nursing Sick Children	20
WHATELY's English Synonymes	5
———— Logic	5
———— Rhetoric	5
WHITE and RIDDLE's Latin Dictionaries	6
WILCOCKS's Sea Fisherman	19
WILLIAMS's Aristotle's Ethics	5
WILLIAMS on Consumption	11
WILLICH's Popular Tables	20
WILLIS's Principles of Mechanism	13
WINSLOW on Light	9
WOOD's (J. G.) Bible Animals	10
———— Homes without Hands	9
———— Insects at Home	10
———— Insects Abroad	10
———— Strange Dwellings	9
———— (T.) Chemical Notes	11
WORDSWORTH's Christian Ministry	14
Yarndale	17
YONGE's History of England	1
———— English-Greek Lexicons	6
———— Horace	18
———— English Literature	5
———— Modern History	3
YOUATT on the Dog	19
———— on the Horse	19
ZELLER's Socrates	3
———— Stoics, Epicureans, and Sceptics	3
Zigzagging amongst Dolomites	15

www.ingramcontent.com/pod-product-compliance
Lightning Source LLC
Chambersburg PA
CBHW032119230426
43672CB00009B/1788